THE GUINNESS BOOK OF
WINNERS

ANNE MARSHALL

GUINNESS PUBLISHING

Anne Marshall has spent most of her life collecting books and has been fortunate enough to have had a career in book and magazine publishing. She has worked for 20 years in the industry, producing recreational, educational and technical magazines and books. For the last ten years she has run her own company, providing a service to publishers and industry, writing articles and features, editing magazines, and packaging books, and is currently writing a novel. She has recently converted from paper to disc and researches and rewrites software packages for the general market. She is co-author of *The Guinness Book of Winners and Champions* and a contributor to *The Guinness Book of Answers*.

ACKNOWLEDGEMENTS

The publisher would like to convey thanks to the many organisations, institutions, libraries and individuals who have provided information, facts and figures and assisted with research during the course of writing this book, particularly Robert Birke; CIN Co. Ltd; Barry Cox; Jackie Cox in the *Mastermind* office at the BBC; Ian Dean, Timeform; Ian Herbert, *Theatre Record*; Steve Holland, *Comic World*; Byron Jacobs, chess correspondent; The Music Publishers' Association Ltd; Perry Robbins, Eurovision Network; Chris Seaber for photographing archival material; David Webster; Malcolm Whyatt, *Health & Strength*. The following Guinness publications should also be acknowledged: *British Hit Albums, British Hit Singles, The Guinness Book of Answers, The Guinness Book of Names, The Guinness Book of Records*.

Editor Beatrice Frei
Design Michael Morey

First published in 1994 by Guinness Publishing Ltd.

Typeset in Sabon and Franklin Gothic
by Ace Filmsetting Ltd, Frome, Somerset
Colour origination by Master Image, Singapore
Printed and bound in Italy by New Interlitho Italia S.p.a.

A catalogue record for this book is available from the British Library.

ISBN 0-85112-791-6

PERMISSIONS

Permission has been granted for use of the following material on the pages indicated:
p.46: excerpt from *Song of Solomon* by Toni Morrison, permission granted by International Creative Management, Inc., ©1977 Toni Morrison; p.51: excerpt from *Rabbit is Rich* by John Updike, Penguin Books, first published by André Deutsch, ©1981 John Updike, reproduced by permission of Hamish Hamilton Ltd; pp.61–65: 'Kevin The Blue', ©1993 Caroline Pitcher, from *Story of the Year*, published by Scholastic Children's Books; p.114: *Through the Looking Glass*, Lewis Carroll, 1872, illustration by John Tenniel; p.149: 'Anamnemonicker', Ted Hughes; p.187: 'Valentine', *Meantime*, ©1993 Carol Ann Duffy, published by Anvil Press Poetry; p.187: 'Protestant Windows', ©1993 Sam Gardiner; p.188: 'A Date Called *Eat Me* ', from First Language, ©1993 Ciaran Carson, reproduced by kind permission of the author and The Gallery Press; p.199: *Mastermind* questions – John D. Bareham (The Crusades 1095–1154), Christine Ansell, Bridget Ardley, Gillian Elston, J. C. G. George, Di Lewis, Philip Pitcher, Dee Wallis (General Knowledge round).

CONTENTS

INTRODUCTION

The aim in writing this book has been to provide, first and foremost, an authoritative reference work for those seeking information on awards, competitions and winners within a wide range of subject areas. The intention has also been to create a book that will fit well into Guinness's successful range of fascinating, fun and informative titles.

The Guinness Book of Winners includes lists, information on awards, competitions and championships, and interactive entries where readers can, for example, attempt *The Times* Championship crossword or try to answer a round of *Mastermind* questions. Examples of winning work, such as poems, stories, and recipes are reproduced, and winners and their achievements are featured. Highlighted boxed items include anecdotal material, quotes, and superlatives, together with statistics on the lists of winners, for example the breed of dog which has most often won Best in Show at Crufts, which Eurovision songs have entered the British charts, and countries which have won most Miss World titles or Nobel Prizes.

The overall criteria for inclusion has been that all 'winners' can be measured in terms of success, either by judging, election, or numerical assessment, for example sales volume, such as in bestselling books, and records. Occasionally, anecdotal material on winners in a more general sense has been included.

Abbreviations for countries have been used throughout, adopting the convention of taking the first three letters. Mention must also be made of the use of imperial and metric units. Conversions have been added where appropriate, adopting the system in which the original measurement was recorded, followed by the conversion in brackets. This system is also applied where countries have been renamed – the name recorded at the time is given.

Finally, I would like to thank the many individuals and organisations who have helped during the research of this book, together with my editor at Guinness, Beatrice Frei, whose suggestions and exacting high standards have been much appreciated. I would also like to thank Claire, Charlotte, Luke and Matthew, and last but not least Chris without whose constant encouragement, enthusiasm and help this book might never have been completed.

ADVERTISING

British Television Advertising Awards

Organised by the British Advertising Broadcast Awards Ltd (BABA) since 1976, the awards honour and recognise the best television commercials made and produced by British advertising agencies and film production companies. The awards – Gold, Silver, Bronze and a Diploma – are spread over many categories.

Each year the awards organiser's directors select a chairman for the jury who in turn selects the jury which is made up of representatives from six production companies, six advertising agencies and six advertisers. Entries to the awards are received from advertising agencies and production companies for the jury's consideration along guidelines set by the chairman. Each year the ITV Award is given for the Best Commercial of the Year:

1977 Sony Television, 'Tuning People In'
1978 EMI The Supremes Greatest Hits, 'Three Little Girls'
1979 EMI Frank Sinatra's Greatest Hits, 'Animals'

1980 Courage Best Bitter, 'Gercha!'
1981 Lego, 'Kipper'
1982 Courage Best Bitter, 'Margate'
1983 Tango, 'Stanley Gimble'
1984 Irn Bru, 'Culprit'
1985 John Smith's Bitter, 'Song and Dance'
1986 Levi 501, 'Russia'
1987 Hamlet Cigars, 'Photobooth'
1988 Whitbread Best Bitter, 'Switcheroo'
1989 K Shoes, 'Creaks'
1990 Maxell Audio Tape, 'Israelites'
1991 Electricity Association, 'Pablo'
1992 Schweppes Tonic, 'Strange Taste Test'
1993 Levi 501, 'The Swimmer'
1994 Levi's, 'Creek'

1994 Awards

TOP ADVERTISING AGENCY
BMP DDB Needham won the highest number of awards overall, including its campaigns for John Smith's Bitter, Barclaycard, and Volkswagen.

TOP PRODUCTION COMPANY
Paul Weiland Film Company, the production company which has worked on the highest number of 1994 winning commercials, including Tesco's image campaign and Volvo's gold winner, 'On Your Side'.

Gold Awards

BEST USE OF PRODUCTION CRAFT
Levi Strauss, 'Creek'
Agency Bartle Bogle Hegarty

BEST SERIES OF COMMERCIALS
Levi Strauss, 'Creek', 'Campfire', 'Tackle'
Agency Bartle Bogle Hegarty
Peperami (Van den Berghs), 'Shopping', 'Arms', 'Jump', 'Crisp', 'Video', 'Wimp'
Agency Still Price Lintas
John Smith's Bitter (Courage), 'Penguins', 'Penguins return', 'Credibility II', 'Sad'
Agency BMP DDB Needham

ABOVE BMP DDB Needham, most successful advertising agency in the 1994 British Television Advertising Awards, won a Gold Award for this John Smith's Bitter 'Penguins' series of ads.

LEFT Tesco Stores 'Baby Face' advertisement which won 1994 Best Retail Commercial award.

BEST BUSINESS, FINANCIAL, GOVERNMENT COMMERCIAL
Barclaycard Purchase Protection, 'Teapot'
Agency BMP DDB Needham

BEST INTERNATIONAL COMMERCIAL
British Telecom, 'Hawking'
Agency Saatchi and Saatchi
Levi Strauss, 'Creek'
Agency Bartle Bogle Hegarty

BEST CORPORATE COMMERCIAL
British Telecom, 'Hawking'
Agency Saatchi and Saatchi

BEST CAR COMMERCIAL AND BEST POST-PRODUCTION COMMERCIAL
SIPS (Volvo), 'On Your Side'
Agency Abbott Mead Vickers BBDO

BEST RETAIL COMMERCIAL
Tesco Stores, 'Baby Face'
Agency Lowe Howard-Spink

BEST ALCOHOL COMMERCIAL
Heineken Lager (The Whitbread Beer Company), 'Incredible Journey'
Agency Lowe Howard-Spink
John Smith's Bitter (Courage), 'Penguins'
Agency BMP DDB Needham

Independent Radio Advertising Awards

Since 1979, an annual competition to find the year's best UK-produced radio commercials has been held. Entries are invited for work transmitted during the past year to be judged by a professional jury. Advertising agencies, production companies, advertisers, radio stations or individuals concerned with the production or creation of radio commercials may enter in any of the listed categories which change from year to year. Each commercial may be entered for as many different Bronze category Awards as appropriate.

In 1993 the awards were given in association with *Campaign* and sponsored by a variety of companies connected with the radio industry. There were five main groups, in each of which an overall Silver Award was made to one of the nominated Bronze Award winners. An overall Gold Award, sponsored by the Association of Independent Radio Companies (AIRC), was made to the best overall advertisement across all groups which is chosen by the jury from the five Silver Award nominations. The

Gold Award winner receives a gold trophy and £5000, the Silver and Bronze Award winners, silver and bronze trophies respectively. The winners in 1993 were (advertising agency/producer in brackets):

GOLD AWARD FOR BEST OVERALL ADVERTISEMENT
RSPCA for 'Injection', an ad that looks at life from the perspective of a dog that has been given as an unwanted Christmas present.
(Abbott Mead Vickers/BBDO)
Sponsored by AIRC

Group 1 – Station Produced
SILVER AWARD
Nescafé, 'Nescafé Big Red Mug Promo – Peter Cook', Virgin Radio

BRONZE AWARDS
Station Produced Commercial Roodhouses, 'Sit-Ron' (Hallam FM, part of the Metro Radio Group)
Station Produced Promotion Nescafé, 'Nescafé Big Red Mug Promo – Peter Cook' (Virgin Radio)
Station Produced Series Cornes Motors, 'Almost Old', 'Jellied Eel Folk', 'Thrust', 'Translation' (Radio Aire)

Group 2 – Retail and Manufacturing
SILVER AWARD
Cadbury Ltd, 'Patch' (Bartle Bogle Hegarty Ltd)

BRONZE AWARDS
Toiletries and Pharmaceuticals Procter & Gamble, 'Carnal Heat' (Saatchi & Saatchi)
Automotive Volvo, 'Mrs Carlsson' and 'Mr Dobie' (Abbott Mead Vickers/BBDO)
Food and Drink Cadbury Ltd, 'Patch' (Bartle Bogle Hegarty Ltd)
Retail BHS, 'Men's Gloves' (Flamingo Productions)

Group 3 – Services
SILVER AWARD
RSPCA, 'Injection' (Abbott Mead Vickers/BBDO)

BRONZE AWARDS
Corporate and Finance TSB, 'Dynorod' (DMB&B)
Community, Government and Public Services RSPCA, 'Injection' (Abbott Mead Vickers/BBDO)
Travel and Transport Qantas, 'Haggle' (DMB&B)
Business to Business Capital Gold, 'Bend It' (Commercial Breaks)

Group 4 – Media and Leisure
SILVER AWARD
TDK, 'Silence' (Reay Keating Hamer)

BRONZE AWARDS
Publishing *Esquire*, 'Flirting' (Bartle Bogle Hegarty Ltd)
Leisure The Coliseum Nightclub, 'Morning Moaning' (The Pulse [part of the Metro Radio Group])
Music and Entertainment TDK, 'Silence' (Reay Keating Hamer)

Group 5 – Use of
SILVER AWARD
RSPCA, 'Swim', 'Drive', 'Injection' (Abbott Mead Vickers/BBDO)

BRONZE AWARDS
Use of Humour Cadbury Ltd, 'Patch' (Bartle Bogle Hegarty Ltd)
Use of Series RSPCA, 'Swim' 'Drive', 'Injection' (Abbott Mead Vickers/BBDO)
Use of Original Music TDK, 'Silence' (Reay Keating Hamer)

The RSPCA's 'Injection', an emotive first-person account of a dog living its last few moments before being 'put down', won the Gold Award in the 1993 Independent Radio Advertising Awards. The advertisement is one of three which all work in the same way – the listener is drawn into the story before it becomes clear what it is actually about. The other two ads tell of a dog being abandoned by a road side and two puppies being drowned in a sack. They are all told in the first person, from the dog's perspective, and in each case the animal completely trusts his owner. The ads are unusual in that they last 60 seconds, designed to get away from the so-called 'fast and frantic syndrome' which tends to be associated with radio ads.

Male Voice-over I'm not very well. At least I don't think I am. Actually I feel fine but I must be ill because I'm here. I'm where you go when you're not very well. I must be really quite bad because I've just had an injection to make me better. My friend brought me here which shows he cares. I didn't think he did at first. But on the way here he was very nice. Very nice. Feel tired now . . . very tired, here on this table where they put me down. Put me down . . . tired . . . make better . . . injection . . . very tired . . .

Female Voice-over Every Christmas the RSPCA has to rescue thousands of unwanted animals. If you give a damn, don't give a pet.

ANIMALS & PETS

Crufts Dog Show

Charles Cruft was born in 1852 in South London, the son of a jeweller. After leaving Birkbeck College, he disregarded his father's wishes to join the family firm and in 1876 joined James Spratt, a company manufacturing 'dog cakes'. He started as an office boy but was quickly promoted to salesman with responsibility for visiting kennels on large estates and dog breeders in England and on the Continent.

In 1878 he was invited by the French dog breeders to undertake the organisation of the canine section of the Paris Exhibition. In 1886, following this success, he managed the 600 dogs entered for the Allied Terrier Club Show held at the Royal Aquarium, Westminster, London.

Charles Cruft worked with Spratts for 30 years and became General Manager. In 1891 he organised the first of the Crufts shows at the Royal Agricultural Hall, Islington, London, in which Queen Victoria entered some of her dogs. It was the first time that a ruling monarch had exhibited dogs at an open show and it helped to encourage dog showing and ensured that each successive year's entrants to Crufts increased.

Cruft died in 1938 and his widow subsequently organised one show in 1939. Three years later, however, Mrs Cruft decided that she could no longer be responsible for the show and, to perpetuate his name, asked the Committee of the Kennel Club to take over its organisation. In 1948 the first Crufts Show under Kennel Club jurisdiction was held at Olympia, London. It moved in 1979 to Earls Court, London, and in its centenary year in 1991 to the National Exhibition Centre, Birmingham, where it attracted a record 22 993 entries. In 1994 there were 19 877 entries.

The show is divided into six groups – three sporting breeds (terrier, hound, gundog) and three non-sporting breeds (toy, utility,

---

FACTS

■ All registered Kennel Club dogs have to have a minimum of two names. The most usual way to register a dog is to use the registered kennel name of the breeder, together with another name of the owner's choice.

■ Ch and Sh stand for 'champion' and 'show champion' respectively. Border collies and all gundog breeds have to have a working qualification before they can be promoted from show champion to champion.

■ H. S. Lloyd has won Best in Show most times, taking the title in six years with three different dogs, all cocker spaniels. They were called Luckystar of Ware (1930, 1931), Exquisite Model of Ware (1938, 1939) and Tracey Witch of Ware (1948, 1950).

Crufts Dog Show in February 1912 at the Agricultural Hall, where 3950 entries competed for a total £2000 in prize money.

CURS OF HIGH DEGREE AT THE AGRICULTURAL HALL
CRUFT'S ANNUAL DOG SHOW AND SOME OF THE BREEDS TO BE SEEN THERE

BULLDOG   BLENHEIM SPANIEL   IRISH TERRIER   DACHSHUND   NEWFOUNDLAND   DEERHOUND   GREAT DANE   WELSH TERRIER   COLLIE   RETRIEVER   SCOTCH TERRIER   ENGLISH SETTER   FOX TERRIER   BORZOI   POINTER   SPANIEL   BLOODHOUND

The great event in the canine year took place this week at the Agricultural Hall, where, from Wednesday to Friday, the aristocracy of the dog world have been holding a reception of their friends and admirers. This year's show constitutes a record, the number of entries being 3950, which is the largest for any dog show ever held in this country. Every breed of dog, from the majestic bloodhound to the tiny toy, has had a chance of distinguishing itself, the list of prizes including some 700 special, in addition to £2000 prize money.

working). Within each class, within a particular breed, the males compete first, followed by the bitches; then the best dog and best bitch compete to decide best of breed. Best of each breed then competes to find the best overall winner in each of the six main groups. These six then go on to compete to decide the overall winner of Best in Show (instigated in 1928).

In 1994 the Best in Show was the winner of the terrier group, a black and brown, four-year-old Welsh terrier, Ch Purston Hit and Miss from Brocolita, commonly called Buttons. Buttons was runner-up in 1993, winning the best in terrier group, but failed to impress the judge sufficiently to clinch the title.

BEST IN SHOW WINNERS BY BREED

6 Spaniel (cocker) (G)
3 Alsatian (GSD) (W)
English setter (G)
Fox terrier (wire) (Tr)
Greyhound (H)
Retriever (Labrador) (G)
Welsh terrier (Tr)
2 Afghan hound (H)
Airedale terrier (Tr)
Irish setter (G)
Lakeland terrier (Tr)
Pointer (G)
Poodle (standard) (U)
Poodle (toy) (U)
West Highland white terrier (Tr)
1 Bearded collie (W)
Bulldog (U)
Bull terrier (Tr)
Cavalier King Charles spaniel (T)
Chow-chow (U)
Dalmatian (U)
Great Dane (W)
Irish wolfhound (H)
Keeshond (U)
Kerry blue terrier (Tr)
Lhasa apso (U)
Pyrenean mountain dog (W)
Retriever (flat-coat) (G)
St Bernard (W)
Scottish terrier (Tr)
Spaniel (clumber) (G)
Whippet (H)

Note: Within the main groupings the breakdown of winners is: Sporting – terrier (Tr) 8, hound (H) 4, gundog (G) 7; Non-sporting – toy (T) 1, utility (U) 7, working (W) 5.

BEST IN SHOW

	Breed	Winner	Owner
1928	Greyhound	Primeley Sceptre	H. Whitley
1929	Scottish terrier	Heather Necessity	E. Chapman
1930	Spaniel (cocker)	Luckystar of Ware	H. S. Lloyd
1931	Spaniel (cocker)	Luckystar of Ware	H. S. Lloyd
1932	Retriever (Labrador)	Bramshaw Bob	Lorna Countess Howe
1933	Retriever (Labrador)	Bramshaw Bob	Lorna Countess Howe
1934	Greyhound	Southball Moonstone	B. Harland Worden
1935	Pointer	Pennine Prima Donna	A. Eggleston
1936	Chow-chow	Ch Choonam Hung Kwong	Mrs V. A. M. Mannooch
1937	Retriever (Labrador)	Ch Cheveralla Ben of Banchory	Lorna Countess Howe
1938	Spaniel (cocker)	Exquisite Model of Ware	H. S. Lloyd
1939	Spaniel (cocker)	Exquisite Model of Ware	H. S. Lloyd
1940–1947	No shows		
1948	Spaniel (cocker)	Tracey Witch of Ware	H. S. Lloyd
1949	No show		
1950	Spaniel (cocker)	Tracey Witch of Ware	H. S. Lloyd
1951	Welsh terrier	Twynstar Dyma-Fi	Capt. and Mrs I. M. Thomas
1952	Bulldog	Ch Noways Chuckles	J. T. Barnard
1953	Great Dane	Ch Elch Elder of Ouborough	W. G. Siggers
1954	No show		
1955	Poodle (standard)	Ch Tzigane Aggri of Nashend	Mrs A. Proctor
1956	Greyhound	Treetops Golden Falcon	Mrs W de Casembroot and Miss H. Greenish
1957	Keeshond	Ch Volkrijk of Vorden	Mrs I M. Tucker
1958	Pointer	Ch Chiming Bells	Mrs W. Parkinson
1959	Welsh terrier	Ch Sandstorm Saracen	Mesdames Leach and Thomas
1960	Irish wolfhound	Sulhamstead Merman	Mrs Nagle and Miss Clark
1961	Airedale terrier	Ch Riverina Tweedsbairn	Miss P. McCaughey and Mrs D. Schutch
1962	Fox terrier (wire)	Ch Crackwyn Cockspur	H. L. Gill
1963	Lakeland terrier	Rogerholm Recruit	W. Rogers
1964	English setter	Sh Ch Silbury Soames of Madavale	Mrs A. Williams
1965	Alsatian (GSD)	Ch Fenton of Kentwood	Miss S. H. Godden
1966	Poodle (toy)	Oakington Puckshill Amber Sunblush	Mrs C. E. Perry
1967	Lakeland terrier	Ch Stingray of Derrabah	Mr and Mrs Postlewaite
1968	Dalmatian	Ch Fanhill Faune	Mrs E. J. Woodyatt
1969	Alsatian (GSD)	Ch Hendrawen's Nibelung of Charavigne	Mr and Mrs E. J. White
1970	Pyrenean mountain dog	Bergerie Knur	Mr and Mrs F. S. Prince
1971	Alsatian (GSD)	Ch Ramacon Swashbuckler	Prince Ahmed Hussain
1972	Bull terrier	Ch Abraxas Audacity	Miss V. Drummond-Dick
1973	Cavalier King Charles spaniel	Alansmere Aquarius	Messrs Hall and Evans
1974	St Bernard	Ch Burtonswood Bossy Boots	Miss M. Hindes
1975	Fox terrier (wire)	Ch Brookewire Brandy of Layven	Messrs Benelli and Dondina
1976	West Highland white terrier	Ch Dianthus Buttons	Mrs K. Newstead
1977	English setter	Bournehouse Dancing Master	G. F. Williams
1978	Fox terrier (wire)	Ch Harrowhill Huntsman	Miss E. Howles
1979	Kerry blue terrier	Eng Am Ch Callaghan of Leander	Miss W. Streatfield
1980	Retriever (flat-coat)	Ch Shargleam Blackcap	Miss P. Chapman
1981	Irish setter	Ch Astley's Portia of Rua	Mrs and Miss Tuite
1982	Poodle (toy)	Ch Grayco Hazlenut	Mrs L. A. Howard
1983	Afghan hound	Ch Montravia Kaskarak Hitari	Mrs P. Gibbs

Breed	Winner	Owner
1984 Lhasa apso	Ch Saxonsprings Hackensack	Mrs J. Blyth
1985 Poodle (standard)	Ch Montravia Tommy-Gun	Miss M. Gibbs
1986 Airedale terrier	Ch Ginger Christmas Carol	Miss A. Livragh
1987 Afghan hound	Ch Viscount Grant	Mr and Mrs C. Amoo
1988 English setter	Sh Ch Starlite Express at Valsett	Mr and Mrs J. W. Watkin
1989 Bearded collie	Ch Potterdale Classic of Moonhill	Mrs B. White
1990 West Highland white terrier	Ch Olac Moon Pilot	D. Tattersall
1991 Spaniel (clumber)	Sh Ch Raycroft Socialite	R. Dunne
1992 Whippet	Ch Pencloe Dutch Gold	Miss M. Bolton
1993 Irish setter	Sh Ch Danaway Debonair	Mrs J. Lorrimer
1994 Welsh terrier	Ch Purston Hit and Miss of Brocolita	Mrs A. J. Maughan

The Welsh terrier bitch Ch Purston Hit and Miss of Brocolita, 1994 Crufts Best in Show, seen here with handler Frank Kellett.

Medals Awarded for the Care and Breeding of Hippopotamuses

The Zoological Society of London (see p. 14) has awarded one Silver and four Bronze Medals for services in the care, breeding and rearing of hippopotamuses at London Zoo.

In 1849 the Society acquired its first hippopotamus – a young male, named Obaysch, presented to HM Queen Victoria by HM Abbas Pasha, Viceroy of Egypt. He was given a stud of greyhounds and deerhounds in the care of an experienced trainer in return. The history of Obaysch's capture is recorded by Samuel Shepheard, founder of Shepheard's Hotel, Cairo, who wrote on 14 November 1849:

'In the spring of the year Inshallah! your London visitors will be gratified with a sight of one of our river monsters – the Hippopotamus. Our consul here, the Honble Mr Murray, having expressed a wish to have one sent to England, where such a thing had never yet been seen, His Highness ordered off a Captain with a troop of twenty men to proceed up to the interior of Africa to follow the course of the white river and not to return without one. After having been five months away they have returned and brought a very fine specimen 5 or 6 months old. He is yet a suckling and drinks 80 pints of milk at a meal and, unwieldy as he is, plays about with the keeper like a great fat pet pig with a square head. The Pasha has presented him to Mr Murray. He was caught with a harpoon.'

The animal was brought back to England in November 1849 on a P & O steamer, the *Ripon*,

ABOVE Ernie Bowman with Bobbie and Joan at London Zoo, 1923, the parents who sired Jimmy, successfully reared by Bowman who was awarded a Bronze Medal.

OPPOSITE The P & O SS *Ripon,* built in 1846, which transported Obaysch in November 1849 back from Egypt.

on which a special tank, holding 400 gallons of water, was built. A special train then took the hippo on the last lap of its journey to London Zoo. This hippo was the first to be seen in Great Britain, and, it is believed, the first to be imported alive into Europe since the Imperial Exhibitions held in the arena of Ancient Rome, between *c.* 50 BC and AD 50. The number of visitors, anxious to see the animal at London Zoo, rose dramatically from 168 895 in 1849 to 360 402 in 1850. Obaysch was accommodated in the new Hippo House, built in 1850, and was very popular, and at first so good natured that he could be ridden around the adjacent Giraffe paddock.

Other hippos were purchased and attempts were made to breed them successfully in captivity, but this was not achieved until 5 November 1872 when 'Guy Fawkes' was born. Bartlett, superintendent from 1859 to 1897, was awarded a Silver Medal on 18 December 1872 for his part in rearing the baby hippo. Michael Prescot and Arthur Thomson, both keepers, received Bronze Medals in the same year for 'successful rearing of young hippopotamus'.

On 18 May 1927, Ernest Bowman, keeper, was awarded a Bronze Medal for the 'successful rearing of young hippopotamus'. He was the eighth Bronze Medal winner since 1866 and the third keeper to win an award for rearing hippopotamuses. He helped to rear successfully a male calf named Jimmy who was born on 20 August 1926 – he received a gratuity of £15.

One other keeper, Gerald C. S. Stanbridge, received a Bronze Medal for 'assiduous care in rearing young hippopotamus' on 20 October 1954.

Pup of the Year

Since 1971 an annual competition has been organised to find Pup of the Year. *Dog World* and Spillers, dog food manufacturers, arrange for a number of heats before the final where a panel of judges selects a winner. Over 10 000 puppies are entered every year into the heats in the hope of winning the title.

FACTS

▪ The 1985 winner, the Afghan hound, Viscount Grant, went on to win Best in Show at Crufts in 1987.

▪ The 1989 winner, the clumber spaniel, Sh Ch Raycroft Socialite, went on to win Best in Show at Crufts in 1991.

BELOW Ch Maid for Gold with Armorique, the Schnauzer who won the 1993 Pup of the Year title and later went on to win Reserve in Best of Group at Crufts in 1994.

WINNERS

	Breed	Winner	Owner
1971	Fox terrier (wire)	Ch Cripsey Townville T'Other Un	Mr and Mrs W. Havenhand
1972	Poodle (standard)	Josato Pink Gin	Mrs A. Timson
1973	Chow-chow	Ch Edlen Crisandra	Mrs E. G. and Miss C. A. Entwis
1974	Alsatian (GSD)	Tracelyn Enterprise	J. Peden and J. Young
1975	Pomeranian	Ch Hadleigh Honey Puff	Mrs G. Dyke
1976	Bull terrier	Ch Kearby's Temptress	Mrs Q. Youatt
1977	Scottish terrier	Brio Chief Barker	Miss J. Miller
1978	Bulldog	Ch Outdoors Jubilant	Mrs G. S. Wakefield
1979	Dachshund (smooth haired)	Turlshill Troubadour	Mrs R. W. B. Pinches
1980	West Highland white terrier	Ch Halfmoon of Olac	D. Tattersall
1981	Greyhound	Ch Rych Pyscador	R. H. Parsons
1982	Pembroke corgi	Belroyd Lovebird	I. Jones and A. Taylor
1983	Poodle (miniature)	Ch Filigran the Master of Valetta	Miss V. M. Dunn
1984	Fox terrier (wire)	Louline Heartstrain	Mr and Mrs G. Pedersen
1985	Afghan hound	Viscount Grant	Mr and Mrs C. Amoo
1986	Scottish terrier	Stuane Enchanted	S. Plane
1987	Poodle (miniature)	Ch Michandy Qui Va La	D. Kitchener
1988	Fox terrier (wire)	Louline High Tide	Mr and Mrs G. Flyckt-Pedersen
1989	Spaniel (clumber)	Sh Ch Raycroft Socialite	R. Dunne
1990	Pekingese	Ch St Sanja Star Attraction of Genderlee	G. Davies
1991	Dachshund (miniature smooth haired)	Jarac Top of the Chocs at Pipersvale	Mrs B. Munt
1992	Airedale terrier	Ch Ballintober Envoy for Joky	Mrs O. Jackson and Mrs M. Swa
1993	Schnauzer	Ch Maid for Gold with Armorique	D. S. Bates and S. R. Frost

Pet Slimmer of the Year

More than 8000 pets from all over Britain weighed in for the 1993 *Weight Watchers Magazine* Pet Slimmer of the Year competition. The 20 cat and dog finalists, all shadows of their former selves, were judged by Jilly Cooper, the novelist.

The winner was 6-year-old Candy the cocker spaniel/collie cross who shed a staggering 24 lb (10.9 kg) to reduce her weight from 57 lb (25.8 kg) to a mere 33 lb (15 kg) over a 12-month period. Her owner, Valerie McMurtrie from Jelliston, Ayr, said: 'The difference in Candy is tremendous. She used to waddle, but now she bounces and gallops along. She used to live with a retired miner who fed her anything and everything.'

OPPOSITE Six-year-old Candie, Pet Slimmer of the Year – before and after!

The Society's medal was designed by Thomas Landseer in the early 1830s and was engraved in 1844. On one side (left) it shows a group of birds, including a crane, stork, swan, spoonbill, pelican, eagle and parrot with the inscription 'Zoological Society of London 1826' and on the other a group of mammals, including an elephant, rhinoceros, cattle and goats. The original dies, made by Benjamin Wyon, recently began to show signs of disintegration, and the medals are now struck from replica dies prepared by the Royal Mint.

The Zoological Society of London Medals

The Zoological Society of London makes a number of awards for contributions to zoology. Six of these are given for outstanding scientific work at various levels of achievement, from school projects to the life's research of the most eminent professors. There are also awards for people who have contributed by helping the public to appreciate the natural world, or by helping or working for the Society itself, particularly in its best-known guise as the body that runs London Zoo and Whipsnade Wild Animal Park. The oldest of the Society's awards are its Gold, Silver and Bronze Medals.

The Gold Medal is awarded to eminent persons as a recognition of outstanding services to the Society or to zoology. Nine medals have been given (end May 1994), the first to HRH Albert, the Prince of Wales, on 18 April 1877 for 'valuable services rendered'. The most recent to HH the Emir of Kuwait in 1993 'in recognition of his contribution to keeping London Zoo open'.

The Silver Medal is awarded in two different categories: to a senior member of staff or an honorary consultant, for long and

Gold Medal Awards

	Recipient	Awarded for
1877	HRH Albert, the Prince of Wales (HM King Edward VII)	Valuable services rendered
1902	Sir Harry H. Johnston	Discovery of the Okapi
1936	The Duke of Bedford	Long service as President and many gifts
1949	Henry G. Maurice	Long and valuable services on Council and as President
1951	Alfred Ezra	Thirty-six years on Council and outstanding donations
1963	Jack Cotton	In recognition of the outstanding help he has given to the Society in its efforts to rebuild the Zoological Gardens, Regent's Park
1970	Professor Sir Solly Zuckerman	In recognition of the outstanding contribution he has made to the scientific development and general progress of the Society's work
1977	HRH Prince Philip, the Duke of Edinburgh	In recognition of his long service as President of the Society
1993	HH the Emir of Kuwait	In recognition of his contribution to keeping London Zoo open

distinguished service to the Society or for some outstanding achievement; to a Fellow of the Society or any other person for contributions to the understanding and appreciation of zoology. A total of 78 medals have been given (end May 1994), the first to Sir Roderick I. Murchison on 1 December 1847 for 'assistance in the introduction of the Aurochs'. The most recent winner is Jonathan Kingdon (writer and artist) for 'contributing by both art and science to the public understanding and appreciation of zoology'.

The Bronze Medal is also awarded to members of staff for long and meritorious service to the Society or for some outstanding achievement. A total of 63 medals (end May 1994) have been given, the first to Henry Hunt, keeper, on 4 July 1866 for 'successful breeding of foreign animals in the Gardens'; most recently to E. Swain, head keeper of the new Lion Terraces, for 'long and meritorious service'.

Simon, the Ship's Cat– Recipient of the Dickin Medal

Simon, a black-and-white tomcat, was awarded the Dickin Medal–the animal equivalent of the Victoria Cross–by the PDSA (People's Dispensary for Sick Animals, see below) on 31 July 1949; it was presented posthumously on 13 April 1950.

Simon was born in 1949 on Stonecutters Island, Hong Kong, and served as a ship's cat on HMS *Amethyst* during the 'Yangtse Incident', 20 April– 31 July 1949. On the night of 19 April, HMS *Amethyst* was proceeding up the Yangtse River to relieve the guard ship HMS *Consort* at Nanking. The ship was trapped by Communist fire and received over 50 direct hits. Simon was wounded and was reportedly buried under wreckage and not discovered for four days. The *Amethyst* was trapped throughout the summer as negotiations between the British government and the Communist People's Liberation Army proved fruitless. During these months the Chinese at Shanghai withheld vital supplies and the crew suffered swarms of mosquitos and a horde of rats. Under these conditions Simon, despite his injuries, disposed of large numbers of rats and thus helped preserve vital food supplies.

In the Public Records Office, London, a letter from the PDSA reads as follows: '. . . As well as being the first time the Dickin Medal has been awarded to a cat, it is also the first time the decoration has gone to the Royal Navy. It is hoped to arrange a special presentation ceremony for Simon when the *Amethyst* returns to this country! A piece of the special Dickin Medal ribbon has been forwarded to Simon together with an elastic collar for him to wear pending the award of the actual medal. Simon's photograph will be placed in the Imperial War Museum, Lambeth as soon as one is available as this is usual with all Dickin Medal animals and birds . . .'

Simon did not fully recover from his wounds, and he died in quarantine at Hackbridge, Surrey, on 28 November 1949. He is buried in plot 281 in the Pets Cemetery, Ilford, Essex.

The Dickin Medal is named after the founder of the PDSA, Maria Elizabeth Dickin, CBE. Born in London in 1870, she devoted her life to philanthropic causes, particularly the welfare of animals. The medal was awarded 53 times between 1943 and 1949 and recipients included 31 pigeons, 18 dogs, 3 horses and Simon, the only cat ever to receive it. It has not been awarded since.

Simon's Dickin Medal sold for a world record price of £23 100 on 23 September 1993 at Christie's – the estimate was £3000–£5000. It was bought by Eton Films, which is making an animated series about animal heroes. (In April 1983 a similar medal, awarded to a pigeon in 1946, was sold at Christie's for £5000.)

15

Top 10 UK Wildlife Attractions

		No. of visitors
1	London Zoo	863 352
2	Chester Zoo, Cheshire	814 883
3	Sea Life Centre, Blackpool, Lancs	592 000
4	Edinburgh Zoo, Lothian, Scotland	515 823
5	Whipsnade Wild Animal Park, Beds	406 912
6	Twycross Zoo, Tamworth, Leics	399 337
7	Knowsley Safari Park, Prescot, Mersey	390 000
8	Bristol Zoo	352 000
9	Cotswold Wildlife Park, Burford, Oxon	330 693
10	Birmingham Nature Centre, W. Midlands	317 684

Source: English Tourist Board, 1993

TOP TWELVE GARDEN BIRDS

For the first time since 1970 the thrush has dropped out of the British Trust for Ornithology's annual winter survey of top 12 birds most commonly seen in British gardens. Published in 1993, the list was headed by the blue tit and blackbird, followed by the robin, house sparrow, chaffinch, dunnock, starling, great tit, greenfinch, song thrush, collared dove and coal tit.

Most Popular Pedigree Cat Breeds, UK

		No. registered
1	Persian long hair	10 991
2	Siamese	5471
3	Burmese	3947
4	British short hair	3727
5	Birman	2152
6	Oriental short hair	1360
7	Maine Coon	1123
8	Exotic short hair	646
9	Abyssinian	603
10	Devon Rex	455

Source: Governing Council of the Cat Fancy, 1993

Most Popular Dog Breeds, UK

		No. registered
1	Labrador	25 261
2	German Shepherd (Alsatian)	19 960
3	Golden retriever	14 685
4	West Highland white terrier	14 468
5	Cavalier King Charles spaniel	13 705
6	Yorkshire terrier	13 041
7	Cocker spaniel	13 002
8	English springer spaniel	11 148
9	Boxer	8139
10	Staffordshire bull terrier	5729

Source: The Kennel Club, 1993

The American Society for the Prevention of Cruelty to Animals instituted a Duncan Gibbins Award for people who show courage in saving an animal, after film director Duncan Gibbins lost his life in a Malibu fire in November 1993 trying to save his cat. Mr Gibbins was fleeing from his house which was on fire when he returned in a vain attempt to find Elsa, the stray he had adopted. Unfortunately, he did not survive the rescue attempt. Elsa was later found cowering underneath the house which survived the fire, nursing burnt paws and singed fur and whiskers.

Ron Langley's scarlet-chested Sunbird, Supreme Champion of the 1993 National Cage & Aviary Birds Exhibition. This show was first held in February 1940 when it attracted 5400 entries. Later the show transferred to Olympia, where huge exhibitions attracted up to 10 000 birds with gates in excess of 30 000. The 50th show was held in December 1993 at the Birmingham National Exhibition Centre. As well as a large variety of exhibited birds, the show introduced performing parrots from the Fantastic Tropical Gardens and Flamingo Land and a Talking Birds Competition.

The 1993 Governing Council of the Cat Fancy, Supreme Grand Champion – Grch Shimileeta Sapphireprince, born 8 May 1992 and owned by Mrs J. A. Bauerfeind. The show, in its 97th year, exhibited many exotic breeds such as the Tonkinese, Ragdoll, Maine Coon and Oriental Spotted. Kari & Oke from *Blue Peter* and Arthur of Spillers 'eat with my paw' fame also attended.

Dog Hero of the Year Award

Ken-L Ration dog food, an American division of the Quaker Oats Company, has made an annual award since 1954 to a dog who under the worst of circumstances comes through with acts of extraordinary bravery. Dogs are nominated and judged by an independent panel of judges on the difficulty/uniqueness of the heroic act (50%), consequence of the act, e.g. saving a life (40%), and the relationship of the dog to the rescued person (10%). The first winner in 1954 was Tang, a collie, who saved a 2-year-old girl from falling off a milk truck. After watching her climb into the back,

Tang blocked the truck's path until the driver discovered the little girl. Tang is also credited with saving the lives of four other children, on separate occasions, by pushing them out of the paths of oncoming vehicles.

WINNERS INCLUDE

Duchess (1958), a German shepherd who watched from shore as her owners sailed across a lake. When the boat overturned, she plunged into the water and rescued one child while the father helped the other two.

Mijo (1967), a St Bernard, who rescued a young girl who fell into a muddy gravel pit filled with water. The frightened child clung to the St Bernard's collar while he towed her safely to dry land.

Grizzly Bear (1970), ironically a St

Bernard, who lived up to his name when he saved his owner from a real grizzly bear. The huge bear was standing in the front door of the house, swinging its paws, until the family dog chased the bear away.

Skippy (1974), a mongrel, to protect his owner, clenched a rattlesnake between his teeth and was bitten in the face several times. He had to spend three days in an animal hospital recovering.

King (1981), a mongrel, who when a fire broke out, clawed and chewed through a plywood door to alert the family.

Bo (1982), a Labrador retriever, and his owner, Laurie, were 'riding rapids' on the Colorado River when their raft overturned. Bo pulled Laurie by the hair out from under the raft and swam to shore with Laurie holding his tail.

17

ARCHITECTURE

Royal Institute of British Architects Awards

The Royal Institute of British Architects (RIBA) has made annual awards since 1966, at a national and regional level. The purpose of the awards is to give public recognition to outstanding examples of current architecture and thereby achieve greater public appreciation of good architectural design. A building is judged on its setting, fitness for purpose, consistency of design, appropriate use of materials, and whether it is likely to remain a fine work of architecture throughout its full working life. Buildings submitted for awards are judged by regional juries.

Since 1988 a 'Building of the Year' has been selected from the national winners:

1988 St Oswald's Hospice, Newcastle upon Tyne (Jane and David Derbyshire)

1989 Nelson Mandela School, Birmingham (City of Birmingham Architect's Department)

1990 Queen's Inclosure Middle School, Cowplain, Hants (Hampshire County Council Architect's Department)

1991 Broadgate Centre, London (Arup Associates)

1992 Sackler Gallery, Royal Academy of Arts, London (Sir Norman Foster & Partners)

1993 Woodlea Primary School, Bordon, Hants (Hampshire County Council Architect's Department)

Financial Times Architecture Award

Since 1967 this award has been given to encourage higher standards of architectural and environmental design for industrial and commercial buildings. The 1993 entries were judged by Sir Simon Hornby (Chairman, Association for Business Sponsorship), Nicholas Grimshaw and John Outram (architects) and the award was given to the Queen's Stand at Epsom Racecourse,

designed by Richard Horden Associates, for its 'stunning geometry and its pure, simple and disciplined design'.

WINNERS (BIENNIAL SINCE 1987)

1967 Reliance Controls Ltd, Swindon, Wilts (Foster Ass.)

1968 Engineering Research Station for the Northern Gas Board,

Killingworth, Newcastle upon Tyne (Ryder & Yates)

1969 Wallace Arnold Quality Tested Used Car Factory, Leeds (Derek Walker & Partners)

1970 Chemical and Administration Building, Bradford Water Supply (Whicheloe & Macfarlane)

1971 Lee Abbey Farm, Lynton, N. Devon (Scarlett Burkett Ass.)

The 1993 National RIBA awards went to Woodlea Primary School, Bordon, Hants (also 'Building of the Year'), the Queen's Stand at Epsom Racecourse, Surrey, and The Fountains Abbey Visitor Centre, Ripon, N. Yorks.

Woodlea Primary School, designed by Hampshire County Council Architect's Department is, as its name suggests, set in densely wooded country on a steep, east-west slope. Following the contours of the land, the school nestles in a naturally created bowl. Designed to accommodate 245 children between the ages of 5 and 11, the school is a robust but simple timber and masonry building. Most of the noisier teaching areas are situated on the outside of the designed curve and open on to paved external areas. Quieter areas by contrast overlook the bowl. A large assembly hall, the only two-storey part of the building complex, is enclosed and rooflit within the brick-walled part of the building. *Jury's comment*: 'The level of invention and sheer exuberance of this building are very compelling. It is a romantic and picturesque ideal that has been lovingly nurtured and crafted by a dedicated team from inception to completion.'

1972 IBM Havant Plant, Hants (Arup Ass.)

1973 Horizon Project for John Player & Sons, Nottingham (Arup Ass.)

1974 Warehouse and office for Modern Art Glass Co., Thamesmead, London (Foster Ass.)

1975 Carlsberg Brewery, Northampton (Knud Munk)

1976 PATS Centre, Industrial Research Laboratory, Melbourn, Herts (Piano & Rogers)

1977 Furniture Factory for Herman Miller Ltd, Bath, Avon (Farrell/Grimshaw Partnership)

1978 Solid Wastes Rail Transfer Station, Brentford, London (Brentford Architects)

1979 St Sergus North Sea Gas Terminal (Area Design Group)

1980 Greene King & Sons Brewery, Cask Department, Bury St Edmunds, Suffolk (Michael Hopkins Architects)

1981 No award

1982 Humber Bridge, Humberside (Freeman, Fox & Partners)
Production plant, Amersham Int., Bucks (Percy Thomas Partnership)

1983 Gateway House, Basingstoke, Hants (Arup Ass.)

1984 Renault Centre, Swindon, Wilts (Foster Ass.)

1985 1 Finsbury Avenue, London (Arup Ass.)
Schlumberger Research Centre, Cambridge (Michael Hopkins & Partners)

1986 Control Building, Megget Reservoir, Selkirk, Borders, Scotland (W. J. Cairns & Partners and R. H. Cuthbertson Partners)

1987 Lloyd's of London (Richard Rogers Partnership)

1989 Courts of Justice, Truro, Cornwall (Evans & Shalev)

1991 RMC House, Egham, Surrey (Edward Cullinan Architects Ltd)

1993 Queen's Stand, Epsom Racecourse, Surrey (Richard Horden Ass.)

The Queen's Stand, designed by Richard Horden Associates, overlooks Epsom Downs and the racecourse. The design won a competition held in 1988 when a decision was made to replace the existing stand. The 5000 club members and visitors enter the stand on the ground floor, a terrace at mezzanine level provides a view of the racecourse, and above is a restaurant, private boxes, hospitality suites, and press facilities. *Jury's comment*: 'A building that more than demonstrates the architects' brilliant assurance and confidence in their ability to contribute to the body of work that distinguishes and nourishes contemporary modernist architecture.' This building also received the 1993 *Financial Times* Architecture Award.

The Fountains Abbey Visitor Centre at Ripon, designed by Edward Cullinan Architects, is the National Trust's (NT) most visited property (see p.246). In 1983 the NT acquired Studley Royal Estate – an extensive, landscaped garden dating from the 18th century and dominated by the ruins of the Cistercian Fountains Abbey. The architects were appointed to design a visitor centre. The main buildings form a cluster reminiscent of farm buildings grouped around a courtyard. The centre has stone-tiled monopitch roofs and dry-stone rainscreen walls which shelter the courtyard within. *Jury's comment*: 'The poetic combination of solid rising walls and delicately poised roofs oversailing into the landscape has immediate appeal; yet this is a building of which one could never tire and where there would always be something new and delightful to discover.'

ART & ILLUSTRATION

The Turner Prize

This prize, established in 1984 by the Patrons of New Art, is intended to encourage discussion about new developments in contemporary British art. It is open to any British artist under 50 for an outstanding exhibition or other presentation of work. The winner receives a prize of £20 000. The prizegiving has been broadcast live by Channel 4 television, who also sponsors the award. The artists are shortlisted by a jury and their work is exhibited at the Tate Gallery, London.

The 1993 jury members, chaired by Nicholas Serota (Director, Tate Gallery), were Iwona Blaswick (Curator, Tate Gallery), Carole Conrad (Patrons of New Art), Declan McGonagal (Director, Irish Museum of Modern Art, Dublin) and David Sylvester (critic).

Winners	Shortlisted artists
1984 Malcolm Morley	Richard Deacon, Gilbert and George, Howard Hodgkin, Richard Long
1985 Howard Hodgkin	Terry Atkinson, Tony Cragg, Ian Hamilton Finlay, Milean Kalinvoska, John Walker
1986 Gilbert and George	Art & Language, Victor Burgin, Derek Jarman, Steven McKenna, Bill Woodrow
1987 Richard Deacon	Patrick Caulfield, Helen Chadwick, Richard Long, Declan McGonagle, Therese Oulton
1988 Tony Cragg	no shortlist
1989 Richard Long	Gillian Ayres, Lucian Freud, Giuseppe Penone, Paula Rego, Sean Scully, Richard Wilson
1990 No award	
1991 Anish Kapoor	Ian Davenport, Riona Rae, Rachel Whiteread
1992 Grenville Davey	Damien Hirst, David Tremlett, Alison Wilding
1993 Rachel Whiteread	Hannah Collins, Vong Phaophanit, Sean Scully

FACTS

- Rachel Whiteread (1993) and Gilbert and George (1986) have both won once and have also been shortlisted in 1991 and 1984 respectively.
- Sean Scully has been shortlisted twice (1989, 1993), but has never won.
- The 1993 shortlisted artists were: Hannah Collins, who has adopted photography as the important medium in her work; Vong Phaophanit, whose installation 'Neon Rice Field' (especially created for the exhibition) is an example of the interaction of materials, in this case the organic (rice) and the man-made (neon tubes); and Sean Scully, whose three large exhibited paintings were composed of wide vertical and horizontal bands of resonant colour.

The John Moores Liverpool Exhibition

The first exhibition in 1957 was organised by John Moores, founder of the Littlewoods Company, and a keen amateur painter. The aims stated in the preface to the first catalogue were: '. . . to give Merseysiders the chance to see an exhibition embracing the best and most vital work being done today throughout the country, and to encourage contemporary artists, especially the young and progressive'. The exhibition has been held at the Walker Art Gallery biennially since then, and is open to all living artists working in the UK. The first prize is £20 000, in return for which the winning painting joins the Walker Art Gallery's permanent collection. There are also 10 prizes of £1000 each.

In 1993, 2013 works were submitted and placed before a jury who selected 54 and awarded the prizes. Peter Doig, born in Edinburgh in 1959, won the 1993 prize with his work entitled 'Blotter'.

Winners

- **1957** Jack Smith (Open)
  - John Bratby (Junior)
- **1959** Patrick Heron (Main Prize)
  - William Scott (British)
  - Paul Rebeyrolle (French)
  - Hubert Dalwood (Sculpture)
- **1961** Henry Mundy (Open)
  - Peter Blake (Junior)
  - Evelyn Williams (Sculpture)
- **1963** Roger Hilton (Open)
  - Stephen McKenna (Junior)
- **1965** Michael Tyzack (Open)
  - Tim Whitmore (Junior)
- **1967** David Hockney
  - Malcolm Hughes
  - Joe Tilson
- **1969** Richard Hamilton
  - Mary Martin
- **1972** Euan Uglow
  - Adrian Henri
  - Noel Forster
- **1974** Myles Murphy
  - John Walker
  - Craigie Aitchison
  - Sean Scully
- **1976** John Walker
  - Howard Hodgkin
  - Laurie Baldwyn
- **1978** Noel Forster
  - William Turnbull
  - Robyn Denny
- **1980** Michael Moon
  - Howard Hodgkin
  - Christopher Le Brun
- **1982** John Hoyland
  - Gillian Ayres
  - Adrian Berg
- **1985** Bruce McLean
  - Stephen Buckley
  - Terry Setch
- **1987** Tim Head
  - Graham Crowley
  - Kate Whiteford
- **1989** Lisa Milroy
  - Basil Beattie
  - Suzanne Treister
- **1991** Andrzej Jackowski
- **1993** Peter Doig

Peter Doig describes his painting: '"Blotter" was painted from a photograph I took of my brother standing on a frozen pond. The reflection was enhanced by pumping water on to the ice. It is a variation of earlier paintings that have been more reliant on the imagination. The title refers to (amongst other things) the notion of one's being absorbed into a place or landscape, and to the process through which the painting developed: soaking paint into canvas. The figure is deliberately shown looking down into the reflection; this is to suggest inward thought, rather than some sort of contemplation of the scene.'

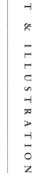

'Blotter' by Peter Doig won first prize in the 1993 John Moores Liverpool Exhibition at the Walker Art Gallery.

▌ The 1993 conditions of entry stated that entrants were limited to submitting one painting, preferably new, in an accepted modern medium, designed to hang on a wall and project no more than six inches. Sculpture, traditional watercolours and graphics were excluded.
▌ The 1993 judging panel: Andrew Brighton (critic and lecturer, Kent Institute of Art & Design), Stephen Farthing (Ruskin Master of Drawing, Oxford University), Paul Huxley (Professor of Painting, Royal College of Art), Catherine Lampert (Director, Whitechapel Art Gallery), and Julian Treuherz (Keeper of art galleries, National Museums and Galleries on Merseyside).

Selection for inclusion in the 1957 John Moores Liverpool Exhibition. Judges (left to right): Eric Newton, Professor Lawrence Gowing, Sir John Rothenstein, Hugh Scrutton.

The Portrait Award

The National Portrait Gallery, London, established this award in 1980 for British artists under 40 years of age. The competition is judged from original paintings which must be in oil, tempera or acrylic, and be painted from life – the human figure predominating. An exhibition of works selected from the entries is mounted annually in the Gallery from June to early September of each year. Since 1990 the competition has received over 600 entries annually, out of which an average of 58 paintings a year have been selected and exhibited. In 1993 a record 79 007 visitors attended the exhibition.

The award consists of a cash prize and a commission to be painted for the Gallery by the winner. Sponsored by John Player from 1980 to 1989, the award is now sponsored by British Petroleum. In 1994 the first prize was £10 000 and a commission worth £2000 (the subject is decided as a result of discussion between the artist, the director and curator of the 20th Century Department at the Gallery); second prize was £4000; and third prize £2000. Up to five special

	Winner	Title of portrait	Commissioned portrait
1980	Margaret Foreman	Sir Richard Southern	Lord Butler
1981	Emma Sergeant	Drinks at Milapote I	Lord David Cecil and Lord Olivier
1982	Humphrey Ocean	Lord Volvo and his Estate	Paul McCartney
1983	Michael Taylor	Caroline Watching Television	Julian Bream
1984	Rosemary Beaton	Paul	Sir Robin Day
1985	Jeff Stultiens	Isobel Work	Cardinal Basil Hume
1986	Ivy Smith	The Smith Family 'Golden Wedding'	Sir Richard and Sir David Attenborough
1987	Alison Watt	Self-Portrait with Tea-Cup	HM Queen Elizabeth The Queen Mother
1988	Allan Ramsay	Self-Portrait	Alan Ayckbourn
1989	Paula MacArthur	Portrait with Brown Overalls	Dr Frederick Sanger
	Tai-Shan Schierenberg	Lynn Dennison	John Mortimer
1990	Annabel Cullen	Self-Portrait	Baroness Blackstone
1991	Justin Mortimer	Three Seated Figures	Harold Pinter
1992	Lucy Willis	Her Majesty's Pleasure	Lord and Lady Longford
1993	Philip Harris	Two Figures Lying in a Shallow Stream	Anthony Dowell
1994	Peter Edwards	An Artist's Model	(to be announced)

commendations are also awarded annually worth £500 each.

The winners are chosen by a distinguished panel of judges, which in 1994 was: Lord Ashburton (chairman, British Petroleum), John Bellany (artist), Richard Calvocoressi (keeper, Scottish National Gallery of Modern Art), Joanna Drew (former director, Hayward Gallery), Robin Gibson (curator, 20th Century Collection, National Portrait Gallery), Philip Harris (winner, Portrait Award 1993), Professor Norbert Lynton (art historian), Humphrey Ocean (artist), and the current director of the National Portrait Gallery.

FAR LEFT 'Self-Portrait', oil on canvas, by Allan Ramsay, winner of the 1988 Portrait Award and **LEFT** 'Alan Ayckbourn', oil on canvas, Ramsay's subsequent commission completed in 1989.

The National Portrait Gallery, London, was founded in 1856 as a 'Gallery of the Portraits of the most eminent persons in British History'. Its aim was to collect the likenesses of famous British men and women. Today, the collection is the most comprehensive of its kind in the world, and constitutes a unique record of the men and women who created British national history. The Gallery houses a primary collection of over 9000 works, only about ten per cent of which are on display at one time, as well as an immense picture archive.

Rachel Whiteread – 'Untitled Room'

Previously shortlisted in 1991, Rachel Whiteread, the 30-year-old artist born in London in 1963, received a cheque for £20 000 when she won the 1993 Turner Prize. Her sculpture is based on taking casts of commonplace objects. However, one of the most remarkable aspects of her work is that these casts are not of the objects themselves but of the space surrounding the object or the inside space of an object. Recently, the artist commented: 'I wanted to use things that already existed. I wanted to get inside them or beneath them and try to reveal something previously unknown. I've cast all sorts of objects, but one that recurs is the space beneath a bed – a sinister place. To cast that space and make it solid transformed it into something with a presence rather than something forgotten.' Over the past five years she has undertaken such works as casting the inside of a wardrobe and covering it with black felt, and using rubber and plaster to cast the bottoms of baths and the inside of hot-water bottles.

Her new work which was shown at the Tate in the Turner Prize exhibition, 'Untitled Room', was a development of the sculpture 'Ghost' – a plaster cast of the four walls of a living room of a deserted 1930s terraced house in North London. In contrast, this new sculpture was cast from a room constructed by the artist herself in Berlin where she had been living for the last year.

At the time of the award, her most recent work was 'House' which was situated near the corner of Grove Road and Roman Road in the East End of London, isolated in a small park where once a Victorian terrace stood. Before the last house was demolished she managed to cast the interior. She constructed a reinforced sprayed concrete lining inside the walls. The empty house was then sealed off and left to let the mould separate from the outer walls. Finally the exterior walls were dismantled, leaving Whiteread's grey, eerie, stark sculpture as a memorial to the Victorian house that went before. 'House' was sponsored to the tune of £60 000 and survived several stays of execution before demolition on 11 January 1994.

Rachel Whiteread's 'House' – a negative impression of a Victorian terraced house – door panels, fireplaces and window frames that obtrude; door handles and architraves that have become intrusions into the structure of the building – a stark, eerie monument to the house that went before.

Rachel Whiteread also received another award on the same night as the Turner Prize – the K Foundation prize for the 'worst artist on the shortlist'. For this she received a further £40 000. The K Foundation, set up by the pop group KLF to satirise the Turner Prize, took 25 journalists and guests on a mystery tour in stretch limousines to a field in Surrey where each person was given £1600 to pin to a board. This was then driven to the Tate Gallery where it was chained to the railings. A masked man from the Foundation then announced that if the artist did not claim her prize within five minutes he was going to set fire to it – with seconds to spare Whiteread appeared and collected the money. The Foundation had purportedly spent an estimated £200 000, including the prize money, on advertising their award in both the national press and on Channel 4 television.

Royal Academy Summer Exhibition

'*The toil of months, experience of years
Before the dreaded Council now appears.*'

Thus run the first lines of a pamphlet written in 1875 by a disappointed painter. The 'Council' in question are the artists governing the Royal Academy who, for a few weeks each year, take on the long and arduous task of selecting pictures for the Summer Exhibition. In April, the alley at the side of Burlington House becomes a bustling stream of people bringing oils, watercolours, drawings, prints, sculpture and architectural designs to the Academy for the annual ritual of selection and hanging. Many of them will not be lucky, on average only one in ten is finally included.

In 1994 this remarkable open exhibition will have been held every year for 226 years –

'We . . . beg leave to inform your Majesty, that the two principal objects we have in view are the establishing of a well-regulated School or Academy of Design, and an Annual Exhibition, open to all artists of distinguished merit, where they may offer their performances to public inspection and acquire that degree of reputation and encouragement which they shall be deemed to deserve.'

The charter containing these words was signed by 22 artists and submitted to King George III on 28 November 1768. It stated the aims of the proposed Royal Academy of Arts and sought permission for the foundation of the Institution. The King's response was favourable; and the 'Royal Academy of Arts in London, for the purpose of cultivating the Arts of Painting, Sculpture and Architecture' came into being soon afterwards, on 10 December 1768.

In the earlier years of the 18th century, contemporary works were rarely exhibited. There were no public art galleries in Britain until 1814 when the Dulwich Picture Gallery opened in London, Britain's oldest purpose-built picture gallery, designed by Sir John Soane. The Royal Academy's annual exhibition of the work of living artists was to have a remarkable impact on this unhappy situation.

The first of the annual exhibitions in 1769, held in a hired room in Pall Mall, London, comprised only 136 works. The following year, the Academy came into the possession of splendid new apartments in Somerset House, London. For over half a century the exhibitions were held on the top floor. To reach these rooms, visitors had to climb a superb staircase. This presented problems to some of the more elderly or corpulent among them. Queen Charlotte had to recuperate on each floor before ascending further and Doctor Johnson regarded the climb as a major test of endurance.

The small South Room with paintings hung with their entry labels, awaiting the 1993 Summer Exhibition.

The youngest exhibitor at the Royal Academy of Arts Annual Summer Exhibition was Lewis Melville 'Gino' Lyons. He was born on 30 April 1962, painted 'Trees and Monkeys' on 4 June 1965, and submitted it on 17 March 1967 at just under five years of age. It was exhibited on 29 April 1967.

Though the number of artists who wished to exhibit increased, the space available at the Academy remained the same, and more works were crowded on to the walls of Somerset House. Prints of the period, notably by Rowlandson and Pietro Martini, show great crowds of fashionable visitors attending the exhibition, peering at walls hung floor to ceiling with paintings.

Despite the confusion caused by the proximity of the paintings to one another, it began to be customary for a picture to emerge as 'Picture of the Year' due to its great popular appeal. In 1813, when Wilkie's 'Blind Man Buff' earned this title, a fellow painter wrote to a friend '[it] has ever a crowd round it closely packed, and some of those in the rear, in vain struggling for a view, console themselves for the disappointment by looking upwards at my Shakespeare subject . . .'. Frith's painting 'The Private View of the Royal Academy' in 1881 is evidence of the Academy as the art establishment, including portraits of Lillie Langtry, Oscar Wilde and Lord Gladstone as they peruse the year's successes.

The Academy's move to Trafalgar Square in 1837 and Burlington House, Piccadilly, London, in 1869 (where the galleries were built on the gardens) helped to alleviate the problem of overcrowding. In the first year at Burlington House, there were over 4500 works submitted and the exhibition drew a remarkable 315000 visitors. Since then the exhibition has survived two world wars, the advent of modern, then abstract, art and a quantity of critical contempt. In the last decade the Academy has made the exhibition more accessible to the general public and around 100000 visitors attend the exhibition each year.

Thomas Rowlandson's painting of the Exhibition Room, Somerset House, showing the crowds of visitors attending the early, packed Summer Exhibitions, with paintings hanging from floor to ceiling.

Award	Prize	Awarded for	Winner	Judges
Charles Wollaston Award	£10 000	Most distinguished work in the exhibition	Robert Medley 'Preparation for the Execution'	Frank Auerbach, John Bellany RA, Jeremy Isaacs, Sir Eduardo Paolozzi RA, David Sylvester
Korn / Ferry Award	£10 000	Picture of the Year	Norman Adams RA 'Cycle of Love and Death' (watercolour)	Norman Ackroyd RA, Sir Alan Bowness, Jeffery Camp RA, Joanna Drew
Bovis / *Architects' Journal* Awards for Architecture	£3500	Exhibit of architectural merit which successfully communicates the architect's intention to the public	Andrew Wright 'The Holy Island' (models)	Committee from *Architects' Journal* and Bovis Construction Ltd
	£1500	Exhibit submitted by a non-member of the Academy	Daniel Libeskind 'The Extension of the Berlin Museum with the Jewish Museum' (model)	
	£750	Model, drawing or other graphic representation executed by exhibitor or in his office	Eva Jiriona Architects 'The Stairs I' and 'The Stairs: Studies' (model)	
The Worshipful Company of Chartered Architects	£1000	Measured drawing (or set of drawings) or work of architecture	Jason Oliver 'Axonometric of Fothergill Watson's Office, Nottingham' (watercolour)	
Jack Goldhill Award for Sculpture	£5000	Sculpture	Neil Taylor 'Kara'	Jack Goldhill, Anish Kapoor, John Wragg RA
Guinness Award	A comm. for £5000 to be acquired by the Guinness Art Collection	First-time exhibitor	Timur Iskhakov 'The Autumn Dream' (oil)	Sir Philip Dowson PRA, Lord McFarlane
London Original Print Fair Award	£1000	Print in any medium	John Loker 'Double Crossover Entry' (monoprint)	Gordon Cooke, John Hoyland RA, Mick Moon, Helen Rosslyn
House & Garden Award	£1000	Work in any medium depicting an interior	Fred Cuming RA 'Window: April Evening' (oil)	Sister Wendy Beckett, Ken Howard RA
The Arts Club Prize	Purchase price paid for work	Picture chosen to be added to collection at the Arts Club, Dover Street, London	Francis Bowyer 'Studio Window' (watercolour)	Committee from The Arts Club

The Singer & Friedlander first prize of £15 000 in 1993 went to Martin Aubert for his painting 'After The Hurricane' – an atmospheric stack of deck chairs on Brighton beach after one of the famous hurricane storms. His most difficult problem in this picture was getting the stripes to come out the other side, and not have the green where the white should be. Aubert had never previously entered an art competition.

Topselling Art Postcards

| Tate Gallery | | National Gallery | |
Title	Artist	Title	Artist
1 Ophelia	Millais	Sunflowers	Van Gogh
2 Lady of Shalott	Waterhouse	The Thames Below Westminster	Monet
3 The Snail	Matisse	The Water-Lily Pond	Monet
4 Carnation Lily, Lily	Sargent	A Wheatfield with Cypresses	Van Gogh
5 The Window	Bonnard	The Umbrellas	Renoir
6 The Table	Bonnard	Van Gogh's Chair and Pipe	Van Gogh
7 Farm near Auvers	Van Gogh	The Toilet of Venus	Velazquez
8 Whaam!	Lichtenstein	Bathers at Asnières	Seurat
9 Metamorphosis	Dali	The Fighting Temeraire	Turner
10 Weeping Woman	Picasso	Boating on the Seine	Renoir

ABOVE 'Sunset Song', painted in oil by John Bellany RA, won the Korn / Ferry Award for Picture of the Year at the 1993 Summer Exhibition.

LEFT 'Sunflowers' by Vincent van Gogh – topselling postcard at the National Gallery.

BELOW 'Ophelia' by Sir John Millais topselling postcard at the Tate Gallery.

The Singer & Friedlander/Sunday Times *Award for Watercolours*

The Sunday Times and Singer & Friedlander, the City merchant bank, sponsor this annual competition to promote the continuance of fine watercolour painting. The sixth annual awards for watercolour painting were made in 1993, offering £25 000 in prize money – the winner received £15 000, second prizewinner £5000 and five runners-up £1000 each. The competition is open to all artists born or resident in the UK who may enter up to two of their works. The 1993 competition attracted 1400 entrants from which approximately 200 paintings were selected.

WINNERS
1988 Tom Coates
1989 Sandra Walker
1990 David Prentice
1991 Guy Noble
1992 David Curtiss
1993 Martin Aubert

W. H. Smith Illustration Awards

These annual awards, first given in 1987, are organised by the National Art Library at the Victoria and Albert Museum, London, and are intended to encourage the illustration of published books and magazines. A prize of £4000 is awarded to the best overall illustration and two second prizes of £1500 are each given to a book and magazine illustration. The judging panel is made up of three illustrators, one painter and one writer.

WINNERS

1987 Overall Ralph Steadman, *I, Leonardo*
Book Justin Todd, *Alice's Adventures in Wonderland* and *Through the Looking-Glass and What Alice Found There*, by Lewis Carroll
Magazine No award

1988 Overall No award
Book Charles Keeping, *Classic Tales of the Macabre*
Magazine Richard Parent, *The Chernobyl effect: lessons from a nuclear disaster*

1989 Overall Jeff Fisher, *A Better Beast of Burden* (*New Scientist* cover, No. 1609)
Book Charlotte Voake, *The Mighty Slide*, by Alan Ahlberg
Magazine Richard Parent, *Breakdown: Out of Sight, Out of Mind* (*Director*, vol. 41, no. 11, May 1988)

1990 Overall John Vernon Lord, *Aesop's Fables: retold in verse by James Michie*
Book Michael Foreman, *War Boy: A Country Childhood*
Magazine Jamel Akib, *Crisis in food* (*Marketing*, 26 October 1989; *Director*, vol. 41, no. 11, May 1988)

1991 Overall Angela Barrett, *The Hidden House*
Book Christopher Mormell, *An Alphabet of Animals*
Magazine Christopher Brown, *Cut d'Azur* (*Sunday Times Magazine*, spring 1990)

1992 Overall Charlotte Knox, *Fruit: a connoisseur's guide and cookbook*
Book Angela Barrett, *Snow White*
Magazine Dolores Fairman, *The Cure is Green* (*Observer Magazine*, 21 April 1991)

The most valuable painting in the world is the 'Mona Lisa' by Leonardo da Vinci (1452–1519) which hangs in the Louvre, Paris, France. For insurance purposes it was valued at $100 million when it was moved from Washington, DC, USA, to New York City for an exhibition which ran from 14 December 1962 to 12 March 1963. This insurance was not taken up because the premiums outweighed the cost of providing round-the-clock security precautions. Da Vinci painted the Mona Lisa in *c.* 1503–7 and it measures 30.5 x 20.9 in (77.5 x 53.1 cm). It is believed to be a portrait of either Mona (short for Madonna) Lisa Gherardini, the wife of Francesco del Giocondo of Florence, or Constanza d'Avalos, mistress of Giuliano de Medici. King Francis I of France bought the painting for his bathroom in 1517 for 4000 gold florins.

1993 Overall Tony Meeuwissen, *The Key to the Kingdom*
Book Louise Brierley, *Songs from Shakespeare*
Magazine Sarah Ball, *Christmas Books* (*Times Saturday Review*, 28 November 1992)

Tony Meeuwissen's *The Key to the Kingdom*, published by Pavilion in 1992, winner of the overall 1993 W. H. Smith Illustration Award.

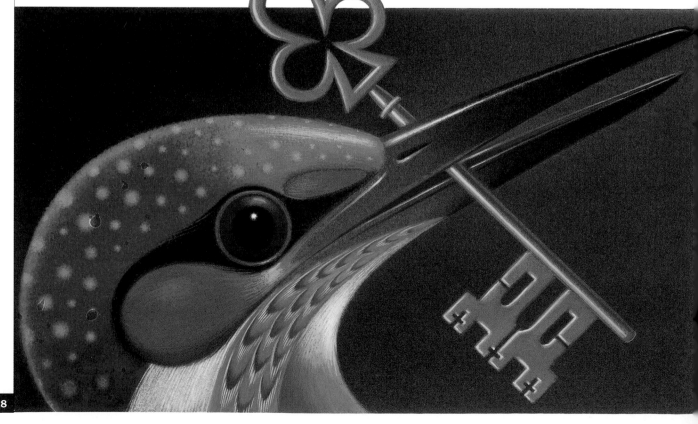

AUCTIONS

World Auction Records

The largest auction company in the world is the Sotheby Group of London and New York which was founded in 1744 (until 1778 it dealt mainly in books). The other major auction house, Christie's of London, held its first art auction in 1766. The following selection of world auction records is derived from these two houses. Prices quoted are hammer prices.

Antiquity £2 000 000, 9 December 1993. A Caeretan hydria Greek vase, attributed to the Eagle Painter, late 6th century BC (Sotheby's, London)

Armour £1 750 000, 5 May 1983. A Milanese three-quarter armour, made for Henri II, King of France, by Giovanni Paolo Negroli, c. 1540–45 (from the Hever Castle Collection) (Sotheby's, London)

ABOVE Chinese Tang dynasty horse sold for £3 400 000.
BELOW 'Portrait of Dr Gachet' by Vincent van Gogh sold for a record £44 589 774.

Art – any work £44 589 774, 15 May 1990. 'Portrait of Dr Gachet', Vincent van Gogh (Christie's, New York)

Art – old master drawing £3 800 000, 6 July 1993. 'The Holy Family on the Flight into Egypt', Michelangelo Buonarroti (Christie's, London)

Art – old master painting £17 121 455, 31 May 1989. 'Cosimo de Medici', Jacopo Pontormo (Christie's, New York)

Art Nouveau £1 023 672, 2 December 1989. A Daum Nancy and Louis Majorelle wheel-carved cameo glass and bronze three-branch Lotus Lamp, c. 1900 (Sotheby's, New York)

Barometer £310 000, 5 December 1991. From the Messer Collection by Quare (Christie's, London)

Printed book £2 817 713, 22 October 1987. *The Gutenberg Bible*, vol. 1, Doheny Collection, Gutenberg & Fust (Christie's, New York)

Camera £36 000, 25 November 1993. Opulent gold camera made specifically for Sultan Abdel Aziz of Morocco in 1901 (Christie's, London)

Car £5 775 401, 21 May 1990. 1962 Ferrari 250 Gran Turismo Berlinetta Competition GTO (Sotheby's, Monaco)

Car registration number £185 000, 10 December 1993. K1 NGS (Christie's, London)

Carpet £605 060, 21 May 1992. A Louis XIV Savonnerie carpet, c. 1670 (Sotheby's, New York)

Ceramic £3 400 000, 12 December 1989. A Chinese Tang dynasty (AD 618–906) horse sold by the British Rail Pension Fund (Sotheby's, London)

Clock £800 000, 5 July 1989. 'Night' miniature longcase clock, Charles II, 6 ft 1 in (1.85 m) high, Thomas Tompion (Christie's, London)

Historical Costume £55 000, 23 May 1989. Gentleman's doublet of ivory silk woven in pink, yellow, blue, mauve and green, Italian or French c. 1625 (Christie's, London)

Diamond £5 930 470, 14 November 1990. An 11-sided pear-shaped mixed cut diamond – 101.84 carats (Sotheby's, Geneva)

Doll's House £135 000, 10 January 1978. Titania's Palace, designed by Major Sir Neville Wilkinson. It took 15 years to complete, 1907–22 (Christie's, London)

Furniture £7 800 000, 5 July 1990. The Badminton Cabinet, The Grand Ducal Workshops (Christie's, London)

Glass £520 000, 4 June 1979. A hitherto unrecorded late Roman cage-cup or diatretum, c. AD 200 (Sotheby's, London)

Globes (a pair) £930 000, 30 October 1991. Magnificent pair of gilt-metal globes by Gerard Mercator (Christie's, London)

Islamic Art £2 200 000, 19 October 1993. Islamic bronze lion produced in Moorish Spain, dating from the 11/12th century (Christie's, London)

Islamic Work of Art £850 000, 8 July 1980. *The World History of Rashid al-Din* (text in Arabic), AD 714/1314 (Sotheby's, London)

The Badminton Cabinet sold for £7 800 000.

This unique Kämmer and Reinhardt bisque character doll was sold at Sotheby's, London, for a world record auction price of £170 000 on 8 February 1994. It was made in Germany in c. 1909, bears an impression which reads 'K & R 108', and it is believed to be the only one of its type in the world. The doll was possibly made from an experimental mould, number 108, which was destroyed and never used in production by the company. It has pierced ears unlike others in the series, suggesting that it was meant to portray an older child.

The doll has a well-moulded face with closed, slightly smiling mouth, red dashes in the nostrils and well-painted grey-blue eyes. It has real fair hair, held in plaited bunches by a white bow at each side. Its body is composed of wood and it has a voice box. It is dressed in a white pintucked broderie-anglaise cotton dress with lace cuffs and neck, threaded with blue ribbon, and a blue sash, white petticoat and blue-threaded bloomers, with a blue-ribboned straw bonnet, and is 25¼ in (64 cm) high.

Manuscript £7 400 000, 6 December 1983. *The Gospels of Henry the Lion*, written in Helmershausen Abbey, Germany, c. 1173–75 (Sotheby's, London)

Medals – Victoria Cross (and for any group of medals) £120 000, 19 September 1992. The VC, DSO and two Bars, MC and Bar Group awarded posthumously to Major Edward 'Mick' Mannock, Royal Air Force, the highest scoring and most decorated British pilot of World War I (Sotheby's, Sussex)

Musical Instrument £820 000, 21 November 1990. 'Mendelssohn' Stradivarius violin – Antonio Stradivari (Christie's, London)

Photograph £235 294, 8 October 1993. Georgia O'Keefe: 'A portrait – Hands with Thimble', by Alfred Stieglitz (Christie's, New York)

Russian Work of Art £1 581 674, 10 June 1992. Fabergé Imperial Easter Egg – 'The Love Trophy' – commissioned by Tsar Nicholas II, workmaster: Henrik Wigström, St Petersburg, c. 1905 (Sotheby's, New York)

Sculpture £6 200 000, 7 December 1989.

This snuff box made £1 050 228 at auction.

A Prague bronze statue of the 'Dancing Faun', *c.* 1610–15, by Adrien de Vries (Sotheby's, London)
Silver £2 045 454, 4 December 1993. The Hanover Chandelier – a magnificent silver chandelier executed by Balthasar Friedrich Behrens in 1736, after a design by William Kent (Christie's, Monaco)
Snuff Box £1 050 228, 17 November 1992. A jewelled gold and hardstone snuff box made for Frederick II, King of Prussia, after a design by Jean Guillaume George Krüger, Berlin, *c.* 1770 (Sotheby's, Geneva)
British 20th-century Stamp £33 000, 21 November 1991. 1902–04, 6d dull purple postage stamp issued on 14 March 1904 (Sotheby's, London)
Teddy Bear £55 000, 19 September 1989. A dual-plush Steiff teddy bear, German, *c.* 1920 – blonde and brown plush (Sotheby's, London)
Toy £115 257, 16 December 1991. George Brown handpainted tin plate replica of the 'Charles' hose reel, a piece of fire-fighting equipment, measuring 15 × 23 in (38 × 58 cm), built *c.* 1870 (Christie's, New York)
Tribal Art £1 890 243, 21 April 1990. A Bangwa Memorial Figure of a Royal Titled Wife, 21 April 1990 (Sotheby's, New York)
Bottle of Wine £105 000, 4 December 1985. Château Lafite initialled Th. J. (Christie's, London)

National Auction Competition

This competition, now in its 41st year, is open to all junior members of the Incorporated Society of Valuers and Auctioneers, under the age of 36. The competitors have to win a series of regional heats to qualify for the final. The subjects of the 'mock' auctions are property, chattels and agriculture and they are rotated tri-annually. In past years the *Cutty Sark* tea clipper, the Euro-

Tunnel and even the knocking-down of the Clifton Suspension Bridge have been featured as items to go under the hammer!

In 1993 the Bristol Zoo Gardens were hypothetically up for sale. The lots consisted of the following, providing the contestants with a barrage of awkward, hostile and just plain difficult questions to answer:

Lot 1 Zoo and Gardens.
Lot 2 A Corn Snake – female, *c.* 5 years old, length *c.* 1 m.
Lot 3 An Asian Elephant (Wendy) – a grey female originally from Thailand, 32 years old, weight *c.* 3500 kg.
Lot 4 West African Lowland Gorilla (Daniel) – 21-year-old male, weight *c.* 190 kg, first gorilla successfully bred in Great Britain

Lot 5 Massey Ferguson 165 Tractor – first registered 2 October 1977, diesel, four-wheel drive.
Lot 6 300 cases of bananas.

The aim of the competition was to get the highest price bid for the lots, with extra points being awarded by the judges for those auctioneers who 'kept their hands out of their pockets and didn't sway about'! Six different awards were made, including an award to the overall winner who, in 1993, was 31-year-old Tom Smith from Nottingham who the judges said: 'struck the right blend of professionalism, approachability and had a cool head'.

The most valuable teddy in the world – sold at auction for £55 000.

BEAUTY

Miss World

The first Miss World contest was organised by Eric Morley and sponsored by Mecca Ltd to coincide with the 1951 Festival of Britain celebrations. The event was held at the Lyceum Ballroom in the Strand, London, with 30 contestants (only five from overseas), compared with 1993 when there were 81 contestants from as many different countries. The 1951 Miss World, Kiki Haakonson from Sweden, won £1000.

The 1993 Miss World contest was held for the second year running in South Africa at Sun City,

Lisa Hanna from Jamaica, Miss World 1993.

the vast gambling and entertainment resort in Bophuthatswana, owned by Sol Kerzner who was once married to the 1976 South African Miss World contestant.

In 1993 live television broadcasts went out on the night of 27 November 1993 to 70 countries with an estimated audience of 1.2 billion (in Britain it could only be viewed on the satellite and cable channel, Sky). The show was compèred by the Irish film-star Pierce Brosnan, with special guest stars – Jacqueline Bisset, the actress, and George Benson, the singer. Other attractions included an African choir, a marching band, a host of South African celebrity singers, and a troupe of traditional African dancers.

WINNERS
1951 Kiki Haakonson (SWE)
1952 May Louise Flodin (SWE)
1953 Denise Perrier (FRA)
1954 Antigone Costanda (EGY)
1955 Carmen Susana Duijm Zubillaga (VEN)
1956 Petra Schurmann (GER)
1957 Marita Lindahl (FIN)
1958 Penelope Anne Coelen (SA)
1959 Corine Rottschafer (NETH)
1960 Morma Gladys Cappagli (ARG)
1961 Rosemarie Frankland (UK)
1962 Catharina Lodders (NETH)
1963 Carole Joan Crawford (JAM)
1964 Ann Sidney (UK)
1965 Lesley Langley (UK)
1966 Reita Faria (IND)
1967 Madeleine Hartog Bell (PERU)
1968 Penelope Plummer (AUS)
1969 Eva Rueber Staier (AUT)

Miss World – Most Wins by Country

5 United Kingdom 1961, 1964, 1965, 1974 (resigned), 1983

4 Venezuela 1955, 1981, 1984, 1991

3 Jamaica 1963, 1976, 1993, **Sweden** 1951, 1952, 1977

2 Argentina 1960, 1978, **Australia** 1968, 1972, **Austria** 1969, 1987, **Germany** 1956, 1980 (resigned), **Iceland** 1985, 1988, **Netherlands** 1959, 1962, **South Africa** 1958, 1974 (came second, took over from Helen Morgan (UK) who resigned), **USA** 1973, 1990

1 Bermuda 1979, **Brazil** 1971, **Dominican Republic** 1982, **Egypt** 1954, **Finland** 1957, **France** 1953, **Greece** 1970, **Guam** 1980 (came second, took over from Gabriella Brum (Ger) who resigned), **India** 1966, **Peru** 1967, **Poland** 1989, **Puerto Rico** 1975, **Russia** 1992, **Trinidad and Tobago** 1986.

1970 Jennifer Hosten (GRENADA)
1971 Lucia Tavares Petterle (BRA)
1972 Belinda Green (AUS)
1973 Marjorie Wallace (USA)
1974 Helen Morgan (UK) (resigned)
　　　 Anneline Kriel (SA)
1975 Wilnelia Merced (PR)
1976 Cindy Breakspear (JAM)
1977 Mary Stavin (SWE)
1978 Silvana Suarez (ARG)
1979 Gina Swainson (BER)
1980 Gabriella Brum (GER) (resigned)
　　　 Kimberly Santos (GUAM)
1981 Pilin Leon (VEN)
1982 Mariasela Alvarez (DOM)

In the first Miss World contest in 1951, all the girls had to appear in bikinis, a new form of swimwear in Britain. The bikini, considered to be an extremely daring two-piece, had been introduced on 5 July 1946 by the Frenchman Louis Réard in his swimwear collection. He named it the 'bikini' because he considered it as explosive in its own way as the American atomic bomb which had been detonated four days earlier at Bikini Atoll in the Marshall Islands, in the western Pacific Ocean. It was so daring that he was unable to persuade his professional models to wear it and had to enlist the help of Micheline Bernardini, a dancer from the Casino in Paris, to model it for him. The first record of the use of the word was in the August 1947 issue of Le Monde Illustré. Réard's creation was subsequently patented and soon entered the dictionary.

1983 Sarah-Jane Hutt (UK)
1984 Astrid Herrera (VEN)
1985 Hofi Karlsdottir (ICE)
1986 Giselle Laronde (TRI)
1987 Ulla Weigerstorfer (AUT)
1988 Linda Petursdottir (ICE)
1989 Aneta Kreglicka (POL)
1990 Gina Marie Tolleson (USA)
1991 Ninibeth Jiminez Leal (VEN)
1992 Julia Kourotchina (RUS)
1993 Lisa Hanna (JAM)

Miss United Kingdom

This contest originated in 1958 and is organised by Eric Morley. The winner gains direct entry into the Miss World contest representing the UK.

1958 Eileen Sheridan, Walton-on-Thames, Surrey
1959 Anne Thelwell, Heswall, Mersey
1960 Hilda Fairclough, Lancaster, Lancs
1961 Rosemarie Frankland*, Lancaster, Lancs
1962 Jackie White, Alvaston, Derbys
1963 Diane Westbury, Ilkeston, Derbys
1964 Ann Sidney*, Parkstone, Dorset
1965 Lesley Langley*, London
1966 Jennifer Lowe, Warrington, Cheshire
1967 Jennifer Lewis, Leicester, Leics
1968 Kathleen Winstanley, Wigan, Gt Man
1969 Sheena Drummond, Tullibody, Scotland
1970 Yvonne Ormes, Nantwich, Cheshire
1971 Marilyn Ward, New Milton, Hants
1972 Jenny McAdam, London
1973 Veronica Cross, London

1974 Helen Morgan*, Barry, Tayside
1975 Vicki Harris, London
1976 Carol Grant, Glasgow, Strathclyde
1977 Madeleine Stringer, North Shields, Tyne & Wear
1978 Ann Jones, Welshpool, Powys
1979 Carolyn Seawood, Yelverton, Norfolk
1980 Kim Ashfield, Buckley, Wales
1981 Michele Donelly, Cardiff, Wales
1982 Della Dolan, Grimsby, Humberside
1983 Sarah-Jane Hutt*, Poole, Dorset
1984 Vivienne Rooke, Weston-super-Mare, Avon
1985 Mandy Shires, Bradford, W. Yorks
1986 Alison Slack, Sheffield, S. Yorks
1987 Karen Mellor, Derby, Derbys
1988 Kirsty Roper, Manchester, Gt Man
1989 Suzanne Younger, Wales
1990 Helen Upton, Blackpool, Lancs
1991 Joanne Lewis, Mansfield, Notts
1992 Claire Smith, Chester, Cheshire
1993 Amanda Johnson, Nottingham, Notts

* Crowned Miss World (in 1974 Helen Morgan resigned)

Miss America

Held in 1921, this was the world's first bathing beauty contest; that is, the first to be held with the contestants wearing swimsuits. In 1993 it achieved another record by becoming the first 'politically correct' beauty contest.

Each contestant was asked to state her 'special cause' which she would promote if voted Miss America 1993. The winner, 18-year-old Kimberly Aiken from South

Line-up of the finalists in the 1961 Miss World contest in which the United Kingdom, represented by 18-year-old Rosemarie Frankland, won for the first time. Grace Li from Free China came second and Carmen Cervera from Spain came third.

Miss Aiken received a $35 000 college scholarship, a car and an estimated $200 000 for public engagements during the forthcoming year.

Miss Pears

The first Miss Pears competition was held in 1958. The competition originated from an advertising campaign – 'Preparing to be a Beautiful Lady' which featured a series of little girls who were doing just that – with the help of Pears soap. In 1958 the chance to feature in an advertisement was opened up by the introduction of the Miss Pears competition. The first winner was 3-year-old Susan Cadge from Bristol.

The competition is open to girls aged 3 to 9, with the winner becoming 'princess for a day' and the holder of the title for that year. Over 23 000 photographs are received each year and one child is selected from ten regions to go forward to the final. The finalists are then judged to find a natural, attractive, and photogenic winner. Miss Pears receives £1000 and has her portrait painted.

Candice Carpenter, aged four years, from Harlow, Essex, crowned Miss Pears 1993.

Carolina, pledged a commitment to the homeless, which proved more successful than other contestants, who chose subjects such as 'maths literacy' and 'adult day care'. Miss Aiken even backed up her pledge by disclosing that she had an uncle who lives in a homeless shelter in New York.

None of the 50 participants took advantage of the new rule which allowed trousers to be worn in the evening-wear section, and it was alleged after the event that some contestants failed to abide by another new rule which stated that they had to style their own hair. It was suggested that some contestants smuggled their own hair stylists into the hotel bedrooms. There was some discussion about whether swimwear was still appropriate. However, a viewers' telephone poll, undertaken during the contest, indicated that 60 per cent of callers wished it to remain.

Preparing to be a Beautiful Lady

This very attractive Junior Miss was christened Catherine, but since childhood she has been known to everyone as "Freckles"! But no one minds, least of all Catherine, because a few freckles look perfectly natural with that lovely auburn colouring. Like most titian-haired young ladies, Catherine has fair, delicate skin that must be guarded carefully. This is a job for Mummy, who sees to it that Pears Soap and clear water are surely preparing Catherine to be a beautiful lady.

PEARS SOAP

We regret that Pears Transparent Soap is in short supply just now

This Pears advertisement helped launch the 'Miss Pears' competition. Young girls were invited to enter in the hope of featuring in the advertisement. (During the war toilet soap was considered to be something of a luxury and the subsequent restrictions brought an apology at the end of the advertisement for the problems in supply.)

BODYBUILDING

> *'No pain, No gain.'*
> Arnold Schwarzenegger's motto

Mr Universe

In 1901 the discipline of bodybuilding, as it is known today, began with an event organised by Eugen Sandow. At a cost of £1700, including the trophies, he organised 'The most perfectly proportioned subject of the king' contest at London's Royal Albert Hall. A total of 150 competitors lined up to compete for the three Sandow statuettes (Gold, Silver and Bronze).

Today, there are two Mr Universe titles – Amateur and Professional. The Amateur originated in 1948, organised by *Health & Strength* magazine, to coincide with the 1948 Olympic Games held in London.

Founded in 1892, *Health & Strength* also founded NABBA (National Amateur Bodybuilders Association) in 1950 which took over staging the contest in that year. NABBA is the oldest bodybuilding association and has the largest membership (the late John Paul Getty was a patron and Jimmy Savile was its president from 1968 to 1980). Although it is an amateur body (unincorporated association), it also stages the Professional Universe contest which was launched in 1952.

There is no difference in the standard and quality of Amateur and Professional competitors – a bodybuilder is defined as a

Professional if he has competed for prize money. Competitors in the Amateur contest qualify from their respective associations around the world and compete for a trophy and the honour of being crowned Mr Universe. Professionals do not qualify as such, but obviously have to be of a standard that gives them a chance to win not only the trophy, but the prize money obtained from the various sponsors of the event. However, Amateurs can and do appear as 'guest stars' at various functions and receive expenses in kind. For example, several of the LWT television's 'Gladiators' are former NABBA title holders (Universe or Britain titles).

The first big-time bodybuilding contest (see above), organised by Eugen Sandow, was held in the Albert Hall, London, in front of 15 000 spectators on Saturday 14 September 1901. The prizes included a solid gold Sandow statuette weighing 12 pounds and valued at £500, a solid silver statuette valued at £60, and a bronze valued at £20. Gold, Silver and Bronze Medals were also given to the winners of the preliminary rounds held in each English county which attracted large numbers of competitors and spectators. For example, the London, South and Western counties final was held at the Crystal Palace with 156 competitors. Ladies were not permitted to watch any of the competitions.

In the final, there were 105 contestants from 52 counties lined up before the judges who included Sir Arthur Conan Doyle, creator of Sherlock Holmes. The musclemen posed

under the lights dressed in black tights, black jockey belt and a leopard-skin leotard. The gold statuette was won by W. Murray of Nottingham and Paisley, the silver by D. Cooper of Birmingham and the bronze by A. C. Smyth of Middlesex (see above left [left to right] Murray, Sandow, Cooper and Smyth). Murray, on the strength of his success,

turned professional and performed a Roman speciality act entitled 'Grand entry of the gladiators' which took place in a Roman courtyard. Murray, billed as 'The Most Perfectly Developed Athlete of Modern Times', followed the Roman act with physical drill, dumbell work, and 'herculean deeds of daring'.

Muscle and Movies

Since the early days of cinema, 'muscle movies' have met with box office success, featuring bodybuilding, strong men such as Sandow in the early days to Schwarzenegger most recently. Some of the great stars from early days until recently have been:

Eugen Sandow (1867–1925) This first 'monarch of muscle' (see Mr Universe above) was one of the first to be filmed.

Josef Grafl (1872–1915) An Austrian who was five times world weightlifting champion between 1907 and 1913. He is widely credited as filling the role of Ursus in the 1913 version of *Quo Vadis?*, acting as the mighty slave and bodyguard to the Christian heroine. In this epic of the silent screen, Grafl had a fight in the arena with a large lion and also had to subdue a raging bull to which his mistress, Lygia, was tied. According to a reporter, the bout with the lion was particularly tricky and Grafl was covered in real wounds before a satisfactory 'take' was achieved.

Bartolomeo Pagano (d. 1946) An illiterate, Italian, strongman wrestler who captivated audiences worldwide with his performance in *Cabiria*, released in 1914, in which he played the role of Maciste. One of his party pieces was to rip open a can of sardines with his bare hands.

Francis X. Bushman (1883–1966) Considered to be the first American screen idol, a well-known bodybuilder, and once known as the handsomest man in the world. His last major appearance was in the 1925 version of *Ben Hur* (US) when he played the part of Messala.

Victor McLaglen (1886–1959) A popular figure in Hollywood with a well-earned reputation as a good actor with more than 150 films to his credit. In the early 1920s he worked in a travelling sideshow as a strong man. To attract audiences he would allow his chest to be used as an anvil, supporting large rocks which were then shattered by sledge hammers.

Nat Pendleton (1895–1967) The handsome and muscular wrestling American champion of the 1920 Olympics. His most memorable role was as strongman, Eugen Sandow, in *The Great Ziegfield* (US 36) – a strongman playing a strongman – which won the 1936 Oscar for Best Picture.

Joe Bonomo (1901–78) Billed as 'the Hercules of the Screen' and the greatest stuntman of his time.

Steve Reeves (b. 1926) Won Mr California 1946, Mr America 1947, Mr World 1948 and the first NABBA Mr Universe contest in 1950, before becoming an actor. The first *Hercules* (ITA 57) film, initiated a craze and, through a subsequent run of a further 20 such films, made him an internationally acclaimed star.

Reg Park (b. 1928) Became the idol of British bodybuilders and won the Mr Universe title three times (1951, 1958, 1965 [Professional]). Between 1961 and 1965 he made five or six *Hercules* films, being one of the most 'muscular' stars ever to appear.

LEFT Lou Ferrigno – 'The Incredible Hulk'.

INSET RIGHT Reg Park in his *Hercules* film role – he was one of the most 'muscular' stars to feature in this role.

INSET BOTTOM Nat Pendleton, as Sandow, the world's strongest man, grapples with a full-grown lion in a scene from *The Great Ziegfeld* (US 36).

BELOW Joe Bonomo – the greatest stuntman of his time.

THE STRONGMAN

THE STRONGMAN JOE BONOMO

A PICTORIAL AUTOBIOGRAPHY

THE DAREDEVIL EXPLOITS OF THE MIGHTIEST MAN IN THE MOVIES
JOE BONOMO

Sean Connery (b. 1930) Former Mr Universe competitor in 1953, prior to becoming a cult figure as James Bond. Long before he became famous, he was a member of the Dunedin Weightlifting Club in Edinburgh.

Arnold Schwarzenegger (b. 1947) Born in Austria, he became an American citizen in September 1983. Having won more major physique titles than anybody else, including Junior Mr Europe 1965, Mr Europe 1966, Mr Universe 1967 (Amateur) and 1968, 1969 and 1970 (Professional), he channelled his energies into becoming an actor. He became a worldwide cult figure when he made *Conan the Barbarian* (US 81) and *Conan the Destroyer* (US 84).

MR UNIVERSE

	Amateur	Professional		Amateur	Professional
1948	John Grimek (USA)		1971	Ken Waller (USA)	Bill Pearl (USA)
1949	No contest		1972	Elias Petsas (SA)	Frank Zane (USA)
1950	Steve Reeves (USA)		1973	Chris Dickerson (USA)	Boyer Coe (USA)
1951	Reg Park (ENG)		1974	Roy Duval (ENG)	Chris Dickerson (USA)
1952	Mohamed Nasr (EGY)	Juan Ferrero (SPA)	1975	Ian Lawrence (SCO)	Boyer Coe (USA)
1953	Bill Pearl (USA)	Arnold Dyson (ENG)	1976	Sigeru Sugita (JAP)	Serge Nubret (FRA)
1954	Enrico Thomas (USA)	Jim Park (USA)	1977	Bertil Fox (ENG)	Tony Emmott (ENG)
1955	Mickey Hargitay (USA)	Leo Robert (CAN)	1978	Dave Johns (USA)	Bertil Fox (ENG)
1956	Ray Schaeffer (USA)	Jack Dellinger (USA)	1979	Ahmet Enunlu (TUR)	Bertil Fox (ENG)
1957	John Lees (ENG)	Arthur Robin (FRA)	1980	Bill Richardson (ENG)	Tony Pearson (USA)
1958	Earl Clark (USA)	Reg Park (ENG)	1981	John Brown (USA)	Robbie Robinson (USA)
1959	Len Sell (ENG)	Bruce Randel (USA)	1982	John Brown (USA)	Edward Kawak (FRA)
1960	Henry Downs (ENG)	Paul Wynter (ANT)	1983	Jeff King (USA)	Edward Kawak (FRA)
1961	Ray Routledge (USA)	Bill Pearl (USA)	1984	Brian Buchanan (ENG)	Edward Kawak (LEB/GER)
1962	Joe Abbenda (USA)	Len Sell (USA)	1985	Tim Belknap (USA)	Edward Kawak (LEB/GER)
1963	Tom Sansome (USA)	Joe Abbenda (USA)	1986	Charles Clairmonte (ENG)	Lance Dreher (USA)
1964	John Hewlett (ENG)	Earl Maynard (USA)	1987	Basil Francis (ENG)	Olev Annus (FIN)
1965	Elma Santiago (USA)	Reg Park (ENG)	1988	Victor Terra (USA)	Charles Clairmonte (ENG)
1966	Chester Yorton (USA)	Paul Wynter (WIN)	1989	Matt Dufresne (USA)	Charles Clairmonte (ENG)
1967	Arnold Schwarzenegger (AUT)	Bill Pearl (USA)	1990	Peter Reid (ENG)	Charles Clairmonte (ENG)
1968	Dennis Tinerino (USA)	Arnold Schwarzenegger (AUT)	1991	Reiner Jorbracht (GER)	Victor Terra (USA)
1969	Boyer Coe (USA)	Arnold Schwarzenegger (AUT)	1992	Mohammad Mustafa (AUT)	Peter Reid (ENG)
1970	Frank Zane (USA)	Arnold Schwarzenegger (AUT)	1993	Dennis Francis (ENG)	Edward Kawak (FRA)

'The first Professional winner of Mr Universe had 17-inch arms and a 47½-inch chest and since then arms of 21 inches plus and chests of 56 inches plus have been recorded several times, with other body part measurements in proportion. However, it's not only muscles that win, as competitive bodybuilding can be described as 'expression of an art form'. An athlete seeks to impress the judges and captivate the audience by displaying the physique/figure to its best advantage, in rhythmic harmony to well-chosen music. Accentuating the good points, disguising perhaps a weak one, the performance can be sensational, a revelation in power, grace and beauty. Such a presentation often moves an audience to dramatic and tumultuous applause.'

Malcolm Whyatt, 1987 Mr Universe programme

Edward Kawak (FRA) holds the record for having won the Mr Universe title most – five times.

FACTS

■ To 1993 there have been a total of 2073 competitors in the Amateur contest and 495 in the Professional.

■ England have won the Amateur title 13 times, and the Professional 10 times.

■ Edward Kawak of France has won most times, gaining five titles (Professional: 1982, 1983, 1984, 1985, 1993).

■ The most successful British bodybuilder is Charles Clairmonte who has won four titles (Amateur: 1986; Professional: 1988, 1989, 1990).

■ In 1993 there were a record number of entrants for the Mr and Miss Universe contest – 136 contestants from 25 countries.

■ *Health and Strength*'s motto is 'Sacred Thy Body Even As Thy Soul' and NABBA's motto is 'Through Effort to Perfection'.

■ Sean Connery, of James Bond fame, entered the Mr Universe Amateur contest in 1953, but was not placed.

Miss Universe

Previously known as Miss Bikini International, Miss Universe was introduced by NABBA in 1966. Up until the early 1980s, it was judged more or less as a 'beauty' contest, e.g. face, figure, attire. Today, the emphasis is similar but the 'trained' condition is also taken into consideration, as is the mode of display, i.e. choreography of the posing routine. In 1986 two separate categories were introduced – Miss Figure (F) and Miss Physique (P):

1966 Elizabeth Lamb (Eng)
1967 Kathleen Winstanley (Eng)
1968 Silvia Hibbert (Eng)
1969 Jean Galston (Eng)
1970 Christine Zane (USA)
1971 Linda Thomas (Eng)
1972 Christine Charles (Eng)
1973 Jean Galston (Eng)
1974 Linda Cheesman (Eng)
1975 Linda Cheesman (Eng)
1976 Cindy Breakspear (Jam)
1977 Bridget Gibbons (Eng)
1978 Sandra Kong (Jam)
1979 Karen Griffiths (Nir)
1980 Erika Mes (Hol)
1981 Jocelyne Pigeonneau (Fra)
1982 Jocelyne Pigeonneau (Fra)
1983 Mary Scott (Sco)
1984 Mary Scott (Sco)
1985 Jocelyne Pigeonneau (Fra)
1986 Heidi Thomas (Eng) (F)
         Monika Steiner (Ger) (P)
1987 Sonia Walker (Eng) (F)
         Connie McClosky (USA) (P)

Susana Perez (Spa), 1993 Miss Universe Figure champion.

1988 Sarah Staunton (Eng) (F)
         Lisa Campbell (Aus) (P)
1989 Tracey Citrone (Eng) (F)
         Tatjana Scholl (Ger) (P)
1990 Bronwyn O'Brien (Aus) (F)
         Monika Debatin (Ger) (P)
1991 Helen Madderson (Eng) (F)
         Uta Geisel (Ger) (P)
1992 Anita Lawrence (Aus) (F)
         Bernie Price (Eng) (P)
1993 Susana Perez (Spa) (F)
         Deborah Compton (Aus) (P)

Mr and Miss Britain

This contest for the two titles was started by *Health & Strength* magazine in 1930. The National Amateur Bodybuilders Association (NABBA) took the event over in 1950. In 1983 a Physique category was added to the original Figure category for Miss Britain. Winners since 1983:

	MR BRITAIN	MISS BRITAIN	
		Figure	Physique
1983	Brian Buchanan	Joanne Day	Christine Hall
1984	Eugene Laviscount	Mary Scott	No contest
1985	Linkie Wilson	Mary Scott	Carol Bennett
1986	Owen Neil	Mary Scott	Carol Bennett
1987	Basil Francis	Heidie Thomas	Robina Harvey
1988	Simon Lancaster	Kathy Titherington	Donna Hartley
1989	Eddie Ellwood	Kathy Titherington	Bernie Price
1990	Tony Francis	Evelin Lees	Bev Hahn
1991	Francis Rainford	Jane Louise Johns	Linda Mason
1992	Dennis Francis	Jackie Young	Linda Middleton
1993	Eamon McGauley	Pauline Oliver	Jane Arthur
1994	Ernie Taylor	Caroline Smith	Lynn McBride

BOOKS & LITERATURE

The Booker McConnell Prize

This annual literary event celebrated its 25th anniversary in 1993 by awarding a 'Booker of Books' prize to Salman Rushdie for his novel *Midnight's Children* which originally took the 1981 prize. The novel tells the story of 1001 supernaturally gifted children born in the first hour of 15 August 1947 at the precise moment of independent India's birth. Their turbulent lives are portrayed and the book shows the progress of a nation and the betrayal of its young. Rushdie lives under an Iranian death threat (a *fatwa*) as a consequence of his novel *The Satanic Verses*, shortlisted for the Booker in 1989.

The Booker prize is awarded to the best novel, published in English, written by a citizen of Britain, the Commonwealth, the Republic of Ireland or South Africa. The prize was first awarded in 1969 by Booker plc, a company which started in Demerara (now Guyana) 160 years ago. It owned sugar estates, ships to transport the produce to England and the shops to distribute the goods. Today Booker is the UK's leading food wholesaler.

Each year a shortlist is drawn up by the panel of judges from which the final winner is selected.

Salman Rushdie was awarded the 'Booker of Bookers' prize in 1993 for *Midnight's Children*.

THE 1993 SHORTLIST WAS:
Roddy Doyle, *Paddy Clarke Ha Ha Ha*
Tibor Fischer, *Under the Frog*
Michael Ignatieff, *Scar Tissue*
David Malouf, *Remembering Babylon*
Caryl Phillips, *Crossing the River*
Carol Shields, *The Stone Diaries*

WINNERS

1993 Roddy Doyle, *Paddy Clarke Ha Ha Ha*
1992 Barry Unsworth, *Sacred Hunger*
Michael Ondaatje, *The English Patient*
1991 Ben Okri, *The Famished Road*
1990 A. S. Byatt, *Possession*
1989 Kazuo Ishiguro, *The Remains of the Day*
1988 Peter Carey, *Oscar and Lucinda*

1987 Penelope Lively, *Moon Tiger*
1986 Kingsley Amis, *The Old Devils*
1985 Keri Hulme, *The Bone People*
1984 Anita Brookner, *Hôtel du Lac*
1983 J. M. Coetzee, *Life and Times of Michael K*
1982 Thomas Keneally, *Schindler's Ark*
1981 Salman Rushdie, *Midnight's Children*
1980 William Golding, *Rites of Passage*
1979 Penelope Fitzgerald, *Offshore*
1978 Iris Murdoch, *The Sea, The Sea*
1977 Paul Scott, *Staying On*
1976 David Storey, *Saville*
1975 Ruth Prawer Jhabvala, *Heat and Dust*
1974 Nadine Gordimer, *The Conservationist*
Stanley Middleton, *Holiday*
1973 J. G. Farrell, *The Siege of Krishnapur*

1972 John Berger, *G*
1971 V. S. Naipaul, *In a Free State*
1970 Bernice Rubens, *The Elected Member*
1969 P. H. Newby, *Something to Answer For*

Booker Shortlisted Authors and Winners

The following is a list of authors and the number of titles each has had shortlisted for the Booker Prize since inception in 1969. The date in brackets following the titles refers to the year the title was nominated and the asterisk denotes the winner for that year.

6 Iris Murdoch – *The Nice and the Good* (1969), *Bruno's Dream* (1970), *The*

FACTS

▪ The cash prize was initially £5000. It was increased to £10 000 in 1978, £15 000 in 1984 and £20 000 in 1989.

▪ In 1993, each member of the judging panel had five months to read a record 110 submissions for a sum of £2500.

▪ The 1993 judging panel of five, headed by Lord Gowrie (former Minister of the Arts), included Gillian Beer (Professor of English, Cambridge University), Anne Chisholm (journalist and author), Nicholas Clee (Book News Editor, *The Bookseller*), and Olivier Todd (French writer, journalist and broadcaster).

Iris Murdoch has had more titles shortlisted for the Booker Prize than any other author. She has only won the Prize once, in 1978 for *The Sea, The Sea*.

Black Prince (1973), *The Sea, The Sea* (1978*), *The Good Apprentice* (1985), *The Book and the Brotherhood* (1987)

4 Penelope Fitzgerald – *The Bookshop* (1978), *Offshore* (1979*), *The Beginning of Spring* (1988), *The Gate of Angels* (1990)

Thomas Keneally – *The Chant of Jimmy Blacksmith* (1972), *Gossip from the Forest* (1975), *Confederates* (1979), *Schindler's Ark* (1982*)

3 Kingsley Amis – *Ending Up* (1974), *Jake's Thing* (1978), *The Old Devils* (1986*)

Beryl Bainbridge – *The Dressmaker* (1973), *The Bottle Factory Outing* (1974), *An Awfully Big Adventure* (1990)

Doris Lessing – *Briefing for a Descent into Hell* (1971), *The Sirian Experiments* (1981), *The Good Terrorist* (1985)

Penelope Lively – *The Road to Lichfield* (1977), *According to Mark* (1984), *Moon Tiger* (1987*)

Timothy Mo – *Sour Sweet* (1982), *An Insular Possession* (1986), *The Redundancy of Courage* (1991)

Brian Moore – *The Doctor's Wife* (1976), *The Colour of Blood* (1987),

Lies of Silence (1990)

Salman Rushdie – *Midnight's Children* (1981*), *Shame* (1983), *The Satanic Verses* (1988)

William Trevor – *Mrs Eckdorf in O'Neill's Hotel* (1970), *The Children of Dynmouth* (1976), *Reading Turgenev (from Two Lives)* (1991)

2 Margaret Atwood – *The Handmaid's Tale* (1986), *Cat's Eye* (1989)

Paul Bailey – *Peter Smart's Confession* (1977), *Gabriel's Lament* (1986)

André Brink – *An Instant in the Wind* (1976), *Rumours of Rain* (1978)

Peter Carey – *Illywhacker* (1985), *Oscar and Lucinda* (1988*)

J. L. Carr – *A Month in the Country* (1980), *The Battle of Pollocks Crossing* (1985)

Anita Desai – *Clear Light of Day* (1980), *In Custody* (1984)

Roddy Doyle – *The Van* (1991), *Paddy Clarke Ha Ha Ha* (1993*)

Kazuo Ishiguro – *An Artist of the Floating World* (1986), *The Remains of the Day* (1989*)

David Lodge – *Small World* (1984), *Nice Work* (1988)

Ian McEwan – *The Comfort of Strangers* (1981), *Black Dogs* (1992)

V. S. Naipaul – *In a Free State* (1971*), *A Bend in the River* (1979)

THE SEA: TURBULENT AND LEADEN; TRANSPARENT AND OPAQUE; MAGICIAN AND MOTHER.

When Charles Arrowby, over sixty, a demi-god of the theatre – director, playwright and actor – retires from his glittering London world in order to, 'abjure magic and become a hermit', it is to the sea that he turns.

He hopes at least to escape from 'the women' – but unexpectedly meets one whom he loved long ago. His Buddhist cousin, James, also arrives. He is menaced by a monster from the deep. Charles finds his 'solitude' peopled by the drama of his own fantasies and obsessions.

'Such richness of imagination and such grandeur of intellect' – Francis King in the *Spectator*

The cover shows a detail from 'Perseus and Andromeda' by Titian in the Wallace Collection, London.

Cover painting of Dame Iris Murdoch by Tom Phillips © National Portrait Gallery

A PENGUIN BOOK
Fiction

U.K. £5.99
AUST. $13.99 (recommended)
CAN. $11.95
N.Z. $21.95 (incl. GST)
U.S.A. $8.95

ISBN 0-14-005199-6

9 780140 051995   91001

IRIS MURDOCH
THE SEA, THE SEA

ISBN 0 14 005199 6

IRIS Murdoch

THE SEA, THE SEA

A RICH, CROWDED, MAGICAL LOVE STORY

To give weight to the myth that nobody ever reads the Booker novels, the *Mail on Sunday* inserted special slips in 40 bookshop copies of each of the 1991 shortlisted titles, promising a £5 note to the finders. Only 12 readers claimed this prize, and in the case of Ben Okri's *The Famished Road*, which later went on to win the prize, there was not a single claimant.

The Commitments (US/GB 91) is the story of Jimmy Rabbitte (Robert Arkins) and his quest to bring soul music to Dublin, Ireland, in the form of a diverse 10-piece group. The film is taken from Roddy Doyle's book of the same name.

Julian Rathbone – *King Fisher Lives* (1976), *Joseph* (1979)
Mordecai Richler – *St Urbain's Horseman* (1971), *Solomon Gursky Was Here* (1990)
Bernice Rubens – *The Elected Member* (1970*), *A Five Year Sentence* (1978)
Muriel Spark – *The Public Image* (1969), *Loitering with Intent* (1981)
David Storey – *Pasmore* (1972), *Saville* (1976*)
Barry Unsworth – *Pascali's Island* (1980), *Sacred Hunger* (1992* [joint])
1 Chinau Achebe – *Anthills of the Savannah* (1987)
Peter Ackroyd – *Chatterton* (1987)
Martin Amis – *Time's Arrow* (1991)
John Arden – *Silence Among the Weapons* (1982)
J. G. Ballard – *Empire of the Sun* (1984)
John Banville – *The Book of Evidence* (1989)
A. L. Barker – *John Brown's Body* (1970)
Julian Barnes – *Flaubert's Parrot* (1984)

Nina Bawden – *Circles of Deceit* (1987)
Sybille Bedford – *Jigsaw* (1989)
John Berger – *G* (1972*)
Caroline Blackwood – *Great Granny Webster* (1977)
Elizabeth Bowen – *Eva Trout* (1970)
William Boyd – *An Ice-Cream War* (1982)
Malcolm Bradbury – *Rates of Exchange* (1983)
Anita Brookner – *Hôtel du Lac* (1984*)
Anthony Burgess – *Earthly Powers* (1980)
A. S. Byatt – *Possession* (1990*)
Bruce Chatwin – *Utz* (1988)
J. M. Coetzee – *Life and Times of Michael K* (1983*)
Robertson Davies – *What's Bred in the Bone* (1986)
Lawrence Durrell – *Constance or Solitary Practices* (1982)
Alice Thomas Ellis – *The 27th Kingdom* (1982)
Barry England – *Figures in a Landscape* (1969)
J. G. Farrell – *The Siege of Krishnapur* (1973*)
Tibor Fischer – *Under the Frog* (1993)
John Fuller – *Flying to Nowhere* (1983)
Jane Gardam – *God on the Rocks* (1978)
William Golding – *Rites of Passage* (1980*)
Nadine Gordimer – *The Conservationist* (1974* [joint])
Susan Hill – *Bird of the Night* (1972)
Christopher Hope – *Serenity House* (1992)
Keri Hulme – *The Bone People* (1985*)
R. C. Hutchinson – *Rising* (1976)
Michael Ignatieff – *Scar Tissue* (1993)
Ruth Prawer Jhabvala – *Heat and Dust* (1975*)
Jennifer Johnston – *Shadows on Our Skin* (1977)
Molly Keane – *Good Behaviour* (1981)

James Kelman – *A Disaffection* (1989)
Thomas Kilroy – *The Big Chapel* (1971)
Patrick McCabe – *The Butcher Boy* (1992)
John McGahern – *Amongst Women* (1990)
David Malouf – *Remembering Babylon* (1993)
Anita Mason – *The Illusionist* (1983)
Elizabeth Mayor – *The Green Equinox* (1973)
Stanley Middleton – *Holiday* (1974* [joint])
Rohinton Mistry – *Such a Long Journey* (1991)
Jan Morris – *Last Letters from Hav* (1985)
Nicholas Mosley – *Impossible Object* (1969)
Alice Munro – *The Beggar Maid* (1980)
P. H. Newby – *Something to Answer For* (1969*)
Julia O'Faolain – *No Country for Young Men* (1980)
Ben Okri – *The Famished Road* (1991*)
Michael Ondaatje – *The English Patient* (1992* [joint])
Caryl Phillips – *Crossing the River* (1993)
Barbara Pym – *Quartet in Autumn* (1977)
Michèle Roberts – *Daughters of the House* (1992)
Derek Robinson – *Goshawk Squadron* (1971)

BOOKER RUSSIAN NOVEL PRIZE

Booker expanded the scope of its literary prizes in 1992 by creating a new Russian book prize. Offering £10 000, half that offered in Britain, the prize is open to any 'citizen of the world', the only condition being that it is written in Russian. It was set up to encourage and stimulate a wider knowledge of modern Russian fiction in the western world. The winner is selected by an international panel of five judges from entries which are submitted by 40 nominators who are representatives of the Russian-language literary world. The first winner announced in 1993 was the Russian, Mark Kharitonov, for *Lines of Fate*.

'Our difficulty this year was the strength and professionalism of the entry. In the end what we all went for was passion.'

Lord Gowrie, chairman of the judges, 1993

Ann Schlee – *Rhine Journey* (1981)
Paul Scott – *Staying On* (1977*)
Carol Shields – *The Stone Diaries* (1993)
C. P. Snow – *In Their Wisdom* (1974)
Graham Swift – *Waterland* (1983)
Elizabeth Taylor – *Mrs Palfrey at the Claremont* (1971)
D. M. Thomas – *The White Hotel* (1981)
Rose Tremain – *Restoration* (1989)
Marina Warner – *The Lost Father* (1988)
Fay Weldon – *Praxis* (1979)
T. W. Wheeler – *The Conjunction* (1970)
G. M. Williams – *From Scenes Like These* (1969)

Nobel Prize for Literature

Awarded annually since 1901 for outstanding achievement in the field of literature, this prize was endowed by Alfred Nobel in 1896. (See separate section, Nobel Prizes.)

1901 Armand Sully-Prudhomme (FRA) – Poet. Noted for later philosophical poetry

1902 Theodor Mommsen (GER) – Historian. *History of Rome* (1854–56, 1885)

1903 Björnstjerne Björnsen (NOR) – Novelist, poet and dramatist. Helped revive Norwegian as a literary language

1904 Frédéric Mistral (FRA) – Poet. Promoted Provençal as a literary language

Juan Echegaray (SPA) – Dramatist *The World and His Wife* (1881)

1905 Henryk Sienkiewicz (POL) – Novelist. *Quo Vadis?* (1895)

1906 Giosuè Carducci (ITA) – Classical poet. *Inno a Satana/Hymn to Satan* (1865)

1907 Rudyard Kipling (UK) – Novelist and poet. *Jungle Books* (1894–95); *Just So Stories* (1902)

1908 Rudolf Eucken (GER) – Idealist philosopher

1909 Selma Lagerlöf (SWE) – Novelist. Famous for novels based on legends and sagas

1910 Paul von Heyse (GER) – Poet, novelist and dramatist

1911 Maurice Maeterlinck (BEL) – Symbolist poet and dramatist. *Pelléas et Mélisande* (1892) and *The Blue Bird* (1908)

1912 Gerhart Hauptmann (GER) – Dramatist, novelist and poet. Introduced Naturalism to German theatre

(continued on p. 46)

Top UK Literary Prizes

Prize/Award	Category	Latest winner	First prize
David Cohen British Literature Prize (biennial)	Recognition of a living British writer's lifetime achievement	V. S. Naipaul (1993)	£40 000
NCR Book Award	Best non-fiction work	*Edward Heath*, John Campbell (1994)	£25 000
Whitbread Book of the Year	Chosen from five different categories: novel, first novel, biography, children's novel and poetry	*Theory of War*, Joan Brady (1993)	£21 000
Booker Prize for Fiction	Best full-length novel	*Paddy Clarke Ha Ha Ha*, Roddy Doyle (1993)	£20 000
Sunday Express Book of the Year	Most stylish, literate and readable work of fiction	*The Blue Afternoon*, William Boyd (1993)	£20 000
Commonwealth Writers' Prize	Work of fiction – novel or collection of short stories	*The Ancestor Game*, Alex Miller (1993)	£10 000
Catherine Cookson Fiction Prize	Unpublished full-length novel	*Mariana*, Susanna Kearsley (1993)	£10 000
Forward Poetry Prize*	Best collection of poems	*Meantime*, Carol Ann Duffy (1993)	£10 000
W. H. Smith Literary Award	Most outstanding contribution to English literature	*A Suitable Boy*, Vikram Seth (1994)	£10 000
Wolfson History Prize	Historical book	*Living and Dying in England 1100–1540*, Barbara Harvey (1994)	£10 000

*See separate section, Poetry

Cyrus Cuneo's portrait of the popular poet and storyteller surrounds Rudyard Kipling with many of his creations, including Mowgli, Kim and the Soldiers Three. Kipling won the UK's first Nobel Prize for Literature in 1907.

UK Bestselling Fiction Hardbacks, 1993

1. *Paddy Clarke Ha Ha Ha*, Roddy Doyle (Secker & Warburg / £12.99)
2. *Honour Among Thieves*, Jeffrey Archer (HarperCollins / £14.99)
3. *Adrian Mole: The Wilderness Years*, Sue Townsend (Methuen / £8.99)
4. *The Man Who Made Husbands Jealous*, Jilly Cooper (Bantam Press / £15.99)
5. *Decider*, Dick Francis (Michael Joseph / £14.99)
6. *A Suitable Boy*, Vikram Seth (Phoenix House / £20.00)
7. *Mrs de Winter*, Susan Hill (Sinclair-Stevenson / £12.99)
8. *The Night Manager*, John le Carré (Hodder / £15.99)
9. *River God*, Wilbur Smith (Macmillan / £15.99)
10. *A Spanish Lover*, Joanna Trollope (Bloomsbury / £14.99)

Source: Bookwatch

Roddy Doyle was born in Dublin in 1958. Both his first two books, *The Commitments* and *The Snapper*, were made into films, his third novel, *The Van*, was shortlisted for the 1991 Booker Prize, and *Paddy Clarke Ha Ha Ha* won the Prize in 1993. The book charts the triumphs, indignities and bewilderment of Patrick Clarke growing up in North Dublin at the age of ten – as indeed Doyle was in 1968, the year in which the novel is set. Patrick's attempts to keep his parents' marriage together are described in a truly convincing and heartbreaking manner. The text captures the breathless narrative of Patrick, evoking childhood brilliantly.

RODDY DOYLE
Paddy Clarke Ha Ha Ha

Secker & Warburg

UK Bestselling Non-Fiction Hardbacks, 1993

1. *Delia Smith's Summer Collection*, Delia Smith (BBC Books / £14.99)
2. *The Downing Street Years*, Margaret Thatcher (HarperCollins / £25.00)
3. *Some Other Rainbow*, John McCarthy & Jill Morrell (Bantam Press / £14.99)
4. *Bravo Two Zero*, Andy McNab (Bantam Press / £14.99)
5. *Taken on Trust*, Terry Waite (Hodder / £14.99)
6. *The Guinness Book of Records*, ed. Peter Matthews (Guinness Publishing / £14.99)
7. *Hugh Johnson's Pocket Wine Book*, (Mitchell Beazley / £6.99)
8. *Diaries*, Alan Clark (Weidenfeld / £20.00)
9. *Delia Smith's Christmas*, Delia Smith (BBC Books / £12.95)
10. *Delia Smith's Complete Illustrated Cookery Course*, Delia Smith (BBC Books / £22.99)

Source: Bookwatch

Delia Smith's cookery books have sold over five million copies in Britain. This new book, also available on a BBC video, is a celebration of summer and all its ingredients. From early May to September Delia Smith details a progression of summer produce, introducing unusual ingredients such as rocket leaves and lemon grass. She includes sections on new techniques for grilling and roasting vegetables, home-made ice creams, barbecues for meat-eaters and vegetarians, a feast of fresh fruit, as well as preserving fruits to enjoy through the dull days of winter. The book includes 50 colour photographs.

BBC

Delia
SMITH'S
SUMMER COLLECTION

140 recipes for summer

UK Bestselling Fiction Paperbacks, 1993

1 *Jurassic Park*, Michael Crichton (Arrow / £4.99)
2 *The Firm*, John Grisham (Arrow / £4.99)
3 *The Bridges of Madison County*, Robert James Waller (Mandarin / £3.99)
4 *The Men and the Girls*, Joanna Trollope (Black Swan / £5.99)
5 *The House of Women*, Catherine Cookson (Corgi / £4.99)
6 *The Pelican Brief*, John Grisham (Arrow / £4.99)
7 *The Copper Beech*, Maeve Binchy (Orion / £4.99)
8 *The Maltese Angel*, Catherine Cookson (Corgi / £4.99)
9 *Jewels*, Danielle Steel (Corgi / £4.99)
10 *The Queen and I*, Sue Townsend (Mandarin / £4.99)

Source: Bookwatch

The paperback version of *Jurassic Park* – you've seen the film now read the book – headed Britain's fiction list for 1993. It recounts the story of a remote jungle island where genetic engineers create a dinosaur game park. Originally published in 1991, it sold 175 000 copies. On release of Steven Spielberg's film in 1993, sales rocketed to over 695 000 copies. The junior version of the book also appeared at No. 10 in the 1993 UK Bestselling Children's Book list. Author Michael Crichton, born in 1942, is an American living in California. He has also directed films, including the movie version of his own *The First Great Train Robbery* (GB 79), starring Sean Connery and Donald Sutherland, and *Coma* (US 78), starring Genevieve Bujold and Michael Douglas.

A STEVEN SPIELBERG Film

JURASSIC PARK

The Bestselling Novel by
MICHAEL CRICHTON

UK Bestselling Non-Fiction Paperbacks, 1993

1 *Wild Swans*, Jung Chang (Flamingo / £7.99)
2 *An Evil Cradling*, Brian Keenan (Vintage / £6.99)
3 *Fever Pitch*, Nick Hornby (Gollancz / £4.99)
4 *Food Combining for Health*, Doris Grant and Jean Joice (Thorsons / £4.99)
5 *Diana: Her True Story*, Andrew Morton (O'Mara / £6.99)
6 *The Rock and Water Garden Expert*, D. G. Hessayon (Expert / £4.99)
7 *Every Living Thing*, James Herriot (Pan / £4.99)
8 *The Lost Continent*, Bill Bryson (Abacus / £5.99)
9 *Paperweight*, Stephen Fry (Mandarin / £4.99)
10 *Your Driving Test*, Driving Standards Agency (HMSO / £2.75)

Source: Bookwatch

Wild Swans, written by Jung Chang, is a real-life saga of three generations of a Chinese family. It tells the story of three women – Jung Chang, her mother and her grandmother – whose fortunes mirror the tumultuous history of 20th-century China. The author was born in Yibin, Sichuan Province, China, in 1952. She was a Red Guard at the age of 14 and then worked as a peasant, a 'barefoot doctor', a steelworker and an electrician before leaving China for Britain in 1978 where she obtained a PhD in Linguistics in 1982. She now lives in London and teaches at London University.

WILD SWANS

Three Daughters of China

'It is impossible to exaggerate the importance of this book.'
Mary Wesley

JUNG CHANG

Winner of the 1992 NCR Book Award

flamingo

Nobel Prize for Literature (continued)

1913 Rabindranath Tagore (IND) – Poet and playwright. One of the most influential Indian authors of the 20th century

1914 No award

1915 Romain Rolland (FRA) – Novelist and biographer. *Jean-Christophe* (1904–12) – 10 volumes

1916 Verner von Heidenstam (SWE) – Lyric poet

1917 Karl Gjellerup (DEN) – Novelist
  Henrik Pontoppidan (DEN) – Novelist. *Lucky Peter* (1898–1904)

1918 No award

1919 Carl Spitteler (SWI) – Poet and novelist. *The Olympic Spring* (1900–05)

1920 Knut Hamsun (NOR) – Novelist. *Pan* (1894); *The Growth of the Soil* (1917)

1921 Anatole France (FRA) – Novelist

1922 Jacinto Benavente y Martinez (SPA) – Dramatist. Social satires

1923 William Butler Yeats (IRE) – Poet

1924 Wladyslaw Stanislaw Reymont (POL) – Novelist. *The Promised Land* (1895); *The Peasants* (1904–05)

1925 George Bernard Shaw (IRE) – Dramatist

1926 Grazia Deledda (ITA) – Naturalist novelist

1927 Henri Bergson (FRA) – Philosopher

1928 Sigrid Undset (NOR) – Novelist. Novels about women and religion

1929 Thomas Mann (GER) – Novelist. *Buddenbrooks* (1901); *Der Zauberberg/ The Magic Mountain* (1924)

1930 Sinclair Lewis (USA) – Satirical novelist. *Babbitt* (1922)

1931 Erik Axel Karlfeldt (SWE) – Lyric poet. Wrote about love, nature and peasant life

1932 John Galsworthy (UK) – Novelist and dramatist. *The Forsyte Saga* (1906–28)

1933 Ivan Bunin (USSR) – Novelist. Famous for his short stories

1934 Luigi Pirandello (ITA) – Dramatist

1935 No award

1936 Eugene O'Neill (USA) – Dramatist. Often regarded as leading US dramatist between two world wars

1937 Roger Martin du Gard (FRA) – Novelist. *Les Thibaults* (1922–40)

1938 Pearl Buck (USA) – Novelist. Famous for novels about China

1939 Frans Eemil Sillanpää (FIN) – Novelist. *Meek Heritage* (1919); *People of the Summer Night* (1934)

1940-43 No awards

1944 Johannes V. Jensen (DEN) – Writer. Travel books and essays

1945 Gabriela Mistral (CHL) – Poet. *Sonnets of Death* (1915)

1946 Hermann Hesse (GER/SWI) –

'The fact that the Nobel Prize was not accorded to me was doubly pleasant: first, because it saved me from the painful necessity of dealing in some way with money – generally regarded as very necessary and useful, but which I regard as the source of every kind of evil; and secondly, because it has afforded to people whom I respect the opportunity of expressing their sympathy with me, for which I thank you all from my heart.'

Leo Tolstoy

Novelist. *Steppenwolf* (1927); *Das Glasperlenspiel/The Glass Bead Game* (1943)

1947 André Gide (FRA) – Novelist and essayist. Largely autobiographical, concerned with themes of self-fulfilment and renunciation

1948 T. S. Eliot (USA/UK) – Poet, playwright and critic. *The Waste Land* (1922); *Old Possum's Book of Practical*

FIRST BLACK WOMAN TO WIN NOBEL PRIZE

Toni Morrison, an American aged 62, won the 1993 Nobel Prize for Literature, becoming the first black woman and only the eighth woman ever to do so (the first being Selma Lagerlöf, the Swedish novelist in 1909). She was awarded the prize of $825 000 (£550 000) for her depiction of black America in novels which are 'characterised by visionary force and poetic import' and which give life 'to an essential aspect of American reality'.

She is author of six novels, her fifth, *Beloved,* won the Pulitzer Prize in 1988. She was brought up in a steel town near Cleveland, second child in a family of four, during the Depression. Her mother believed that race relations in America would improve but her father distrusted 'every white man on earth'. Consequently she grew up with a sense of resentment towards white people.

Her writing is full of rich prose as can be seen in the following excerpt taken from *Song of Solomon* (1978):

'Pretty woman, he thought. Pretty little black-skinned woman. Who wanted to kill for love, die for love. The pride, the conceit of these doormat women amazed him. They were always women who had been spoiled children. Whose whims had been taken seriously by adults and who grew up to be the stingiest, greediest people on earth and out of their stinginess grew their stingy little love that ate everything in sight.

'They could not believe or accept the fact that they were unloved . . . Why did they think they were so lovable? Why did they think their brand of love was better than, or even as good as, anybody else's? But they did. And they loved their love so much they would kill anybody who got in its way.'

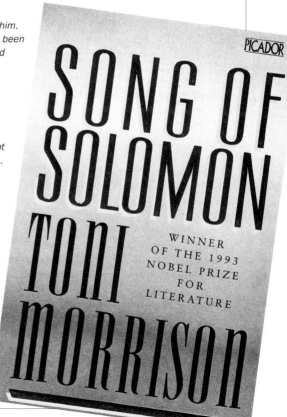

PICADOR

SONG OF SOLOMON

TONI MORRISON

WINNER OF THE 1993 NOBEL PRIZE FOR LITERATURE

Cats (1939)

1949 **William Faulkner** (USA) – Novelist. Wrote in an experimental stream-of-consciousness style

1950 **Bertrand Russell** (UK) – Philosopher and mathematician. *A History of Western Philosophy* (1945)

1951 **Pär Lagerkvist** (Swe) – Novelist. Work concerned man's search for God and good and evil

1952 **François Mauriac** (Fra) – Novelist, poet and dramatist. Famous for Catholic novels

1953 **Sir Winston Churchill** (UK) – Politician, historian. Six-volume history of World War II (1948–54); four-volume *History of the English-Speaking Peoples* (1956–58)

1954 **Ernest Hemingway** (USA) – Novelist. *A Farewell to Arms* (1929); *For Whom the Bell Tolls* (1940); *The Old Man and the Sea* (1952)

1955 **Halldór Laxness** (Ice) – Novelist. Wrote about Icelandic life in the style of the early sagas

1956 **Juan Ramón Jiménez** (Spa) – Poet

1957 **Albert Camus** (Fra) – Novelist and dramatist. His novels owe much to existentialism

1958 **Boris Pasternak** (USSR) – Novelist and poet. *Dr Zhivago* (1957) – declined award

1959 **Salvatore Quasimodo** (Ita) – Poet

1960 **Saint-John Perse** (Fra) – Lyric poet

1961 **Ivo Andric** (Yug) – Novelist. Famous for Bosnian historical trilogy

1962 **John Steinbeck** (USA) – Novelist. *Of Mice and Men* (1937); *The Grapes of Wrath* (1939)

1963 **George Seferis** (Gre) – Poet and essayist. Introduced Symbolism to Greek literature

1964 **Jean-Paul Sartre** (Fra) – Philosopher and writer. Declined award for 'personal reasons' but allegedly changed his mind later, saying he wanted it, or the money

1965 **Mikhail Sholokhov** (USSR) – Novelist. *And Quiet Flows the Don* (1926–40) – depicts the Don Cossacks through World War I and the Russian Revolution

1966 **Shmuel Yosef Agnon** (Isr) – Novelist. Considered to be the leading writer in Hebrew

Nelly Sachs (Ger / Swe) – Jewish poet. Wrote about persecution of Jews

1967 **Miguel Angel Asturias** (Guatemala) – Novelist and poet. Wrote poetry, Guatemalan legends and novels attacking Latin-American dictatorships and American imperialism

1968 **Kawabata Yasunari** (Jap) – Novelist

1969 **Samuel Beckett** (Ire) – Novelist and dramatist. *En attendant Godot / Waiting for Godot* (1952) – possibly the best-known example of Theatre of the Absurd (in which life is taken to be meaningless)

1970 **Aleksandr Solzhenitsyn** (USSR) – Novelist. *One Day in the Life of Ivan Denisovich* (1962); *The Gulag Archipelago* (1973); *Cancer Ward* (1968)

1971 **Pablo Neruda** (Chl) – Poet. *Canto General* (1950)

1972 **Heinrich Böll** (Ger) – Novelist. Poems, short stories and novels which satirise German society

1973 **Patrick White** (Aus) – Novelist. *The Aunt's Story* (1948); *Voss* (1957)

1974 **Eyvind Johnson** (Swe) – Novelist. Famous for four autobiographical novels

Harry Martinson (Swe) – Novelist and poet. *The Road* (1948) and the poem *Aniara* (1956)

1975 **Eugenio Montale** (Ita) – Poet. Pessimistic poetry

1976 **Saul Bellow** (USA) – Novelist. *Humboldt's Gift* (1975)

1977 **Vicente Aleixandre** (Spa) – Poet

1978 **Isaac Bashevis Singer** (USA) – Author. Wrote in Yiddish; described Jewish life in Poland

1979 **Odysscus Elytis** (Gre) Poet

1980 **Czeslaw Milosz** (Pol / USA) – Poet and novelist. *The Captive Mind* (1953)

1981 **Elias Canetti** (Bul / Ger) – Writer. *Auto da Fè* (1935); *Crowds and Power* (1960)

1982 **Gabriel Garcia Márquez** (Col) – Novelist

1983 **William Golding** (UK) – Novelist. *Lord of the Flies* (1954); *Rites of Passage* (1980)

1984 **Jaroslav Seifert** (Cze) – Poet. *Switch off the Lights* (1938)

1985 **Claude Simon** (Fra) – Novelist

1986 **Wole Soyinka** (Nig) – Playwright and poet. Work merges Nigerian and Western traditions

1987 **Joseph Brodsky** (USA / USSR) – Poet and essayist. His work often deals with themes of exile

1988 **Naguib Mahfouz** (Egy) – Novelist. *Children of Gebelawi* (1959) (banned in Egypt because of its treatment of religious themes)

1989 **Camilo José Cela** (Spa) – Novelist

1990 **Octavio Paz** (Mex) – Poet. Exponent of Magic Realism

1991 **Nadine Gordimer** (SA) – Novelist. An opponent of apartheid

1992 **Derek Walcott** (St Lucia) – Poet

1993 **Toni Morrison** (USA) – Novelist. Famous for depicting black America in novels

Hidden Clues, Prizes and Buried Treasure

The publication of books containing competitions inbuilt into both text and illustrations has been a recent innovation. The publication of *Masquerade* in 1979 set a precedent and was followed by a spate of other books endeavouring to capitalise on *Masquerade*'s success, but none engaged the reader in quite the same way. *The Piper of Dreams* was one such example – however, the hidden treasure, a flute made of gold, silver and diamonds, was found within three weeks of burial.

More recently, two other remarkable titles by Mike Wilks – *The Ultimate Alphabet* (1986) and *The Ultimate Noah's Ark* (1993), have been published. These two titles each offered not buried treasure but a prize of £10 000. The first title awarded the prize to the first person to identify all the alliterative elements in 26 detailed drawings of the alphabet. The second was zoological rather than linguistic. Some 707 creatures appear in 16 paintings, two of each except one. The challenge was to identify which animal had been excluded.

Masquerade – THE SEARCH FOR THE GOLDEN HARE

The forerunner of these two books, Kit Williams's *Masquerade*, published in 1979 by Jonathan Cape, caused large areas of England to be dug up by frantic treasure-seekers in search of the buried treasure – a golden hare. Tom Maschler, having seen one of Williams's paintings in a London gallery, approached him about publishing a book containing his illustrations, but had difficulty persuading him. Williams felt that the task would be daunting since each one of his paintings took

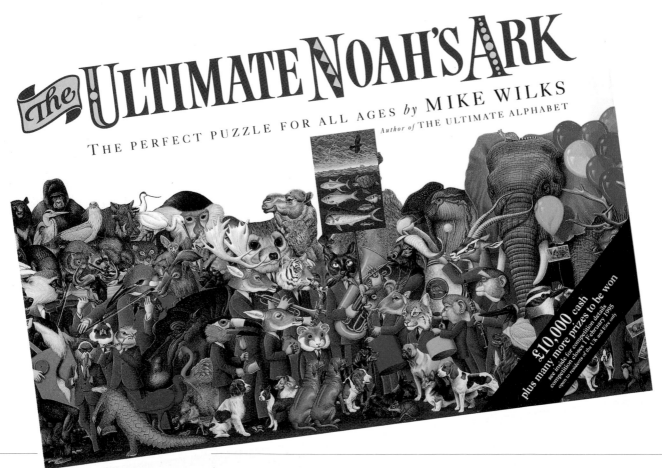

In the picture (left), taken from the book, following the solution given on p. 50, the letters 'LOOK YOU' are spelt out by:

Puppet

1 **L**–left eye to left middle finger

2 **O**–left eye to left big toe

3 **O**–right eye to right middle finger

4 **K**–right eye to right big toe

Bird (left)

5 left eye to left foot – points to no letter

6 **Y**–right eye to right foot

Bird (right)

7 **O**–left eye to left foot

8 **U**–right eye to right foot

There are also other riddles and clues built into the pictures and text which serve to confirm the above solutions. The complete perfect solution is included in the paperback edition of *Masquerade*, published by Cape.

more than a month to complete. He also disliked the way many readers flip through books and he felt strongly that he wanted his pictures to be examined closely. As a child he loved Victorian books which contained hidden elements and it was from this that the idea of a book of pictures with riddles, hidden clues and buried treasure grew. He eventually approached Maschler with the concept that the book, in his words, 'would do something for my lost childhood. Real treasure, real gold, buried in cold dark earth.'

It took Kit three years to complete the pictures containing the riddles and solutions which, once solved, would reveal the whereabouts of the golden

hare. They were delivered to Cape wrapped in army blankets and old carpets in a large wooden chest. He had insured them for £25 000 during the journey from Gloucestershire to Bedford Square, London.

Kit Williams then personally fashioned the golden hare out of 18-carat gold, adorned with precious stones – ruby, moonstone, citrines, turquoise, mother of pearl and a rare compound called faience, used by the ancient Egyptians to grace the Pharaohs. On 7 August 1979, before publication, Bamber Gascoigne (who was later to write a book entitled *Quest for the Golden Hare*) and Kit Williams buried the hare at dead of night on a windswept hillside at Ampthill, Bedfordshire. It was only then that Kit explained to Gascoigne how the clues in the book worked.

The book was published in 1979, and nearly 40 000 copies of the original print run were bought in advance by bookshops. By the afternoon of publication day, 8000 orders had arrived at Cape's trade counter and an immediate reprint of 50 000 copies was ordered. This was followed by two further reprints of 50 000, making a total of 210 000 pre-Christmas sales. The final number of copies sold worldwide was well in excess of a million.

The search for the hare then began in earnest. From September 1979 to March 1982 millions of people worldwide began to examine the book in detail, trying to make sense of the pictures and riddles. At various locations throughout Britain, people thought they had found the correct position of the golden hare. The Haresfield Beacon, a National Trust property in Gloucestershire, attracted much attention because of its name. Many treasure-seekers proceeded to dig up areas of this spot. The National Trust eventually charged Kit £50 for the cost of a notice informing people that the hare was definitely not to be found there! In America, airline companies even offered hunt-the-hare flights to England.

Eventually, on 24 February 1982, more by luck than judgement, the hare was dug up by Ken Thomas who had jumped to certain lucky conclusions – he had still not come up with several of the solutions to the clues included in the book. Ironically, only two days later, the perfect solution to the riddles arrived at the offices of Jonathan Cape, submitted by Mike Barker and John Rousseau, two school teachers.

THE SOLUTION

This hinges on the relationship between the eyes and fingers and toes of all the characters within the paintings and the letters that appear around the border. Lines drawn from the characters' eyes through their middle fingers or big toes (or in the case of animals, from their eyes to front and rear paws, feet [bird], or top then bottom fin of tail [fish]) point towards specific letters around the border. These letters spell out the 16 clues which lead to the treasure. These are as follows:

C atherine's
L ong finger
O ver
S hadows
E arth

B uried
Y ellow

A mulet
M idday
P oints
T he
H our
I n
L ight of equinox
L ook you

A certain hierarchy exists, not only within the order of lines drawn, but within the order of animals. These are as follows:

Animals
adults, children, frog, hare, mammals, birds, fish.

Lines
Left eye to *left* middle finger, front paw or hoof
Left eye to *left* big toe, rear paw, hoof or foot (bird)
Right eye to *right* middle finger, front paw or hoof
Right eye to *right* big toe, rear paw, hoof or foot (bird)
Fish takes either eye to top fin of tail and then to bottom fin

Literature Nobel Prize Winners by Country

Country	Total	Year first awarded prize
France	12	1901
USA	10	1930
Germany*	7	1902
Sweden	7	1909
UK	7	1907
Italy	5	1906
Spain	5	1904
USSR	5	1933
Denmark	3	1917
Ireland	3	1923
Norway	3	1903
Chile	2	1945
Greece	2	1963
Poland	2	1905
Switzerland	2	1919
Australia	1	1973
Belgium	1	1911
Colombia	1	1982
Czechoslovakia	1	1984
Egypt	1	1988
Finland	1	1939
Guatemala	1	1967
Iceland	1	1955
India	1	1913
Israel	1	1966
Japan	1	1968
Mexico	1	1990
Nigeria	1	1986
St Lucia	1	1992
South Africa	1	1991
Yugoslavia	1	1961
Total	**91**	

*Includes both West and East Germany
Notes
1 Nobel Prizes are actually awarded to individuals rather than the countries from which they come.
2 Figures include 1993 prizewinners.

Pulitzer Prize

Awarded annually for achievement in American literature and journalism. The prizes were endowed by the American publisher, Joseph Pulitzer, in 1917. (See separate section, Pulitzer Prizes.)

Fiction
For distinguished fiction by an American author, preferably dealing with American life.

1917 No award
1918 Ernest Poole, *His Family*
1919 Booth Tarkington, *The Magnificent Ambersons*
1920 No award
1921 Edith Wharton, *The Age of Innocence*
1922 Booth Tarkington, *Alice Adams*
1923 Willa Cather, *One of Ours*
1924 Margaret Wilson, *The Able McLaughlins*

Wilbur Minafer (Donald Dillaway), Isabel Amberson (Dolores Costello) and Eugene Morgan (Joseph Cotten) in a scene from *The Magnificent Ambersons* (US 42). Booth Tarkington won the Pulitzer Prize for Fiction in 1919 for her book of the same name.

1925 Edna Ferber, *So Big*
1926 Sinclair Lewis, *Arrowsmith*
1927 Louis Bromfield, *Early Autumn*
1928 Thornton Wilder, *The Bridge of San Luis Rey*
1929 Julia Peterkin, *Scarlet Sister Mary*
1930 Oliver LaFarge, *Laughing Boy*
1931 Margaret Ayer Barnes, *Years of Grace*
1932 Pearl S. Buck, *The Good Earth*
1933 T. S. Stribling, *The Store*
1934 Caroline Miller, *Lamb in His Bosom*
1935 Josephine Winslow Johnson, *Now in November*
1936 Harold L. Davis, *Honey in the Horn*
1937 Margaret Mitchell, *Gone with the Wind*
1938 John Phillips Marquand, *The Late George Apley*
1939 Marjorie Kinnan Rawlings, *The Yearling*
1940 John Steinbeck, *The Grapes of Wrath*
1941 No award
1942 Ellen Glasgow, *In This Our Life*
1943 Upton Sinclair, *Dragon's Teeth*
1944 Martin Flavin, *Journey in the Dark*
1945 John Hersey, *A Bell for Adano*
1946 No award
1947 Robert Penn Warren, *All the King's Men*
1948 James Michener, *Tales of the South Pacific*

'The day is still golden outside, old gold now in Harry's lengthening life. He has seen summer come and go until its fading is one in his heart with its coming, though he cannot yet name the weeds that flower each in its turn through the season, or the insects that also in ordained sequence appear, eat, and perish. He knows that in June school ends and the play-grounds open, and the grass needs cutting again and again if one is a man, and if one is a child games can be played outdoors while the supper dishes tinkle in the mellow parental kitchens, and the moon is discovered looking over your shoulder out of a sky still blue, and a silver blob of milkweed spittle has appeared mysteriously on your knee.'

Rabbit is Rich, John Updike, 1982 Pulitzer Prize; he also won the 1991 Prize for *Rabbit at Rest*

1949 James Gould Cozzens, *Guard of Honor*
1950 A. B. Guthrie Jr, *The Way West*
1951 Conrad Richter, *The Town*
1952 Herman Wouk, *The Caine Mutiny*
1953 Ernest Hemingway, *The Old Man and the Sea*
1954 No award
1955 William Faulkner, *A Fable*
1956 MacKinlay Kantor, *Andersonville*
1957 No award
1958 James Agee, *A Death in the Family*
1959 Robert Lewis Taylor, *The Travels of Jaime McPheeters*
1960 Allen Drury, *Advise and Consent*
1961 Harper Lee, *To Kill a Mockingbird*
1962 Edwin O'Connor, *The Edge of Sadness*
1963 William Faulkner, *The Reivers*
1964 No award
1965 Shirley Ann Grau, *The Keepers of the House*
1966 Katherine Anne Porter, *The Collected Stories of Katherine Anne Porter*
1967 Bernard Malamud, *The Fixer*
1968 William Styron, *The Confessions of Nat Turner*
1969 N. Scott Momaday, *House Made of Dawn*
1970 Jean Stafford, *Collected Stories*
1971 No award

The Guinness Book of Records gives the highest price ever paid for a book as £8.14 million for the 226-leaf manuscript, *The Gospel Book of Henry the Lion, Duke of Saxony*. It was auctioned by Sotheby's in London on 6 December 1983. The book was illuminated in *c.* 1173 by the Monk Herimann at Helmershausen Abbey, Germany.

1972 Wallace Stegner, *Angle of Repose*
1973 Eudora Welty, *The Optimist's Daughter*
1974 No award
1975 Michael Shaara, *The Killer Angels*
1976 Saul Bellow, *Humboldt's Gift*
1977 No award
1978 James Alan McPherson, *Elbow Room*
1979 John Cheever, *The Stories of John Cheever*
1980 Norman Mailer, *The Executioner's Song*
1981 John Kennedy Toole, *A Confederacy of Dunces*
1982 John Updike, *Rabbit is Rich*
1983 Alice Walker, *The Color Purple*
1984 William Kennedy, *Ironweed*
1985 Alison Lurie, *Foreign Affairs*
1986 Larry McMurtry, *Lonesome Dove*
1987 Peter Taylor, *A Summons to Memphis*
1988 Toni Morrison, *Beloved*
1989 Anne Tyler, *Breathing Lessons*
1990 Oscar Hijuelos, *The Mambo Kings Play Songs of Love*
1991 John Updike, *Rabbit at Rest*
1992 Jane Smiley, *A Thousand Acres*
1993 Robert Olen Butler, *A Good Scent from a Strange Mountain*
1994 E. Annie Proulx, *The Shipping News*

General Non-Fiction

First awarded in 1962 for a distinguished book by an American author.

1962 Theodore H. White, *The Making of the President 1960*
1963 Barbara W. Tuchman, *The Guns of August*
1964 Richard Hofstadter, *Anti-intellectualism in American Life*
1965 Howard Mumford Jones, *O Strange New World*
1966 Edwin Way Teale, *Wandering Through Winter*
1967 David Brion Davis, *The Problem of Slavery in Western Culture*
1968 Will and Ariel Durant, *Rousseau and Revolution*
1969 Rene Dubos, *So Human an Animal: How we are Shaped by Surroundings and Events*
1970 Erik H. Erikson, *Gandhi's Truth*
1971 John Toland, *The Rising Sun*
1972 Barbara W. Tuchman, *Stilwell and the American Experience in China, 1911–1945*
1973 Frances Fitzgerald, *Fire in the Lake*; Robert Coles, *Children of Crisis*
1974 Ernest Becker, *The Denial of Death*
1975 Annie Dillard, *Pilgrim at Tinker Creek*
1976 Robert N. Butler, *Why Survive? Being Old in America*

The smallest book ever printed, measuring 1 x 1 mm, was the children's story *Old King Cole,* published in March 1985 by The Gleniffer Press of Paisley, Strathclyde. A total of 85 copies were printed on 22 gsm paper in March 1985. The pages can only be turned by using a needle.

1977 William W. Warner, *Beautiful Swimmers: Watermen, Crabs and the Chesapeake Bay*
1978 Carl Sagan, *The Dragons of Eden*
1979 Edward O. Wilson, *On Human Nature*
1980 Douglas R. Hofstadter, *Godel, Escher, Bach: An Eternal Golden Braid*
1981 Carl E. Schorske, *Fin-de-Siècle Vienna: Politics and Culture*
1982 Tracy Kidder, *The Soul of a New Machine*
1983 Susan Sheehan, *Is There No Place on Earth for Me?*
1984 Paul Starr, *The Social Transformation of American Medicine*
1985 Studs Terkel, *The Good War: An Oral History of World War Two*
1986 Joseph Lelyveld, *Move Your Shadow: South Africa, Black and White*; J. Anthony Lukas, *A Turbulent Decade in the Lives of Three American Families*
1987 David K. Shipler, *Arab and Jew: Wounded Spirits in a Promised Land*
1988 Richard Rhodes, *The Making of the Atomic Bomb*
1989 Neil Sheehan, *A Bright Shining Lie: John Paul Vann and America in Vietnam*
1990 Dale Maharidge and Michael Williamson, *And Their Children After Them*
1991 Bert Holldobler and Edward O. Wilson, *The Ants*
1992 Daniel Yergin, *The Prize: The Epic Quest for Oil, Money and Power*
1993 Garry Wills, *Lincoln at Gettysburg: The Words that Remade America*
1994 David Remnick, *Lenin's Tomb: The Last Days of the Soviet Empire*

The slowest selling book must be the record-breaking effort by David Wilkins whose translation of the New Testament from Coptic into Latin was published by Oxford University Press in 1716. When it went out of print in 1907 it had sold only 500 copies. This represents sales of about two and a half copies each year!

Most Borrowed Authors from UK Libraries

1 Catherine Cookson
2 Danielle Steel
3 Dick Francis
4 Agatha Christie
5 Ruth Rendell
6 Enid Blyton
7 Roald Dahl
8 Wilbur Smith
9 Ellis Peters
10 Jack Higgins

Note: Each author's book has been borrowed from a library in excess of one million times.
Source: Public Lending Right, 1993

Most Borrowed Non-Fiction Titles from UK Libraries

1 *Diana: Her True Story*, Andrew Morton
2 *Toujours Provence*, Peter Mayle
3 *Nancy Reagan: The Unauthorized Biography*, Kitty Kelly
4 *Innocent Abroad*, Hannah Hauxwell and Barry Cockcroft
5 *Daughter of the Dales*, Hannah Hauxwell and Barry Cockcroft
6 *Seasons of My Life*, Hannah Hauxwell and Barry Cockcroft
7 *A Brief History of Time*, Stephen Hawking
8 *A Year in Provence*, Peter Mayle
9 *The Blue Peter Green Book*, BBC
10 *One Lifetime is not Enough*, Zsa Zsa Gabor

Source: Public Lending Right, 1993

Most Borrowed Classic Titles from UK Libraries

1 *Lord of the Rings, 1*, J. R. R. Tolkien
2 *Animal Farm*, George Orwell
3 *Wuthering Heights*, Emily Brontë
4 *Catcher in the Rye*, J. D. Salinger
5 *Pride and Prejudice*, Jane Austen
6 *Rebecca*, Daphne du Maurier
7 *Jane Eyre*, Charlotte Brontë
8 *Emma*, Jane Austen
9 *Lord of the Rings, 2*, J. R. R. Tolkien
10 *Nineteen Eighty-four*, George Orwell

Source: Public Lending Right, 1993

> 'From the moment I picked your book up until I laid it down I was convulsed with laughter. Someday I intend reading it.'
>
> Groucho Marx

Top 10 Bestselling Penguin Paperbacks Worldwide

	Title	Author	Date first published
1	*Animal Farm*	George Orwell	July 1951
2	*Nineteen Eighty-four*	George Orwell	February 1954
3	*Lady Chatterley's Lover*	D. H. Lawrence	November 1960
4	*The Odyssey*	Homer	January 1946
5	*The Catcher in the Rye*	J. D. Salinger	May 1958
6	*The F-Plan Diet*	Audrey Eyton	May 1982
7	*Wuthering Heights*	Emily Brontë	March 1946
8	*Pride and Prejudice*	Jane Austen	February 1972
9	*Great Expectations*	Charles Dickens	February 1955
10	*Jane Eyre*	Charlotte Brontë	June 1953

Most Borrowed Classic Authors from UK Libraries

1 Daphne du Maurier
2 Beatrix Potter
3 Thomas Hardy
4 J. R. R. Tolkien
5 Charles Dickens
6 Anthony Trollope
7 Jane Austen
8 A. A. Milne
9 William Shakespeare
10 D. H. Lawrence

Note: Each author's book has been borrowed from a library between 200 000 and 500 000 times.
Source: Public Lending Right, 1993

Cover of the first edition of *Animal Farm* by George Orwell, bestselling Penguin paperback worldwide.

PENGUIN BOOKS

FICTION

ANIMAL FARM
—
GEORGE ORWELL

FICTION

COMPLETE UNABRIDGED

1/6

The British Book Design and Production Exhibition

In its current form, this exhibition has been held since 1973. It was originally administered by the National Book League, but since 1987 has been jointly co-sponsored by the British Printing Industries Federation and the Publishers Association; in 1993 the Book Trust also became involved. Books, published or printed in the UK, are submitted by publishers, printers or designers, and a selection of about 100 books is chosen by a panel of experts. An exhibition then tours the country and the books also make an appearance at the Frankfurt Book Fair. The 1993 awards were made in seven categories:

In Lewis Carroll's diary on 2 August 1882, he estimated that if he sold the complete 2000 first print run of *Alice in Wonderland* he would lose £200. If he sold another 2000 copies he would make £200. If he sold further copies he would make even more money, but 'that I can hardly hope for'. The book had sold approximately 180 000 copies by the time of his death in 1898!

Category	Title and selectors' comments	Author	Publisher	Designer
General Hardback	*Images of Science: A History of Scientific Illustration* Diverse range of scientific illustration skilfully brought together by the designer and fully supported by consistent printing	Brian J. Ford	The British Library	John Mitchell
General Paperback	*The Ninety-Nine Beautiful Names of God* Outstanding title page	Al-Ghazali	The Islamic Texts Soc.	Brian Keeble
Educational and Technical	*The Cambridge Encyclopedia of Human Evolution* Clarity of design and line illustrations combine with consistent black-and-white printing	–	Cambridge University Press	Dale Tomlinson
Children's	*Tigers* The only book in this category which all the judges viewed as successful. Illustration, typeface and size, balance together	Roland Edwards	All Books for Children	Jennifer Campbell
Illustrated	*David Bailey: If We Shadows* Exceptional quality of reproduction and printing of duo-tones, restrained typography	–	Thames & Hudson	Johanna Neurath
Limited Editions	*The Stanbrook Abbey Press 1956-1990* Outstanding design, beautifully printed and bound. A 'true' limited edition. Very carefully thought out, particularly in respect of the numerous tip-ins.	David Butcher	Whittington Press	John Randle
Exhibition Catalogues	*Allan Ramsay 1713-1784* Classic typography, careful letter spacing. Sympathetic choice of paper and even, consistent quality of printing	Alistair Smart	Trustees of The National Galleries of Scotland	Dalrymple

Redwood Books Award

This is an overall award, given by Redwood Books, book manufacturers in Wiltshire. The award is given for excellence in book production combined with value for money, to a title manufactured wholly in the UK.

Winning titles and publishers since inception are:

1980 *British Art from Holbein to the Present Day*, Tate Gallery Publications

1981 *The Art of Hokusai in Book Illustration*, Philip Wilson Publishers

1982 *Nature Lover's Library Field Guides*, Reader's Digest Association

1983 *The Kelmscott Chaucer*, Gordon Fraser Gallery

1984 *Engravings of Eric Gill*, Skelton's Press Ltd

1985 *The Nonsense Verse of Edward Lear*, Jonathan Cape Ltd

1986 *Land*, William Heinemann Ltd

Realms of the Russian Bear, winner of the Redwood Books Award for excellence in book production. Selectors' comments: 'An exceptionally well-designed and produced book at an attractive price. Text typography balances with outstanding and well-reproduced photographs; somewhat eccentric margins.'

Accompanies the major TV series

REALMS OF THE RUSSIAN BEAR

A natural history of Russia and the Central Asian Republics

JOHN SPARKS

1987 *Oxford Italian Mini Dictionary*, Oxford University Press

1988 *Classic Tales of the Macabre*, Blackie Children's Books

1989 *Archbold: Pleading*, Sweet & Maxwell Ltd

1990 *The Longman Encyclopedia*, Longman Group UK

1991 *The Plastics Age*, V & A Museum Publications Ltd

1992 *Anita Roddick: Body and Soul*, Ebury Press

1993 *Realms of the Russian Bear*, BBC Books

NCR Book Award

This award, sponsored by AT&T since 1988, was set up with the aim of stimulating an interest in non-fiction. Publishers submit books which are then assessed by a panel of judges and a first prize of £25 000 goes to the winner. The 1994 members of the jury were Sue Lawley and Sir Robin Day (TV presenters), Clare Short (Labour politician), Steve Jones (Professor of Genetics, University College London) and Simon Heffer (political journalist).

WINNERS

1988 *Nairn in Darkness and Light*, David Thomson

1989 *Touching the Void*, Joe Simpson

1990 *Citizens*, Simon Schama

1991 *The Invisible Woman*, Claire Tomalin

1992 *Wild Swans*, Jung Chang

1993 *Never Again*, Peter Hennessy

1994 *Edward Heath*, John Campbell

Whitbread Literary Awards

These awards have been organised since 1971 by the Booksellers Association of Great Britain and Ireland, and have been sponsored by Whitbread & Co. The awards are made in five categories – novel, first novel, children's novel, poetry, and biography/autobiography – to writers who live and work in the UK or Ireland, and each receive £2000 in prize money. In 1985 a Whitbread Book of the Year Award was introduced with a prize of £21 000, the winner being selected from the five category winners.

Within each category there are three judges who select the winning title, and these five winners go on to be judged by an 11-member panel for the overall award, comprised of one representative from each of the five category panels and a further six drawn from other fields. The panels have included members such as the Archbishop of Canterbury, Shirley Williams, Ken Livingstone, Ludovic Kennedy, Kate Adie and Gerald Durrell.

WINNERS IN 1993

Novel *Theory of War*, Joan Brady

First Novel *Saving Agnes*, Rachel Clusk

Children's Novel *Flour Babies*, Anne Fine

Poetry *Meantime*, Carol Ann Duffy

Biography *Philip Larkin, A Writer's Life*, Andrew Motion

Whitbread Book of the Year winners

1985 *Elegies*, Douglas Dunn (Poetry)

1986 *An Artist of the Floating World*, Kazuo Ishiguro (Novel)

1987 *Under the Eye of the Clock*, Christopher Nolan (Biography)

1988 *The Comforts of Madness*, Paul Sayer (First Novel)

1989 *Coleridge: Early Visions*, Richard Holmes (Biography)

1990 *Hopeful Monsters*, Nicholas Mosley (Novel)

1991 *A Life of Picasso*, John Richardson (Biography)

1992 *Swing Hammer Swing!*, Jeff Torrington (First Novel)

1993 *Theory of War*, Joan Brady (Novel)

W. H. Smith Literary Award

In January 1959, W. H. Smith announced its intention to present an annual literary award for a book by a British author, which, in the opinion of three independent judges, had made the most outstanding contribution to literature in the previous year. The award is not limited to any specific field of literature.

Winners

1959 *Voss*, Patrick White (novel)

1960 *Cider with Rosie*, Laurie Lee (semi-autobiographical novel)

1961 *Friday's Footprint*, Nadine Gordimer (short stories)

1962 *We Think the World of You*, J. R. Ackerley (novel)

1963 *The Birthday King*, Gabriel Fielding (novel)

1964 *Meditations on a Hobby-Horse*, Ernst H. Gombrich

1965 *Beginning Again*, Leonard Woolf (autobiography)

1966 *A Child Possessed*, R. C. Hutchinson (novel)

1967 *Wide Sargasso Sea*, Jean Rhys (novel)

1968 *The Mimic Men*, V. S. Naipaul (novel)

1969 *John Keats*, Robert Gittings (biography)

1970 *The French Lieutenant's Woman*, John Fowles (novel)

1971 *New Lives, New Landscapes*, Nan Fairbrother (non-fiction)

1972 *The Lost Country*, Kathleen Raine (poetry)

1973 *Catholics*, Brian Moore (novel)

1974 *Temporary Kings*, Anthony Powell (novel)

1975 *Wilfred Owen*, Jon Stallworthy (biography)

1976 *North*, Seamus Heaney (poetry)

1977 *Slim: The Standardbearer*, Ronald Lewin (biography)

1978 *A Time of Gifts*, Patrick Leigh Fermor (autobiography)

1979 *Life in the English Country House*, Mark Girouard (non-fiction)

1980 *Selected Poems 1950–1975*, Thom Gunn (poetry)

1981 *The Shooting Party*, Isabel Colegate (novel)

1982 *Last Waltz in Vienna*, George Clare (biography)

1983 *Wise Virgin*, A. N. Wilson (novel)

1984 *Required Writing*, Philip Larkin (poetry)

1985 *The Pork Butcher*, David Hughes (novel)

1986 *The Good Terrorist*, Doris Lessing (novel)

1987 *Collected Poems 1953–1985*, Elizabeth Jennings (poetry)

1988 *The Fatal Shore*, Robert Hughes (non-fiction)

1989 *A Turbulent, Seditious and Factious People – John Bunyan and His Church*, Christopher Hill (biography)

1990 *A Careless Widow and Other*

Stories, V.S Pritchett (short stories)

1991 *Omeros*, Derek Walcott (poetry)

1992 *The Scramble for Africa*, Thomas Pakenham (non-fiction)

1993 *Daughters of the House*, Michèle Roberts (novel)

1994 *A Suitable Boy*, Vikram Seth (novel)

Sunday Express Book of the Year

An annual award given by the *Sunday Express* for the most stylish and compulsively readable novel published in Britain. It was launched in 1987 and was at the time Britain's richest fiction prize. It offers a first prize of £20 000 and shortlisted titles receive £1000 each – all authors also receive leather-bound, gold embossed copies of their books.

The judges in 1993 were John Mortimer, Jeremy Paxman, David Mellor, Hilary Mantel (last year's winner) and Eve Pollard and the shortlisted titles were:

Asta's Book, Barbara Vine
Birdsong, Sebastian Faulks
The Blue Afternoon, William Boyd
Guppies for Tea, Marika Cobbold
In the Place of Fallen Leaves, Tim Pears
Paddy Clarke Ha Ha Ha, Roddy Doyle.

Winners

1987 *The Colour of Blood*, Brian Moore

1988 *Nice Work*, David Lodge

1989 *Restoration*, Rose Tremain

1990 *Age of Iron*, J. M. Coetzee

1991 *A Landing on the Sun*, Michael Frayn

1992 *A Place of Greater Safety*, Hilary Mantel

1993 *The Blue Afternoon*, William Boyd

FACTS

▪ Roddy Doyle's *Paddy Clarke Ha Ha Ha*, 1993 shortlisted title, won the 1993 Booker Prize.

▪ William Boyd (winner 1993) and Tim Pears (shortlisted 1993) were both also shortlisted for the 1993 Whitbread Awards.

Diagram Competition for the Oddest Title

In 1978, The Diagram Group, book designers and creators, organised a search to find the book with the oddest title at the Frankfurt Book Fair. It unearthed titles such as *Making Money out of Worms*,

Having Fun with Rats, and *The Interpretation of Geological Time from the Study of Fossilised Elephant Droppings*. This competition has been run every year since then, with *The Bookseller* organising an extra competition in 1993 to find the 'Oddest of the Odd' from previous winners and runners up. Readers were asked to vote for their top three in order of preference from the list of winners below:

1978 *Proceedings of the Second International Workshop on Nude Mice* (University of Tokyo Press)

1979 *The Madam as Entrepreneur: Career Management in House Prostitution* (Transaction Press)

1980 *The Joy of Chickens* (Prentice-Hall)

1981 *Last Chance at Love – Terminal Romances* (Pinnacle Press)

1982 *Population and Other Problems* (China National Publications)
Braces Owners Manual: A Guide to the Wearing and Care of Braces (Patient Information Library)

1983 *The Theory of Lengthwise Rolling* (MIR)

1984 *The Book of Marmalade: Its Antecedents, Its History and Its Role in the World Today* (Constable)
Big and Very Big Hole Drilling (Technical Publishing House, Bucharest)

1985 *Natural Bust Enlargement with Total Power: How to Increase the Other 90% of Your Mind to Increase the Size of Your Breasts* (Westwood Publishing Co.)

1986 *Oral Sadism and the Vegetarian Personality* (Brunner/Mazel)

1987 No award

1988 *Versailles: The View from Sweden* (University of Chicago Press)

1989 *How to Shit in the Woods: An Environmentally Sound Approach to a Lost Art* (Ten Speed Press)

1990 *Lesbian Sadomasochism Safety Manual* (Lace Publications)

1991 No award

1992 *How to Avoid Huge Ships* (Cornell Maritime Press)

1993 *American Bottom Archaeology* (University of Illinois Press)
Liturgy of the Opening of the Mouth for Breathing (Griffith Institute)

The winning title was *Proceedings of the Second International Workshop on Nude Mice*, a work resulting from a symposium on the health of mice, published by the University of Tokyo Press.

CHILDREN'S BOOKS

Carnegie and Kate Greenaway Awards

These awards are made annually by the Library Association, the professional body for librarians which was established in 1877 and now has 24 000 members. Library services and individual members of the Association, throughout the UK, submit a shortlist to a panel of 15 judges who are all members of the Youth Libraries Group. The two winners are each presented with a golden medal and from 1991 have been able to nominate an organisation of their choice to receive £750 worth of books.

Carnegie Medal

This is the oldest British children's book award, and is named after Andrew Carnegie, the Scottish-born philanthropist who provided funding for many British and American public libraries. In 1935, the centenary of his birth, the Library Association decided that a medal should be instituted in celebration of this. It is awarded for an outstanding book for children written in English.

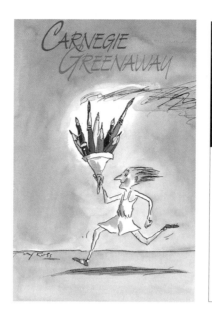

FACTS

▍ Six authors have been awarded the Carnegie Medal twice: Peter Dickinson (1979, 1980); Berlie Doherty (1986, 1991); Anne Fine (1989, 1992); Margaret Mahy (1982, 1984); Jan Mark (1976, 1983); Robert Westall (1975, 1981).

▍ The following titles have been made into a television series: *The Borrowers* (1952); *Tom's Midnight Garden* (1958); *Goggle-Eyes* (1989). *Watership Down* has been made into an animated film.

WINNERS

1936 *Pigeon Post*, Arthur Ransome
1937 *The Family from One End Street*, Eve Garnett
1938 *The Circus is Coming*, Noel Streatfeild
1939 *Radium Woman*, Eleanor Doorly
1940 *Visitors from London*, Kitty Barne
1941 *We Couldn't Leave Dinah*, Mary Treadgold
1942 *The Little Grey Men*, B.B. (D. J. Watkins-Pitchford)
1943 No award
1944 *The Wind on the Moon*, Eric Linklater
1945 No award

1946 *The Little White Horse*, Elizabeth Goudge
1947 *Collected Stories for Children*, Walter De La Mare
1948 *Sea Change*, Richard Armstrong
1949 *The Story of Your Home*, Agnes Allen
1950 *The Lark on The Wing*, Elfrida Vipont Foulds
1951 *The Woolpack,* Cynthia Harnett
1952 *The Borrowers*, Mary Norton
1953 *A Valley Grows Up*, Edward Osmond

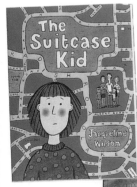

Shortlisted titles for the 1992 Carnegie Medal, including: *Flour Babies* (winner), *Gulf* (highly commended), *A Bone From a Dry Sea* and *The Great Elephant Chase* (commended).

- **1954** *Knight Crusader*, Ronald Welch
- **1955** *The Little Bookroom*, Eleanor Farjeon
- **1956** *The Last Battle*, C. S. Lewis
- **1957** *A Grass Rope*, William Mayne
- **1958** *Tom's Midnight Garden*, Philippa Pearce
- **1959** *The Lantern Bearers*, Rosemary Sutcliff
- **1960** *The Making of Man*, Dr I. W. Cornwall
- **1961** *A Stranger at Green Knowe*, Lucy M. Boston
- **1962** *The Twelve and The Genii*, Pauline Clarke
- **1963** *Time of Trial*, Hester Burton
- **1964** *Nordy Bank*, Sheena Porter
- **1965** *The Grange at High Force*, Philip Turner
- **1966** No award
- **1967** *The Owl Service*, Alan Garner
- **1968** *The Moon in the Cloud*, Rosemary Harris
- **1969** *The Edge of the Cloud*, Kathleen Peyton
- **1970** *The God Beneath the Sea*, Leon Garfield and Edward Blishen
- **1971** *Josh*, Ivan Southall
- **1972** *Watership Down*, Richard Adams
- **1973** *The Ghost of Thomas Kempe*, Penelope Lively
- **1974** *The Stronghold*, Mollie Hunter
- **1975** *The Machine Gunners*, Robert Westall
- **1976** *Thunder and Lightnings*, Jan Mark
- **1977** *The Turbulent Term of Tyke Tiler*, Gene Kemp
- **1978** *The Exeter Blitz*, David Rees
- **1979** *Tulku*, Peter Dickinson
- **1980** *City of Gold*, Peter Dickinson
- **1981** *The Scarecrows*, Robert Westall
- **1982** *The Haunting*, Margaret Mahy
- **1983** *Handles*, Jan Mark
- **1984** *The Changeover*, Margaret Mahy
- **1985** *Storm*, Kevin Crossley-Holland
- **1986** *Granny was a Buffer Girl*, Berlie Doherty
- **1987** *The Ghost Drum*, Susan Price
- **1988** *A Pack of Lies*, Geraldine McCaughrean
- **1989** *Goggle-Eyes*, Anne Fine
- **1990** *Wolf*, Gillian Cross
- **1991** *Dear Nobody,* Berlie Doherty
- **1992** *Flour Babies*, Anne Fine
- **1993** *Stone Cold*, Robert Swindells

Kate Greenaway Medal
This Medal, instituted in 1955, is awarded to an illustrator for an outstanding illustrated book for children. It is named after the English artist and illustrator Kate Greenaway (1846–1901), the daughter of an engraver, known for her children's books. She made her name with *Under the Window* (1878). Twenty thousand copies were sold immediately and a Greenaway craze began, followed by *Mother Goose* (1881) and *Marigold Garden* (1885).

ARTHUR RANSOME'S PIGEON POST – FIRST CARNEGIE MEDAL WINNER

Arthur Ransome won this first Medal in 1935 for *Pigeon Post* and it was presented at the Library Association Conference in Scarborough in 1937. Mr Woodfield of Woodfield & Stanley Ltd, specialist printers in children's books, was present and gives an account of the occasion in *The Junior Bookshelf*:

'Among the high spots at Scarborough was a half-hour on a quiet afternoon when Arthur Ransome was talking.

'As he talked I knew why he wrote such children's books as he does. Behind those spectacles of his were eyes sparkling with a boyish enthusiasm. He looked able to enjoy every moment of life and its experiences. Although in most of the photographs I had seen he wears an expression of seriousness and the sparkle is not apparent, in this half-hour all gravity had gone and we began to share the excitement of taking The Teazel on its first voyage through Yarmouth bridges or Swallow on its night run from Amazon River to Wild Cat Island. . . .

'In reply to our suggestions, he confessed that it certainly is good to be able to earn one's living in such pleasant circumstances, to write books for children and to write them while enjoying one's favourite sport of sailing or in a three hundred-year-old cottage in the Lakeland Fells with a view over forty miles of glorious country from one's front door.

'When we hoped he would give us more books of the type we had come to expect of him, he looked whimsically at the row of volumes displayed on our stand and waving a hand in their direction. "Look at all those," he said. "You don't really want more of them do you?" But he confessed to being engaged on another one which, he remarked, will make him still more unpopular among parents who want to keep their boys and girls on land while he lures them to the sea. One passage in it, he said, is so vivid that in writing it he himself had to get up and walk about because it made him feel seasick.'

A Kate Greenaway illustration taken from *Mother Goose,* engraved and printed by Edmund Evans, London, 1881.

■ Four illustrators have been awarded the Greenaway Medal twice:
Raymond Briggs (1966, 1973);
Jan Pienkowski (1971, 1979);
Anthony Browne (1973, 1992);
Michael Foreman (1982, 1989).

WINNERS

1955 No award
1956 *Tim All Alone*, Edward Ardizzone
1957 *Mrs Easter and the Storks*, V. H. Drummond
1958 No award
1959 *Kashtanka and a Bundle of Ballads*, William Stobbs
1960 *Old Winkle and the Seagulls*, Gerald Rose, by Elizabeth Rose
1961 *Mrs Cockle's Cat*, Antony Maitland
1962 *A.B.C.*, Brian Wildsmith
1963 *Borka: The Adventures of a Goose With No Feathers*, John Burningham
1964 *Shakespeare's Theatre*, C. Walter Hodges
1965 *The Three Poor Tailors*, Victor Ambrus
1966 *Mother Goose Treasury*, Raymond Briggs
1967 *Charley, Charlotte and the Golden Canary*, Charles Keeping
1968 *Dictionary of Chivalry*, Pauline Baynes, by Grant Uden
1969 *The Quangle Wangle's Hat*, Helen Oxenbury, by Edward Lear
The Dragon of an Ordinary Family, Margaret Mahy
1970 *Mr Gumpy's Outing*, John Burningham
1971 *The Kingdom Under the Sea*, Jan Pienkowski, by Joan Aiken
1972 *The Woodcutter's Duck*, Krystyna Turska
1973 *Father Christmas*, Raymond Briggs
1974 *The Wind Blew*, Pat Hutchins
1975 *Horses in Battle and Mishka*, Victor Ambrus
1976 *The Post Office Cat*, Gail Haley
1977 *Dogger*, Shirley Hughes
1978 *Each Peach Pear Plum*, Janet Ahlberg
1979 *The Haunted House*, Jan Pienkowski
1980 *Mr Magnolia*, Quentin Blake
1981 *The Highwayman*, Charles Keeping
1982 *Long Neck and Thunder Foot and Sleeping Beauty and Other Favourite Fairy Tales*, Michael Foreman
1983 *Gorilla*, Anthony Browne
1984 *Hiawatha's Childhood*, Errol Le Cain
1985 *Sir Gawain and the Loathly Lady*, Juan Wjingaard
1986 *Snow White in New York*, Fiona French
1987 *Crafty Chameleon*, Adrienne Kennaway, by Mwenye Hadithi
1988 *Can't You Sleep Little Bear?*, Barbara Firth, by Martin Waddell
1989 *War Boy, A Country Childhood*, Michael Foreman
1990 *The Whales' Song*, Gary Blythe, by Dyan Sheldon
1991 *The Jolly Christmas Postman*, Janet and Allan Ahlberg
1992 *Zoo*, Anthony Browne
1993 *Black Ships Before Troy*, Alan Lee, by Rosemary Sutcliffe

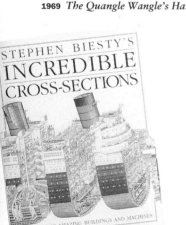

Shortlisted titles for the 1992 Kate Greenaway Medal, including: *Zoo* (winner), *The Pig in the Pond* and *Hue Boy* (highly commended).

UK Bestselling Children's Books, 1993

1. *Only You Can Save Mankind*, Terry Pratchett (Corgi / £3.99)
2. *After the Storm*, Nick Butterworth (Picture Lions / £3.99)
3. *The Very Hungry Caterpillar*, Eric Carle (Puffin / £3.99)
4. *The Window*, Carol Ellis (Hippo / £2.99)
5. *The Animals of Farthing Wood*, Colin Dann (Mammoth / £3.99)
6. *Take That: Our Story*, Piers Morgan (Boxtree / £5.99)
7. *Where's Wally?* Mini edition, Martin Handford (Walker / £4.25)
8. *Junglebook*, Disney Series (Ladybird / £4.99)
9. *Incredible Cross Sections*, Stephen Blesty (Dorling Kindersley / £12)
10. *Jurassic Park: The Junior Novelisation* (Red Fox / £2.99)

Source: Bookwatch

As the mighty alien fleet from the very latest computer game thunders across the computer screen, Johnny Maxwell prepares to blow them into the usual million pieces. And they send him a message: 'We surrender.' They're not supposed to do that! They're supposed to die. And computer joysticks don't have 'Don't Fire' buttons. . . . It's hard enough, trying to save Mankind from the Galactic Hordes. It's even harder trying to save the Galactic Hordes from Mankind. . . . An entertaining and thought-provoking new adventure from Terry Pratchett. He also wrote the children's novel *Truckers* which was serialised for television in 1992.

Mother Goose Award

Established in 1979 as an award for 'the most exciting newcomer to British children's book illustration', its aim is to encourage children's book illustrators at the beginning of their careers by drawing serious critical attention to their work, and to encourage children's book publishers to continue to foster new talent. The award takes the form of a bronzed goose egg, a scroll and £1000.

WINNERS

1979 Michelle Cartlidge, *Pippin and Pod*
1980 Reg Cartwright, *Mr Potter's Pigeon*
1981 Juan Wijngaard, *Green Finger House*
1982 Jan Ormerod, *Sunshine*
1983 Satoshi Kitamura, *Angry Arthur*
1984 Patrick Benson, *The Hob Stories*
1985 Susan Varley, *Badger's Parting Gifts*
1986 No award
1987 Patrick James Lynch, *A Bag of Moonshine*
1988 Emma Chichester-Clark, *Listen to This*
1989 Charles Fuge, *Bush Vark's First Day Out*
1990 David Hughes, *Strat and Chatto*
1991 Amanda Harvey, *A Close Call*
1992 Ted Dewan, *Inside the Whale*
1993 Claire Fletcher, *The Seashell Song*
1994 Lisa Flather, *Where the Great Bear Watches*

'As I was walking by the sea, I found a shell which sang to me; it sang the story of the sea . . .'. Claire Fletcher's illustrations in the *The Seashell Song* (by Susie Jenkin-Pearce, published by The Bodley Head) won the 1993 Mother Goose Award.

It sang of calms.

Scholastic/Independent *Story of the Year*

This competition, launched in 1993, aims to encourage new good stories for six- to nine-year-olds. Nearly 4000 stories were received and judged by a panel; the top ten were published in an anthology by Scholastic Publications and five were broadcast on Radio 5's 'Book at Bedtime'.

The winner, Caroline Pitcher, received a prize of £2000. Her story, 'Kevin the Blue', is reproduced on pp. 62–5.

FACTS

A panel of seven judged the final shortlist of 20 stories which had been selected from the 3712 entries received in the 1993 Scholastic/*Independent* Story of the Year competition. The judges were:

- Michael Rosen, children's writer and presenter of BBC Radio 4's 'Treasure Islands'
- Julia Eccleshare, children's correspondent of *The Bookseller*
- Judge Stephen Tumim, HM Chief Inspector of Prisons
- Elizabeth Hammill, Waterstones
- Angela Lambert, feature writer and columnist, *The Independent*
- Suggs, lead singer, Madness
- Sue Bates, chair, Federation of Children's Book Groups

KEVIN THE BLUE

by Caroline Pitcher

Harry crept across the kitchen floor. His wellingtons squeaked like a finger rubbing a balloon and she heard him. 'Where do you think you're going, Harry Hodgkin?' she called.

'I'm going to see Kevin,' he said and ran out of the back door.

'Who's Kevin?' she cried.

Harry kept on running, across the garden, through the gate, down the hillside speckled with cowslips to the stream.

'She can stay with that baby,' he muttered. 'I'm going to see Kevin the Blue. He isn't sick on me, he doesn't dribble and he doesn't need nappies. All she ever says is "Not now, Harry, I'm busy with the baby." Now I know how my old teddy felt when I sent him to the jumble sale.'

On the banks of the stream the willow trees trailed their yellowgreen leaves in the water, like girls leaning forward to brush their hair. There were tall plants called policemen's helmets which would have pink flowers, then seed-pods which exploded when you touched them.

Harry settled in his secret den to wait for Kevin.

It didn't look like a den. Three trees grew close together and made a perfect place to hide. Harry kept an old ice-cream box under a root. Inside was half a packet of soggy custard creams and a hat.

It was a fisherman's hat. Harry had found it further along the bank, among the wild forget-me-nots. It was too big so he had to perch it right on the back of his head to see out, but it was a dull green colour and good camouflage.

Harry's other camouflage was silence. There must only be the running of the stream on the stones.

In the chocolate-brown mud of the bank opposite there was a hole. Harry stared at it for so long that he saw an odd little face grinning back at him, a cross between a goblin and a water-rat. Harry blinked and shook his head.

There was no face after all.

'Come on, Kevin,' said Harry. 'I'm cold.' The willows met over the water as if they were playing 'Here's the church, here's the steeple' and they kept out the warmth of the sun.

Just when Harry thought he couldn't stay still for one more second, a dazzling blue light darted down the flightpath of the stream like a tiny turquoise Concorde, then hovered by the hole in the bank.

Kevin was here!

Of course, it might have been Kathleen, because there were two kingfishers. Harry had watched them flying at the bank, digging out mud with their bills to make a tunnel.

Kevin disappeared inside.

'Perhaps Kathleen's sitting on the eggs and he's brought her a fish supper,' whispered Harry.

Seconds later the kingfisher was back. He paused, then whizzed upstream, swift as a stained-glass arrow.

Harry felt a firebomb of joy explode in his chest. It was river magic! He had his very own secret, his king and queen birds. Kingfishers were rare and rich as jewels.

Back home, he sat on the doorstep to pull off his muddy wellies.

'Hello, Harry!' said his mother behind him. 'Dad's home. He's looking after the baby so why don't we read a book? Or play a game. We never get a chance to do things together now.'

'No thank you,' said Harry. She would just have to wait.

He ran upstairs and opened his bird book at the kingfisher page for the umpteenth time. It said that kingfishers laid six or seven white eggs. They hatched after about three weeks. Then the parents fed the fledglings with small fish and water creatures for another three weeks. They would have to rush in and out, stuffing food into gaping bills.

'A bit like Mum and her baby,' giggled Harry.

The next day at school, Harry drew kingfishers in his Special Topic book. It was difficult to get the colour right, especially the brilliant blue upper parts with the emerald gloss on the wings and top of the head. Underneath was a chestnut-orange colour like the cinnamon Harry's mum put in apple cake.

Harry wrote about the birds digging out their nest, and then hid his book right at the bottom of his drawer. He didn't want anyone to see it.

Especially David Snaddlethorpe.

Some children were scared of David Snaddlethorpe. He walked with his arms stuck out and he had a big face with little eyes like currants in a Sally Lunn.

David Snaddlethorpe liked birds, but not in the same way as Harry. David Snaddlethorpe collected birds' eggs like other children collect badges or toy cars.

He's like a great greedy cuckoo, thought Harry. If he ever robbed the kingfishers' nest I'd want to kill him.

Just before playtime Mrs Green gathered everyone together for news. John Campbell's stick insect had laid lots of eggs, Judith Pottle had been sick all over the new sheepskin covers in her dad's car, and Michael Stenson's little brother had stuck a coffee bean up his nose.

'How's *your* little brother Harry?'

Harry said, 'I've been down to the stream and found a –'

He stopped. All the children were waiting. He saw David Snaddlethorpe's little eyes fixed on him, hard as burned currants.

'I've found an interesting plant,' he mumbled. 'It's called policeman's helmet.'

David Snaddlethorpe snorted like a pig.

'What a stupid name for a flower,' he sneered. 'Are the police down there guarding something?'

He looked round to see who thought he was funny. Some children did.

Harry hung his head in shame. He had almost given away his dearest secret, just to show off.

Mrs Green said, 'I hope you're careful near the stream, Harry. It's dangerous.'

'Mum could hear me scream,' he said, thinking, it's the kingfishers who are in danger.

Harry went down to the stream each day on his way home from school. The grass grew long and lush in the spring rain. Harry took an old cycling cape of his dad's to keep in the den. When he put on the cape it was like sitting inside a tepee with your head poking out of the smoke hole.

One afternoon he saw Kevin and Kathleen whizzing in and out with food in their bills and he knew the eggs had hatched. There would be three more weeks before the fledglings were ready to leave.

At school, Harry worked in his kingfisher book but at home those weeks were so boring! Mum and Dad only noticed him when he slammed out of the room or when he was pulling his wide-mouthed frog face. The thing that wound them up most of all was his joke eyeballs on springs. Harry loved to frighten his mum with them, turning round suddenly so that the eyeballs bounced out at her. One night she tore them off and shouted, 'These will go in the dustbin if you do that to me again!'

So Harry took them to the den. He made a bird-watcher to keep him company. The silly bird-watcher was made from the cycling cape draped over some branches, with the fisherman's hat perched on top. Harry hooked the eyeballs so that they dangled down beneath the hat. He named the bird-watcher Bobby, so that B.E. could watch K.K. with H.H.

Now it looked as if someone had been plastering under Kevin's doorway, because the bank was white with droppings. Harry's bird book said that the tunnel would be slippery too, and littered with bones and bits of minnow and stickleback. Every time Kevin and Kathleen emerged they took quick baths in the stream.

That evening Mum said, 'Why don't you ask Kevin home to play?'

'He won't be able to come,' muttered Harry.

'But you're always on your own,' she said.

Rubbish, thought Harry. The kingfisher darted through his mind all the time. He longed for the fledglings to come out into the daylight to learn to fly. That time would be so short. He musn't miss it. He had a terrible dream. David Snaddlethorpe was waiting for the fledglings too. When they came out he snatched their little blue bodies out of the air and dashed them down into the mud. Harry woke up trembling.

Harry was beginning to like baby-watching as well as bird-watching. The baby noticed him now and Harry was learning how to look after babies. When Mum went to Parents' Evening Harry said to his dad, 'You'd better get him clean clothes before she gets back. He's covered in banana and she says it stains.'

Dad disappeared for clean clothes. Harry knelt down and brushed bits of banana and soggy biscuit off the baby. He whispered, 'I've got a friend called Kevin the Blue. He's a kingfisher and he's got babies. You're the only one who knows, Humphrey.'

He sang,

> 'Kingfisher blue, dilly dilly,
>   Kingfisher green,
> No one but you, little brother,
>   Knows who I've seen.'

Humphrey gave him a big smile. There was one tooth in his pink mouth, like a sharp, peeled almond.

When Mum came home she looked hard at Harry.

She said, 'There isn't anyone in your class called Kevin, is there?'

'No,' said Harry.

'In fact there isn't a Kevin in the whole school, is there?'

'Don't think so', he muttered.

She wasn't cross. She said, 'Your books are beautiful, Harry. I'm proud of you.'

Mum wasn't the only one who had looked at Harry's books. When he arrived at school the next morning he saw that Mrs Green had put his kingfisher book on full display for Parents' Evening. David Snaddlethorpe was peering at it and licking his lips.

'Found a kingfisher's hole have you Hodgkin?' he smirked. 'I knew there was something up. You've been acting sneaky.'

'Don't you dare go near it!' cried Harry.

'Will if I like. It's not yours.'

Yes it is! Well, in a way it is. And anyway, they've hatched so you can't steal the eggs.'

'I could have the babies though,' whispered David Snaddlethorpe. 'I've got a stick like a shepherd's crook and it's good for hooking things, specially things out of nests down tunnels. I could keep some chicks in my old budgie cage now the dog's had the budgie. I could get them stuffed and sell them.'

'It's against the law to catch kingfishers!' cried Harry.

David Snaddlethorpe just laughed.

Harry could hardly breathe. What could he do? David would go looking for the kingfishers after school. Harry would have to get there first. He must protect them, even if it meant sitting up all night long.

Harry's eyes hardly left the clock all day. To make things worse, a storm was brewing and he began to get a headache.

Just before hometime Mrs Green sent him to the headteacher to ask for more pastels to finish his kingfisher colouring. The headteacher searched for ages and then said, 'Sorry, Harry, we must have used them all up.'

When Harry ran into the classroom, only Mrs Green was there. Everyone else had gone home.

He fled without even a goodbye, out into the wind and slanting rain, remembering too late that his anorak was still on its peg. The sky was dark and full of storm. On the hillside the long grass soaked his legs. He slipped and fell and rolled to the bottom. He lay there panting for breath. What terrible things had Snaddlethorpe done by now? If he had hooked the babies out of the tunnel they might have fallen in the water and drowned, with poor Kevin and Kathleen fluttering over them, crying in small shrill voices for their children.

'Why didn't I get Mum?' cried Harry.

There was a great splash and an eerie wail.

Harry scrambled to his feet and stared.

David Snaddlethorpe came crashing through the policemen's helmets, setting off a hundred little explosions like bursting pepperpots. He was splattered all over with mud and his eyes stretched wide with terror.

'Bogey man!' he gasped. 'Bogey man, lying in wait to get me!'

He staggered past Harry and floundered up the hillside through the long grass. The wind carried his wail, 'Bogey man, Bo-gey man . . .'

Harry heard another sound. Flapping.

He hesitated. Then, with his heart beating like a bird trapped against glass, he stalked that sound through the willow trees.

It was coming from his den.

There was a bogey man all right.

It was a bogey bird-watcher called Bobby.

The wind had got inside the cape and blown it out like a balloon and the eyeballs rolled madly.

Harry sank to the ground with relief.

'Thanks for keeping them safe, Bobby,' he said.

The storm rolled away and the pale sun swam into the sky.

Harry felt the river magic.

He watched spellbound.

The little kingfishers came out of the tunnel into the sunlight and clung to the low branches of a willow tree, iridescent as dragonflies.

Then, as if they had been given a secret sign, they burst over the stream in a shower of brilliant blue sparks.

They hovered and turned, Harry tried to count them but they flashed away before he could finish.

Kevin and Kathleen hovered above the water, watching and guiding the flying practice.

'It's like a firework display,' whispered Harry. 'They're even more beautiful than I dreamed.'

He decided there were six fledglings just before they finished their display and vanished into the tunnel.

Harry was exhausted, and happy, and hungry too. He set off up the hill for home.

Someone was coming to look for him. It was his mum, with Humphrey clinging to her side like a baby monkey. Harry grinned.

'Come and meet Kevin, Mum!', he said.

The Children's Book Award

The Federation of Children's Book Groups has made this unique annual award since 1980. Unique because the winners are chosen primarily by children who allocate points from 1 to 10 to each book. Books are judged on production, illustrations and content by a network of children nationwide, in three categories: picture books for younger and older readers; shorter novels for less experienced readers; and longer novels for fluent readers.

Ten titles are drawn together as a shortlist, from which an overall winner is selected:

1980 *Mister Magnolia*, Quentin Blake
1981 *Fair's Fair*, Leon Garfield and Margaret Chamberlain
1982 *The B.F.G.*, Roald Dahl and Quentin Blake
1983 *Erik the Viking*, Terry Jones and Michael Foreman
1984 *Brother in the Land*, Robert Swindells
1985 *Arthur*, Amanda Graham and Donna Gynell
1986 *The Jolly Postman*, Janet and Allan Ahlberg
1987 *Winnie the Witch*, Korky Paul and Valerie Thomas
1988 No award
1989 *Matilda*, Roald Dahl and Quentin Blake
1990 *Room 13*, Robert Swindells
1991 *Threadbear*, Mick Inkpen
1992 *Kiss the Dust*, Elizabeth Laird
1993 *The Suitcase Kid*, Jacqueline Wilson
1994 *The Boy in the Bubble*, Ian Strachan

Most Borrowed Children's Fiction from UK Libraries

1 *Matilda*, Roald Dahl
2 *The BFG*, Roald Dahl
3 *The Twits*, Roald Dahl
4 *Esio Trot*, Roald Dahl
5 *The Witches*, Roald Dahl
6 *The Very Hungry Caterpillar*, Eric Carle
7 *George's Marvellous Medicine*, Roald Dahl
8 *Peace at Last*, Jill Murphy
9 *A Piece of Cake*, Jill Murphy
10 *Whatever Next!* Jill Murphy
11 *The Minpins*, Roald Dahl
12 *Dear Zoo*, Rod Campbell
13 *Superfudge*, Judy Blume
14 *Charlie and the Great Glass Elevator*, Roald Dahl
15 *Dogger*, Shirley Hughes

Source: Public Lending Right, 1993

The Children's Book Award magnificent oak and silver tree trophy awarded to the annual overall winner.

WINNER OF THE 1993 CHILDREN'S BOOK AWARD

The Suitcase Kid

JACQUELINE WILSON
ILLUSTRATED BY NICK SHARRATT

ROALD DAHL
Matilda
Illustrated by Quentin Blake

Matilda by Roald Dahl, the book children most often borrow from their public library. The next four most popular titles listed are also written by Roald Dahl.

The Top Ten Children's Books of 1993

Books selected by children nationwide – organised by The Federation of Children's Book Groups.

PICTURE BOOKS
The Bee's Sneeze, Ellis Nadler
Amazing Anthony Ant, Lorna and Graham Philpot
Tippu, David Day

SHORTER NOVELS
The Incredible Reversing Peppermints, Paul Adshead
War Game, Michael Foreman
The Finders, Nigel Hinton

LONGER NOVELS
Kezzie, Theresa Breslin
Street Child, Berlie Doherty
See Ya, Simon, David Hill
The Boy in the Bubble, Ian Strachan

The Smarties Book Prize

Sponsored by Nestlé Rowntree and organised by the Book Trust since 1985, this is the biggest children's book prize in the world, set up to stimulate interest in children's books and encourage children to enjoy reading. A total of £12 000 prize money is offered for books written for three age groups: 0–5, 6–8 and 9–11 years. Each category winner receives £2000 and the overall winner, chosen from one of the category winners, receives an extra £6000 and the Book Prize Trophy for the year.

The judging panel is made up of children's writers, illustrators, booksellers and children's television personalities.

OVERALL WINNERS
1985 *Gaffer Samson's Luck*, Jill Paton Walsh
1986 *The Snow Spider*, Jenny Nimmo
1987 *A Thief in the Village*, James Berry
1988 *Can't You Sleep Little Bear*, Martin Waddell and Barbara Firth
1989 *We're Going on a Bear Hunt*, Michael Rosen, and Helen Oxenbury
1990 *Midnight Blue*, Pauline Fisk
1991 *Farmer Duck*, Martin Waddell and Helen Oxenbury
1992 *The Great Elephant Chase*, Gillian Cross
1993 *War Game*, Michael Foreman

1993 Smarties Book Prize Shortlist

0–5 YEARS AGE GROUP
Winner **Hue Boy**, Rita Phillips Mitchell (illustrated by Caroline Binch)
Grandfather's Pencil and the Room of Stories, Michael Foreman
Come Back, Grandma, Sue Limb (illustrated by Claudio Munoz)
Get Lost, Laura!, Jennifer Northway
The Bear Under the Stairs, Helen Cooper

6–8 YEARS AGE GROUP
Winner **War Game**, Michael Foreman
Mummy Laid an Egg, Babette Cole
The Enchanted Horse, Magdalen Nabb (illustrated by Julek Heller)
Henry's Baby, Mary Hoffman (illustrated by Susan Winter)
Grandpa Chatterji, Jamila Gavin
Bully, David Hughes

9–11 YEARS AGE GROUP
Winner **Listen to the Dark**, Maeve Henry
The Boggart, Susan Cooper
The Frozen Waterfall, Gaye Hicyilmaz
Hiding Out, Elizabeth Laird
The War of Jenkin's Ear, Michael Morpurgo
Double Image, Pat Moon

Disagreements reigned within the judging panel for the 1993 Smarties children's book prize (the Baby Booker). The judges disagreed over a title included in the shortlist – *Mummy Laid an Egg* by Babette Cole, an informative book about sex written for children. It was originally included in the under-five section, but some of the judges felt that sex education should not start so early – so, it was shifted to the six- to eight-year-old category.

BRAVERY

Binney Memorial Medal Awards

The Binney Medal has been awarded since 1947 for the bravest action in support of law and order performed during the year in the areas controlled by the City of London Police or by the Metropolitan Police, by any person who is not a member of a police force. A number of Certificates of Merit are also awarded each year for similar acts of courage for which the medal cannot be awarded, but which deserve special recognition. Individuals are put forward for the award by the City and Metropolitan Police.

HRH Prince Charles, the Prince of Wales, presented the 1993 Binney Medal to Marjorie Condie from Elstree, Herts (see below). Sixteen Binney Memorial Award Certificates were also presented. The official citation relates Mrs Condie's act of bravery:

'On the afternoon of 20 November 1991 a man entered the Pinner Medical Centre and asked to see a particular doctor. When told the doctor was not on duty he became agitated and produced a gun. He forced the Practice manager, Mrs Condie, and two members of staff into a section of the reception area that was out of sight. His objective was to gain publicity in the media over the recent death of his wife.

'At this point an elderly patient entered the surgery and the man agreed that Mrs Condie could escort the patient out of the centre. Mrs Condie took this opportunity to ask the patient to inform the police. Mrs Condie was then allowed to answer the telephone and again took the opportunity to inform other members of staff what was going on. The man then threatened Mrs Condie with a knife held at her throat. Mrs Condie was sent upstairs to get keys to lock the centre and while doing so rang the police herself.

'When the police arrived the man again held a knife to Mrs Condie's throat. After negotiations the man agreed to release the other two members of staff. Eventually he agreed to release Mrs Condie in exchange for a police officer but not before she had been forced to tie up and handcuff the officer.

'For her courage and calmness in dealing with a dangerous armed man, and for her concern of the safety of others Mrs Condie is given this award.'

BELOW Marjorie Condie receives the 1993 Award from HRH the Prince Charles.

The award was instituted as a memorial to Captain Ralph D. Binney who lost his life in 1944 when he made a gallant and single-handed attempt to prevent the escape of 'smash and grab' thieves in the City of London. Captain Binney's friends in the Royal Navy wanted to commemorate his bravery in some way which would never be forgotten and so they subscribed to a Trust Fund to found a medal which could be awarded each year.

The thieves tackled by Captain Binney had robbed a jeweller's shop in the City and at the suggestion of Sir Hugh Turnbull (formerly commissioner of the City Police), the Naval Officers who had collected the Memorial Fund invited the Goldsmiths' Company to act as trustees.

The awards are made by a selection committee consisting of the Chief Metropolitan Stipendiary Magistrate, the Commissioner of the Metropolitan Police, the Commissioner of City Police, the Chief of Fleet Support and the Clerk of the Goldsmiths' Company.

Since 1963 the awards have been presented at the Goldsmiths Hall. The medal is not necessarily awarded every year, if, in the opinion of the committee, the recommendations put to them do not justify awarding a medal; on the other hand, two medals were awarded in 1964. The number of certificates of merit awarded each year varies up to a total of twenty.

■ The total number of medals awarded to end 1993: 46 (representing only 45 ceremonies – in 1964 two medals were awarded).

■ Five women have won the award: Mrs P. H. Richards (1951); Mrs W. Myers (1955); Mrs E. M. Moss (1957); Mrs J. Burns (1973); and Mrs M. Condie (1993).

■ Four recipients of the medal have died as a direct result of their act of bravery. Mr Munnelly (1964) was kicked in the face, hit with milk bottles and stabbed twice, as a result of which he died almost immediately. Mr Barton (1974) died eleven days after his act of bravery and died without regaining consciousness. Mr Chesworth (1979) died seven days after being injured. Mr Kell (1989), an old-age pensioner, was walking along with some wooden shelving when security guards were robbed and he intervened. He was shot and fatally wounded, dying almost immediately.

THE FIRST BINNEY MEDAL AWARD

The first medal was awarded to Thomas Arthur Beall in 1947. The official citation reads:

'Mr Thomas Arthur Beall reported to the police on Friday 23 May 1947 that his bicycle had been stolen. On the way home he saw his bicycle standing outside a telephone box inside which a man was telephoning. He opened the door of the kiosk to make enquiries and after some conversation the man pushed his way out as if to run away. At this moment Mr Beall noticed that the man had a gun in his pocket and he immediately flung his arms around the villain from behind pinioning his arms above the elbows. A fierce struggle followed during which the man was able to take out his gun and point it upwards towards Mr Beall's head. A shot was fired and the struggle went on. Mr Beall could now see that the weapon was in fact a sawn-off rifle but with complete disregard for his own safety he continued to hold on shouting for help. A second shot was fired before assistance came, by which time Mr Beall was becoming exhausted. He nevertheless kept his hold until the police arrived and he continued to help until the man, after firing two more shots, was eventually overpowered. Mr Beall displayed great courage and determination in tackling singlehanded a dangerous criminal whom he knew to be armed and who was obviously prepared to go to any length to avoid arrest.'

Champion Children of the Year

These awards, organised by Barnardo's, the child-care charity, were created in 1977 and launched in association with BBC Television's 'Nationwide'. Sponsored by Woolworths and assisted by 'Good Morning with Anne and Nick' the awards aim to highlight the achievements of British kids today. Nominations are received from parents, friends, etc. and Barnardo's compiles a shortlist which is passed to a panel of judges. There are seven categories – Bravery, Sport, Art, Dance, Music, Triumph over Adversity and Young Carer – and each has a well-known judge who has experience in the relevant field. The 1993 awards were presented by the Princess of Wales.

1993 Bravery Awards

Judged by Raymond Fayers, Hong Kong and Shanghai Bank Security Guard, on duty when the IRA bomb exploded in April in the City of London.

Christopher Oliver, aged 11, from Jarrow, Tyne & Wear. He was fishing with friends, when a group of youths began taunting them and throwing stones. A stone hit one of Christopher's friends on the head and the force knocked her into the river. Christopher immediately waded out into the water and pulled her back to safety. He then carried her to a nearby caravan site to find help.

John Race, aged 14, from Hartlepool, Cleveland. He saw a man entering the water in a gravel pit to try and drown himself. John swam out to the man and started to drag him back to the bank; his friend John Forster waded out to help him. The man began to struggle violently, so John twisted his arm behind his back, forced him to the ground and sat on him until the police arrived.

Paul Carlton, aged 13, from Paignton, Devon. When he saw his brother fall into a fast-flowing river he did not stop to think of himself but jumped in to save him, shouting to get the attention of the family nearby. Paul grabbed hold of his brother and held on to a rock while he waited for help. He did not stop to consider his own safety, only the danger that his brother faced, and it was this reflex action which saved his brother's life.

CARS

European Car of the Year

The Ford Mondeo was voted European Car of the Year 1994 by a panel of 58 motor journalists from 20 European countries, from a final list of 15 cars (chosen by a committee of 10). Each member of the jury had 25 marks to allocate to at least five cars on the list, with a maximum of 10 marks per car. The rules for entry were: cars could be manufactured anywhere in the world but had to have sold more than 5000 a year; and had to be on sale in a minimum of six European markets. The main criteria on which each car was judged were: general design, comfort, safety, economy, handling and general roadworthiness, performance, functionality, drive satisfaction and price; value for money being a major factor.

The award has been given for 31 years and is now run by an Organising Committee which represents a group of seven European publications: *Sunday Express Magazine* (Great Britain); *Stern* (Germany); *L'Equipe* (France); *Vi Bilägare* (Sweden); *AM* (Italy); *Autovisie* (Holland) and *Autopista* (Spain). Each publication appoints a senior staff member to represent it on the Committee.

WINNERS

1964	Rover 2000	1980	Lancia Delta
1965	Austin 1800	1981	Ford Escort
1966	Renault 16	1982	Renault 9
1967	Fiat 124	1983	Audi 100
1968	NSU Ro 80	1984	Fiat Uno
1969	Peugeot 504	1985	Opel Kadett
1970	Fiat 128	1986	Ford Scorpio
1971	Citroën GS	1987	Opel Omega
1972	Fiat 127	1988	Peugeot 405
1973	Audi 80	1989	Fiat Tipo
1974	Mercedes 450	1990	Citroën XM
1975	Citroën CX	1991	Renault Clio
1976	Simca 1307-1308	1992	VW Golf
		1993	Nissan Micra
1977	Rover 3500	1994	Ford Mondeo
1978	Porsche 928		
1979	Simca-Chrysler Horizon		

The Ford Mondeo, 1994 European Car of the Year

Top 20 Selling Cars in the UK, 1993

		Total sales
1	Ford Escort	122 002
2	Ford Fiesta	110 449
3	Vauxhall Astra	108 204
4	Vauxhall Cavalier	104 104
5	Ford Mondeo	88 660
6	Rover 200	77 745
7	Rover Metro	57 068
8	Peugeot 405	52 184
9	Vauxhall Corsa	51 608
10	Renault Clio	45 269
11	Nissan Micra	38 117
12	Volkswagen Golf	36 404
13	Peugeot 106	35 918
14	Citroën ZX	33 283
15	Rover 400	33 146
16	BMW 3 Series	29 065
17	Renault 19	26 492
18	Volvo 400	26 218
19	Citroën AX	24 578
20	Ford Orion	23 972

Source: The Society of Motor Manufacturers and Traders Ltd, 1993

Top 10 Money Saving Cars

		Running cost per mile (pence)
1	Citroën AX	24.4
2	Fiat Cinquecento	24.4
3	Rover Metro 1.1 Quest	25.0
4	Vauxhall Corsa 1.2i	25.7
5	Renault Clio Prima 1.2	26.1
6	Ford Fiesta 1.1CFi	26.7
7	Nissan Micra 1.0L	26.7
8	Peugeot 106XN 1.1i	26.9
9	Rover Mini Mayfair	27.4
10	Rover Metro 1.1C	27.6

Source: Leasecontracts, 1993

FACTS

■ The Ford Mondeo appeared in first place in 19 of the jurors' voting lists; in second, 19; in third, 11; in fourth and fifth, 4; and in one list, no placing.

■ The Citroën Xantia appeared first in 10 lists; the Renault Twingo in 9; the Mercedes-Benz C in 8; the Opel / Vauxhall Corsa in 6; the Saab 900 in 4; and the Peugeot 306 and Seat Ibiza in 1.

'EUROPEAN CAR OF THE YEAR 1994' VOTING

		Points awarded
1	Ford Mondeo	290
2	Citroën Xantia	264
3	Mercedes-Benz C	192
4	Opel / Vauxhall Corsa	185
5	Renault Twingo	174
6	Peugeot 306	108
7	Saab 900	87
8	Seat Ibiza	64
9	Rover 600	33
10	Honda Accord	28
11	Lancia Delta	11
	Mitsubishi Galant	11
13	Subaru Impreza	2
14	Daihatsu Charade	1
15	Nissan Serena	0

Cartoons & Comics

Golden Jester Award

The Cartoonists' Club of Great Britain has made this award since 1974 to individuals who it feels have best supplied cartoonists with material for gags during the year. The recipient of the award receives a small tie-tack in gold in the form of the club motif – a jester's head with a paint brush in its mouth – and is made an Honorary member of the Club.

WINNERS

1974 Enoch Powell, Cons. politician and scholar

1975 Brian Clough, footballer and manager

1976 Margaret Thatcher, Cons. stateswoman, PM 1979–90

1977 Richard Ingrams, co-founder and co-publisher of *Private Eye*

1978 Sir Freddie Laker, chairman and man. dir., Laker Airways Ltd.

1979 Tony Benn, Lab. politician

1980 No award

1981 The Emanuels, dress designers

1982 Hercules the Bear, famous for his escape from a zoo into the Scottish Highlands

1983 Ken Livingstone, Lab. politician

1984 Robert Maxwell, publisher and politician

1985 Jeffrey Archer, author and politician

1986 Terry Waite, religious adviser

1987 Lester Piggott, jockey

1988 Terry Wogan, broadcaster and writer

1989 Derek Jameson (on behalf of Fleet Street)

1990 Ken Dodd, stand-up comedian, singer, actor

1991 Terry Waite, religious adviser

1992 No award

1993 Frank Bruno, professional boxer

UK Comic Art Awards

The awards, organised by Rusty Staples Ltd, were instituted in 1989 and presented in 1990, and were originally sponsored by Penguin Books. They are presented annually at the Glasgow Comic Art Convention. The results are compiled by tabulating the votes of

Each year, members of the Cartoonists' Club of Great Britain submit ideas for a new pub sign to be hung outside their headquarters – the Cartoonist Pub, Shoe Lane, off Fleet Street, London. This sign is changed every year – the winning design is copied by a signwriter on to the inn sign. The 1993 winning pub sign (above) was drawn by David Gaskill, Political / Editorial cartoonist for the *Today* newspaper.

those involved in Britain's comic industry on a professional basis. Writers, artists, editors, letterers and colourists are polled by circulating forms to the comic companies and to individuals listed on the Rusty Staples mailing list. Each specialist comic shop in Britain also receives a form. Votes can be cast for any title published worldwide, or for anyone making a significant contribution to the comic art world during the previous year.

1994 WINNERS

Best writer Pete Milligan, *Shade the Changing Man; Enigma; The Extremist*

Best artist Duncan Fegredo, *Enigma; Shade the Changing Man*

Best writer/artist Frank Miller, *Daredevil Man Without Fear; Sin City*

Best newcomer Frank Quitely (artist), 'Shimura' and 'The Missionary Man', *Judge Dredd Megazine*

Best auxiliary contributor Ellie de Ville (letterer)

Best company D.C. Comics

Best graphic novel (original material) *Vendetta*

in Gotham, John Wagner, Alan Grant, Cam Kennedy

Best book collection *Hugo Tate – O, America*, Nick Abadzis

Best ongoing publication *Judge Dredd Megazine*

Best new publication *Daredevil Man Without Fear*

Special career achievement award Will Eisner, creator of 'The Spirit' in the 1940s, a masked adventurer, which is still reprinted today. Pioneer of the graphic novel with *A Contract with God*, published in 1977. He now produces one graphic novel a year, some autobiographical material (e.g. *The Heart of the Storm*) and some fiction (e.g. *The Building*).

Comic Creators Guild Awards

These annual awards, first made in 1992, are given by a panel of judges who are drawn from committee members and other members of the Guild.

1993 WINNERS

Frank Bellamy Lifetime Achievement award Jack Kirby, co-creator of Captain America, the Fantastic Four, the Hulk and many other Marvel characters

Special award *Understanding Comics*, Scott McCloud

Best ongoing title *Cud*, Terry Laban

Best cover *Dark Horse Presents*, No. 75, Charles Vess

Best newspaper strip 'Calvin and Hobbes', Bill Watterson

Best monthly title *Action Comics*, Roger Stern and Jackson Guice

Best humour strip 'Hate', Peter Bagge

Best weekly strip 'Firekind', John Smith and Paul Marshall (in *2000 AD*)

Best one-off *Casanova's Last Stand*, Hunt Emerson

Best limited series *Enigma*, Pete Milligan and Duncan Fegredo

Best anthology *Gay Comics*, edited by Andy Mangels

Best small press/self-published title *Exit*, Nabiel Kanan

Best foreign work worthy of translation into English *Les Lutins*, Pierre Dubois and Stéphane Duval

Comic World *Readers Poll*

Comic World was launched in 1992 as the only British newsstand magazine about comic strips and comic books. The poll was introduced in 1993, readers voting in a variety of categories for their choice of best and most promising creators, characters and titles of the previous year, the categories recognising the wide variety of talent involved in putting together a comic. The award is the only one in Britain for comic creators which is decided on by votes from the comic fans themselves.

1994 WINNERS

Best ongoing title *The Sandman*. Long-running, dark fantasy series featuring Morpheus – the Sandman of the title – and the family of The Endless, the immortal beings – Death, Despair, etc. – set partly in the mystical land of The Dreaming. The series has explored the relationship between The Endless and man throughout time and myth. Co-created by Neil Gaiman and Sam Kieth in 1988, the series has proved to be the most critically successful title of the early 1990s.

Best one-shot/graphic novel *Cerebus* No. 0. Gathering together previously unreprinted episodes of Dave Sim's popular Cerebus series. Cerebus the

LEFT Detail from *The Sandman* comic, No. 50, which featured prominently in the list of winners in the 1993 *Comic World* Readers Poll.

Aardvark began as a parody of the sword and sorcery genre but quickly established both Sim's often scathing satirical wit with a fascinating continuous storyline which he plans to write for exactly 300 issues – with a large party planned for the year 2004.

Best limited series *Death: The High Cost of Living*. Spin-off from *The Sandman* comic strip, Neil Gaiman's vision of Death is as a teenage girl. The series is notable for Gaiman's humorous dialogue. Death can be at times endearing for her fascination with old movies like *Mary Poppins,* as well as her 'cut out the rubbish' attitudes to life, sex and death.

Best story in a single issue *The Sandman* No. 50. A celebratory issue of Gaiman's series. Issue No. 50, drawn by P. Craig Russell, featured 'Ramadan', a mythological fantasy set in Baghdad, the heavenly city, the jewel of Arabia, its troubled king, Haroun Al Raschid, and his attempt to make a bargain with the Sandman.

Best penciller Chris Bachalo. American artist who first came to prominence in 1990 with his work on *Shade the Changing Man,* and has subsequently drawn episodes of *Sandman*, the mini-series *Death: The High Cost of Living,* *X-Men Unlimited* and currently draws *Ghost Rider 2099.*

Best inker Mark Buckingham. British artist who gained attention in 1988 with his work on *Hellblazer* and artwork for *Miracleman, Death: The High Cost of Living,* 'Tyranny Rex' (in *2000 AD*), and *Immortalis.* Currently inking *Ghost Rider 2099.*

Best penciller/inker Glenn Fabry. Very popular artist who leapt to fame for his highly rendered black and white artwork for 'Slaine' in *2000 AD*. He returned to the series recently producing fully-painted artwork. His covers regularly appear on *Hellblazer, Scarab,* and he is currently painting a *Batman/Judge Dredd* graphic novel.

Best writer Neil Gaiman. Freelance writer who has written *The Sandman* since 1988, the most widely applauded comic book currently in production. Gaiman has also written numerous other strips and was co-author with Terry Pratchett of the novel *Good Omens.* (Terry Pratchett is author of the 1993 UK bestselling children's book, *Only You Can Save Mankind.*)

Best writer/artist Frank Miller. Extremely popular writer whose comic work first appeared in the 1970s. His bestselling graphic novels include *Batman: The Dark Knight Returns, Give Me Liberty, Sin City,* etc. He was the screenwriter of *Robocop 2* (US 90) and *Robocop 3* (US 93).

Jeff Smith, most promising new writer, 1994 *Comic World* Readers Poll.

Best colourist Steve Oliff. American comic book colourist whose Olyoptics group are responsible for work on the bestselling *Spawn* comic, as well as the above award-winning *Death: The High Cost of Living.*

Best letterer Todd Klein. American writer and letterer who has worked on thousands of pages for D.C. Comics since 1978. His work can be found in *Batman: Year One, Batman/Judge Dredd: Judgement in Gotham, Black Orchid, Books of Magic,* and most notably appears each month in *The Sandman.*

Best editor Karen Berger. American, group editor of the Vertigo line of titles for D.C. Comics, one-time editor of the award-winning *Swamp Thing* and current editor of *The Sandman.*

Most promising new title Catwoman. A long-time antagonist of Batman, Catwoman's popularity rose even higher following her portrayal by Michelle Pfeiffer in the movie *Batman Returns* (US 92). The *Catwoman* comic book is written by Jo Duffy and drawn by Jim Balent.

Most promising new writer Jeff Smith. Jeff Smith's *Bone*, comedic tales of the inhabitants of Boneville, has its roots in Walt Kelly's 'Pogo' newspaper strip. Smith himself has a background in animated movies.

Most promising new artist Frank Quitely. Quitely is the pen name of Vincent Douhan whose work first appeared nationally in *Electric Soup* where his 'The Greens' parodied the famous Scottish newspaper strip 'The Broons'. He is currently drawing two strips for the *Judge Dredd Megazine*, 'Missionary Man' and 'Shimura'.

BRITAIN'S OLDEST COMICS

▌ *The Dandy* is Britain's oldest comic still being published. It was launched on 4 December 1937 by D.C. Thomson & Co. and has been issued weekly (apart from during World War II). 'Desperate Dan' stories have appeared in every issue.

▌ *The Beano* is Britain's second oldest comic still being published. It was launched on 30 July 1938 by D.C. Thomson & Co. and is issued weekly and 'Dennis the Menace' stories have appeared in every issue except one since 17 March 1951. The Dennis The Menace Fan Club (founded in 1976) has over one and a quarter million members.

▌ *The Dandy* and *The Beano* recorded their highest combined weekly sale on 22 April 1950 when the figure exceeded 4 000 000 – *The Dandy*, 2 035 310; *The Beano*, 1 974 072.

▌ Both comics have produced Christmas annuals each year without a break. The first *Dandy* annual, *The Dandy Monster Comic,* was published in 1938, and the first *Beano* annual, *The Beano Book,* was published in 1939.

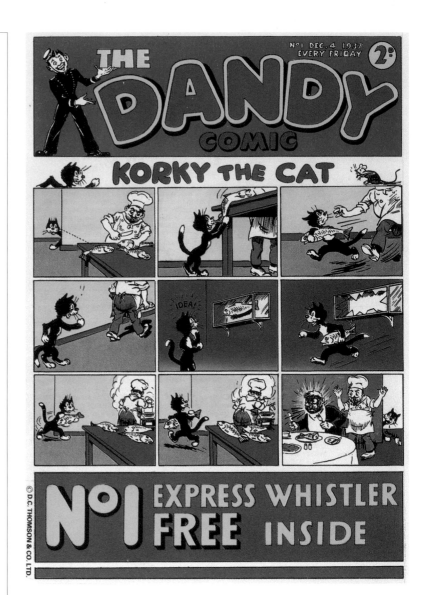

Front cover of the first issue of *The Dandy*.

The original artwork for 'Hey Sonia!', one of the most popular postcard cartoons ever printed, was sold at Christie's on 17 February 1994 for £3850 – a world record price for postcard artwork. The estimate set by the auctioneers was £150 to £250 – the artwork was bought by an anonymous English collector living in America. The new owner said: 'This card has been seen in schoolboys' lockers and workmen's huts all over the world. In my view it is just as important as the Mona Lisa.'

'Hey Sonia!', drawn by Arnold Taylor, was one of the most successful cards ever produced by James Balmforth, a company based in Holmfirth, W. Yorks, founded in the 1860s. By the beginning of World War II, Bamforth was printing an estimated 20 million cards a year. Over a period of 90 years, the company produced about 50 000 comic designs. Balmforth is now owned by E. T. W. Dennis of Scarborough who made £80 033 from this sale for 3000 original pieces of artwork divided into 210 lots.

CHEMISTRY

Nobel Prize

Awarded annually since 1901 for outstanding achievement in the field of chemistry, this prize was endowed by Alfred Nobel in 1896. (See separate section, Nobel Prizes.)

1901 Jacobus Henricus van't Hoff (NETH). Discovery of laws of chemical dynamics and osmotic pressure in solutions

1902 Hermann Emil Fischer (GER). Work on sugar and purine syntheses

1903 Svante August Arrhenius (SWE). Electrolytic theory of dissociation

1904 Sir William Ramsay (UK). Discovery of inert gaseous elements in air, and determination of their place in the periodic system

1905 Johann Adolf von Baeyer (GER). Work on organic dyes and hydroaromatic compounds

1906 Henri Moissan (FRA). Investigation and isolation of fluorine element, and 'Moissan' electric furnace

1907 Eduard Buchner (GER). Discovery of non-cellular fermentation

1908 Lord Ernest Rutherford (UK). Atomic structure and chemistry of radioactive substance

1909 Wilhelm Ostwald (GER). Work on catalysis and investigations into chemical equilibria and rates of reaction

1910 Otto Wallach (GER). Work in field of alicyclic compounds

1911 Marie Curie (FRA). Discovery of radium and polonium elements by isolation of radium

1912 Victor Grignard (FRA). Discovery of 'Grignard' reagents

Paul Sabatier (FRA). Method of hydrogenating organic compounds

1913 Alfred Werner (SWI). Work on linkage of atoms in molecules

1914 Theodore William Richards (USA). Precise determinations of atomic weight of many chemical elements

1915 Richard Martin Willstätter (GER). Research on plant pigments, especially chlorophyll

1916–17 No awards

1918 Fritz Haber (GER). Synthesis of ammonia

1919 No award

1920 Walther Hermann Nernst (GER). Work in thermochemistry

1921 Frederick Soddy (UK). Studied radioactive materials and investigated occurrence and nature of isotopes

1922 Francis William Aston (UK). Work on mass spectrography and whole-number rule

1923 Fritz Pregl (AUT). Invention of method of microanalysis of organic substance

1924 No award

1925 Richard Adolf Zsigmondy (GER). Demonstration of heterogenous nature of colloidal solutions

1926 Theodor Svedberg (SWE). Work on disperse systems

1927 Heinrich Otto Wieland (GER). Investigations of constitution of bile acids and related substances

1928 Adolf Otto Reinhold Windaus (GER). Research into constitution of sterols and their connection with vitamins

1929 Sir Arthur Harden (UK) and Hans von Euler-Chelpin (Swe). Studied fermentation of sugar and enzymes involved in the process

1930 Hans Fischer (GER). Chlorophyll research, and discovery of haemoglobin in blood

1931 Karl Bosch and Friedrich Bergius (GER). Invention and development of chemical high-pressure methods

1932 Irving Langmuir (USA). Discoveries and investigations in surface chemistry

1933 No award

1934 Harold Clayton Urey (USA). Discovery of heavy hydrogen

1935 Frédéric Joliot and Irène Joliot-Curie (FRA). Synthesis of new radioactive elements

1936 Peter Josephus W. Debye (NETH). Investigations on dipole moments and diffraction of X-rays and electrons in gases

1937 Sir Walter Norman Haworth (UK). Carbohydrate and vitamin C research

Paul Karrer (SWI). Carotenoids, flavins and vitamins A and B2 research

1938 Richard Khun (GER). Work on carotenoids and vitamins (Award declined – Hitler forbade Germans to accept Nobel prizes)

1939 Adolf Fridrich Johann Butenandt (GER). Work on sex hormones (Award declined – Hitler forbade Germans to accept Nobel prizes)

Leopold Ruzicka (SWI). Work on polymethylenes and higher terpenes

1940–42 No awards

1943 George de Hevesy (HUN). Work on use of isotopes as tracers in research

1944 Otto Hahn (GER). Discovery of fission of heavy nuclei

1945 Arturri Ilmari Virtanen (FIN). Invention of fodder preservation method

1946 James Batcheller Sumner (USA). Discovery that enzymes can be crystallised

John Howard Northrop and Wendell Meredith Stanley (USA). Preparation of enzymes and virus proteins in a pure form

1947 Sir Robert Robinson (UK). Research on alkaloids and plant biology

1948 Arne Wilhelm Kaurin Tiselius (SWE). Electrophoretic and absorption analysis research; serum proteins

1949 William Francis Giauque (USA). Contributions in field of chemical thermodynamics, particularly concerning behaviour of substances at extremely low temperatures

1950 Otto Diels and Kurt Alder (GER). Discovery and development of diene synthesis

1951 Edwin Mattison McMillan and Glenn Theodore Seaborg (USA). Discoveries of and research on transuranium elements

1952 Archer John Porter Martin and Richard Laurence Millington Synge (UK). Invention of partition chromatography

1953 Hermann Staudinger (GER). Discoveries in field of macromolecular chemistry

1954 Linus Carl Pauling (USA). Research into nature of chemical bond

---

Glenn Theodore Seaborg, American joint winner of the 1951 Nobel Prize, announced his discovery of element 95, americium, and element 96, curium, on an early American question-and-answer radio programme called 'Quiz Kids'. On this programme, a panel of bright children were asked difficult questions and received prizes for correct answers. The news of Seaborg's discovery was due to be announced at a future meeting of the American Chemical Society, but on the programme, in 1944, as a guest, Seaborg was asked if there were any new elements. Seaborg and his co-workers had just witnessed the discovery of these two new elements and he announced this news in response to the question posed.

The Dating of the Turin Shroud

In 1960 Willard Frank Libby, an American chemist, won the Nobel Prize for Chemistry for his development of the theory and practice of the use of carbon-14 for determining the age of objects in archaeology, geology, geophysics and other areas of scientific interest. Refinements of this technique have been used for accurate determination of objects of ages up to around 70 000 years.

Carbon-14 is a radioactive form (isotope) of the common element carbon (main form carbon-12), which is formed in very low concentrations in the upper atmosphere due to collisions of cosmic rays with atmospheric nitrogen. Living organisms (plants and animals) exchange carbon with the atmosphere and therefore have small quantities of carbon-14 in their systems. When the organism dies, it no longer takes up carbon-14 and the small amount in the body decays away. Accurate measurement of the proportion of carbon-14 in a sample of the organism may therefore be used to date the sample.

One of the most famous examples of work undertaken recently with an advanced form of this method of carbon dating is the investigation of the Turin Shroud which was thought by many Christians to be Christ's shroud. This new method measures the ratio of carbon-14 to carbon-12.

In 1898 Secondo Pia, an Italian lawyer and amateur photograher, set up his box camera in Turin cathedral and proceeded to photograph the piece of cloth now well known as the Turin Shroud. When he developed the first plate he was amazed to find that the reversal of tones, light to dark and dark to light, revealed a lifelike image of a bearded man laid out who bore the marks of death by crucifixion. Later, Pia recorded in his diary: 'Closed up in my darkroom I experienced such an intense emotion when I saw for the first time the Holy Face appear with such clearness that I remained as if frozen.'

The first mention of Christ's burial shroud is in the New Testament gospels (Mark 15:45/6): 'And when he knew it of the centurion, he gave the body to Joseph. And he bought fine linen, and took him down, and wrapped him in the linen, and laid him in a sepulchre which was hewn out of a rock, and rolled a stone unto the door of the sepulchre.' Mention is also made of a cloth which bore the imprint of Jesus's face found in the ancient city of Edessa (now Urfa, Turkey) in the first century AD. No mention is made then until the discovery in about 1350 of the shroud by Geoffrey de Charny.

In the mid-1970s, two researchers from the National Aeronautical and Space Administration in the United States discovered that the image had mysterious three-dimensional properties, which allegedly could not have been created by an artist. Other scientists entered the debate and claimed that the injuries depicted on the shroud were too accurate to have been painted.

Carbon dating, which is recognised as being the most accurate means of determining the age of such objects, was not considered earlier since a large amount of cloth would have had to be removed to complete the process. However, new techniques developed at Oxford University, involving AMS (accelerated mass spectrometry), can give accurate results from only a few threads of cloth. Subsequently, in 1988, three centimetre squares of the 14 ft 6 in (4.4 m) shroud, which is kept in Turin's Royal Chapel, were cut from the left-hand hem and put into sealed steel containers. They were shipped to laboratories in Oxford, Arizona and Zürich for analysis. Two other pieces of ancient linen were also included in the containers so that no bias could be given to the shroud.

The results obtained from the three laboratories were very close and the overall conclusion was that the shroud was a clever medieval hoax. All three laboratories dated the shroud to be between AD 1000 and 1500. Who produced the shroud is a mystery and one that is unlikely ever to be solved.

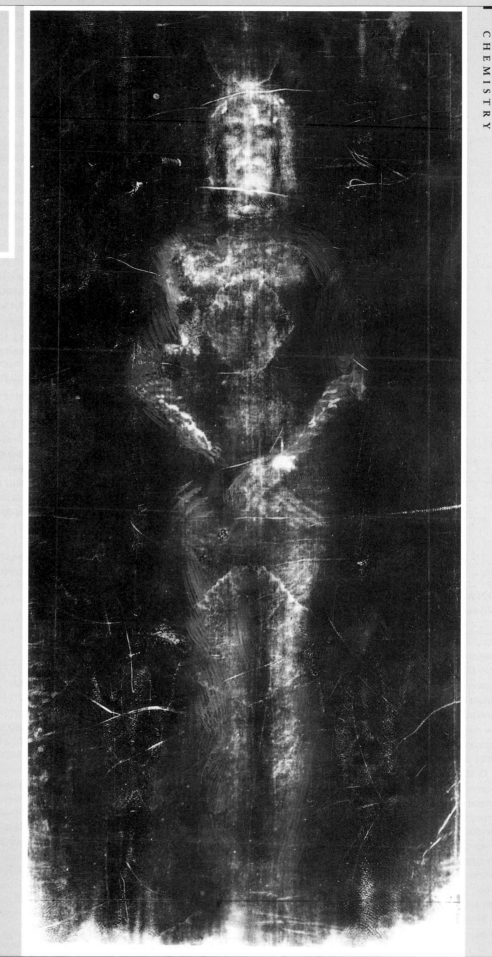

'Seldom has a single discovery in chemistry had such an impact on the thinking of so many fields of human endeavour. Seldom has a single discovery generated such wide public interest.'

Nobel Foundation on Willard Frank Libby's discovery of carbon dating, 1960

The Turin Shroud – in the photographic negative of the face there are clear marks around the forehead – said by some to have been made by a crown of thorns.

ECONOMICS

Nobel Prize

Established in 1968, the Nobel Memorial Prize in Economic Science was introduced by the Swedish National Bank and is awarded annually for outstanding achievement in the field of economics. (See separate section, Nobel Prizes.)

1969 Ragnar Frisch (NOR) and Jan Tinbergen (NETH). Work in econometrics
1970 Paul A. Samuelson (USA). Scientific analysis in economic theory
1971 Simon Kuznets (USA). Work on use of gross national product as a measure of economic growth
1972 Kenneth J. Arrow (USA) and Sir John R. Hicks (UK). Contributions to equilibrium and welfare theories
1973 Wassily Leontief (USA). Developing the input-output technique
1974 Gunnar Myrdal (SWE) and Friedrich A. von Hayek (AUT). Work on interdependence of economic, institutional, and social phenomena
1975 Tjalling C. Koopmans (USA) and Leonid V. Kantorovich (USSR). Contributions to theory of optimum allocation of resources
1976 Milton Friedman (USA). Work in consumption analysis, monetary theory and economic stabilisation

1977 Bertil Ohlin (SWE) and James Meade (UK). Contributions to international trade theory
1978 Herbert A. Simon (USA). Research in economic decision-making
1979 Theordore W. Schultz (USA) and Sir Arthur Lewis (UK). Research in economics of developing countries
1980 Lawrence R. Klein (USA). Development and analysis of empirical models of business fluctuations
1981 James Tobin (USA). Empirical macro-economic theories
1982 George Stigler (USA). Work on economic effects of governmental regulation
1983 Gerard Debrau (USA). Mathematical proof of supply and demand theory
1984 Sir Richard Stone (UK). Development of a national income accounting system
1985 Franco Modigliani (USA). Analysis of household savings and financial markets
1986 James McGill Buchanan (USA). Political theories advocating limited government role in the economy
1987 Robert M. Solow (USA). Contributions to theory of economic growth
1988 Maurice Allais (FRA). Contributions to theory of markets and efficient use of resources

1989 Trygve Haavelmo (NOR). Testing fundamental econometric theories
1990 Harry Markowitz, Merton Miller and William Sharpe (USA). Pioneering theories on managing investment portfolios and corporate finances
1991 Ronald H. Coase (UK). Work on the value and social problems of companies
1992 Gary S. Becker (USA). Work linking economic theory to aspects of human behaviour, drawing on other social sciences
1993 Robert Fogel and Douglass North (USA). Applying quantitative methods to economic history to explain long-term economic development and decline – first economic historians to win

Economics Nobel Prize Winners by Country

Country	Total	Year first awarded Prize
USA	21	1970
UK	5	1972
Norway	2	1969
Sweden	2	1974
Austria	1	1974
France	1	1988
Netherlands	1	1969
USSR	1	1975
Total	**34**	

Notes
1 Nobel Prizes are actually awarded to individuals rather than the countries from which they come.
2 Figures include 1993 prizewinners.

'Economic theory is a systematic application and critical evaluation of the basic analytic concepts of economic theory, with an emphasis on money and why it's good.'

Woody Allen (1970)

'If all economists were laid end to end, they would not reach a conclusion.'

G. B. Shaw

FASHION

Best and Worst Dressed Personalities

Since 1981, the American magazine *People* has annually produced lists of the ten best and ten worst dressed personalities. The 1993 lists read as follows:

10 Best Dressed
Joan Rivers, talk show hostess
Sharon Stone, actress
Charles Barkley, basketball player
Natalie Cole, singer
Connie Chung, newscaster
Warren Christopher, US Secretary of State
Janine Turner, actress
Wesley Snipes, costume designer
Mayim Bialik, television actress
Princess Caroline of Monaco

BELOW Chris Evans, voted Britain's 1993 worst dressed man and Gary Oldman, best dressed man, by *Esquire* magazine.

10 Worst Dressed
Daryl Hannah, actress
Whoopi Goldberg, actress
Heidi Fleiss, Hollywood hostess
Diane Keaton, actress
Burt Reynolds, actor
Julia Roberts, actress
Robert Downey Jr, actor
Garth Brooks, country singer
Marisa Tomei, actress
Anthony Kiedis, rock star

Britain's Best and Worst Dressed Men

Esquire's annual round-up of best and worst dressed men for 1993 looked like this:

Best Dressed

Best Dressed Man Gary Oldman
Rock 'n' Roll Bryan Ferry, David Bowie, Eric Clapton
Great British Individual George Melly, John McCririck, George O'Dowd (Boy George)
Flair and Flamboyance Ian Wright, John Fashanu, Linford Christie
Sports Football Kit Newcastle (home), Spurs (home), Manchester United (away), Blackburn (home)
Urban Creatives Salman Rushdie, Steven Berkoff, Alan Yentob
Beautiful Boffins Nigel Short, Patrick Moore, Bamber Gascoigne
Establishment Chic Michael Heseltine, Stephen Fry, Prince Charles
Glamorous Slobs Peter O'Toole, Tim Roth, Daniel Day Lewis
Smart Music Neil Tennant, The Kemp Brothers, George Michael, Charlie Watts

Worst Dressed

Worst Dressed Man Chris Evans
Political Suicide MPs Bill Cash, Nicholas Fairbairn, Ken Livingstone

Mr Slobby Bob Geldof, Andrew Lloyd Webber, Sir John Harvey Jones, Ian McShane, Peter Cook
Professional Foul Ian Botham, Nigel Benn, Nick Faldo
Get Your Kit Off Liverpool, Manchester City, Wolves, Coventry City
Where Did You Get that Hat? Prince Edward, David Bailey, Jonathan King
Rockers' Revenge Bill Wyman, Status Quo, Mick Jagger
Tries too Hard Chris Eubank, Tony Slattery, Brett Anderson
Jacket In Terry Christian, Angus Deayton, Nick Owen, Richard Madeley, Jeff Banks
Designer Victims Elton John, Richard O'Brien, Bono, Dave Stewart, Mick Hucknall, Simon LeBon

Designer of the Year Award

Introduced in 1983, this award is organised by the British Fashion Council, the organising body for London Fashion Week and the British Fashion Awards. Over 400 senior press and buyers annually submit nominations to establish the designer of the year.

WINNERS
1984 Katharine Hamnett
1985 Betty Jackson
1986 Jasper Conran
1987 John Galliano
1988 Rifat Ozbek
1989 Workers for Freedom
1990 Vivienne Westwood
1991 Vivienne Westwood
1992 Rifat Ozbek
1993 John Rocha

1993 DESIGNER OF THE YEAR

John Rocha, born in Hong Kong in 1953 to a Chinese mother and Portuguese father and based in Dublin, has woven Irish fabrics and rustic colours into chic wearable clothes and come up with the title of 1993 Designer of the Year. He came to London at the age of eighteen to study fashion design – his degree show featuring Irish fabrics to such tremendous effect that the Irish Export Board encouraged him to base his career in Ireland, where he has lived for the last 14 years. In the late 1980s he attracted the attention of the prestigious Irish retailer, the Brown Thomas Group, who decided to back him, and the successful John Rocha label was launched on to the international market.

His 1993 autumn/winter collection which gained him the nomination, was called Dochas (Gaelic for hope) and used Celtic imagery with Irish linen, tweeds, and traditional knits in cream and marl grey. His 1994 spring / summer men's collection (appearing in Britain for the first time) and women's collection evoked an awareness of 'Saoirse' (the celtic word for 'freedom') – independent, unconstrained and uncomplicated clothes, a designer whose simple, understated approach made the most of natural fibres and fabrics. His collection created aesthetic contrasts, mixing hard and soft textures, defined shapes with sheer fabrics and purity of design with a contemporary edge. He continued to refine and develop his existing strengths – combining Celtic inspiration and introducing new shapes and textures.

His structured shapes were diffused with diaphanous fabrics – cream chiffon and organza, layered and sheer but not transparent. Soft tiered silhouettes were defined with tailored black suiting – structured jackets and waistcoats combined with dramatic handpainted poppies on bright red silk and organza. As a contrast, loose pure linen was highlighted with encrusted beading – tunics worn under cream hand-crocheted knitwear emblazoned with the Celtic cross, wrapped in raw cobweb lace.

John Rocha now shows twice a year in Milan, Paris, London, Amsterdam and Düsseldorf and has over 400 retail outlets in 21 countries worldwide.

ABOVE Sheer fabrics overlaid with cream hand-crocheted knitwear – designed by John Rocha, 1993 Designer of the Year.

FILM & VIDEO

Royal Film Performance

The very first Royal Command Film Performance was held at Marlborough House, London, on 21 July 1896 before 40 guests gathered for the marriage of Princess Maud (Queen of Norway) the following day. This showing was requested by Birt Acres, a pioneer cinematographer, who had taken a film the previous month of the Prince and Princess of Wales attending the Cardiff Exhibition and wanted permission to exhibit it publicly. The Prince of Wales (later King Edward VII) requested that he first see Acres's film. It was shown in a specially erected marquee together with 20 other short films, including *Tom Merry the Lightning Artist drawing Mr Gladstone and Lord Salisbury*, the 1895 and 1896 Derby Races, Henley Regatta, and scenes showing a boxing kangaroo, a Great Northern Railway express train and the pursuit of a pickpocket. The royal film was so popular it was shown twice.

The following year, on 23 November 1897, a selection of Diamond Jubilee and other films taken for the Lumière Cinematographe was shown to Queen Victoria by H. J. Hitchins. They were accompanied by a full orchestra conducted by Leopold Wenzel.

The first feature film presented by Royal Command was *Comin' Thro' the Rye* (GB 16), produced by Cecil Hepworth and starring Alma Taylor (a later version of this was made in GB 23 with the same producer and leading actress). This was shown on 4 August 1916 before Queen Alexandra in the State Dining Room of Marlborough House. Hepworth, who attended, was also present at the very first Command Performance in 1896 when he acted as assistant to Birt Acres.

The first feature film to be presented by command of the sovereign was *Tom Brown's Schooldays* which Lew Waren exhibited for King George V and Queen Mary at Buckingham Palace on 24 February 1917.

The current 'run' of Royal Film Performances (named the Royal Command Film Performance for 1946 and 1947 only) began on 1 November 1946 when the film was shown at a public cinema – the Empire, Leicester Square, London. King George VI and Queen Elizabeth, with Princesses Elizabeth and Margaret, attended a viewing of *A Matter of Life and Death* (GB 46), starring David Niven and Marius Goring. It was something of a first for the King to be seen 'going to the pictures' and crowds gathered ten hours before the performance was due to start, just to see the King entering a public cinema.

Since this date, a film has been selected annually by a committee of executives from the film and television industry, headed by the President of the Cinema and Television Benevolent Fund. The films selected each year are shown at a London West End cinema and the performances have been attended by either The Queen, Queen Elizabeth The Queen Mother, or other members of the Royal Family.

FACTS

▮ To date the following number of films to have been selected, by country, are: GB 23, US 22, ITA/US 1, Panama 1.

▮ The first X-rated film was shown in 1969 – *The Prime of Miss Jean Brodie* (GB)

▮ The Queen attends even-numbered years and other members of the royal family odd years.

SELECTED FILMS

1946 *A Matter of Life and Death* (GB)
1947 *The Bishop's Wife* (US)
1948 *Scott of the Antarctic* (GB)
1949 *The Forsyte Saga* (US)
1950 *The Mudlark* (GB)
1951 *Where No Vultures Fly* (GB)
1952 *Because You're Mine* (US)
1953 *Rob Roy the Highland Rogue* (GB)
1954 *Beau Brummel* (GB)
1955 *To Catch a Thief* (US)
1956 *The Battle of the River Plate* (GB)
1957 *Les Girls* (US)
1958 No performance
1959 *The Horse's Mouth* (GB)
1960 *The Last Angry Man* (US)
1961 *The Facts of Life* (US)

(continued on p.90)

Comin' Thro' the Rye (GB 16) starring Alma Taylor (right), the first feature film to be presented by Royal Command.

Jurassic Park

'Imagine that you are one of the first visitors to Jurassic Park – a melding of scientific discovery and visual imagination.

'Entering the gates of the park, your senses are overwhelmed by the world that surrounds you; the sounds, the smells, even the feel of the earth is curiously different. Somewhere in the distance, you hear the movement of huge animals – the ground shakes with their passing. You are a stranger in an alien world.

'You look into the night sky, at stars whose light was born long before humans ever existed; born when a different race of being walked the planet – swift, powerful animals, rulers of the earth for 160 million years. Like those ancient stars, the Jurassic has left only faint traces of itself – fossils, footprints, relics of blood cells encased in amber. A time capsule that has remaind closed for countless millennia.

'Now the time capsule has been opened, and man and dinosaurs, the two rulers of the earth, will meet for the first time.

'All our scientific resources have been dedicated to bring Jurassic Park to reality; a childhood fantasy made real, a place where wonders come to life. It was created to be the ultimate amusement. But someone forgot to tell the dinosaurs.

*J*urassic Park (US 93) is based on Michael Crichton's novel, and was adapted for the screen by Crichton and David Ashton. It was directed by Steven Spielberg at a reported cost of $68 million. Richard Attenborough, in his first screen role for 14 years, plays John Hammond, a billionaire who invests his money in developing a theme park on an island near Costa Rica which features genetically engineered dinosaurs.

> 'This is not science fiction; it's science eventually.'
>
> Steven Spielberg

The film incorporates stunning special effects which were created by the Industrial Light and Magic Company, a studio founded by George Lucas of *Star Wars* (US 77) fame. The dinosaurs are amazingly impressive as prehistoric creatures – quite the most believable ever created on film. They were developed using a computer software package which was written and created by the British company Parallax. The film-makers combined digital computer graphics with models and live action – in all, 54 sequences, totalling over six minutes of screen time, were created, featuring dinosaurs generated solely by the use of computer graphics.

Steven Spielberg's *Jurassic Park* began its record-breaking career with its US release on Friday 11 June 1993, earning US$50 159 460 over the first three days, the highest-ever opening weekend gross for a film. This included the highest single day's gross of all time at $18 million on Saturday 12 June.

1993 OSCARS

OPPOSITE

A Tyrannosaurus Rex advances on two stranded cars in a scene from *Jurassic Park* (US 93).

Jurassic Park won an Oscar in each of the categories it was nominated for:

- Best Visual Effects
- Best Sound
- Best Sound Effects Editing

When the film opened in the UK on Friday 16 July 1993, the figures were equally spectacular – the opening weekend grossing an incredible £4 875 137 at the box office. This exceeded by more than £2 million the previous all-time opening weekend record, held by *Batman Returns* (US 92); and also surpassed the seven-day opening week box office record, previously held by *Terminator 2* (US 91). In total, more than 1.7 million people in the UK saw *Jurassic Park* on its opening weekend.

Twenty days after the film's release it became the UK's highest grossing picture of all time when gross box off receipts reached £24 248 031. This exceeded the current *lifetime* receipts of the previous top five UK box office grossers: *Ghost*

John Hammond (Richard Attenborough), owner of the dinosaur amusement park, examines a newly hatched egg with the two recently arrived palaeontologists, Ellie Sattler (Laura Dern) and Dr Alan Grant (Sam Neill).

(US 90) £23 341 465; *E.T. The Extra Terrestrial* (US 82) £21 696 809; *Crocodile Dundee* (Aus 86) £21 526 574; *Robin Hood – Prince of Thieves* (US 91) £20 491 099; and *Terminator 2* (US 91) £18 397 499.

By 1 June 1994 the film had grossed at the box office over £47 million in the UK, over US$345 million in America, and over US$900 million worldwide.

After the opening of the film, licensed products arrived, supported by companies such as Kenner Parker, Sega, Marks and Spencer, Wall's Ice Cream and Coca-Cola. Kenner Parker sold over one million dinsosaur toys, Marks and Spencer sold around 8000 *Jurassic Park* cakes a week, and the Natural History Museum saw a 33 per cent increase in people visiting the dinosaur exhibition since the film première.

The novel by Michael Crichton, on which the film was based, sold over 695 000 copies in the first two months after the film was released, compared with lifetime sales of 175 000 in its original edition. It headed the list of 1993 UK Bestselling Fiction Paperbacks and the junior version was No. 10 in the 1993 UK Bestselling Children's Books list.

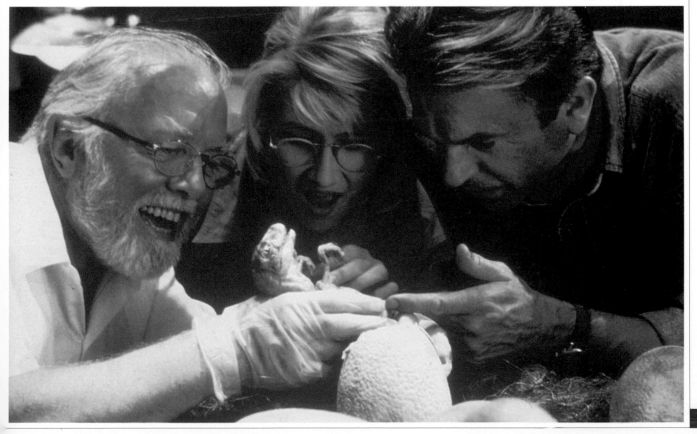

Selected Films (continued)

1962 *West Side Story* (US)
1963 *Sammy Going South* (GB)
1964 *Move Over Darling* (US)
1965 *Lord Jim* (GB)
1966 *Born Free* (GB)
1967 *The Taming of the Shrew* (ITA / US)
1968 *Romeo and Juliet* (GB)
1969 *The Prime of Miss Jean Brodie* (GB)
1970 *Anne of the Thousand Days* (GB)
1971 *Love Story* (US)
1972 *Mary Queen of Scots* (GB)
1973 *Lost Horizon* (US)
1974 *The Three Musketeers* (PAN)
1975 *Funny Lady* (US)
1976 *The Slipper and the Rose* (GB)
1977 *Silver Streak* (US)
1978 *Close Encounters of the Third Kind* (US)
1979 *California Suite* (US)
1980 *Kramer vs Kramer* (US)
1981 *Chariots of Fire* (GB)
1982 *Evil under the Sun* (GB)
1983 *Table for Five* (US)
1984 *The Dresser* (GB)
1985 *A Passage to India* (GB)
1986 *White Nights* (US)
1987 *84 Charing Cross Road* (GB)
1988 *Empire of the Sun* (US)
1989 *Madame Sousatzka* (GB)
1990 *Always* (US)
1991 *Hot Shots* (US)
1992 *Chaplin* (GB)
1993 *The Man without a Face* (US)

BELOW Orson Welles (Kane) and Ruth Warrick (Emily Norton) in a scene from *Citizen Kane* (US 41) – first choice in the *Sight and Sound* Survey listings.

Sight and Sound
Survey of the World's Top 10 Films

Every ten years since 1952, *Sight and Sound*, the British Film Institute's quarterly journal, invites *c.* 200 critics, film scholars and archivists from around the world to nominate their ten best films. If one is to believe their selection, no great film has been released since *2001: A Space Odyssey* (GB) in 1968.

The polls are unanimous in their best film of all times – for four out of five decades, Orson Welles's *Citizen Kane* (US 41) comes in as first choice. (In the lists that follow, at first mention of a film the director is given; each successive appearance is denoted by a figure in brackets which indicates the total number of appearances in the list.)

1952

1 *Bicycle Thieves* (ITA 49), Vittorio de Sica
2 *City Lights* (US 31), Charles Chaplin
   The Gold Rush (US 25), Charles Chaplin
4 *Battleship Potemkin* (USSR 25), Sergei Eisenstein
5 *Intolerance* (US 16), D. W. Griffith
   Louisiana Story (US 47), Robert Flaherty
7 *Greed* (US 24), Erich von Stroheim
   Le Jour se lève (FRA 39), Marcel Carné
9 *The Passion of Joan of Arc* (FRA 28), Carl Dreyer
   Brief Encounter (GB 45), David Lean
11 *Le Million* (FRA 30), René Clair
   La Règle du jeu (FRA 39), Claude Renoir

1962

1 *Citizen Kane* (US 41), Orson Welles
2 *L'Avventura* (ITA 60), Michelangelo Antonioni
3 *La Règle du jeu* (FRA 39) – (2)
4 *Greed* (US 24) – (2)
   Ugetsu Monogatari (JAP 53), Kenji Mizoguchi
6 *Battleship Potemkin* (USSR 25) – (2)
   Bicycle Thieves (ITA 49) – (2)
   Ivan the Terrible (USSR 43–46), Sergei Eisenstein
9 *La terra trema* (ITA 48), Luchino Visconti
10 *L'Atalante* (FRA 34), Jean Vigo

1972

1 *Citizen Kane* (US 41) – (2)
2 *La Règle du jeu* (FRA 39) – (3)
3 *Battleship Potemkin* (USSR 25) – (3)

■ The earliest film included in the selection is *Intolerance* (US 16).

■ America leads the way with 19 selections (11 different films); France 12 (5 different); Italy 8 (4 different); USSR 6 (2 different); Japan 4 (3 different); Sweden and Britain 2 (each 2 different) and India 1.

■ Two films appear in all five lists: *La Règle du jeu* (FRA 39) and *Battleship Potemkin* (USSR 25).

4 *8½* (ITA 63), Federico Fellini
5 *L'Avventura* (ITA 60) – (2)
   Persona (SWE 67), Ingmar Bergman
7 *The Passion of Joan of Arc* (FRA 28) – (2)
8 *The General* (US 26), Buster Keaton and Clyde Bruckman
   The Magnificent Ambersons (US 42), Orson Welles
10 *Ugetsu Monogatari* (JAP 53) – (2)
   Wild Strawberries (SWE 57), Ingmar Bergman

1982

1 *Citizen Kane* (US 41) – (3)
2 *La Règle du jeu* (FRA 39) – (4)
3 *Seven Samurai* (JAP 54), Akira Kurosawa
   Singin' in the Rain (US 52), Stanley Donen and Gene Kelly
5 *8½* (ITA 63) – (2)
6 *Battleship Potemkin* (USSR 25) – (4)
7 *L'Avventura* (ITA 60) – (3)
   The Magnificent Ambersons (US 42) – (2)
   Vertigo (US 58), Alfred Hitchcock
10 *The General* (US 26) – (2)
   The Searchers (US 56), John Ford

1992

1 *Citizen Kane* (US 41) – (4)
2 *La Règle du jeu* (FRA 39) – (5)
3 *Tokyo Story* (JAP 53), Yasujiro Ozu
4 *Vertigo* (US 58) – (2)
5 *The Searchers* (US 56) – (2)
6 *L'Atalante* (FRA 34) – (2)
   The Passion of Joan of Arc (FRA 28) – (3)
   Pather Panchali (IND 55), Satyajit Ray
   Battleship Potemkin (USSR 25) – (5)
10 *2001: A Space Odyssey* (GB 68), Stanley Kubrick

OPPOSITE The magnificent Babylonian sequence from *Intolerance* (US 16), the earliest film included in the *Sight and Sound* selection.

Sight and Sound
Directors' Top Ten

In 1992 *Sight and Sound* extended the voting to include a film-makers poll of Top Ten films. This makes an interesting comparison with the critics' list, not least because the critics include no post-1960s film, while three later films are included in the directors' list.

1 *Citizen Kane* (US 41), Orson Welles
2 *Raging Bull* (US 80), Martin Scorsese
  8½ (ITA 63), Federico Fellini
4 *La strada* (ITA 54), Federico Fellini
5 *L'Atalante* (FRA 34), Jean Vigo
6 *Modern Times* (US 36), Charles Chaplin
  The Godfather (US 72), Francis Ford Coppola
  Vertigo (US 58), Alfred Hitchcock
9 *Seven Samurai* (JAP 54), Akira Kurosawa
  The Passion of Joan of Arc (FRA 28), Carl Dreyer
  The Godfather Part II (US 74), Francis Ford Coppola
  Rashomon (JAP 50), Akira Kurosawa

Top 20 Films at the UK Box Office, 1993

		Opened
1	*Jurassic Park* (US 93)	16 July 1993
2	*The Bodyguard* (US 92)	25 December 1992
3	*The Fugitive* (US 93)	24 September 1993
4	*Indecent Proposal* (US 93)	14 May 1993
5	*Bram Stoker's Dracula* (US 92)	29 January 1993
6	*Sleepless in Seattle* (US 93)	24 September 1993
7	*Cliffhanger* (US 93)	25 June 1993
8	*A Few Good Men* (US 92)	1 January 1993
9	*Aladdin* (US 93)	19 November 1993
10	*The Jungle Book* (US 67)	26 March 1993
11	*In the Line of Fire* (US 93)	27 August 1993
12	*The Firm* (US 93)	10 September 1993
13	*Forever Young* (US 92)	26 March 1993
14	*Sommersby* (US 93)	23 April 1993
15	*Home Alone 2: Lost in New York* (US 92)	11 December 1992
16	*Demolition Man* (US 93)	12 November 1993
17	*Under Siege* (US 92)	26 February 1993
18	*Much Ado About Nothing* (GB/US 93)	27 August 1993
19	*Groundhog Day* (US 93)	7 May 1993
20	*Made in America* (US 93)	13 August 1993

Notes:
1 Listing also takes into account figures from the Republic of Ireland.
2 The chart positions in the above listing are determined by the gross box office receipts during the calendar period 1993. Had the lifetime income of the film been taken into consideration, i.e. income generated by the film prior to 1993, then the chart positions might be different.
Source: © Entertainment Data International

Top 20 Films at the US and Canada Box Office, 1993

		Opened
1	*Jurassic Park* (US 93)	11 June 1993
2	*The Fugitive* (US 93)	6 August 1993
3	*The Firm* (US 93)	30 June 1993
4	*Sleepless in Seattle* (US 93)	25 June 1993
5	*Aladdin* (US 93)	11 November 1992
6	*Indecent Proposal* (US 93)	7 April 1993
7	*In the Line of Fire* (US 93)	9 July 1993
8	*Mrs Doubtfire* (US 93)	24 November 1993
9	*Cliffhanger* (US 93)	28 May 1993
10	*A Few Good Men* (US 92)	11 December 1992
11	*Free Willy* (US 93)	16 July 1993
12	*Groundhog Day* (US 93)	12 February 1993
13	*Dave* (US 93)	7 May 1993
14	*Rising Sun* (US 93)	30 July 1993
15	*Scent of a Woman* (US 92)	23 December 1992
16	*Cool Runnings* (US 93)	1 October 1993
17	*The Crying Game* (GB 92)	25 November 1992
18	*Demolition Man* (US 93)	8 October 1993
19	*Rookie of the Year* (US 93)	7 July 1993
20	*Dennis the Menace* (US 93)	25 June 1993

Note: The chart positions in the above listing are determined by the gross box office receipts during the calendar period 1993. Had the lifetime income of the film been taken into consideration, i.e. income generated by the film prior to 1993, then the chart positions might be different.
Source: © Entertainment Data International

Top 10 Non-English Language Films at the UK Box Office, 1993

1 *Tous les Matins du Monde* (Fra 92)
2 *Un Coeur en Hiver* (Fra 92)
3 *The Wedding Banquet* (partly subtitled) (HK 93)
4 *Indochine* (Fra 92)
5 *Jamon Jamon* (Spa 93)
6 *Three Colours Blue* (Fra 93)
7 *Tango* (Spa 93)
8 *The Story of Qiu Ju* (Chi/HKG 92)
9 *Like Water for Chocolate* (Mex 93)
10 *Conte d'Hiver* (Fra 92)

Notes:
1 Listing also takes into account figures from the Republic of Ireland.
2 The chart positions in the above listing are determined by the gross box office receipts during the calendar period 1993. Had the lifetime income of the film been taken into consideration, i.e. income generated by the film prior to 1993, then the chart positions might be different.
Source: © Entertainment Data International

The greatest loss ever incurred in the making of a film was $57 million. *Hudson Hawk* (US 91), made by Columbia Tri-Star, directed by Michael Lehman and starring Bruce Willis, cost $65 million to make, and returned $8 million in North America and hardly anything anywhere else.

Academy Awards – Oscars

The Oscars are awarded annually by the Academy of Motion Picture Arts and Sciences to the film world in recognition of artistic merit and success. It is Hollywood's glitziest night out and the award ceremony is viewed on television by more than one billion people in over 100 countries worldwide.

The American Academy of Motion Picture Arts and Sciences was established by 36 leading figures in the film industry who met on 4 May 1927 and selected Douglas Fairbanks as their first president. Three hundred guests attended an industry banquet one week later to discuss the Academy's aims and purposes. Louis B. Mayer, the American film producer and distributor, suggested that the Academy should sponsor awards to celebrate outstanding achievement.

At this event, the art director, Cedric Gibbons, sketched the outline of a statuette on his tablecloth that was later to be sculpted by George Stanley into the 'Oscar' – a gold-plated figure, carrying a sword, standing on a reel of film. It weighs 8½ lb (3.8 kg) and is 13½ in (34 cm) high. The origin of the term 'Oscar' is obscure, but the most likely explanation is that the Academy librarian, Margaret Herrick, declared that it resembled her Uncle Oscar – and so from 1931 this name stuck.

In July 1928 the Academy announced the 12 categories for its first awards – any film produced in the 12 months between 1 August 1927 and 31 July 1928 was eligible. (Since 1935 the awards cover a calendar year.) The ballot forms were sent to every member of the Academy along with a list of eligible films, still a part of the Oscar voting system today. Nearly 1000 suggested nominations were received in the first year.

Awards are given in the following main categories, although from year to year these have varied: Picture, Foreign-Language Film, Director, Actor in a Leading Role, Actress in a Leading Role, Actor in a Supporting Role, Actress in a Supporting Role, Original Screenplay, Adapted Screenplay, Cinematography, Editing, Original Score, Original Song, Art Direction, Costume Design, Make-up, Visual Effects, Sound, Sound Effects Editing, Animated Short Film, Live Action Short Film, Documentary Feature, Documentary Short, Honorary Award, Gordon E. Sayer Award.

OPPOSITE PAGE The Oscar for best actress won in 1940 by the British actress Vivien Leigh for her performance as Scarlett O'Hara in *Gone With the Wind* was sold at Sotheby's in New York on 15 December 1993 for a record $563 500 (£378 750). The previous record was $110 000 for John Lennon's Oscar for best score in *Let It Be* (GB 70).

RIGHT Clark Gable's herringbone riding jacket (left), Vivien Leigh's shantytown antebellum travelling suit (right and below) and Cammie King's (Bonnie Blue Butler) two-piece velvet riding suit – costumes from *Gone With The Wind* (US 39) – were sold for record prices in 1993 by Butterfield & Butterfield Auctioneers, Los Angeles. They were owned by the Western Costume Company and made $19 550, $33 350 (record selling price in the auction for a single garment) and $9775, respectively.

Oscars – Academy Awards

The main awards are listed below (unless otherwise indicated, all films are American):

Year	Picture	Actor	Actress	Director	Screenplay*	
					Original Story	Adaptation
1927–28	*Wings*	Emil Jannings *The Way of All Flesh*	Janet Gaynor *Seventh Heaven*	Frank Borzage *Seventh Heaven* Lewis Milestone *Two Arabian Knights*	Ben Hecht *Underworld*	Benjamin Glazer *Seventh Heaven*
					Achievement	
1928–29	*Broadway Melody*	Warner Baxter *In Old Arizona*	Mary Pickford *Coquette*	Frank Lloyd *The Divine Lady*	Hans Kraly *The Patriot*	
1929–30	*All Quiet on the Western Front*	George Arliss *Disraeli*	Norma Shearer *The Divorcee*	Lewis Milestone *All Quiet on the Western Front*	Frances Marion *The Big House*	
					Original Story	Adaptation
1930–31	*Cimarron*	Lionel Barrymore *Free Soul*	Marie Dressler *Min and Bill*	Norman Taurog *Skippy*	John Monk Saunders *The Dawn Patrol*	Howard Estabrook *Cimarron*
1931–32	*Grand Hotel*	Fredric March *Dr Jekyll and Mr Hyde* Wallace Beery *The Champ*	Helen Hayes *Sin of Madelon Claudet*	Frank Borzage *Bad Girl*	Frances Marion *The Champ*	Edwin Burke *Bad Girl*
1932–33	*Cavalcade*	Charles Laughton *Private Life of Henry VIII* (GB)	Katharine Hepburn *Morning Glory*	Frank Lloyd *Cavalcade*	Robert Lord *One Way Passage*	Victor Heerman and Sarah Y. Mason *Little Women*
1934	*It Happened One Night*	Clark Gable *It Happened One Night*	Claudette Colbert *It Happened One Night*	Frank Capra *It Happened One Night*	Arthur Caesar *Manhattan Melodrama*	Robert Riskin *It Happened One Night*
					Original Story	Screenplay
1935	*Mutiny on the Bounty*	Victor McLaglen *The Informer*	Bette Davis *Dangerous*	John Ford *The Informer*	Ben Hecht and Charles MacArthur *The Scoundrel*	Dudley Nichols *The Informer*
1936	*The Great Ziegfeld*	Paul Muni *The Story of Louis Pasteur*	Luise Rainer *The Great Ziegfeld*	Frank Capra *Mr Deeds Goes to Town*	Pierre Collings and Sheridan Gibney *The Story of Louis Pasteur*	Pierre Collings and Sheridan Gibney *The Story of Louis Pasteur*
1937	*Life of Emile Zola*	Spencer Tracy *Captains Courageous*	Luise Rainer *The Good Earth*	Leo McCarey *The Awful Truth*	William A. Wellman and Robert Carson *A Star is Born*	Heinz Herald, Geza Herczeg and Norman Reilly Raine *The Life of Emile Zola*
					Original Story	Adaptation
1938	*You Can't Take It With You*	Spencer Tracy *Boys Town*	Bette Davis *Jezebel*	Frank Capra *You Can't Take It With You*	Eleanore Griffin and Dore Schary *Boys Town*	Ian Dalrymple, Cecil Lewis and W. P. Lipscomb *Pygmalion* (GB) (by George Bernard Shaw)
					Original Story	Screenplay
1939	*Gone With the Wind*	Robert Donat *Goodbye Mr Chips* (GB)	Vivien Leigh *Gone With the Wind*	Victor Fleming *Gone With the Wind*	Lewis R. Foster *Mr Smith Goes to Washington*	Sidney Howard *Gone With the Wind*
1940	*Rebecca*	James Stewart *The Philadelphia Story*	Ginger Rogers *Kitty Foyle*	John Ford *The Grapes of Wrath*	Benjamin Glazer and John S. Toldy *Arise, My Love*	Donald Ogden Stewart *The Philadelphia Story*
1941	*How Green Was My Valley*	Gary Cooper *Sergeant York*	Joan Fontaine *Suspicion*	John Ford *How Green was My Valley*	Harry Segall *Here Comes Mr Jordan*	Sidney Buchman and Seton I. Miller *Here Comes Mr Jordan*

Year	Picture	Actor	Actress	Director	Screenplay* Original Story	Adaptation
1942	*Mrs Miniver*	James Cagney *Yankee Doodle Dandy*	Greer Garson *Mrs Miniver*	William Wyler *Mrs Miniver*	Emeric Pressburger *The Invaders* (GB)	George Froeschel, James Hilton, Claudine and Arthur Wimperis *Mrs Miniver*
1943	*Casablanca*	Paul Lukas *Watch on the Rhine*	Jennifer Jones *The Song of Bernadette*	Michael Curtiz *Casablanca*	William Saroyan *The Human Comedy*	Julius J. Epstein, Philip G. Epstein and Howard Koch *Casablanca*
1944	*Going My Way*	Bing Crosby *Going My Way*	Ingrid Bergman *Gaslight*	Leo McCarey *Going My Way*	Leo McCarey *Going My Way*	Frank Butler and Frank Cavett *Going My Way*
1945	*The Lost Weekend* *The Lost Weekend*	Ray Milland *Mildred Pierce*	Joan Crawford *The Lost Weekend*	Billy Wilder *The House on 92nd Street*	Charles G. Booth Billy Wilder	Charles Brackett and *The Lost Weekend*
1946	*The Best Years of Our Lives*	Fredric March *The Best Years of Our Lives*	Olivia de Havilland *To Each His Own*	William Wyler *The Best Years of Our Lives*	Clemence Dane *Vacation from Marriage* (GB)	Robert E. Sherwood *The Best Years of Our Lives*
1947	*Gentleman's Agreement*	Ronald Colman *A Double Life*	Loretta Young *The Farmer's Daughter*	Elia Kazan *Genetleman's Agreement*	Valentine Davies *Miracle on 34th Street*	George Seaton *Miracle on 34th Street*
1948	*Hamlet* (GB)	Laurence Olivier *Hamlet* (GB)	Jane Wyman *Johnny Belinda*	John Huston *The Treasure of the Sierra Madre*	**Motion Picture Story** Richard Sweizer and David Wechsler *The Search* (US/SWI)	**Screenplay** John Huston *The Treasure of the Sierra Madre*
1949	*All the King's Men*	Broderick Crawford *All the King's Men*	Olivia de Havilland *The Heiress*	Joseph L. Mankiewicz *A Letter to Three Wives*	Douglas Morrow *The Stratton Story*	Joseph L. Mankiewicz *A Letter to Three Wives*
1950	*All About Eve*	José Ferrer *Cyrano de Bergerac*	Judy Holliday *Born Yesterday*	Joseph L. Mankiewicz *All About Eve*	Edna and Edward Anhalt *Panic in the Streets*	Joseph L. Mankiewicz *All About Eve*
1951	*An American in Paris*	Humphrey Bogart *The African Queen* (GB)	Vivien Leigh *A Streetcar Named Desire*	George Stevens *A Place in the Sun*	Paul Dehn and James Bernard *Seven Days to Noon* (GB)	Michael Wilson and Harry Brown *A Place in the Sun*

Mrs Miniver (US 42), a story of middle-class family life in war-torn England, starring Walter Pidgeon and Greer Garson as Mr and Mrs Miniver. The film won Oscars for Best Picture, Best Actress (Greer Garson), Best Supporting Actress (Teresa Wright), Best Director (William Wyler), Best Screenplay and Best Cinematography.

Year	Picture	Actor	Actress	Director	Screenplay*	
					Motion Picture Story	**Screenplay**
1952	*The Greatest Show on Earth*	Gary Cooper *High Noon*	Shirley Booth *Come Back, Little Sheba*	John Ford *The Quiet Man*	Frederic M. Frank, Theodore St John and Frank Cavett *The Greatest Show on Earth*	Charles Schnee *The Bad and the Beautiful*
1953	*From Here to Eternity*	William Holden *Stalag 17*	Audrey Hepburn *Roman Holiday*	Fred Zinnemann *From Here to Eternity*	Ian McLellan Hunter *Roman Holiday*	Daniel Taradash *From Here to Eternity*
1954	*On the Waterfront*	Marlon Brando *On the Waterfront*	Grace Kelly *The Country Girl*	Elia Kazan *On the Waterfront*	Philip Yordan *Broken Lance*	George Seaton *The Country Girl*
1955	*Marty*	Ernest Borgnine *Marty*	Anna Magnani *The Rose Tattoo*	Delbert Mann *Marty*	Daniel Fuchs *Love Me or Leave Me*	Paddy Chayefsky *Marty*
					Original Screenplay	**Adapted Screenplay**
1956	*Around the World in 80 Days*	Yul Brynner *The King and I*	Ingrid Bergman *Anastasia* (GB)	George Stevens *Giant*	Albert Lamorisse *The Red Balloon* (FRA)	James Poe, John Farrow and S. J. Perelman *Around the World in 80 Days*
1957	*The Bridge on the River Kwai* (GB)	Alec Guinness *The Bridge on the River Kwai* (GB)	Joanne Woodward *The Three faces of Eve*	David Lean *The Bridge on the River Kwai* (GB)	George Wells *Designing Woman*	Pierre Boulle, Michael Wilson and Carl Foreman *The Bridge on the River Kwai* (GB)
1958	*Gigi*	David Niven *Separate Tables*	Susan Hayward *I Want to Live*	Vincente Minnelli *Gigi*	Nathan E. Douglas and Harold Jacob Smith *The Defiant Ones*	Alan Jay Lerner *Gigi*
1959	*Ben Hur*	Charlton Heston *Ben Hur*	Simone Signoret *Room at the Top* (GB)	William Wyler *Ben Hur*	Russell Rouse and Clarence Greene (story), Stanley Shapiro and Maurice Richlin (screenplay) *Pillow Talk*	Neil Paterson *Room at the Top* (GB)
1960	*The Apartment*	Burt Lancaster *Elmer Gantry*	Elizabeth Taylor *Butterfield Eight*	Billy Wilder *The Apartment*	Billy Wilder and I. A. L. Diamond *The Apartment*	Richard Brooks *Elmer Gantry*
1961	*West Side Story*	Maximilian Schell *Judgment at Nuremberg*	Sophia Loren *Two Women* (ITA/FRA)	Jerome Robbins Robert Wise *West Side Story*	William Inge *Splendor in the Grass*	Abby Mann *Judgment at Nuremberg*
1962	*Lawrence of Arabia* (GB)	Gregory Peck *To Kill a Mockingbird*	Anne Bancroft *The Miracle Worker*	David Lean *Lawrence of Arabia* (GB)	Ennio de Concini, Alfredo Giannetti and Pietro Germi *Divorce – Italian Style* (ITA)	Horton Foote *To Kill a Mockingbird*
1963	*Tom Jones* (GB)	Sidney Poitier *Lilies of the Field*	Patricia Neal *Hud*	Tony Richardson *Tom Jones* (GB)	James R. Webb *How the West was Won*	John Osborne *Tom Jones* (GB)
1964	*My Fair Lady*	Rex Harrison *My Fair Lady*	Julie Andrews *Mary Poppins*	George Cukor *My Fair Lady*	S. H. Barnett (story), Peter Stone and Frank Tarloff (screenplay) *Father Goose*	Edward Anhalt *Becket* (GB)
1965	*The Sound of Music*	Lee Marvin *Cat Ballou*	Julie Christie *Darling* (GB)	Robert Wise *The Sound of Music*	Frederic Raphael *Darling* (GB)	Robert Bolt *Dr Zhivago*
1966	*A Man for All Seasons* (GB)	Paul Scofield *A Man for All Seasons* (GB)	Elizabeth Taylor *Who's Afraid of Virginia Woolf*	Fred Zinnemann *A Man for All Seasons* (GB)	Claude Lelouch (story) Pierre Uytterhoeven and Claude Lelouch (screenplay) *A Man and a Woman* (FRA)	Robert Bolt *A Man for All Seasons* (GB)

ar	Picture	Actor	Actress	Director	Screenplay* Original Story	Adaptation
67	In the Heat of the Night	Rod Steiger *In the Heat of the Night*	Katharine Hepburn *Guess Who's Coming to Dinner*	Mike Nichols *The Graduate*	William Rose *Guess Who's Coming to Dinner*	Stirling Silliphant *In the Heat of the Night*
68	Oliver (GB)	Cliff Robertson *Charly*	Katharine Hepburn *The Lion in Winter* (GB)	Sir Carol Reed *Oliver* (GB)	Mel Brooks *The Producers*	James Goldman *The Lion in Winter* (GB)
69	Midnight Cowboy	John Wayne *True Grit*	Maggie Smith *The Prime of Miss Jean Brodie* (GB)	John Schlesinger *Midnight Cowboy*	William Goldman *Butch Cassidy and the Sundance Kid*	Waldo Salt *Midnight Cowboy*
70	Patton	George C. Scott *Patton* (refused)	Glenda Jackson *Women in Love* (GB)	Franklin Schaffner *Patton*	Francis Ford Coppola and Edmund H. North *Patton*	Ring Lardner Jr *M*A*S*H*
71	The French Connection	Gene Hackman *The French Connection*	Jane Fonda *Klute*	William Friedkin *The French Connection*	Paddy Chayefsky *The Hospital*	Ernest Tidyman *The French Connection*
72	The Godfather	Marlon Brando *The Godfather* (refused)	Liza Minnelli *Cabaret*	Bob Fosse *Cabaret*	Jeremy Larner *The Candidate*	Mario Puzo and Francis Ford Coppola *The Godfather*
73	The Sting	Jack Lemmon *Save the Tiger*	Glenda Jackson *A Touch of Class* (GB)	George Roy Hill *The Sting*	David S. Ward *The Sting*	William Peter Blatty *The Exorcist*
74	The Godfather, Part II	Art Carney *Harry and Tonto*	Ellen Burstyn *Alice Doesn't Live Here Anymore*	Francis Ford Coppola *The Godfather Part II*	Robert Towne *Chinatown*	Francis Ford Coppola and Mario Puzo *The Godfather Part II*
75	One Flew Over the Cuckoo's Nest	Jack Nicholson *One Flew Over the Cuckoo's Nest*	Louise Fletcher *One Flew Over the Cuckoo's Nest*	Milos Forman *One Flew Over the Cuckoo's Nest*	Frank Pierson *Dog Day Afternoon*	Lawrence Hauben and Bo Goldman *One Flew Over the Cuckoo's Nest*
76	Rocky	Peter Finch *Network*	Faye Dunaway *Network*	John G. Avildsen *Rocky*	Paddy Chayefsky *Network*	William Goldman *All the President's Men*
77	Annie Hall	Richard Dreyfuss *The Goodbye Girl*	Diane Keaton *Annie Hall*	Woody Allen *Annie Hall*	Woody Allen and Marshall Brickman *Annie Hall*	Alvin Sargent *Julia*

The costumes worn by the Von Trapp children and Christopher Plummer in *The Sound of Music* (US 65), designed by Dorothy Jeakins and nominated for an Oscar for Best Costumes. They were owned by The Western Costume Company in Los Angeles and sold in 1993 by Butterfield & Butterfield Auctioneers for a record sum of $28 175, far exceeding the estimated $3700.

Year	Picture	Actor	Actress	Director	Screenplay* Original Story	Adaptation
1978	*The Deer Hunter*	Jon Voight *Coming Home*	Jane Fonda *Coming Home*	Michael Cimino *The Deer Hunter*	Nancy Dowd (story), Waldo Salt and Robert C. Jones (screenplay) *Coming Home*	Oliver Stone *Midnight Express* (GB)
1979	*Kramer vs Kramer*	Dustin Hoffman *Kramer vs Kramer*	Sally Field *Norma Rae*	Robert Benton *Kramer vs Kramer*	Steve Tesich *Breaking Away*	Robert Benton *Kramer vs Kramer*
1980	*Ordinary People*	Robert DeNiro *Raging Bull*	Sissy Spacek *Coal Miner's Daughter*	Robert Redford *Ordinary People*	Bo Goldman *Melvin and Howard*	Alvin Sargent *Ordinary People*
1981	*Chariots of Fire* (GB)	Henry Fonda *On Golden Pond*	Katharine Hepburn *On Golden Pond*	Warren Beatty *Reds*	Colin Welland *Chariots of Fire* (GB)	Ernest Thompson *On Golden Pond*
1982	*Gandhi* (GB)	Ben Kingsley *Gandhi* (GB)	Meryl Streep *Sophie's Choice*	Richard Attenborough *Gandhi* (GB)	John Briley *Gandhi* (GB)	Costa-Gavras and Donald Stewart *Missing*
1983	*Terms of Endearment*	Robert Duvall *Tender Mercies*	Shirley MacLaine *Terms of Endearment*	James L. Brooks *Terms of Endearment*	Horton Foote *Tender Mercies*	James L. Brooks *Terms of Endearment*
1984	*Amadeus*	F. Murray Abraham *Amadeus*	Sally Field *Places in the Heart*	Milos Forman *Amadeus*	Robert Benton *Places in the Heart*	Peter Shaffer *Amadeus*
1985	*Out of Africa* (US/GB)	William Hurt *Kiss of the Spider Woman* (US/Bra)	Geraldine Page *The Trip to Bountiful*	Sydney Pollack *Out of Africa* (US/GB)	William Kelley, Pamela Wallace and Earl W. Wallace *Witness*	Kurt Luedtke *Out of Africa* (US/GB)
1986	*Platoon*	Paul Newman *The Color of Money*	Marlee Matlin *Children of a Lesser God*	Oliver Stone *Platoon*	Woody Allen *Hannah and Her Sisters*	Ruth Prawer Jhabvala *A Room with a View* (GB)
1987	*The Last Emperor* (Ita/HKG/GB)	Michael Douglas *Wall Street*	Cher *Moonstruck*	Bernardo Bertolucci *The Last Emperor* (Ita/HKG/GB)	John Patrick Shanley *Moonstruck*	Mark Peploe and Bernardo Bertolucci *The Last Emperor* (Ita/HKG/GB)
1988	*Rain Man*	Dustin Hoffman *Rain Man*	Jodie Foster *The Accused*	Barry Levinson *Rain Man*	Ronald Bass and Barry Morrow *Rain Man*	Christopher Hampton *Dangerous Liaisons*
1989	*Driving Miss Daisy*	Daniel Day-Lewis *My Left Foot* (GB)	Jessica Tandy *Driving Miss Daisy*	Oliver Stone *Born on the Fourth of July*	Tom Schulman *Dead Poets Society*	Alfred Uhry *Driving Miss Daisy*
1990	*Dances with Wolves*	Jeremy Irons *Reversal of Fortune*	Kathy Bates *Misery*	Kevin Costner *Dances with Wolves*	Bruce Joel Rubin *Ghost*	Michael Blake *Dances with Wolves*
1991	*The Silence of the Lambs*	Anthony Hopkins *The Silence of the Lambs*	Jodie Foster *The Silence of the Lambs*	Jonathan Demme *The Silence of the Lambs*	Callie Khouri *Thelma and Louise*	Ted Tally *The Silence of the Lambs*
1992	*Unforgiven*	Al Pacino *Scent of a Woman*	Emma Thompson *Howards End* (GB)	Clint Eastwood *Unforgiven*	Neil Jordan *The Crying Game* (GB)	Ruth Prawer Jhabvala *Howards End* (GB)
1993	*Schindler's List*	Tom Hanks *Philadelphia*	Holly Hunter *The Piano* (Aus)	Steven Spielberg *Schindler's List*	Jane Campion *The Piano* (Aus)	Steven Zaillian *Schindler's List*

* The titles of the screenplay awards have changed several times over the years. Where these changes are significant, the new title has been added in the columns in the relevant years. In several years, a third writing award was given as follows:

Screenplay – 1938 George Bernard Shaw, *Pygmalion* (GB).

Original Screenplay – 1940 Preston Sturges, *The Great McGinty*; 1941 Herman J. Mankiewicz and Orson Welles, *Citizen Kane*; 1942 Michael Kanin and Ring Lardner Jr, *Woman of the Year*; 1943 Norman Krasna, *Princess O'Rourke*; 1944 Lamar Trotti, *Wilson*; 1945 Richard Schweizer, *Marie-Louise* (Swi); 1946 Muriel Box and Sydney Box, *The Seventh Veil* (GB); 1947 Sidney Sheldon, *The Bachelor and the Bobbysoxer*.

Story and Screenplay – 1949 Robert Pirosh, *Battleground*; Charles Brackett, Billy Wilder and D. M. Marshman Jr, *Sunset Boulevard*; 1951 Alan Jay Lerner, *An American in Paris*; T. E. B. Clark, *The Lavender Hill Mob* (GB); 1953 Charles Brackett, Walter Reisch and Richard Breen, *Titanic*; 1954 Budd Schulberg, *On the Waterfront*; 1955 William Ludwig and Sonya Levien, *Interrupted Melody*; 1956 Dalton Trumbo, *The Brave One*.

OSCARS – THE SUCCESS STORIES

Ben Hur (US 59) holds the record for winning more Oscars than any other film. In 1959 it received 11 awards out of the 12 categories for which it was nominated – Best Picture, Best Director, Best Actor, Best Supporting Actor, Cinematography, Art Direction, Sound, Music Score, Film Editing, Special Effects, and Costume Design. It grossed an estimated $37 million in the domestic market and $80 million worldwide, breaking all box-office records at the time. It cost an estimated $15 million to produce.

Other films which have won more than five Oscars are:

	Oscars	Nominations
West Side Story (US 61)	10	11
Gigi (US 58)	9	9
The Last Emperor (Ita/GB/Chi 87)	9	9
Gone With the Wind (US 39)	8	13
From Here to Eternity (US 53)	8	13
On the Waterfront (US 54)	8	12
My Fair Lady (US 64)	8	12
Cabaret (US 72)	8	10
Gandhi (GB 82)	8	11
Amadeus (US 84)	8	11
Schindler's List (US 93)	7	12
Going My Way (US 44)	7	10
The Best Years of our Lives (US 46)	7	8
The Bridge on the River Kwai (GB 57)	7	8
Lawrence of Arabia (GB 62)	7	10
Patton (US 70)	7	10
The Sting (US 73)	7	10
Out of Africa (US 85)	7	11
Dances with Wolves (US 90)	7	12
Mrs Miniver (US 42)	6	12
All About Eve (US 50)	6	14
An American in Paris (US 51)	6	8
A Place in the Sun (US 51)	6	9
A Man for All Seasons (GB 66)	6	8
The Godfather Part II (US 74)	6	11
Star Wars (US 77)	6	10

ABOVE *Ben Hur* (US 59) has won more Oscars than any other film. Charlton Heston (seen above) played Ben Hur and starred in this spectacular film about life under the Romans, overshadowed by the birth and crucifixion of Christ.

BELOW Shirley Temple presenting Walt Disney with his Special Award for *Snow White and the Seven Dwarfs* (US 37).

FACTS

■ *Gigi* (US 59) and *The Last Emperor* (Ita/GB/Chi 87) won all nine Oscar nominations. Both these films also won the Best Picture award but received no acting nominations.

■ *A Place in the Sun* (US 51), *Cabaret* (US 72) and *Star Wars* (US 77) won six or more Oscars without winning Best Picture.

■ *Gone With the Wind* (US 39) was the first colour film to win Best Picture.

■ *The Godfather Part II* (US 74) has been the only sequel to win Best Picture.

Walt Disney has won most awards overall, receiving 32, including 12 for Best Cartoon. In 1938 he was given a Special Award for *Snow White and the Seven Dwarfs* in recognition of a significant screen innovation which charmed millions. He had announced his intention to make a long-form fairytale in 1934 and estimated a budget of $500 000.

By the time it was premièred at the Cathay Circle Theater in Hollywood in 1937 it had cost some $1 500 000. The film employed 570 artists who produced 250 000 drawings. The young star Shirley Temple presented Walt Disney with the specially designed Oscar representing Snow White, and seven dwarf Oscars.

The youngest winners of the Best Actor and Actress awards, respectively, are Richard Dreyfuss at 29 years, 156 days – *The Goodbye Girl* (US 77) and Marlee Matlin at 21 years, 218 days – *Children of a Lesser God* (US 86).

The youngest person ever to win an Oscar is Shirley Temple who received a Special Award in 1934 at the tender age of 5 years, 10 months. When Irvin Cobb, host of the 1934 ceremony, awarded her the Oscar he said: 'Listen, you-all ain't old enough to know what this is all about. But, honey, I want to tell you that when Santa Claus wrapped you-all up in a package and dropped you down creation's chimney, he brought the loveliest Christmas present that was ever given to the world.' Evidently she did not understand what it was all about because she tried to snatch the small version of the Oscar, made especially for her, out of Cobb's hand before he finished speaking!

The youngest person in competition to win an Oscar is Tatum O'Neal (born on 5 November 1963) who was aged 10 when she received the award in 1974 for Best Supporting Actress in *Paper Moon* (US 73).

The oldest recipients are George Burns (born on 20 January 1896) who won Best Supporting Actor for *The Sunshine Boys* (US 75) in 1976, and Jessica Tandy (born on 7 June 1909) who won Best Actress for *Driving Miss Daisy* (US 89) in 1990, both were 80 at the time of their presentation, although Miss Tandy was the elder by five months.

Oscars–Academy Awards 1993

Steven Spielberg's film, *Schindler's List*, won most awards, receiving seven Oscars from 12 nominations. *Jurassic Park*, also directed by Spielberg, won three Oscars along with *The Piano* (Aus), directed by Jane Campion.

Best Picture *Schindler's List*

Best Actor Tom Hanks, *Philadelphia*

Best Actress Holly Hunter, *The Piano* (Aus)

Best Director Steven Spielberg, *Schindler's List*

Best Supporting Actor Tommy Lee Jones, *The Fugitive*

Best Supporting Actress Anna Paquin, *The Piano* (Aus)

Best Art Direction Allan Starski (art), Ewa Braun (set), *Schindler's List*

Best Visual Effects Dennis Muren, Stan Winston, Phil Tippett, Michael Lantieri, *Jurassic Park*

Best Make-up Greg Cannom, Ve Neill, Yolanda Toussieng, *Mrs Doubtfire*

Best Sound Effects Editing Gary Rydstrom, Richard Hymns, *Jurassic Park*

Best Animated Short Film *The Wrong Trousers* (GB), Nicholas Park (producer)

Best Live Action Short Film *Black Rider*, Pepe Danquart (producer)

Best Sound Gary Summers, Gary Rydstrom, Shawn Murphy, Ron Judkins, *Jurassic Park*

Best Costume Design Gabriella Perscucci, *The Age of Innocence*

Best Documentary Short Subject *Defending Our Lives*, Margaret Lazarus, Renner Wunderlich (producers)

Best Documentary Feature *I Am A Promise: The Children of Stanton Elementary School*, Susan Raymond, Alan Raymond (producers)

Best Original Score John Williams, *Schindler's List*

Best Cinematography Janusz Kaminski, *Schindler's List*

Best Foreign Language Film *Belle Epoque* (Spa)

Best Film Editing Michael Kahn, *Schindler's List*

Best Original Song 'Streets of Philadelphia', from *Philadelphia*, Bruce Springsteen

Best Original Screenplay Jane Campion, *The Piano* (Aus)

Best Screenplay Adaptation Steven Zaillian, *Schindler's List*

Note: Unless otherwise indicated all films are American

OSCAR FACTS

■ The only films to have won Best Picture, Director, Actor, Actress and Screenplay: *It Happened One Night* (US 34); *One Flew Over the Cuckoo's Nest* (US 75); *The Silence of the Lambs* (US 91).

■ The film which acquired most nominations but did not win an Oscar: *The Turning Point* (US) – 11 nominations in 1977.

■ The only silent film ever to win Best Picture: *Wings* (US) in 1927–28.

■ The first sound film to win Best Picture: *Broadway Melody* (US) in 1928–29.

■ The last black-and-white film to win Best Picture: *The Apartment* (US) in 1960.

■ The first colour film to win Best Picture: *Gone With the Wind* (US) in 1939.

■ The only animated film nominated for Best Picture: *Beauty and the Beast* (US) in 1991.

■ The first British film to win Best Picture: *Hamlet* in 1948.

■ Only films to have won both Best Actor and Actress: *It Happened One Night* (US 34) – Clark Gable and Claudette Colbert; *One Flew Over the Cuckoo's Nest* (US 75) – Jack Nicholson and Louise Fletcher; *Network* (US 76) – Peter Finch and Faye Dunaway; *Coming Home* (US 78) – Jon Voight and Jane Fonda; *On Golden Pond* (US 81) – Henry Fonda and Katharine Hepburn; *The Silence of the Lambs* (US 91) – Anthony Hopkins and Jodie Foster.

■ Most acting nominations without a single win: 7, jointly held by Richard Burton and Peter O'Toole.

The Wrong Trousers (GB), produced by Nicholas Park, won an Oscar in 1993 for Best Animated Short Film. He also won an Oscar in 1990 for Creature Comforts (GB).

Top Money-Making Box-Office Stars

Quigley Publications undertakes an annual poll of exhibitors to ascertain the top box-office stars. A list of 97 film stars is sent out, with three blank spaces to add any additional names, to exhibitors and theatre owners. They then send back their top ten stars who they feel have been the biggest box-office success in that year. The results are added together to determine the winners. The poll is not divided by sex and therefore the following list has extracted the first male and female to appear in each year's listings. The actual rating achieved, apart from that of number 1, is included in brackets.

'Bette Davis drops in at these affairs every year for a cup of coffee and another Oscar.'

Bob Hope

	Male	Female
1915	William S. Hart	Mary Pickford (2)
1916	William S. Hart	Mary Pickford (2)
1917	Douglas Fairbanks	Anita Stewart (3)
1918	Douglas Fairbanks	Mary Pickford (2)
1919	Wallace Reid	Mary Pickford (3)
1920	Wallace Reid	Marguerite Clark (2)
1921	Douglas Fairbanks (2)	Mary Pickford
1922	Douglas Fairbanks (2)	Mary Pickford
1923	Thomas Meighan	Norma Talmadge (2)
1924	Rudolph Valentino (3)	Norma Talmadge
1925	Rudolph Valentino	Norma Talmadge (2)
1926	Tom Mix (2)	Colleen Moore
1927	Tom Mix	Colleen Moore (2)
1928	Lon Chaney (2)	Clara Bow
1929	Lon Chaney (2)	Clara Bow
1930	William Haines (2)	Joan Crawford
1931	Charles Farrell (2)	Janet Gaynor
1932	Charles Farrell (4)	Marie Dressler
1933	Will Rogers (2)	Marie Dressler
1934	Will Rogers	Janet Gaynor (3)
1935	Will Rogers (2)	Shirley Temple
1936	Clark Gable (2)	Shirley Temple
1937	Clark Gable (2)	Shirley Temple
1938	Clark Gable (2)	Shirley Temple
1939	Mickey Rooney	Shirley Temple (5)
1940	Mickey Rooney	Bette Davis (9)
1941	Mickey Rooney	Bette Davis (8)
1942	Abbott and Costello	Betty Grable (8)
1943	Bob Hope (2)	Betty Grable
1944	Bing Crosby	Betty Grable (4)
1945	Bing Crosby	Greer Garson (3)
1946	Bing Crosby	Ingrid Bergman (2)
1947	Bing Crosby	Betty Grable (2)

Male	Female		Male	Female
1948 Bing Crosby	Betty Grable (2)		**1971** John Wayne	Ai MacGraw (8)
1949 Bob Hope	Betty Grable (7)		**1972** Clint Eastwood	Barbra Streisand (5)
1950 John Wayne	Betty Grable (4)		**1973** Clint Eastwood	Barbra Streisand (6)
1951 John Wayne	Betty Grable (3)		**1974** Robert Redford	Barbra Streisand (4)
1952 Dean Martin, Jerry Lewis	Doris Day (7)		**1975** Robert Redford	Barbra Streisand (2)
1953 Gary Cooper	Marilyn Monroe (6)		**1976** Robert Redford	Tatum O'Neal (8)
1954 John Wayne	Marilyn Monroe (5)		**1977** Sylvester Stallone	Barbra Streisand (2)
1955 James Stewart	Grace Kelly (2)		**1978** Burt Reynolds	Diane Keaton (7)
1956 William Holden	Marilyn Monroe (8)		**1979** Burt Reynolds	Jane Fonda (3)
1957 Rock Hudson	Kim Novak (11)		**1980** Burt Reynolds	Jane Fonda (4)
1958 Glenn Ford	Elizabeth Taylor (2)		**1981** Burt Reynolds	Dolly Parton (4)
1959 Rock Hudson	Doris Day (4)		**1982** Burt Reynolds	Dolly Parton (6)
1960 Rock Hudson (2)	Doris Day		**1983** Clint Eastwood	Meryl Streep (12)
1961 Rock Hudson (2)	Elizabeth Taylor		**1984** Clint Eastwood	Sally Field (5)
1962 Rock Hudson (2)	Doris Day		**1985** Sylvester Stallone	Meryl Streep (10)
1963 John Wayne (2)	Doris Day		**1986** Tom Cruise	Bette Midler (5)
1964 Jack Lemmon (2)	Doris Day		**1987** Eddie Murphy	Glenn Close (7)
1965 Sean Connery	Doris Day (3)		**1988** Tom Cruise	Bette Midler (7)
1966 Sean Connery (2)	Julie Andrews		**1989** Jack Nicholson	Kathleen Turner (10)
1967 Lee Marvin (2)	Julie Andrews		**1990** Arnold Schwarzenegger	Julia Roberts (2)
1968 Sidney Poitier	Julie Andrews (3)		**1991** Kevin Costner	Julia Roberts (4)
1969 Paul Newman	Katharine Hepburn (9)		**1992** Tom Cruise	Whoopi Goldberg (6)
1970 Paul Newman	Barbra Streisand (9)		**1993** Clint Eastwood	Julia Roberts (6)

FACTS

TOP BOX-OFFICE STARS

▌ Of the 80 polls undertaken, 58 men and 22 women have come top of the list.

▌ Three male stars have appeared at No. 1 in the poll, five times: Bing Crosby (1944–48); Clint Eastwood (1972–73, 1983–84, 1993); and Burt Reynolds (1978–82). A further two have made five appearances as 'top man': John Wayne (1950–51, 1954, 1963 (2), 1971); and Rock Hudson (1957, 1959, 1960–62 (2)).

▌ Two female stars have appeared at No. 1 in the poll, four times: Doris Day (1960, 1962–64); and Shirley Temple (1935–38). Betty Grable has made eight appearances as 'top woman' in the poll: 1942 (2), 1943, 1944 (4), 1947 (2), 1948 (2), 1949 (7), 1950 (4), and 1951 (3).

▌ Since Julie Andrews headed the poll in 1967, no woman has been No. 1 in the listing.

US Top All-Time Box Office Rental Successes, By Decade

Variety magazine has compiled lists of the most successful films released in terms of film rentals generated at the box office in the US and Canada, by decade. The top ten is listed for all decades except the nineties where the top 20 is listed. Because of ticket price inflation, different release patterns and the advantage of older films which are reissued periodically, films from different eras cannot be compared directly. Figures displayed represent either exact figures provided by the distribution companies or *Variety's* estimates. Older films on the charts with reissue value, such as Disney films, dominate. This reflects the ultimate earning power of films that can continue to attract audiences long after their initial release.

BELOW A scene from *The Birth of a Nation* (US 15) – a success at the box office at the beginning of this century and said to have cost $300 000 to make.

The Teens/Twenties
1	*The Birth of a Nation* (US 15)	$10 000 000
2	*The Big Parade* (US 25)	5 120 791
3	*Ben Hur* (US 25)	4 578 634
4	*The Ten Commandments* (US 23)	4 100 000
5	*The Covered Wagon* (US 23)	4 000 000
6	*What Price Glory?* (US 26)	4 000 000
7	*Hearts of the World* (US 18)	3 900 000
8	*Way Down East* (US 20)	3 900 000
9	*The Singing Fool* (US 28)	3 821 000
10	*The Four Horsemen of the Apocalypse* (US 21)	3 800 000

The Thirties
1	*Gone With the Wind* (US 39)	$79 375 077
2	*Snow White and the Seven Dwarfs* (US 37)	61 752 000
3	*The Wizard of Oz* (US 39)	4 759 888
4	*King Kong* (US 33)	4 000 000
5	*San Francisco* (US 36)	3 785 868
6	*Hell's Angels* (US 30)	3 500 000
7	*Lost Horizon* (US 37)	3 500 000
8	*Mr Smith Goes to Washington* (US 39)	3 500 000
9	*Maytime* (US 37)	3 400 000
10	*City Lights* (US 31)	3 300 000

The Forties
1	*Bambi* (US 42)	$47 265 000
2	*Fantasia* (US 40)	41 660 000
3	*Cinderella* (US 49)	41 087 000
4	*Pinocchio* (US 40)	40 442 000
5	*Song of the South* (US 46)	29 228 717
6	*Mom and Dad* (US 44)	16 000 000
7	*Samson and Delilah* (US 49)	11 500 000
8	*The Best Years of Our Lives* (US 46)	11 300 000
9	*Duel in the Sun* (US 46)	11 300 000
10	*This is the Army* (US 43)	8 500 000

The Fifties
1	*The Ten Commandments* (US 56)	$43 000 000
2	*Lady and the Tramp* (US 55)	40 249 000
3	*Peter Pan* (US 53)	37 584 000
4	*Ben Hur* (US 59)	36 992 088
5	*Around the World in Eighty Days* (US 56)	23 120 000
6	*Sleeping Beauty* (US 59)	21 998 000
7	*The Robe* (US 53)	17 500 000
8	*South Pacific* (US 58)	17 500 000
9	*Bridge on the River Kwai* (GB 57)	17 195 000
10	*This is Cinerama* (US 52)	15 400 000

The Sixties
1	*The Sound of Music* (US 65)	$79 975 000
2	*101 Dalmatians* (US 61)	68 648 000

'That was my one big Hollywood hit, but, in a way, it hurt my picture career. After that, I was typecast as a lion, and there just weren't many parts for lions.'

Bert Lahr on his role in *The Wizard of Oz*

3 *The Jungle Book* (US 67)		60 964 000
4 *Doctor Zhivago* (US 65)		47 253 762
5 *Butch Cassidy and the Sundance Kid* (US 69)		45 953 000
6 *Mary Poppins* (US 64)		45 000 000
7 *The Graduate* (US 67)		44 090 729
8 *My Fair Lady* (US 64)		34 000 000
9 *Thunderball* (GB 65)		28 621 434
10 *Funny Girl* (US 68)		26 325 000

The Seventies

1 *Star Wars* (US 77)	$193 777 000
2 *Jaws* (US 75)	129 549 325
3 *Grease* (US 78)	96 300 000
4 *The Exorcist* (US 73)	89 000 000
5 *The Godfather* (US 72)	86 275 000
6 *Superman* (US/GB 78)	82 800 000
7 *Close Encounters of the Third Kind* (US 77/80)	82 750 000
8 *The Sting* (US 73)	78 212 000
9 *Saturday Night Fever* (US 77)	74 100 000
10 *National Lampoon's Animal House* (US 78)	70 826 000

The Eighties

1 *E.T. The Extra Terrestrial* (US 82)	$228 618 939
2 *Return of the Jedi* (US 83)	169 193 000
3 *Batman* (US 89)	150 500 000
4 *The Empire Strikes Back* (US 80)	141 672 000
5 *Ghostbusters* (US 84)	132 720 000
6 *Raiders of the Lost Ark* (US 81)	115 598 000
7 *Indiana Jones and the Last Crusade* (US 89)	115 500 000
8 *Indiana Jones and the Temple of Doom* (US 84)	109 000 000
9 *Beverly Hills Cop* (US 84)	108 000 000
10 *Back to the Future* (US 85)	105 496 267

The Nineties*

1 *Jurassic Park* (US 93)**	$205 000 000
2 *Home Alone* (US 90)	140 099 000
3 *Terminator 2* (US 91)	112 500 000

4 *Home Alone 2: Lost in New York* (US 92)	103 377 614
5 *Batman Returns* (US 92)	100 100 000
6 *Mrs Doubtfire* (US 93)**	98 331 240
7 *Ghost* (US 90)	98 200 000
8 *The Fugitive* (US 93)**	92 600 000
9 *Robin Hood: Prince of Thieves* (US 91)	86 000 000
10 *Aladdin* (US 92)	82 539 083
11 *Pretty Woman* (US 90)	81 905 530
12 *Dances with Wolves* (US 90)	81 537 971
13 *Lethal Weapon 3* (US 92)	80 000 000
14 *Snow White and the Seven Dwarfs* (US 37)	77 156 754
15 *The Firm* (US 93)**	77 047 044
16 *A Few Good Men* (US 92)	71 000 000
17 *Beauty and the Beast* (US 91)	69 415 000
18 *101 Dalmatians* (US 61)	68 648 000
19 *Teenage Mutant Ninja Turtles* (US 90)	67 650 000
20 *Die Hard 2* (US 90)	67 512 000

*Figures to 13 February 1994
** Still on release
Note: Earnings are actual and have not been adjusted for inflation, and are based on estimated rentals.

UK All-Time Top Grossing Films

1 *Jurassic Park* (US 93)	£47 140 000
2 *Ghost* (US 90)	23 341 465
3 *E.T. The Extra Terrestrial* (US 82)	21 697 000
4 *Crocodile Dundee* (Aus 86)	21 527 000
5 *Robin Hood: Prince of Thieves* (US 91)	20 491 000
6 *Terminator 2* (US 91)	18 398 000
7 *The Silence of the Lambs* (US 91)	17 113 000
8 *The Bodyguard* (US 92)	16 801 000
9 *Mrs Doubtfire* (US 93)	16 700 000
10 *Aladdin* (US 93)	16 314 252

Note: approximate grosses to 1 March 1994
Source: © *Screen International*

British Academy of Film and Television Arts Awards

Formerly the Society of Film and Television Arts, this organisation was formed in 1959 by the amalgamation of the British Film Academy (founded in September 1948) and the Guild of Television Producers and Directors (formed in 1954). Membership is open to senior creative workers in both industries. A further reorganisation in 1975 resulted in a change in title to the British Academy of Film and Television Arts (BAFTA). Branches of the Academy exist throughout the world with the aim of raising standards in all aspects of film-making and television.

Each year BAFTA presents a series of awards in various categories. Formerly, these were given as The British Film Academy Awards (1947–68), The Society of Film and Television Arts Awards (1969–74) and, from 1975, the BAFTA awards. Winners from selected categories follow (all are listed from inception [except where stated otherwise], although this date varies from category to category).

Michael Balcon Award

For outstanding British contribution to the cinema

1978 Les Bowie, Colin Chilvers, Denys Coop, Roy Field, Derek Meddings, Zorin Perisic, Wally Veevers
1979 The Children's Film Foundation
1980 Kevin Brownlow
1981 David Puttnam
1982 Arthur Wooster
1983 Colin Young
1984 Alan Parker, Alan Marshall
1985 Sydney Samuelson
1986 The Film Production Executives
1987 The Monty Python team
1988 Charles Crichton
1989 Lewis Gilbert
1990 Jeremy Thomas
1991 Derek Jarman
1992 Kenneth Branagh
1993 Ken Loach

Fellows of BAFTA

1971 Sir Alfred Hitchcock
1972 Freddie Young
1973 Grace Wyndham Goldie
1974 Sir David Lean
1975 Jacques Cousteau
1976 Lord Olivier, Sir Charles Chaplin
1977 Sir Denis Forman
1978 Fred Zinnemann, Sir Huw Wheldon

> '*I am a typed director. If I made Cinderella, the audience would immediately be looking for a body in the coach.*'
>
> Alfred Hitchcock

Butch Cassidy and the Sundance Kid (US 69), starring Paul Newman (Butch Cassidy), Katharine Ross (Etta Place) and Robert Redford (The Sundance Kid), won the 1970 BAFTA Best Film award.

1979 Lord Grade
1980 Sir David Attenborough, John Huston
1981 Michael Powell, Emeric Pressburger, Abel Gance
1982 Andrzej Wajda
1983 Sir Richard Attenborough
1984 Sir Hugh Greene, Sam Spiegel
1985 Jeremy Isaacs
1986 Steven Spielberg
1987 Federico Fellini
1988 Ingmar Bergman
1989 Sir Alec Guinness
1990 Paul Fox
1991 Louis Malle
1992 Sir John Gielgud, David Plowright
1993 Sydney Samuelson, Colin Young
1994 Michael Grade

Best Film
1947 *The Best Years of Our Lives* (US)
1948 *Hamlet* (GB)
1949 *Bicycle Thieves* (ITA)
1950 *All About Eve* (US)
1951 *La Ronde* (FRA)
1952 *The Sound Barrier* (GB)
1953 *Jeux Interdits* (FRA)
1954 *Le Salaire de la Peur* (FRA)
1955 *Richard III* (GB)
1956 *Gervaise* (FRA)
1957 *The Bridge on the River Kwai* (GB)
1958 *Room at the Top* (GB)
1959 *Ben Hur* (US)

1960 *The Apartment* (US)
1961 *Ballad of a Soldier* (USSR), *The Hustler* (US)
1962 *Lawrence of Arabia* (GB)
1963 *Tom Jones* (GB)
1964 *Dr Strangelove* (GB)
1965 *My Fair Lady* (US)
1966 *Who's Afraid of Virginia Woolf?* (US)
1967 *A Man For All Seasons* (GB)
1968 *The Graduate* (US)
1969 *Midnight Cowboy* (US)
1970 *Butch Cassidy and the Sundance Kid* (US)
1971 *Sunday, Bloody Sunday* (GB)
1972 *Cabaret* (US)
1973 *Day For Night* (FRA)
1974 *Lacombe Lucien* (FRA)
1975 *Alice Doesn't Live Here Anymore* (US)
1976 *One Flew Over the Cuckoo's Nest* (US)
1977 *Annie Hall* (US)
1978 *Julia* (US)
1979 *Manhattan* (US)
1980 *The Elephant Man* (GB)
1981 *Chariots of Fire* (GB)
1982 *Gandhi* (GB)
1983 *Educating Rita* (GB)
1984 *The Killing Fields* (GB)
1985 *The Purple Rose of Cairo* (US)
1986 *A Room with a View* (GB)
1987 *Jean de Florette* (FRA)

1988 *The Last Emperor* (ITA/GB/CHI)
1989 *Dead Poets Society* (US)
1990 *Goodfellas* (US)
1991 *The Commitments* (US/GB)
1992 *Howards End* (GB)
1993 *Schindler's List* (US)

Best Film not in the English Language
Until 1988, Best Foreign Language Film
1982 *Christ Stopped at Eboli* (ITA/FRA)
1983 *Danton* (FRA/POL)
1984 *Carmen* (SPA)
1985 *Colonel Redl* (HUN/GER/AUT)
1986 *Ran* (JAP)
1987 *The Sacrifice* (SWE)
1988 *Babette's Feast* (DEN)
1989 *Life and Nothing But* (FRA)
1990 *Cinema Paradiso* (ITA/FRA)
1991 *The Nasty Girl* (GER)
1992 *Raise the Red Lantern* (HKG)
1993 *Farewell My Concubine* (CHI)

'I'm looking for Commander James Bond, not an overgrown stunt man.'

Ian Fleming, on meeting Sean Connery, '007' star

BAFTA Awards

	Actor	Actress	Direction	Screenplay
1968	Spencer Tracy *Guess Who's Coming to Dinner* (US)	Katharine Hepburn *Guess Who's Coming to Dinner* (US) *The Lion in Winter* (GB 68)	Mike Nichols *The Graduate* (US)	Calder Willingham and Buck Henry *The Graduate* (US)
1969	Dustin Hoffman *Midnight Cowboy* (US), *John and Mary* (US)	Maggie Smith *The Prime of Miss Jean Brodie* (GB)	John Schlesinger *Midnight Cowboy* (US)	Waldo Salt *Midnight Cowboy* (US)
1970	Robert Redford *Butch Cassidy and the Sundance Kid* (US), *Tell Them Willie Boy is Here* (US), *Downhill Racer* (US)	Katharine Ross *Tell Them Willie Boy is Here* (US), *Butch Cassidy and the Sundance Kid* (US)	George Roy Hill *Butch Cassidy and the Sundance Kid* (US)	William Goldman *Butch Cassidy and the Sundance Kid* (US)
1971	Peter Finch *Sunday, Bloody Sunday* (GB)	Glenda Jackson *Sunday, Bloody Sunday* (GB)	John Schlesinger *Sunday, Bloody Sunday* (GB)	Harold Pinter *The Go-Between* (GB)
1972	Gene Hackman *The French Connection* (US), *The Poseidon Adventure* (US)	Liza Minnelli *Cabaret* (US)	Bob Fosse *Cabaret* (US)	Paddy Chayevsky *The Hospital* (US) Larry McMurtry and Peter Bogdanovich *The Last Picture Show* (US)
1973	Walter Matthau *Pete 'n Tillie* (US), *Charley Varrick* (US)	Stephane Audran *The Discreet Charm of the Bourgeoisie* (FRA/SPA/ITA), *Just Before Nightfall* (FRA)	Francois Truffaut *Day For Night* (FRA)	Luis Buñuel and Jean-Claude Carrière *The Discreet Charm of the Bourgeoisie* (FRA/SPA/ITA)
1974	Jack Nicholson *The Last Detail* (US), *Chinatown* (US)	Joanne Woodward *Summer Wishes, Winter Dreams* (US)	Roman Polanski *Chinatown* (US)	Robert Towne *Chinatown* (US), *The Last Detail* (US)
1975	Al Pacino *The Godfather Part II* (US), *Dog Day Afternoon* (US)	Ellen Burstyn *Alice Doesn't Live Here Anymore* (US)	Stanley Kubrick *Barry Lyndon* (GB)	Robert Getchell *Alice Doesn't Live Here Anymore* (US)
1976	Jack Nicholson *One Flew Over the Cuckoo's Nest* (US)	Louise Fletcher *One Flew Over the Cuckoo's Nest* (US)	Milos Forman *One Flew Over the Cuckoo's Nest* (US)	Alan Parker *Bugsy Malone* (GB)
1977	Peter Finch *Network* (US)	Diane Keaton *Annie Hall* (US)	Woody Allen *Annie Hall* (US)	Woody Allen and Marshall Brickman *Annie Hall* (US)
1978	Richard Dreyfuss *The Goodbye Girl* (US)	Jane Fonda *Julia* (US)	Alan Parker *Midnight Express* (GB)	Alvin Sargent *Julia* (US)
1979	Jack Lemmon *The China Syndrome* (US)	Jane Fonda *The China Syndrome* (US)	Francis Coppola *Apocalypse Now* (US)	Woody Allen and Marshall Brickman *Manhattan* (US)
1980	John Hurt *The Elephant Man* (GB)	Judy Davis *My Brilliant Career* (AUS)	Akira Kurosawa *Kagemusha* (JAP)	Jerzy Kosinski *Being There* (US)
1981	Burt Lancaster *Atlantic City USA* (CAN/FRA)	Meryl Streep *The French Lieutenant's Woman* (GB)	Louis Malle *Atlantic City USA* (CAN/FRA)	Bill Forsyth *Gregory's Girl* (GB)
1982	Ben Kingsley *Gandhi* (GB)	Katharine Hepburn *On Golden Pond* (US)	Richard Attenborough *Gandhi* (GB)	Costa Gavras and Donald Stewart *Missing* (US)

	Actor	Actress	Direction	Original	Adapted
1983	Michael Caine *Educating Rita* (GB), Dustin Hoffman *Tootsie* (US)	Julie Walters *Educating Rita* (GB)	Bill Forsyth *Local Hero* (GB)	Paul Zimmermann *The King of Comedy* (US)	Ruth Prawer Jhabvala *Heat and Dust* (GB)
1984	Dr Haing S. Ngor *The Killing Fields* (GB)	Maggie Smith *A Private Function* (GB)	Wim Wenders *Paris, Texas* (GER/FRA)	Woody Allen *Broadway Danny Rose* (US)	Bruce Robinson *The Killing Fields* (GB)

	Actor	Actress	Direction	Screenplay	
1985	William Hurt *Kiss of the Spider Woman* (US/BRA)	Peggy Ashcroft *A Passage to India* (GB)	No award	Woody Allen *The Purple Rose of Cairo* (US)	Richard Condon and Janet Roach *Prizzi's Honor* (US)
1986	Bob Hoskins *Mona Lisa* (GB)	Maggie Smith *A Room with a View* (GB)	Woody Allen *Hannah and Her Sisters* (US)	Woody Allen *Hannah and Her Sisters* (US)	Kurt Luedtke *Out of Africa* (US/GB)
1987	Sean Connery *The Name of the Rose* (US)	Ann Bancroft *84 Charing Cross Road* (GB)	Oliver Stone *Platoon* (US)	David Leland *Wish You Were Here* (GB)	Claude Berri and Gera Brach *Jean de Florette* (FRA)
1988	John Cleese *A Fish Called Wanda* (US)	Maggie Smith *The Lonely Passion of Judith Hearne* (GB)	Louis Malle *Au Revoir Les Enfants* (FRA)	Shawn Slovo *A World Apart* (GB)	Jean-Claude Carrière and Philip Kaufman *The Unbearable Lightness of Being* (US)
1989	Daniel Day Lewis *My Left Foot* (GB)	Pauline Collins *Shirley Valentine* (US)	Kenneth Branagh *Henry V* (GB)	Nora Ephron *When Harry Met Sally* (US)	Christopher Hampton *Dangerous Liaisons* (US)
1990	Philippe Noiret *Cinema Paradiso* (ITA/FRA)	Jessica Tandy *Driving Miss Daisy* (US)	Martin Scorsese *Goodfellas* (US)	Giuseppe Tornatore *Cinema Paradiso* (ITA/FRA)	Nicholas Pileggi and Martin Scorsese *Goodfellas* (US)
1991	Anthony Hopkins *The Silence of the Lambs* (US)	Jodie Foster *The Silence of the Lambs* (US)	Alan Parker *The Commitments* (US/GB)	Anthony Minghella *Truly, Madly, Deeply* (GB)	Dick Clement, Ian La Frenais and Roddy Doyle *The Commitments* (US/GB)
1992	Robert Downey Jr *Chaplin* (GB)	Emma Thompson *Howards End* (GB)	Robert Altman *The Player* (US)	Woody Allen *Husbands and Wives* (US)	Michael Tolkin *The Player* (US)
1993	Anthony Hopkins *The Remains of the Day* (GB)	Holly Hunter *The Piano* (AUS)	Steven Spielberg *Schindler's List* (US)	Danny Rubin, Harold Ramis *Groundhog Day* (US)	Steven Zaillian *Schindler's List* (US)

BAFTA 1993 Awards

Alexander Korda Award For Outstanding British Film of the Year *Shadowlands* (GB), Richard Attenborough, Brian Eastman

Lloyds Bank People's Vote for the Most Popular Film *Jurassic Park* (US)

Best Supporting Actor Ralph Fiennes, *Schindler's List* (US)

Best Supporting Actress Miriam Margolyes, *The Age of Innocence* (US)

Best Score John Williams, *Schindler's List* (US)

Best Short Film *Franz Kafka's It's A Wonderful Life* (GB), Ruth Kenley-Letts, Peter Capaldi

Best Short Animated Film *The Wrong Trousers* (GB), Christopher Moll, Nick Park

Best Editing Michael Kahn, Schindler's List (US)

Best Sound John Leveque, Bruce Stambler, Becky Sullivan, Scott D. Smith, Donald O. Mitchell, Michael Herbick, Frank A. Montano, *The Fugitive* (US)

Best Cinematography *Schindler's List* (US), Janusz Kaminski

Best Production Design *The Piano* (AUS), Andrew McAlpine

Best Costume Design *The Piano* (AUS), Janet Patterson

Best Achievement in Special Effects Dennis Muren, Stan Winston, Phil Tippett, Michael Lantieri, *Jurassic Park* (US)

Best Make-Up Artist Morag Ross, *Orlando* (GB/RUS/ITA/FRA/NETHS)

Cannes Film Festival

Established in 1939 by the French government, the first festival did not take place until 1946 because of World War II. Awards vary from year to year, although the Palme d'Or awarded for Best Film has been made annually:

Palme d'Or

1946 *La Bataille du Rail* (FRA)
1947 *Antoine et Antoinette* (FRA)
1948 No festival
1949 *The Third Man* (GB)
1950 No festival
1951 *Miracle in Milan* (ITA), *Miss Julie* (SWE)
1952 *Othello* (MOR), *Two Cents Worth of Hope* (ITA)
1953 *Wages of Fear* (FRA)
1954 *Gate of Hell* (JAP)
1955 *Marty* (US)
1956 *World of Silence* (FRA)
1957 *Friendly Persuasion* (US)
1958 *The Cranes are Flying* (USSR)
1959 *Black Orpheus* (FRA)
1960 *La Dolce Vita* (ITA)
1961 *Viridiana* (SPA), *Une aussi longue absence* (FRA)
1962 *The Given Word* (BRA)
1963 *The Leopard* (ITA)
1964 *The Umbrellas of Cherbourg* (FRA)
1965 *The Knack* (GB)
1966 *A Man and a Woman* (FRA), *Signore e Signori* (ITA)
1967 *Blow-Up* (GB)
1968 Festival disrupted – no awards
1969 *If* (GB)
1970 *M*A*S*H* (US)
1971 *The Go-Between* (GB)
1972 *The Working Class Goes to Paradise* (ITA), *The Mattei Affair* (ITA)
1973 *Scarecrow* (US), *The Hireling* (GB)
1974 *The Conversation* (US)
1975 *Chronicle of the Burning Years* (ALG)

1976 *Taxi Driver* (US)
1977 *Padre Padrone* (Ita)
1978 *L'Albero Degli Zoccoli* (Ita)
1979 *The Tin Drum* (Ger), *Apocalypse Now* (US)
1980 *All That Jazz* (US), *Kagemusha* (Jap)
1981 *Man of Iron* (Pol)
1982 *Missing* (US), *Yol* (Tur)
1983 *The Ballad of Narayama* (Jap)
1984 *Paris, Texas* (Ger)
1985 *When Father Was Away on Business* (Yug)
1986 *The Mission* (GB)
1987 *Under the Sun of Satan* (Fra)
1988 *Pelle the Conqueror* (Den)
1989 *Sex, Lies and Videotape* (US)
1990 *Wild at Heart* (US)
1991 *Barton Fink* (US)
1992 *Best Intentions* (Swe)
1993 *Farewell My Concubine* (Chi), *The Piano* (Aus)
1994 *Pulp Fiction* (US)

Berlin Film Festival

When the Festival was established in 1951, there was no overall best film award made, and in the years from 1952 to 1955 this award was voted for by the audience. From 1956 The Golden Bear for Best Picture was introduced:

The Golden Bear

1952 *She Danced for the Summer* (Swe)
1953 *The Wages of Fear* (Fra)
1954 *Hobson's Choice* (GB)
1955 *The Rats* (Ger)
1956 *Invitation to the Dance* (GB)
1957 *Twelve Angry Men* (US)
1958 *The End of the Day* (Swe)
1959 *The Cousins* (Fra)
1960 *Lazarillo de Tormes* (Spa)
1961 *La Notte* (Ita)
1962 *A Kind of Loving* (GB)
1963 *Oath of Obedience* (Ger), *The Devil* (Ita)
1964 *Dry Summer* (Tur)
1965 *Alphaville* (Fra)
1966 *Cul de Sac* (GB)
1967 *Le Départ* (Bel)
1968 *Ole Dole Doff* (Swe)
1969 *Early Years* (Yug)
1970 No award
1971 *The Garden of the Finzi-Continis* (Ita)
1972 *The Canterbury Tales* (Ita)

1973 *Distant Thunder* (Ind)
1974 *The Apprenticeship of Duddy Kravitz* (Can)
1975 *Orkobefogadas* (Hun)
1976 *Buffalo Bill and the Indians* (US) – declined award
1977 *The Ascent* (USSR)
1978 *The Trouts* (Spa), *The Words of Max* (Spa)
1979 *David* (Ger)
1980 *Heartland* (US), *Palermo oder Wolfsburg* (Ger)
1981 *Di Presa Di Presa* (Spa)
1982 *Die Sehnsucht der Veronica Voss* (Ger)
1983 *Ascendancy* (GB), *The Beehive* (Spa)
1984 *Love Streams* (US)
1985 *Wetherby* (GB), *Die Frau und der Fremde* (Ger)
1986 *Stammheim* (Ger)
1987 *The Theme* (USSR)
1988 *Red Shorghum* (Chi)
1989 *Rain Man* (US)
1990 *Music Box* (US), *Larks on a String* (Cze)
1991 *House of Smiles* (Ita)
1992 *Grand Canyon* (US)
1993 *The Woman from the Lake of Scented Souls* (Chi), *The Wedding Banquet* (Tai/US)
1994 *In the Name of the Father* (GB)

Venice Film Festival

This event was the first ever regular film festival, held as part of the Venice Biennale. It took place at the Hotel Excelsior from 6 to 21 August 1932 and was initially intended to revive the tourist trade. In the first year, America, France, Germany, Italy and Britain entered a total of 18 films, but no awards were made.

Golden Lion

Best Foreign Film (1934–42)
Best Film Award (1946–48)
Golden Lion for Best Film (1980 onwards)

1932 No award
1933 No festival
1934 *Man of Aran* (GB)
1935 *Anna Karenina* (US)
1936 *Der Kaiser von Kalifornien* (Ger)
1937 *Un Carnet de Bal* (Fra)
1938 *Olympia* (Ger)
1939 No award
1940 *Der Postmeister* (Ger)
1941 *Ohm Kruger* (Ger)
1942 *Der grosse König* (Ger)
1943 No festival
1944 No festival
1945 No festival
1946 *The Southerner* (US)
1947 *Sirena* (Cze)

1948 *Hamlet* (GB)
1949 *Manon* (Fra)
1950 *Justice is Done* (Fra)
1951 *Rashomon* (Jap)
1952 *Forbidden Games* (Fra)
1953 No award
1954 *Romeo and Juliet* (Ita/GB)
1955 *Ordet* (Den)
1956 No award
1957 *Aparajito* (Ind)
1958 *Muhomatsu no Issho* (Jap)
1959 *Il Generale della Rovere* (Ita)
1960 *Le Passage du Rhin* (Fra)
1961 *Last Year at Marienbad* (Fra)
1962 *Childhood of Ivan* (USSR)
1963 *Le Mani sulla città* (Ita)
1964 *Red Desert* (Ita)
1965 *Of a Thousand Delights* (Ita)
1966 *Battle of Algiers* (Ita)
1967 *Belle de Jour* (Fra)
1968 *Die Artisten in der Zirkuskuppel* (Ger)
1969–79 Discontinued
1980 *Gloria* (US), *Atlantic City* (Fra/Can)
1981 *Die Bleierne Zeit* (Ger)
1982 *The State of Things* (Ger)
1983 *Prénom Carmen* (Fra/Swi)
1984 *Year of the Quiet Sun* (Pol)
1985 *Sans toit ni loi* aka *Vagabonde* (Fra)
1986 *Le Rayon Vert* (Fra)
1987 *Au Revoir les Enfants* (Fra)
1988 *The Legend of the Holy Drinker* (Ita)
1989 *A City of Sadness* (Tai)
1990 *Rosencrantz and Guildenstern Are Dead* (GB)
1991 *Urga* (Rus/Fra)
1992 *Qiu Ju Da Guansi* (Chi)
1993 *Short Cuts* (US), *Three Colours Blue* (Fra)

Top 20 Video Sales, 1993

1 *The Jungle Book* (US 67)
2 *Peter Pan* (US 53)
3 *Beauty and The Beast* (US 91)
4 *The Muppet Christmas Carol* (US 92)
5 *Home Alone 2 – Lost in New York* (US 92)
6 *The Bodyguard* (US 92)
7 *Lethal Weapon 3* (US 92)
8 *Sister Act* (US 92)
9 *Take That – Take That and Party*
10 *Cherfitness – Body Fitness*

'A celebrity is a person whose name is in everything except the phone directory.'

Anon

'I used to be Snow White . . . but I drifted.'

Mae West

THE JUNGLE BOOK

The Jungle Book (US 67) was the last animated movie that Walt Disney supervised – he died just before it was finished. It is based on the book of the same title written in 1894 by Rudyard Kipling to which it bears scant resemblance apart from having some characters with the same names. As Walt said to storyman Larry Clemmons in 1963, having finally succeeded in purchasing the rights to Kipling's book: 'Here is the original by Rudyard Kipling. The first thing I want you to do is not to read it.'

This was the first of the Disney animated films in which the major characters were based solidly on the personas of the voice-artists employed to bring them to life. Shere Khan the tiger *is* George Sanders, the bear *is* Phil Harris, and King Louie *is* Louis Prima. Wolfgang Reitherman, the movie's director, explained: 'In *The Jungle Book* we tried to incorporate the personalities of the actors that do the voices into the cartoon characters, and we came up with something totally different.' The film was enormously successful.

In 1993 *The Jungle Book* video was released, and within two weeks four million copies had been sold. This was the largest initial order ever for any entertainment product, let alone video, In the UK. By the time this first batch had been sold, one in 14 Britons owned a copy. It quite easily takes first place in the list of bestselling videos for 1993. (The Disney Series *Junglebook* also appeared in the 1993 UK Bestselling Children's Books in position No. 8.)

11 *Blade Runner – The Director's Cut* (US 82/91)
12 *Star Trek VI – The Undiscovered Country* (US 91)
13 *Red Dwarf 1 – The End*
14 *Red Dwarf 1 – Confidence and Paranoia*
15 *Full Metal Jacket* (GB 87)
16 *The Shape Challenge*
17 *Wayne's World* (US 92)
18 *Cinderella* (US 50)
19 *The Merry Mishaps of Mr Bean*
20 *The Terrible Tales of Mr Bean*

Source: Compiled by MRIB, 1993

Top 20 Video Rentals, 1993

1 *Sister Act* (US 92)
2 *The Bodyguard* (US 92)
3 *Universal Soldier* (US 92)
4 *Under Siege* (US 92)
5 *Lethal Weapon 3* (US 92)
6 *Single White Female* (US 92)
7 *Home Alone 2 – Lost in New York* (US 92)
8 *Patriot Games* (US 92)
9 *A Few Good Men* (US 92)
10 *The Last of the Mohicans* (US 92)
11 *Unforgiven* (US 92)
12 *Alien 3* (US 92)
13 *The Hand that Rocks the Cradle* (US 91)
14 *Basic Instinct* (US 91)
15 *Death Becomes Her* (US 92)
16 *Unlawful Entry* (US 92)
17 *Housesitter* (US 92)
18 *Bram Stoker's Dracula* (US 92)
19 *White Men Can't Jump* (US 92)
20 *Far and Away* (US 92)

Source: Compiled by MRIB, 1993

British Film Institute Awards

The British Film Institute (BFI) was founded in 1933 to support all aspects of film culture. It has presented various awards since 1984 to recognise outstanding achievement in film and television, in areas not usually acknowledged by other international awards. In 1991 seven main awards were introduced and made together with

'Making a funny film provides all the enjoyment of getting your leg caught in the blades of a threshing machine. As a matter of fact, it's not even that pleasurable; with the threshing machine the end comes much quicker.'

Woody Allen, *Esquire* (1975)

the prestigious BFI Fellowships which were introduced in 1983 to celebrate the 50th anniversary of the BFI. In this first year they were presented by the BFI's patron, HRH The Prince of Wales.

BFI Fellowships
Unique contribution to the moving image culture
1983 Marcel Carné, Sir David Lean, Michael Powell, Emeric Pressburger, Satyajit Ray, Orson Welles
1984 Lord Bernstein, Akira Kurosawa
1985 Lord Brabourne, Lord Olivier
1986 Jeremy Isaacs, Deborah Kerr, Dilys Powell
1987 Dirk Bogarde, Bette Davis, Elem Klimov
1988 Graham Greene, Vanessa Redgrave, Anthony Smith
1989 Dame Peggy Ashcroft, Gérard Depardieu
1990 Derek Jarman, Krzysztof Kieslowski, Jeanne Moreau, Fred Zinnemann
1991 Sir Alec Guinness, Leslie Hardcastle
1992 Sir Richard Attenborough, Dame Maggie Smith
1993 Clint Eastwood, Sir Denis Forman, Maureen O'Hara

BFI Award for Innovation
1991 *Video Diaries*, BBC TV, series producer: Jeremy Gibson
1992 Chris Newby
1993 *Sweet Thames*, BBC TV, director: Mark Harrison

Archival Achievement Award
1991 University of California, Los Angeles Film and Television Archive

1992 *Selling Murder: The Killing Films of the Third Reich*, director: Joanna Mack
1993 *Pandora's Box*, BBC TV, producer: Adam Curtis

Michael Powell Book Award
1991 *Behind the Mask of Innocence*, Kevin Brownlow
1992 *Projections: A Forum for Filmmakers*, John Boorman and Walter Donohue
1993 *Showman: The Life of David O Selznick*, David Thomson

Mari Kuttna Award
Best animated film
1991 *Manipulation*, director: Daniel Greaves
1992 *A is for Autism*, Channel 4 TV, director: Tim Webb
1993 *Little Wolf*, director: An Vrombaut

Grierson Award
Best documentary
1991 *Absurdistan*, BBC TV, producer: John Whiston
1992 *Children of Chernobyl*, Yorkshire TV for Channel 4, director: Clive Gordon
1993 *Aileen Wuornos: The Selling of a Serial Killer*, Channel 4 TV, director: Nick Broomfield

Sutherland Trophy
Best first feature premièred at the National Film Theatre
1991 *On the Wire*, director: Elaine Proctor
1992 *Proof*, director: Jocelyn Moorhouse
1993 *Vacas*, director: Julio Medem

Career in the Industry Award
1991 David Tomblin, first assistant director

> 'You can pick out actors by the glazed look that comes into their eyes when the conversation wanders away from themselves.'
> Michael Wilding

1992 Douglas Slocombe, director of photography
1993 Eleanor Fazan, choreographer

Evening Standard British Film Awards

These awards have been given annually, since 1973, in various categories, for outstanding contributions to the British cinema year. They include awards to British films and British actors, actresses, technicians, etc. who have contributed towards a film, British or otherwise. The winners are decided by a panel of film critics which in 1993 had the following members: Alexander Walker (film critic, *Evening Standard*), Iain Johnstone (film critic, *The Sunday Times*), Sheila Johnston (film correspondent, *The Independent*), Nigel Andrews (film critic, *Financial Times*), and Ann Billson (film critic, *The Sunday Telegraph*). Until 1979 they were known as *The Evening News* British Film Awards. Winners of Best Film, Comedy, Actor, Actress, Screenplay (given from 1981), Special Award (given from 1975) are listed below:

	Film	Comedy*	Actor	Actress	Screenplay	Special Award
1973	*Ryan's Daughter* (GB 70)	*The National Health* (GB 73)	Keith Michell *Henry VIII and His Six Wives* (GB 72)	Glenda Jackson *Mary Queen of Scots* (GB 71)		
1974	*Live and Let Die* (73)	*The Three Musketeers* (PAN 73)	Michael Caine *Sleuth* (GB 72)	Glenda Jackson *A Touch of Class* (GB 73)		
1975	*Murder on the Orient Express* (GB 74)	*The Four Musketeers* (PAN 74)	Albert Finney *Murder on the Orient Express* (GB 74)	Dame Wendy Hiller *Murder on the Orient Express* (GB 74)		Peter Hall
1976	*Aces High* (GB 76)	*The Return of the Pink Panther* (GB 74)	Peter Sellers *The Return of the Pink Panther* (GB 74)	Annette Crosbie *The Slipper and the Rose* (GB 76)		Stuart Cooper
1977	*A Bridge Too Far* (US/GB 77)	*The Pink Panther Strikes Again* (GB 76)	John Thaw *Sweeney!* (GB 76)	Billie Whitelaw *The Omen* (US 76)		James Mason
1978	*Star Wars* (US 77)	*The Revenge of the Pink Panther* (US 78)	Alec Guinness *Star Wars* (US 77)	Nanette Newman *International Velvet* (GB 78)		David Puttnam

	Film	Comedy*	Actor	Actress	Screenplay	Special Award
1979	*Death on the Nile* (GB 78)	*Porridge* (GB 79)	Peter Ustinov *Death on the Nile* (GB 78)	Maggie Smith *California Suite* (US 78)		Sir John Mills
1980	*Yanks* (GB 79)	*Rising Damp* (GB 80)	Denholm Elliott *Bad Timing* (GB 80), *Rising Damp* (GB 80), *Zulu Dawn* (US / NET 79)	Frances de La Tour *Rising Damp* (GB 80)		David Niven
1981	*The French Lieutenant's Woman* (GB 81)	Bill Forsyth	Bob Hoskins *The Long Good Friday* (GB 80)	Maggie Smith *Quartet* (GB / FRA 81)	Colin Welland	Roy Walker John Alcott
1982	*Moonlighting* (GB 82)	Michael Blakemore	Trevor Howard *Light Years Away* (FRA)	Jennifer Kendal *36 Chowringhee Lane* (IND 81)	John Krish	No award
1983	*The Ploughman's Lunch* (GB 83)	Bill Forsyth	Ben Kingsley *Gandhi* (GB 82), *Betrayal* (GB 82)	Phyllis Logan *Another Time, Another Place* (GB)	Ian McEwan	Sir Richard Attenborough
1984	*1984* (GB 84)	Denholm Elliott	John Hurt *1984* (GB 84), *Champions* (GB 83), *The Hit* (GB 84)	Helen Mirren *Cal* (GB 84)	Bernard MacLaverty	No award
1985	*My Beautiful Laundrette* (GB 85)	Michael Palin	Victor Banerjee *A Passage to India* (GB 84)	Miranda Richardson *Dance with a Stranger* (GB 85)	Alan Bennett and Malcolm Mowbray	Denis O'Brien George Harrison
1986	*A Room with a View* (GB 85)	John Cleese *Clockwise* (GB 86)	Ray McAnally *The Mission* (GB 86), *No Surrender* (GB 85)	Coral Browne *Dreamchild* (GB 85)	Robert Bolt *The Mission* (GB 86)	Jake Eberts
1987	*Hope and Glory* (GB 87)	David Leland *Personal Services* (GB 87), *Wish You Were Here* (GB 87)	Derek Jacobi *Little Dorrit* (GB 87)	Emily Lloyd *Wish You Were Here* (GB 87)	Alan Bennett *Prick Up Your Ears* (GB 87)	Zenith Films
1988	*A Fish Called Wanda* (US 88)	Charles Crichton *A Fish Called Wanda* (US 88)	Bob Hoskins *Who Framed Roger Rabbit* (US 88), *The Lonely Passion of Judith Hearne* (GB 87)	Maggie Smith *The Lonely Passion of Judith Hearne* (GB 87), Billie Whitelaw *The Dressmaker* (GB 88)	Bruce Robinson *Withnail and I* (GB 87)	Richard Williams
1989	*Henry V* (GB 89)	Mike Leigh *High Hopes* (GB 88)	Daniel Day-Lewis *My Left Foot* (GB 89)	Pauline Collins *Shirley Valentine* (US 89)	Willy Russell *Shirley Valentine* (US 89)	Peter Greenaway
1990	*The Krays* (GB 90)	Robbie Coltrane	Iain Glen *Mountains of the Moon* (US 89), *Fools of Fortune* (GB 90), *Silent Scream* (GB 89)	Natasha Richardson *The Comfort of Strangers* (ITA / GB 90), *The Handmaid's Tale* (US / GER 90)	Michael Eaton *Fellow Traveller* (GB / US 89)	Jeremy Thomas
1991	*Close My Eyes* (GB 91)	Dick Clement, Roddy Doyle, Ian Le Frenais *The Commitments* (US / GB 91)	Alan Rickman *Robin Hood: Prince of Thieves* (US 91), *Close My Eyes* (GB 91), *Truly, Madly, Deeply* (GB 90)	Juliet Stevenson *Truly, Madly, Deeply* (GB 90)	Neil Jordan *The Miracle* (GB 90)	No award
1992	*Howards End* (GB 92)	*Peter's Friends* (GB 92)	Daniel Day-Lewis *The Last of the Mohicans* (US 92)	Emma Thompson *Howards End* (GB 92), *Peter's Friends* (GB 92)	Terence Davies *The Long Day Closes* (GB 92)	No award
1993	*Raining Stones* (GB 93)	Les Blair *Bad Behaviour* (GB 93)	David Thewlis *Naked* (GB 93)	Emma Thompson *Much Ado About Nothing* (GB / US 93), *The Remains of the Day* (GB 93)	Jim Allen *Raining Stones* (GB 93)	Sir Anthony Hopkins

* Renamed the Peter Sellers Award in 1980 after his death

FOOD & DRINK

Evian/Guild of Food Writers Award

The Guild of Food Writers and Evian offered a prize of £1500 in their seventh award made to a non-professional food writer who composed the most imaginative and original essay on 'My Favourite Ingredient'. Entries are judged by a panel of culinary experts who look for imagination and wit rather than precise cooking instructions. 1993 produced two winners, Trish Currie and Mary Overton, writing on lemons and lamb. An extract from 'lemons' appears below.

'My love affair began on our honeymoon on a Greek Island. It was the second morning of my marriage, and we were having breakfast in the October sunshine when the owner of the taverna came out with our black tea. He crossed to a dusty tree on the other side of the road, reached up and pulled off a small greenish-yellow fruit. With a knife from his belt he cut it into slices and plopped them into our cups. It was the most fragrant tea I had every drunk. And so the affair began. I had fallen in love with lemons. Of course we had been acquainted before, but I'd forgotten . . .

'. . . Lemons remain my constant

companions in the kitchen. Squeeze them on to smoked salmon blinis, pan-fried skate wings and charcoaled aubergines. Splash the juice into dressings, sauces, vegetable dips, dhals and salads. Grate the zest and its essential oil into cakes, desserts, pâtés and jellies. Sprinkle it in needle shreds on top of tarts and syllabubs. Slice it, twist it and wedge it.

'. . . I also have a new tipple since I gave up gin. It is a fat chunk of unwaxed lemon, squeezed hard into a tall glass and topped up with ice-cold, sparkling mineral water so that when you drink it the lemon bobs on your nose, the fragrance and flavour fizz

EGON RONAY/CELLNET 1994 CHEF OF THE YEAR

Awarded to Paul Heathcote, Paul Heathcote's Restaurant, Longridge, Lancs. At the 1994 Guide prices, a three-course meal for two, including one of the least expensive bottles of wine, coffee, service and VAT, will cost £90.

'. . . In this pretty, extended whitewashed cottage . . . a new kitchen (visible through the glass frontage), an additional dining room and a reception lounge, all complement the existing decor of beams, exposed stone walls and immaculate candle-lit table settings, further enhanced by delightful flower arrangements . . . Paul decided to return to his native Lancashire to cook with good local produce (such as Goosnargh chickens and ducklings) and the finest-quality ingredients from around the rest of the country. Both the lunch and à la carte menus change quite frequently . . . the result is innovative cooking with flair and great skill in a style best described as ''modern British'' – exemplified by dishes such as ham hock, leek and foie gras terrine served with beetroot and caraway chutney and truffle dressing to start, followed by a main course of roast cutlets of lamb served with baked Lancashire hotpot garnish, braised red cabbage and rosemary-scented juices, and perhaps bread-and-butter pudding served with a sauce anglaise, apricot coulis and clotted cream.'

Egon Ronay's Cellnet Guide 1994

round your mouth and you can feel the sun in your nostrils. The honeymoon continues.'
Trish Currie

British Oyster Opening Championship

In the 1993 championship, sponsored by Tabasco Pepper Sauce, each contestant was given 30 Irish native oysters to shuck and present as quickly and elegantly as possible. A panel of judges examined the trays of opened oysters before making a final decision. The winner was Armando Lema of Green's Restaurant and Oyster Bar in St James's, London who opened the 30 oysters in 3 minutes 28 seconds. He also won the contest in 1989, 1990 and 1991. Shucking techniques varied – Mr Lema did not wear

Jackie Moggan, the first woman ever to enter the British Oyster Opening Championship; she opened 30 oysters in 8 minutes 31 seconds.

EGON RONAY/CELLNET 1994 DESSERT OF THE YEAR

John Burton-Race from L'Ortolan in Shinfield, Berks, was winner of the award, sponsored by Häagen-Dazs. Entitled '*assiette chocolatière*' the judges declared it to be 'a perfect example of attention to detail. It combines a clever mix of white and dark chocolate tastes heightened by exquisite artistry in its presentation on the plate. A fitting end to a meal.'

The *assiette chocolatière* (presented on a white plate) consists of five individual desserts (from left, clockwise):

Coffee Mousse A bitter coffee mousse, wrapped in dark chocolate, topped with a crème mousseline and dusted with cocoa. Garnish with a chocolate coffee bean and coffee bean sauce.

Parfait Chocolat Almond biscuit soaked in poire William eau de vie layered with chocolate and vanilla parfaits. Topped with caramelized sponge soaked in pear syrup. Garnish with vanilla sauce anglaise.

Tour d'Ivoire A white chocolate mousse wrapped in white chocolate and topped with glazed raspberries. Garnish with raspberry sauce.

Larne au Chocolat A chocolate tear filled with chocolate mousse, light vanilla cream studded with griotte cherries finished with a piece of English gold leaf. Garnish with chocolate sauce.

Ice Cream (centre) Langue de chat basket with vanilla ice cream and bitter chocolate sorbet, topped with a caramel cage. Garnish with apricot sauce.

gloves and declared that the secret of his speed was: 'I am not afraid of cutting myself.' However, speed was not all that counted – all oysters were examined by the judges for damage, untidiness, bits of broken shell and blood.

'"O Oysters," said the Carpenter,
"You've had a pleasant run!
Shall we be trotting home again?"
But answer came there none –
And this was scarcely odd, because
They'd eaten every one.'

Through the Looking Glass, Lewis Carroll, 1872

Bettys at Ilkley won the 1993 Top Tea Place award after a nationwide search to find the best cup of tea. In this traditional café, waitresses still wear white headbands and starched aprons, and tea is presented in white Wedgwood china porcelain teapots. The café stands in a row of Victorian shops in the town, overlooking Ilkley Moor. It charges £2.90 for a pot of tea for two and has an estimated three million visitors a year. There are three other branches of Bettys which were started in Harrogate in 1919 by Frederick Belmont, a Swiss confectioner. The secret of their good tea is reckoned to be the quality of the water. Every month the company's tea buyer of 40 years' experience is sent bottles of water from all over Yorkshire to test and mix with Ceylon, East African and Assam teas to make the special Bettys Tea Room Blend. Ten other types of tea are also offered. The café seats 110 and is decorated with hundreds of tea pots.

Bettys at Ilkley, Yorks, 1993 Top Tea Place.

The Tea Council Awards

Launched in 1983 with the Tea Place of the Year and the Airports' Best Cup of Tea, The Tea Council has regularly given awards to promote good quality tea. In 1993 the awards were as follows:

Top Tea Place of the Year

Nominations are received from entries in leading food and drink guides and also those who have won a Tea Council award during that year. The Tea Council sends a panel of professional tea-tasters to visit each establishment. Working incognito to a set criteria, the judges award marks for:

- food, cakes, scones
- hygiene and cleanliness
- type of crockery and cup condition
- sugar and its presentation
- fresh milk and the way tea is made
- appearance of liquor
- temperature and taste of tea
- variety of teas on offer
- helpfulness and efficiency of staff
- ambience of establishment
- overall value for money

From the results a shortlist of ten is drawn up and visits are made once more to decide on a winner.

RECENT WINNERS
1990 Shepherd's Tea Rooms, Chichester, Sussex
1991 The Cake Table, Fishmarket Street, Thaxted, Essex
1992 Shepherd's Tea Rooms, Chichester, Sussex
1993 Bettys, 32 The Grove, Ilkley, W. Yorks

In-Flight Best Cup of Tea

Individuals who fly and love tea have been selected since 1990 to judge the quality of in-flight cups of tea. Winners have been Dan Air (1990), British Airways (1991, 1992), and American Airlines (1993).

Motorways Best Cup of Tea

Awarded since 1983 to motorway cafés, professional tea tasters travel incognito up and down motorways visiting all those who have entered. A shortlist is drawn up and these establishments are visited again before a winner is announced.

In 1993 the first motorway service station to serve Britain's travellers, the Blue Boar at Watford Gap on the M1 southbound near Northampton, won the award. It originally opened in 1959 as a petrol station with a portacabin. Tea is their biggest selling drink and they serve more than 24 000 pots a week.

English Wine of the Year

These awards are given to members of the English Vineyards Association. There are various categories but the most prestigious trophy for English Wine of the Year is the Gore Browne Trophy, instituted in 1974. A judging panel is appointed and over the space of two days all wines are tasted.

WINNERS

1974 Brede Riesling Sylvaner 72 (E. Sussex)
1975 Pilton Manor Riesling Sylvaner 73 (N. Godden, Som)
1976 Pilton Manor Riesling Sylvaner 75 (N. Godden, Som)
1977 Pulham Magdalen Rivaner 76 (P. Cook, Norfolk)
1978 Kelsale Müller-Thurgau 77 (Suffolk)
1979 Adgestone 78 (K. Barlow, Isle of Wight, Hants)
1980 Magdalen Rivaner 79 (P. Cook, Norfolk)
1981 Tenterden Seyvel 80 (S. Skelton, Kent)

1982 Wootton Schönburger 81 (C. L. B. Gillespic, Som)
1983 Lamberhurst Huxelrebe 82 (K. McAlpine, Kent)
1984 Barton Manor Dry 83 (A. H. Goddard, Isle of Wight, Hants)
1985 Lamberhurst Schönburger 84 (K. McAlpine, Kent)
1986 Wootton Seyval 85 (C. L. B. Gillespie, Som)
1987 Biddenden Ortega 86 (R. Barnes, Kent)
1988 Chiltern Valley Old Luxters 87 (D. Ealand, Oxon)
1989 Carr Taylor Reichensteiner 88 (D. Carr Taylor, Sussex)
1990 Lamberhurst Schönburger 88 (K. McAlpine, Kent)
1991 Tenterden Special Reserve 89 (M. Kay, Kent)
1992 Thames Valley Botrytis 91 (J. Leighton, Berks)
1993 Thames Valley Fumé 91 (J. Leighton, Berks)

Rémy Martin Head Waiter of the Year Award

There are many awards given for waiters in the UK, but this is the most prestigious for head waiters. Rémy Martin and *Caterer & Hotelkeeper* organise the award, which seeks to recognise the professional skills, expertise and flair of head waiters.

In 1993 participants were judged in a real-life dining situation, serving a four-course meal to 24 invited guests, having already successfully completed a rigorous paper examination and regional finals. Initially, they prepared the tables and left the room for the judges to carry out a first inspection. Marks were lost for faults such as overfilling the breadbasket, smears on glasses, butter being placed uncovered too early on the tables. All the dishes were selected specifically to test the skills of each head waiter. For example, to start there was a choice of Mediterranean prawns with smoked trout, goose liver pâté in Port with aspic, chicken consommé with ricotta ravioli, and mussels in garlic and herbs. Each competitor had to arrange the prawns and bone the trout at the side table, slice the pâté from a terrine and serve it with hot brioche, and serve both the mussels and consommé from a large dish on to

the guests' plates. Every move by the head waiters was observed by the judges throughout the meal.

Vito Scaduto, born in Siciuliana, Sicily, was announced Head Waiter of the Year, having most successfully kept his nerve throughout the day. He is Manager of Carden Park Hotel's Le Croquet restaurant in Chester. (Previous winners: Saverio Buchicchio [1991], Dormy House Hotel, Broadway, Hereford & Worcs; and Didier Broquerault [1992], Wentworth Club, Virginia Water, Surrey.)

CAMRA *Champion Beer of Britain*

This is the most prestigious brewing title in the UK. Since 1978, the Campaign for Real Ale (CAMRA) awards have been made at the opening of the Great British Beer Festival every August. Cask-conditioned beers are shortlisted and then tasted by a panel of expert judges. A winner is selected in each category, and those beers are then judged to select a 'Champion Beer'. Since receiving the 1993 Champion Beer title, the production of Adnams Extra has trebled.

CHAMPION BEERS
1978 Thwaites Mild/Fuller's ESB
1979 Fuller's London Pride
1980 Thwaites Best Mild
1981 Fuller's ESB
1982 Taylor Landlord
1983 Taylor Landlord
1984 No festival
1985 Fuller's ESB
1986 Bateman's XXXB
1987 Pitfield Dark Star
1988 Ringwood Old Thumper

In 1795 Napoleon, who believed that armies marched on their stomachs, offered a prize for practical ways of preserving food. It was won by a French inventor, Nicolas Appert (1749–1841), who devised a method of sterilising foodstuffs in hermetically sealed containers – jars covered with five layers of cork – away from circulating air.

1989 Fuller's Chiswick Bitter
1990 Ind Coope Burton Ale
1991 Mauldon's Black Adder
1992 Woodeford's Norfolk Nog
1993 Adnams Extra

OTHER 1993 WINNERS
Dark and Light Milds Woodforde's Mardler's Mild
Bitters Taylor's Best Bitter
Best Bitters Adnams Extra
Strong Bitters Exe Valley Exeter Old Bitter
Old Ales and Strong Milds Sarah Hughes Original Mild
Barley Wines Woodeforde's Headcracker
Porters and Stouts Coach House Blunderbus Porter
Bottle-conditioned Beers Thomas Hardy Ale (Eldridge Pope)

EGON RONAY/CELLNET 1994 BRITISH CHEESEBOARD OF THE YEAR

The Lygon Arms, Broadway, Hereford & Worcs, won this award for a cheese trolley offering some 30 British and Irish cheeses, served with walnut bread. Most of the cheeses are unpasteurised, giving a fuller flavour, and at least two are made with vegetarian rennet. Some of the more unusual cheeses featured are Celtic Promise (cow's milk), Golden Cross (goat's milk – log-shaped coated in ash), the semi-hard and mild-tasting Swaledales from Yorkshire, and Devon Ticklemore, a mature hard cheese made from goat's milk. The cheddar is an 18-month-old Montgomery from Somerset, and the Colston Bassett Stilton and Blue Shropshire come from Nottingham.

ANDRÉ SIMON MEMORIAL FUND

In 1972, shortly after the death of André Simon (1877–1970), founder of the International Wine and Food Society, the André Simon Memorial Fund was set up as a charitable trust to perpetuate his memory. One objective of the Fund is to benefit those working in the fields of food and drink, and to this end it makes annual book awards in two categories: food; wine, drinks and beverages. An award of £2000 is made to the winner of each category, and £200 to each shortlisted title. In 1991 a new £1000 prize was instituted, called the Special Commendation, which is awarded to one of the shortlisted books in either category. The books are judged by the trustees of the Memorial Fund and two independent assessors who, in 1993, were Clarissa Dickson Wright (manager, The Cooks Bookshop, Edinburgh) and Paul Henderson (owner, Gidley Park restaurant and hotel).

WINNERS

Food

1978 Alan Davidson, *North Atlantic Seafood*
Jane Grigson, *Vegetable Book*

1979 Josceline Dimbleby, *The Book of Puddings, Desserts and Savouries*

1980 Marcella Hazan, *The Classic Italian Cookbook*

Marika Hanbury Tenison, *Cooking with Vegetables*

1981 Anne Willan, *French Regional Cooking*

1982 Jane Grigson, *Fruit Book*
Barbara Maher, *Cakes*

1983 Roger Phillips, *Wild Food*

1984 Yan-Kit So, *Classic Chinese Cookbook*

1985 Hannah Wright, *Soups*

1986 Harold McGee, *On Food and Cooking*

1987 Henrietta Green, *British Food Finds 1987*

1988 Peter Graham, *Classic Cheese Cookery*

1989 Patrick Rance, *The French Cheese Book*

1990 Jill Norman, *The Complete Book of Spices*

1991 Arabella Boxer, *A Visual Feast*

1992 Pierre Koffman, *La Tante Claire*

1993 Sri Owen, *Rice*

Special Commendation

1991 John and Sally McKenna, *The Bridgestone Irish Food Guide*

1992 Richard Mayson, *Portugal's Wines and Winemakers*

1993 Henrietta Green, *Food Lover's Guide to Britain*

Drink

Nicholas Faith, *The Winemasters*

Joanna Smith, *The New English Vineyard*

Michael Broadbent, *The Great Vintage Wine Book*

John R. Hume and Michael S. Moss, *The Making of Scotch Whisky*
David Peppercorn, *Bordeaux*

Hugh Johnson, *Wine Companion*
Rosemary George, *The Wines of Chablis*
Nicholas Belfrage, *Life Beyond Lambrusco*
Jancis Robinson, *Vines, Grapes and Wines*
Stephen Brook, *Liquid Gold: Dessert Wines of the World*
Tom Stevenson, *Sotheby's World Wine Encyclopedia*
Hugh Johnson, *The Story of Wine*
Burton Anderson, *The Wine Atlas of Italy*
Oz Clarke, *New Classic Wines*
Remington Norman, *Great Domaines of Burgundy*
Michael Jackson, *Beer Companion*

Logis Regional Cuisine Competition

Inaugurated in 1993, this competition is organised by Logis of Great Britain, an independent association representing independently owned and run hotels. Entries were received from 415 hotels throughout the UK and from these nine regional finalists were selected. The intention of the competition was for entrants to produce regional cuisine – a menu featuring dishes and ingredients from their own area and which they would normally serve in their dining rooms.

The finalists were then invited to a 'cook-off', including a starter and main course, at Westminster College, to be judged by a panel of eight experts, including chairman Albert Roux, Jane Owen (editor, *The Times Weekend*), Catey Hillier (editor, *Chef*), Graham Leadham (Westminster College), Linda Astbury (chief inspector, English Tourist Board), Jean Falquet (Logis de France), Malcolm Wood (editor, *The Worcester Evening News*), and Alan Hall (freelance journalist).

Albert Roux, sporting a jacket embroidered with the words 'Académie Culinaire de France UK', urged the judges to look for taste and flavour balance and to award marks for these before considering the presentation. Eighteen dishes were served up by the finalists at 10-minute intervals.

After much deliberation, the winner was declared to be Sandra Bates of the Crown at Whitebrook, near Monmouth, Gwent who cooked 'Wild Mushroom and Scallop Croustade' starter, followed by 'Lamb with a Faggot'. Jane Owen, judge, described the winning dishes: 'a wild mushroom and scallop croustade: a crunchy, thin, wholemeal tartlet base topped with local wild mushrooms in a light cream and ground hazelnut sauce and crowned with scallops. A small, tasty fresh leaf salad kept the tart company. The next course was called 'Lamb with a Faggot' – a somewhat bald description in view of the flavours. The faggots were a rich, moist, aromatic blend of kidney, herbs and liver, a delicate cross between a good sausage and rough country pâté. The lamb was saved from being very slightly on the bland side by a richly flavoured Madeira sauce. The vegetables had that pulled-from-the-earth-and-cooked-to-a-turn quality.'

WELSH ARE WINNERS IN REGIONAL CUISINE

Sandra Bates, winner of the 1993 Logis Regional Cuisine Competition, runs The Crown at Whitebrook, Nr. Monmouth, Gwent, with her husband. She prepared the following dishes for the judges:

Wild Mushroom and Scallop Croustade

A hazelnut and pine kernel croustade, filled with local mixed wild mushrooms in a cream sauce, topped with a scallop and garnished with mixed salad leaves in a hazelnut dressing.

Main ingredients

Breadcrumbs	Cream
Ground hazelnuts	Scallops
Butter	Shallots
Pine kernels	Salad leaves
Mixed herbs	Hazelnut oil
Wild mushrooms – picked locally	Sherry vinegar

Method Prepare individual tartlet cases, part fill with wild mushrooms in cream sauce, top with sliced and lightly sautéed scallop and garnish with mixed salad leaves, tossed in hazelnut dressing.

Lamb with a Faggot

Fillet of Welsh lamb from the best end, served with a faggot of liver and kidneys on a bed of spinach accompanied by a lamb, Madeira, tomato and thyme sauce.

Main ingredients	*Vegetables*
Best end of Welsh lamb	Potatoes
Caul, kidney and lamb's liver	Carrots
Shallots	Fine beans
Fresh garden herbs – thyme,	Swede
sage and parsley	Turnip
Tomatoes	Butter
Spinach	Cream and
Madeira	seasoning
Lamb stock	
Brown breadcrumbs	
Salt and pepper	

Method Prepare a faggot of liver and kidney, place on a bed of spinach at the top of the plate. Cook the lamb fillet until pink, slice and arrange in a fan. Prepare a sauce, keeping the herbs, tomato concasse and shallot visible, and pour over the lamb. Serve with gallet potatoes, glazed turned carrots, green beans, swede and turnip purée.

InterCity Chef of the Year

Sponsored by the Meat and Livestock Commission, this event has taken place annually since 1990. Over 200 InterCity chefs competed in 1993 to win £500 and a silver salver. Every year the focus changes, i.e. one year it might be beef, the next pork, and so on. The finalists are all given a similar list of ingredients to create a dish which is judged on colour, texture, taste and presentation.

In 1993 Billy Smith won the title with his recipe entitled 'Sautéed Strips of Beef Oriental Style' which was added to British Rail's Express diner menu as a lunch. He is a regular chef on the Pullman service between Newcastle and London.

Billy Smith's 'Sautéed Strips of Beef Oriental Style'

▪ Start by preparing a good beef stock.

▪ Fry a selection of favourite spices.

▪ Add garlic.

▪ Put in some ginger.

▪ Pour in a glass of red wine.

▪ Add chopped tomatoes.

▪ Mix with stock in one of the pans and reduce for about 30 minutes.

▪ Mango chutney will add the necessary sweetness.

▪ Meanwhile, sauté slices of beef.

▪ Serve them on a bed of golden rice.

▪ A salad at the side adds the finishing touch.

FACTS

▪ Each year, InterCity serves up 37 tonnes of sausages; 37 tonnes of bacon; one million eggs, 1.2 million pots of jam.

▪ InterCity has more on-board chefs (120) and serves more silver service meals than any other train company in the world.

GAMES

Bridge

There are three main international events in the Bridge calendar: the World Teams Championship (the Bermuda Bowl – open event; and the Venice Cup – women's event); the World Teams Olympiad; and the World Pairs Championships.

Bermuda Bowl

The Bermuda Bowl is held biannually (since 1977) and is contested by zonal champions. The world is split into eight zones for this purpose (see Fact Box) and the champions in each zone compete against each other.

The Bermuda Bowl is the oldest World Bridge Federation championship. It grew out of private initiatives, principally by Norman Bach. The first world championship for the Bermuda Bowl was held in 1950, eight years before the WBF was formed. It was contested by only three zones initially – USA, Europe and Britain. The USA won comfortably, beating Europe by 4720 points and Britain by 3660. The Bermuda Bowl then developed into a regular challenge match beween the USA and the winners of the European Championship, a more logical method than the first three-entry event.

In the sixties, the scope of international bridge was expanded. After the formation of the WBF in 1958, member countries were arranged in the eight geographical zones and the contest

---

---

began to take on its present worldwide characteristics. Prior to 1967, placings were decided by a simple round robin, with two points for a win and one for a tie; since this date there is a round robin in which each team meets each other in three separate matches, with 20 victory points at stake in each match; followed by a two-team final over 128 boards.

WINNERS

1950 USA		**1968** Not held
1951 USA		**1969** Italy
1952 Not held		**1970** North America
1953 USA		**1971** USA
1954 USA		**1972** Not held
1955 Great Britain		**1973** Italy
1956 France		**1974** Italy
1957 Italy		**1975** Italy
1958 Italy		**1976** USA
1959 Italy		**1977** USA
1960 Not held		**1979** USA
1961 Italy		**1981** USA
1962 Italy		**1983** USA
1963 Italy		**1985** USA
1964 Not held		**1987** USA
1965 Italy		**1989** Brazil
1966 Italy		**1991** Iceland
1967 Italy		**1993** Netherlands

Most wins 13 Italy (1957–59; 1961–63; 1965–67; 1969; 1973–75)

Venice Cup

The Venice Cup was presented by the Italian Bridge Federation. Like the Bermuda Bowl, it started with a challenge match between teams representing Europe and the United States. Until 1974 there was no official inter-zonal representative match for women's teams. However, the Italian Bridge Federation, who were hosting the Bermuda Bowl in 1974, instigated a challenge match between Italy's women's team representing Europe and a United States women's team.

In 1985 the Venice Cup was brought on to a par with the Bermuda Bowl, to be held every two years at the same time and place as the Bermuda Bowl, and the two contests were to be in almost all respects similar, including eligibility requirements and format.

WINNERS

1974 USA	**1981** Great Britain	**1989** USA
1976 USA	**1985** Great Britain	**1991** USA
1978 USA	**1987** USA	**1993** USA

Most wins 7 USA

World Team Olympiad

The World Team Olympiad, inaugurated in 1960, was the first competition to be set up by the World Bridge Federation itself. The Bermuda Bowl was already well established by the time the WBF was founded in 1958. Harold S. Vanderbilt, the inventor of modern bridge scoring, provided a cup, the Vanderbilt Trophy, and he continued to provide replicas for each member of the winning team.

This event is open to any affiliated country in the world and is contested by large numbers of teams who play in qualifying groups. The winning groups then go on to play in quarter-finals, semi-finals and the final to establish a winning team. Each team is made up of four members, although in practice countries are allowed to send six. The Olympiad is on a four-year cycle (alternating biennially with the World Pairs Championships) and is made up of an Open Series and a Women's Series.

The first Olympiad was held in Turin, Italy and was contested by 25 countries in the Open and 14 in the Women's. In the 1992 Olympiad, 57 countries participated in the Open, 34 in the Women's.

WINNERS

	Open	Women's
1960	France	United Arab Republic
1964	Italy	Great Britain
1968	Italy	Sweden
1972	Italy	Italy
1976	Brazil	Italy
1980	France	USA
1984	Poland	USA
1988	USA	Denmark
1992	France	Austria

Most wins 3 Italy and France   **Most wins** 2 Italy and USA

World Pairs Championships

These championships are on a four-year cycle, alternating biennially with the Teams Olympiad. They consist of a series of championships and subsidiary events which have the World Open Pairs, the World Women's Pairs and the World Knock-out Teams as the base. Originally they began on a modest scale, simply as a World Open Pairs and a corresponding Women's event, with a Mixed event of one kind or another to round out the programme.

(continued on p. 122)

Chess – the Position of the Pieces

The 1993 world championship match between Garry Kasparov of Russia and Nigel Short of England was the first title match since the war played outside the auspices of FIDE, the world chess federation. Over the years, Garry Kasparov, the reigning world champion, had been involved in a number of disputes with Florencio Campomanes, president of FIDE. The most contentious of these stemmed back to 1985, when his first challenge for the world title, against fellow Russian Anatoly Karpov, was halted by Campomanes in controversial circumstances. The winner of the match would be the first to achieve six wins, draws not counting. The score at the time, after 48 games, was five wins to three in favour of Karpov. However, Kasparov had recovered from a 5–0 deficit and there were rumours that Karpov was near exhaustion. Since this time, Kasparov has attempted more than once to break away from FIDE or to have Campomanes overthrown, but without success.

Early in 1993, FIDE announced its decision for the venue of the impending world championship match. It was to be held in Manchester (Nigel Short's home town, and potential host of the Olympic Games), who had offered a prize fund of £1.1 million. Kasparov was agreeable to this choice, but Short was travelling by car between England and Greece at the time of the announcement, and claims not to have been consulted. FIDE countered that he had been in full knowledge of the date of the decision and had deliberately rendered himself incommunicado.

Short had never seen eye to eye with Kasparov (for example, he had recently called him a baboon and an Asiatic despot), but nevertheless contacted

him to suggest breaking away from FIDE, and playing their match under the auspices of a new organisation, the Professional Chess Association (PCA), which they would form. Kasparov, seeing a chance to ditch FIDE, was naturally delighted and fully agreeable. Thus, the PCA was born and their world championship match was played in London, sponsored by *The Times*, who put up a prize fund of £1.7 million.

The match was contested as the best of 24 games, with the title remaining with Kasparov in the event of a 12–12 tie. All international chess is played to a time limit and if a player carelessly uses up too much of his time allowance in the early stages of the game, he runs into what is known as 'time trouble'. When this happens, a great many moves have to be made very quickly and the chances of error, or even a loss by time forfeit, increase. This was Short's undoing in the first half of the match when he lost games 1, 3, 4, 7 and 9, without winning one in reply. He lost by time forfeit in the first game, missed a chance to draw the third game, and also missed good chances to draw games 7 and 9 and to win games 8 and 10. With the score at 7½–2½ to Kasparov, the match was effectively decided.

Short performed better in the second half of the match when he kept an even score with one win, one loss and eight draws. After 20 games, Kasparov was leading by 12½–7½ and thus won the match, retaining his title of world champion. Kasparov won £1 062 500, while Short took home £637 500.

All international chess players are given a figure, known as an ELO rating, which indicates their strength and can determine the probable score in a match between players of unequal strength. Prior to the match, Kasparov's rating would have been 2815 and Short's 2665. They did not, in fact, have official ratings, because FIDE (which publishes the rating list twice a year) had not only dispossessed them of their titles of world champion and

'It was not to be and I think I did not make the best of my chances.'

Nigel Short on being defeated in the 1993 world championship

Garry Kasparov (Rus) and Nigel Short (UK) during the 1993 PCA world chess championship.

challenger, but had stripped them of their ratings as well. However, on the basis of these ratings, Short had performed higher than expected by scoring 7½–20 and would have gained 13 rating points from the champion (i.e. their updated ratings at the end of the match would have been 2802 and 2678 respectively).

Meanwhile, FIDE, having defaulted Kasparov and Short, had organised its own replacement world championship match, contested between Jan Timman (Holland), whom Nigel Short had defeated in the final eliminator of the FIDE cycle, and Anatoly Karpov, Russian ex-world champion and Kasparov's challenger on the previous three occasions. Timman's rating before the match was 2620 and Karpov's 2760. The match was won by Karpov with a score of 12½–8½, but the initial sponsorship of the match (from the Sultanate of Oman) was withdrawn, and it is not clear if the players were ever paid.

In 1994, Kasparov was, without question, considered to be the strongest player in the world, although both he and Karpov carried the title of world champion of their respective organisations.

The women's world champion in 1994 was Xie Jun of China, who successfully defended her title against Nana Ioseliani of Georgia. Their 1993 (FIDE) match resulted in an easy 8½–2½ for the champion. However, the strongest female player in the world is considered unquestionably to be Judith Polgar of Hungary who, in late 1991, at the age of 15 years, 148 days, became the youngest ever grand master, beating a record held by the famous Bobby Fischer for over 30 years. She is currently ranked 20th in the world and has consistently turned her back on women-only events throughout her career.

The highest ELO rating ever achieved is 2800 by Garry Kasparov in January 1990 when he surpassed the previous best, 2785, achieved by Bobby Fischer. The highest rated women's player is Judith Polgar from Hungary at 2550.

Scrabble – The Game of Words

The National Scrabble Championships have been held annually since 1971. Gyles Brandreth, a leading exponent of the game, first conceived of the idea while writing a book on prisons. He observed, while making prison visits, that both English and American prisoners played Scrabble. He was also aware that the royal family played; thus the game covered the whole social spectrum – so he decided to instigate a championship. He started by placing an advertisement in the personal column of *The Times* inviting people to enter a championship and the first event was subsequently held.

Current entrants for the championship now number between two and three thousand each year. Regional finals are held in five locations in the UK, and 64 qualifiers are chosen to enter the final which is held over two days. On the first day, the 64 qualifiers play knock-out tournaments – four games each which produces four semi-finalists. On the second day, semi-finals are held in the morning, the best of three games played by each contestant, and in the afternoon the two finalists play the best of three games.

The 23rd National Championship was held in 1993. The winner was Allan Saldanha who, at 15, is the youngest-ever champion. He comes from Chelsea, London, and won the title by defeating Karl Khoshnaw, a 38-year-old maths lecturer from Richmond, 2–0. The board and moves of the final game (above right) show Karl's early advantage with the play of CRUSTED. He was comfortably ahead when he made a serious error in playing ICE (26 points on move 8) opening up a triple word for Allan. A better move would have been FECES (A15 across – 35 points).

Subbuteo – Tabletop Football

Subbuteo had humble beginnings back in 1947 when Peter Adolph, the game's inventor, set up a cottage industry in rural south-east England and started selling the Subbuteo

Allan Saldanha

	Rack	Word	Score	Total
1	TTIVNOO	VINT	14	14
2	TOOWER?	TOW	21	35
3	OER?TEG	GROVE	18	53
4	E?TRAED	REAS*TED	73	126
5	HIKATRX	XI	52	178
6	HKATRZA	TAK	24	202
7	HRZANAI	RAH	19	221
8	ZNAIHAN	HARN	14	235
9	ZNAIGES	ZIGAN	60	295
10	SEQUERF	QUEERS	32	327
11	FLAWDIN	DWARF	24	351
12	LINOOYR	NOY	31	382
13	LIORDEI	LILO	8	390
14	RDEILM	DREAM	20	410
15	EIL			−3
				407

Karl Khoshnaw

	Rack	Word	Score	Te
1	TORYBUS	YOB	26	
2	TRUSC?D	CRUSTE*D	99	1
3	POOABEE	BAP	24	1
4	OOEEEEI	ch.OOEEEI	0	1
5	ENNAAJS	JANES	56	2
6	ANEMOIE	MIND	27	2
7	AEESUVI	UVEA	21	2
8	ESIFECG	ICE	26	2
9	ESFGOOI	FOG	23	3
10	ESOIPTI	DIP	20	3
11	ESOITEE	EGO	11	3
12	ESITELL	NULL	8	3
13	ESITEEU	EE	10	3
14	ETUIS	SUITED	14	3

Note: A question mark represents a blank tile drawn. When these are played an asterisk indicates which letter they are used chmeans the player changed the letters indicated.

Definitions of some of the words played: VINT – a card game; REASTED – rancid; XI – a Greek letter; JANES – women; T Scottish form of take; MINO – a raincoat; RAH – short for hurrah; UVEA – part of the iris; HARN – coarse linen; ZIGAN Hungarian gypsy; NOY – to annoy; KEX – corn.

Assembly Set on a mail order basis. The original game was very basic with cardboard teams, a cellulose ball and wire-framed goals with paper nets. There was no playing pitch, just a piece of chalk and instructions to mark out the pitch on an ex-army blanket!

Subbuteo was, however, an instant success – partly as a result of the effort to create football realism on the table top, with a choice of two dozen teams in the most popular team colours of the day. This has been one of the major attractions of Subbuteo and it explains why, today, there are almost 700 team colours to choose from plus a range of other accessories.

The inventor called the game Subbuteo because being a keen ornithologist he wanted to combine his passion for birds with the enthusiasm that he had for his new game. His original intention was to call the game 'The Hobby' after the hobby hawk which now forms part of the Subbuteo logo. This was abandoned however, and the Latin name for the bird (Falco Subbuteo subbuteo), after amendment, was adopted.

Today, there are subbuteo clubs, leagues and associations around the world. There is an International Federation and regular national and international events which are based on the football calendar such as the Subbuteo European Championships (Rome 1980, Paris 1984, Brussels 1988, Hamburg 1992) and the Subbuteo World Cup (Athens 1986, Rome 1990, Chicago 1994). Each country sends its national champion to enter the world championships.

The History of Scrabble

Scrabble was originally conceived in America in the early 1930s by Alfred Butts and James Brunot. Alfred Butts, an unemployed architect, was fascinated with words, crosswords and anagrams and devised a game called Lexiko – the forerunner of Scrabble. Lexiko had letter tiles and racks but no board. The letter tiles had no values and the idea of the game was to make a seven-letter word from the tiles on the rack. If a player could not see a word, he exchanged some of his tiles for others and this exchange of letters continued until one player was able to build a seven-letter word, thus winning the game. A later version of Lexiko introduced point values on the tiles. When a player won with a seven-letter word, other players could make shorter words and the point values were added up.

Butts offered Lexico in this form to several manufacturers, but nobody was interested. He then developed the board with premium squares and the game began to move nearer to the present-day Scrabble. However, this game was again rejected. Butts continued undaunted until 1939 when he met Jim Brunot, introduced by a friend who thought he might be interested in marketing the game, which by now was called Criss-Crosswords. Nothing much came of this meeting and it was not until 1946, after the war, that Brunot and Butts met again and, after further discussion and refinement of the game, renamed it Scrabble. The game went through a number of changes and in 1949 was marketed and sold through James Brunot's Production and Marketing Company.

The game's popularity grew slowly. Sales in 1949 were a little over 2000 sets; 1950, 5000 sets; 1951, 8500 sets; and initially in 1952 sales followed the same pattern until suddenly in the middle of the year the game took off, and in the next couple of years Brunot sold 4½ million sets. The reason behind this sudden dramatic increase in sales was Jack Strauss, chairman of Macy's, a large department store in New York, who played Scrabble with some friends and on returning to his store was amazed to find it did not stock the game. He immediately ran a promotion for Scrabble and sales increased sharply.

By 1954 it found its way to Britain. It is now manufactured in 24 different languages, including Arabic, Russian and Greek.

The final board in the 1993 World Scrabble Championships (held biennially since 1991). The reigning champion is Mark Nyman from Leeds, who beat Joel Wapnick from Canada in this game with a score of 417 against 369.

UK Giant Vegetable, Fruit and Flower Championship

A total of 580 specimens of giant produce were exhibited at the 1993 Championship organised by Bernard Lavery, and held at Baytree Nurseries, Spalding. Lavery is the 'supergrower' and holds many of *The Guinness Book of Records* world records for giant fruit and vegetable. He regularly arrives at the events with a lorry laden with carrots, marrows, radishes, tomatoes, cucumbers, etc., of a size and weight that his fellow competitors know will sweep the board.

A total of £17 000 prize money was offered in 1993, including £10 000 given by Thompson & Morgan, seed merchants, for a world record pumpkin using one of three of their seed varieties. It remained unclaimed.

Vin Throup with his new world record onion, which weighed in at 11 lb 8¼ oz. The previous world record was 11 lb 2 oz.

The heaviest pumpkin at the Championship—Reg Rogerson's 413 lb monster.

Type	1993 UK CHAMPIONSHIP Size		Winner	WORLD RECORDS Current record Size		Record holder
Beetroot (length)	153 in	3.89 m	Norman Hosking	–	–	–
Beetroot (weight)	26 lb 10 oz	12.07 kg	Geoff Wheeler	38 lb 8 oz	17.46 kg	Geoff Wheeler, UK
Cabbage	83 lb	37.65 kg	Richard Hope	124 lb	56.24 kg	Bernard Lavery, UK
Carrot (length)	58¼ in	1.48 m	Norman Hosking	202½ in	5.14 m	Bernard Lavery, UK
Carrot (weight)	8 lb 1¾ oz	3.68 kg	Ian Neale	15 lb 7 oz	7 kg	I. Scott, New Zealand
Celery	42 lb	19.05 kg	Bernard Lavery	46 lb 1oz	20.89 kg	Bernard Lavery, UK
Cucumber (length)	29½ in	74.93 cm	Reg Osborne	–	–	–
Cucumber (weight)	17 lb 15¼ oz	8.14 kg	Bernard Lavery	20 lb 1 oz	9.1 kg	Bernard Lavery, UK
Leek	11 lb 10¾ oz	5.29 kg	Vin Throup	12 lb 2 oz	5.5 kg	Paul Harrigan, UK
Marrow	84 lb	38.10 kg	Ken Dade	108 lb 2 oz	49.04 kg	Bernard Lavery, UK
Marrows, two combined	174 lb	78.93 kg	Geoff Wheeler	–	–	–
Melon	8 lb 3¾ oz	3.74 kg	Ken Dade	–	–	–
Onion	11 lb 8¼ oz	5.22 kg	Vin Throup	11 lb 8¼ oz*	5.22 kg	Vin Throup, UK
Onions, three combined	30 lb 7½ oz	13.82 kg	Keith Foster	–	–	–
Parsnip (length)	161¼ in	4.10 m	Norman Hosking	171¾ in	4.36 m	Bernard Lavery, UK
Parsnip (weight)	9 lb 9 oz	4.34 kg	Ian Neale	–	–	–
Pumpkin	413 lb	187.3 kg	Reg Rogerson	836 lb	379.2 kg	Norman Craven, Canada
Pumpkins or squashes, two combined	644 lb	292.1 kg	John Handbury	–	–	–
Radish	17 lb 5½ oz	7.87 kg	Bernard Lavery	37 lb 15 oz	17.21 kg	Litterini family, Australia
Runner bean	28¾ in	73 cm	Geoff Wheeler	43 in	109.2 cm	Faye Etheridge, USA
Squash	345 lb	156.49 kg	John Handbury	821 lb	250.24 kg	L. Stellpflug, USA
Swede	44 lb	19.96 kg	Richard Hope	48 lb 12 oz	22.11 kg	A. Foster, UK
Tomato	4 lb 5 oz	1.96 kg	Peter Welcome	7 lb 12 oz	3.51 kg	Gordan Graham, USA
Tomatoes, three combined	8 lb 9 oz	3.88 kg	Bernard Lavery	–	–	–
Watermelon	6 lb 4½ oz	2.85 kg	Yvonne Grooby	262 lb	118.84 kg	Bill Carson, USA

* New world record set at the 1993 Championship

CHAMPION FLOWER ARRANGER

Ann Stott from Fulwood, Preston, won this title by winning 'Best in Show' at the National Association of Flower Arrangements Societies National Competition in 1993. The inspiration for her design, entitled 'The Secret Place that is Our Own', came when, in her own words, 'I was in the attic looking for something quite different and came across some old books from my childhood. Looking back over the years I remembered how I used to hide my special treasures in a secret place.

'I felt the overall colour scheme had to be grey foliage – to give the feel of age, dust, and cobwebs. The flowers had to be from a garden – so I tried to keep to soft apricot/browns and pale lavenders with most of the roses a deep terracotta/magenta. I included my own large nursery rhyme book, a wooden toy soldier, a rocking horse and several beautiful old books borrowed from friends, along with the abacus and porcelain doll. I added an extra lace frill to the doll's dress which I trimmed with pressed forget-me-nots and small florets of the hedgerow flower – Queen Anne's Lace.

'The rather dilapidated shelves and box was made for me from very old pieces of pine – complete with a small draw that I left half open to represent a forgotten corner of the attic.'

Some of the plant materials she used in the display were roses (Brown Velvet, Vasper, Magenta, Buff Beauty), pale apricot Foxglove, and brown seedheads along the sprays in the top section of the display.

'The Secret Place that is Our Own'.

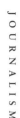

Clare Henderson, *Grimsby Evening Telegraph* reporter, won the 1993 Scoop of the Year award for her world exclusive on Norman Lamont's resignation.

MacKenzie. Our judges argued over the pluses and the minuses and whether the account was in surplus, but no editor we can recall was less in thrall to Government or the establishment and more wedded to the simple philosophy of giving his readers what they wanted. He has been comfortably the most successful newspaper editor of our times.'

What the Papers Say Awards

What the Papers Say is the longest-running regular weekly programme on television. The first edition was broadcast by Granada Television on 5 November 1956 and it is now produced for BBC2. Its awards are made in recognition of special achievement in journalism. The winners are selected by a judging panel made up of senior Granada Television and BBC executives involved in the making of the programme, on the basis of nominations from the journalists who presented the programme in the previous year. The awards vary in category from year to year, although most years there has been a 'Newspaper of the Year' and

(since 1971) a Gerald Barry Award for services to journalism during an individual's career.

Newspaper of the Year
1958 *Daily Mail*
1959 *The Sunday Times*
1961 *Sunday Telegraph*
1965 *Daily Mail*
1967 *The Times*
1968 *Daily Mirror*
1969 *The Guardian*
1970 *The Sun*
1971 *The Guardian*
1972 *Financial Times*
1973 *Washington Post* (US daily newspaper)
Daily Telegraph
1974 *Daily Mail*
1977 *The Daily Telegraph*
1979 *The Guardian*
1981 *Daily Mirror*
1982 *The Observer*
1983 *Financial Times*
1985 *Mail on Sunday*
1986 *The Independent*
1987 *Today*
1989 *Argumenty I. Fakty* (Russian daily newspaper)
1990 *The Guardian*
1991 *Financial Times*
1993 *The Observer*

Gerald Barry Award
Given to an individual for services in journalism
1971 Anthony Mascarenhas
1973 Sir Hugh Cudlipp
1976 Philip Hope-Wallace, *The Guardian*
1977 Terence Kilmartin, *The Observer*
1979 George Hutchinson
1980 James Cameron
1982 David Chipp, Press Association
1983 Ian Aitken, *The Guardian*
1984 Geoffrey Goodman, *Daily Mirror*
1985 Victor Zorza, *The Times*
1987 Alun John
1988 Index on Censorship
1990 Carl Giles
1992 *Oslobodenje* (Bosnia-Herzegovinian daily newspaper printed in Sarajevo)
1993 Jill Tweedie, awarded posthumously

OTHER 1993 AWARDS
Editor Richard Stott, *Today*
Columnist Suzanne Moore, *The Guardian*
Scoop Clare Henderson, *Grimsby Evening Telegraph*
Investigation Robert Peston, *Financial Times*
Cartoonist Steve Bell, *The Guardian*

LIFEBOATS

Royal National Lifeboat Institution Awards

Since the RNLI was founded in 1824, its lifeboats have saved over 124 000 lives. Four main awards are given – Gold, Silver and Bronze Medals and 'Thanks of the Institution on Vellum' (the Bronze was instituted in 1917). The awards are made for acts of outstanding gallantry and skill. The Gold Medal is regarded as the lifeboatman's VC, whilst the Silver is equivalent to the George Medal. To end May 1994, 119 Gold, 1545 Silver, and 747 Bronze Medals, plus 29 Gold and 8 Silver Honorary Medals had been awarded. The 'Thanks on Vellum' award has been made to many thousands of men.

The RNLI has 212 lifeboat stations which provide a 24-hour service to cover search and rescue up to 50 miles out from the coast of the United Kingdom and the Republic of Ireland. It has an active fleet of 278 lifeboats ranging from 16 ft (4.8 m) to 54 ft (16.4 m) in length with a relief fleet of just under 100 additional lifeboats.

First Gold Medal

Captain Charles Howe Fremantle, RN, was Commander of HM Coastguard at Lymington, and was awarded the first Gold Medal for services on 8 March 1824. A Swedish brig, *Carl Jean*, bound from Alicante to Gefle, laden with salt and casks of wine, was seen to be in difficulties broadside on to the shore at Whitepit, near Christchurch, Hants. An account is given in *The Lifeboat* (June 1924) of his actions:

'Captain Fremantle, seeing the brig broadside on the shore, with loss of main mast, and striking on the shore so heavily that it was feared she would go to pieces, thought it practicable to swim on board her, if he could get through the surf, which, fastening a small line to his body, he effected; but the crew were afraid to adopt Captain Fremantle's directions, and (after cutting the boats clear but the decks falling in, and the sea making a breach over her, they filled and were rendered useless) he was compelled, for his own preservation, to leave the wreck, and endeavour to get on shore; which being unable to accomplish by his own exertions, he was hauled on shore by the line, in an exhausted and insensible state. The crew eventually got on shore on the wreck of the mast, after the vessel had parted.'

(In 1829, when in command of the frigate *Challenger*, he was specially selected to take possession of Western Australia, and the port of Fremantle is named after him.)

Captain Charles Howe Fremantle – first RNLI Gold medallist.

Most Gold Medals

Sir William Hillary (1771–1847) not only holds the record for the most Gold Medals but he also founded the Institution. He was awarded the first medal in 1825 (an honorary award) for his services as founder and then three others (1828, 1830 [twice]) for 'gallant and conspicuous service'.

Hillary was a soldier, author and philanthropist who lived in Douglas, the Isle of Man. He witnessed many shipwrecks and felt very determined to do something to diminish the terrible loss of life and property resulting from storms. The year 1822 witnessed a rapid succession of serious wrecks off the Isle of Man in which Hillary assisted in saving 84 lives. It was his experiences in that year that finally impelled him to issue an appeal to the nation. He published a pamphlet in 1823 entitled *An Appeal to the British Nation*, in which he urged every citizen to press for a lifeboat service. Meetings were held and, on 4 March 1824, a resolution was passed to form the 'National Institution for the Preservation of Life from Shipwreck' (the title RNLI was adopted later, in 1854).

The following excerpt from an article in the May 1921 edition of *The Lifeboat* recounts Hillary's achievements:

'. . . In 1825 he helped to rescue sixty-two persons from *The City of Glasgow,* eleven from the brig *Leopard,* and nine from the sloop *Fancy.* His most brilliant service was performed in 1830, when the Royal Mail steamer *St George* was wrecked in Douglas Bay on the 20th November. Her cable parted and she drove on the rocks. The lifeboat was new and not yet ready for service, but Hillary put off, with sixteen other men, and rescued the whole of the twenty-two persons on board. He himself, with three others, was washed overboard. He was rescued with difficulty, and though his chest was crushed and six ribs were broken, he stuck bravely to his task. This is one of the services for which he received the Gold Medal of the Institution.

'In spite of his serious injuries, and, although now sixty-three years of age, he was foremost again in saving life at the wrecks of two vessels in 1831. The next year he again helped to rescue fifty-four men from the Liverpool ship *Parkfield.* This was the last service in which he took part. Altogether he helped to save no fewer than 305 lives from shipwreck, and to the end of his life in 1847, at the age of seventy-eight, he was constantly active in his work on behalf of those in peril on the sea.'

Sir William Hillary was awarded a Gold Medal for his courageous role in rescuing the 22-man crew of The Royal Mail steamer, *St George,* wrecked in Douglas Bay on 20 November 1830.

'*With courage, anything is possible.*'

Motto of Sir William Hillary, founder, RNLI

Most Medals

Henry George Blogg.

Henry George Blogg (1876–1954) holds the record for having been awarded the most medals: the Gold Medal three times (1917, 1927, 1941) and the Silver Medal four times (1932, 1933, 1939, 1941). An account of his gallantry is given in his obituary which appeared in *The Lifeboat* (September 1954):

'. . . His first gold medal was awarded for the rescue of the entire crew of eleven of the Swedish steamer *Fernebo*, which had struck a mine during a gale on the 9th of January, 1917. The *Fernebo* was blown in half. The Cromer life-boat, which had only just returned from a service to a Greek vessel, was immediately launched again in circumstances which led the District Inspector who reported the service to say of Coxswain Blogg: "It was his own remarkable personality and really great qualities of leadership which magnetised tired men into launching, and when the boat was launched it was the consummate skill with which he launched her and the encouragement he gave his crew which brought their efforts to such a successful conclusion."

'Ten years later, on the 22nd of November, 1927, the Cromer life-boat rescued fifteen men from the Dutch tanker *Georgia*, which had broken in half on the Haisborough Sands. The service lasted twenty hours and Coxswain Blogg was awarded a clasp to his gold medal.

'Coxswain Blogg's third gold medal was awarded for services in September, 1941, in which 88 lives were rescued from six steamers of a convoy which had been wrecked on the Haisborough Sands.

'Coxswain Blogg's silver medals were awarded for the rescue of 30 men from the Italian steamer *Monte Nevoso* in 1932; for the rescue of 2 men from the barge *Sepoy* of Dover in 1933; for the rescue of the crew of 29 of the Greek steamer *Mount Ida* in 1939; and for the rescue of the crew of 44 of the steamer *English Trader* in 1941.

'Coxswain Blogg was also awarded the George Cross and the British Empire Medal, and he was presented with a gold watch by the Queen of Holland.'

The barge, the *Sepoy* of Dover, during the storm on 13 December 1933 in which Coxswain Blogg rescued two men and was awarded a Silver Medal for his actions.

'These are among the bravest and most skilful mariners that exist. Let a gale rise and swell into a storm; let a sea run that might appal the stoutest heart that ever beat . . . let them hear through the angry roar the signal guns of a ship in distress, and these men spring up with an activity so dauntless, so valiant and heroic, that the world cannot surpass it.

Charles Dickens, *Household Words*, 1850

LITERACY

Plain English Campaign Awards

Plain English Campaign is an independent organisation, launched in 1979, which fights to stamp out all forms of gobbledygook – legalese, small print and bureaucratic language. The Campaign is funded by its professional services which includes editing, writing, design and training. The awards have been presented annually since 1980, and, in the early years, prizes such as plastic wastebins and bags of tripe were given. Since 1984, the writers of the year's most incomprehensible rubbish have received the Golden Bull award – high-quality plastic trophies from Accrington.

In 1993 there were three categories: Plain English Awards for clear communications; Golden Bulls for gobbledygook; and Media Awards for the clearest television, radio and newspaper reports. A new award was also introduced – the John Smith's No Nonsense Award for the worst recorded public gaffe or case of gobbledygook on television or radio. The winner received a year's supply of John Smith's 'Draught in a can' bitter.

The following is a list of awards made within each category in 1993, including the Plain English Campaign's comments:

THE MEDIA AWARDS

Friends, members and the general public all contribute to these awards by contacting the Plain English Campaign to let them know which programmes and papers explain the news most clearly:

Best national television news **News at Ten**, ITN

Best regional television news **Spotlight**, BBC South West

Best national radio station **News 93**, BBC Radio 1

Best regional radio station **BBC Radio Newcastle**

Best national newspaper **Financial Times**

Best regional newspaper **The Birmingham Evening Mail**

Plain English Awards

INLAND REVENUE: 'ARE YOU PAYING TOO MUCH TAX ON YOUR SAVINGS?'

This leaflet encourages people on low incomes to claim tax back on their savings. In just 12 sentences, it sets out the tax position for savings, explains what action you can take and tells you how to get more information. The humorous cartoons, the friendly language and the simple fact that the leaflet is so short make it one of the least daunting documents you will ever come across. As a result, the Inland Revenue received nearly a quarter of a million claims.

BRITISH LUNG FOUNDATION: 'THE FACTS'

The British Lung Foundation is the only UK charity involved with all lung diseases. These ten leaflets, with individual titles such as 'Asthma' and 'Smoking and Your Lungs', are designed to meet the huge demand for information about lung diseases and related topics. Each leaflet makes the most of the available space, and breaks up the wording with helpful diagrams and straightforward headings. The text is concise and highly informative, with all technical terms carefully explained.

EMPLOYMENT SERVICE: 'JOBSEEKER'S CHARTER'

With full-colour pictures and a crisp, open layout, this booklet clearly explains how the Employment Service helps people to find work, helps to prepare them for work, supports them while they are unemployed and gives them advice on benefits and other matters. The text is broken up well into short sentences and neat lists – and the wording uses only everyday language with a personal style and plenty of active verbs.

WITHINGTON HOSPITAL (MANCHESTER): 'INFORMATION FOR PATIENTS HAVING ERCP'

Members of Withington Hospital's Gastrointestinal Service actually discussed with patients how to produce this information on Endoscopic Retrograde Cholangio-Pancreatography. The result is a short, well-ordered leaflet which gives exactly the information that patients want. Unlike many documents produced by hospitals, the leaflet uses a

THE NO NONSENSE AWARD

This was given to former England cricket boss, Ted Dexter, who was considered to have made the most baffling remark of the year while trying to explain the second test loss to the Australians in June. It was unanimously voted as the worst case of gobbledygook broadcast this year. 'Maybe we are in the wrong sign,' he mused. 'Maybe Venus is in the wrong juxtaposition with something else. I don't know.'

lot of active verbs by referring to 'you' and 'we' instead of 'the patient' and 'the hospital'. This makes the text warm and personal rather than cold and clinical. And there is no medical jargon.

METROPOLITAN POLICE SERVICE: 'ADVICE FOR VICTIMS OF SEXUAL ASSAULT' AND 'OUR PERFORMANCE'

The advice leaflet is a superb example of how to set out sensitive information clearly. The text is excellent – short sentences, short paragraphs, plenty of the personal pronouns 'you' and 'we', and no wasted words. And the design is practical, with well-laid-out lists, 'soft' use of realistic colour photographs and helpful blue boxes that contain key information. Encouraging victims of sexual assault to go to the police or to a hospital, and reassuring them about the procedures they will have to go through, is not easy. But the leaflet manages this with dignity.

'OUR PERFORMANCE'

The Metropolitan Police Service charter. It sets out the Service's principles, role procedures and targets, and asks the public for help, support and opinions. The high-quality design shows that the Metropolitan Police takes the charter seriously. Although the booklet is packed with information, it is easy to read because the wording is so concise.

SHEFFIELD CITY COUNCIL: 'CLAIM FORM FOR COUNCIL BENEFITS'

Many local authorities try to save money by producing their benefit forms in as few pages as possible. However, if a form is squashed up with small type and not enough words to explain things properly, people are less likely to fill it in correctly. This can waste a great deal of money. Sheffield City Council has taken the time and trouble to spread the questions on its benefit form over 12 pages. This has been given space to use a good typesize, to set each section out clearly, to have the right-size box for each answer, to use the right number of words for each question and even to have a page of explanation at the start. It has used colour extremely well to break up the sections, pick out the answer boxes and highlight key information. The wording is unambiguous, straightforward and helpful.

Help the Aged: 'Better Hearing'

This booklet starts with a simple checklist to help you judge whether you might be losing your hearing. After explaining what to do if you think you may have a problem, 'Better Hearing' goes on to explain all about hearing aids. Clear diagrams, an uncomplicated design and sensible, down-to-earth text combine to give an honest account of modern aids.

The Golden Bulls

In a document sent to staff representatives, UNISON Regional Secretary Brian Devine struggled to get to the point

'In examining the intended profile for the post of Information Officer the RMT has been mindful of the residual posts of Organising Assistant the duties and responsibilities attaching thereto and the range of support now required to both the service group and functional elements of the regional structure. With the exception of the IT User Support responsibility within the aforementioned profile and the function of Committee Administration historically embraced by the Organising Assistant remit (both of which would demand specific provision within the administrative resource) it is considered the better option that posts of Organising Assistant (or similar designation) be retained and that an appropriate job profile be designed; this to include items (i)–(iv) in the Information Officer profile and the requirement of generic support to the staffing and lay structures established. In these circumstances I am recommending that a post of Information Officer not be determined at this time and that the requisite number of Organising Assistant posts be reviewed.'

The Value for Money Unit of the NHS Directorate wrote this priceless gem, which was sent out by the Welsh Office

'**Bed** A device or arrangement that may be used to permit a patient to lie down when the need to do so is a consequence of the patient's condition rather than a need for active intervention such as examination, diagnostic investigation, manipulative treatment, obstetric delivery or transport. Beds, couches, or trolleys are also counted as hospital beds where: a) used regularly to permit a patient to lie down rather than for merely examination or transport, (e.g. in a day surgery ward). b) used whilst attending for a specific short procedure taking an hour or less such as endoscopy, provided that such devices are used only because of the active intervention and not because of the patient's condition. c) used regularly as a means of support for patients needing a lengthy procedure such as renal dialysis (includes special chairs etc.). d) used regularly to allow patients to lie down after sedation. NB: A device specifically and solely for the purpose of delivery should not be counted as a bed.'

Southwark Council's Legal Services Department paints a clear picture for its leaseholders

'Lessees decorating obligation (4) To paint with two coats of paint (the paint for the external work to be of a colour and quality to be approved by the Council's Borough Valuer) in a workmanlike manner all the wood iron and other parts of the premises heretofore or usually painted as to the external work in every third successive year and in the last year of the term hereby granted and as to the internal work in every fifth successive year and in the last year of the term hereby granted the time in each case being computed from the commencement of the term hereby granted and after every internal painting to grain varnish distemper wash stop whiten and colour all such parts as have previously been so dealt with and to repaper the parts usually papered with suitable paper of good quality.'

This is how Thorn Security Ltd warns customers that it may have to put up charges for its intruder alarm systems

'(6)(a) In the event of increases in the cost of labour materials or overhead expenses in carrying out the Company's obligations under this Agreement (of the existence and amount of which increase the certificate of the Secretary or other authorised official of the Company shall be conclusive evidence) or in the event of the position of new taxes or the revising of existing taxes the Company shall be entitled to make an increase in the Annual Charge payable hereunder (whether or not such Charge has been paid in advance) such increase to come into effect (when notification to an official body may be required) on the date such notification becomes effective or (when no such notification is required) on the day appointed by the Company whereupon the amount of such increase as applies to the unexpired balance of any period in respect of which any Annual Charge has been paid in advance shall become immediately due and payable.'

In Regulation 10 of 'Management of Health & Safety at Work', the Health & Safety Commission managed to cause confusion among the workers

'(2) Paragraph (1) shall apply to a self-employed person who is working in the undertaking of an employer or a self-employed person as it applies to employees from an outside undertaking who are working therein; and the reference in that paragraph to the employer of any employees from an outside undertaking who are working in the undertaking of an employer or a self-employed person and the references in the said paragraph to employees from an outside undertaking who are working in the undertaking of an employer of a self-employed person shall be construed accordingly.'

The names have been changed to protect the innocent in this letter from The Contributions Agency

'In accordance with Regulation 3(2) of the Social Security (Contributions) Regulations 1979, I hereby give notice to J. Bloggs, M. Bean, C. Chaplin, B. Keaton and Smith & Jones being the secondary contributor, that I am satisfied that the greatest part of the earnings paid to, or for the benefit of, the above employees in respect of employed earner's employment by Smith & Jones is normally paid at intervals of greater length than the shortest interval at which any part of such earnings are normally paid or treated as paid. Accordingly, the length of the earnings period for the purposes of payment of earnings related contributions shall hereafter be the length of that longer interval, that is to say, the earnings period shall be the period of quarterly.'

From the City of Liverpool's Director of Housing and Consumer Services

'In many areas it is unlikely that successful housing renewal programmes can be implemented without increasing the viability of housing association rehabilitation, and in recognising the contribution that housing associations can make particularly in area based programmes, the priority which should be provided when an area is declared should be reflected in an enhancement of housing association funding for rehabilitation.

MAGIC

The Magic Circle Awards

On l July 1905 at Pinoli's restaurant in London, some 23 amateur and professional magicians assembled with the intention of forming a club – The Magic Circle. Later that year, the inaugural meeting was held in a room above the Green Man Public House in Berwick Street, London. In 1906 Nevil Maskelyne edited the first issue of the Society's magazine, *The Magic Circular*, which bore the signs of the zodiac on its cover, and these became the Society's emblem, coupled with its motto, *Indocilis Privata Loqui* (roughly translated: 'not apt to disclose secrets').

In 1970 the Magic Circle introduced an award, The Maskelyne, a trophy sculpted in the form of a head and named after its founder member, to be presented to the magician who had done most for the art of magic, whether in the form of performing, presentation, invention, writing or any other activity which served British magic. The winner is chosen by an awards committee which consists of members of the Magic Circle who are selected by the Magic Circle Council.

WINNERS
The Maskelyne
1970 Robert Harbin
1971 David Nixen
1972 Ali Bongo
1973 John Nevil Maskelyne
1974 Peter Warlock
1978 Goodliffe Neale
1988 Paul Daniels
1989 John Fisher
1990 Gil Leaney
1991 Alan Shaxon
1992 Jeffery Atkins
1993 Harry Devano

The Magic Circle also makes a number of other awards:

The Carlton Award
Arthur Carlton Philps achieved fame during the early part of this century as a 'top of the bill' performer of comedy

MR. MASKELYNE.

Nevil Maskelyne, founder member of The Magic Circle.

magic. His unique appearance, dress and build earned him the title 'The Human Hairpin', outclassing his contemporaries both technically and in his mastery of the throwaway line. This award was instigated in 1989 for comedy and the winner receives a framed print of Philps, the magician. The 1993 winner was Ali Bongo.

The John Nevil Maskelyne Prize
Of the funds administered by The Magic Circle, the John Nevil Maskelyne Memorial Fund provides within its objects a £100 prize for noteworthy contributions by members or non-members of The Magic Circle to the art

of literature of magic. The 1993 winner was Ruth Brandon.

Young Magician of the Year
Inaugurated in 1961, this biennial award is made to an individual between the age of 14 and 18 who receives a trophy. The 1993 winner was Simon Lee.

Cecil Lyle Award
This award is given to the writer of the best trick or illusion printed in *The Magic Circular* during the year. The winner receives a trophy, presented by Cecil Lyle, in the form of a large watch hanging from a large ribbon. The 1993 winner was Richard Wiseman.

MEDICINE

Nobel Prize

Awarded annually since 1901 for outstanding achievement in the field of medicine and physiology, this prize was endowed by Alfred Nobel in 1896. (See separate section, Nobel Prizes.)

1901 Emil von Behring (GER). Work on serum therapy, especially its application against diphtheria

1902 Sir Ronald Ross (UK). Work on malaria, showing how it enters an organism

1903 Niels Ryberg Finsen (DEN). Light radiation treatment of skin diseases

1904 Ivan Petrovic Pavlov (USSR). Work on physiology of digestion

1905 Robert Koch (GER). Investigations and discoveries in relation to tuberculosis

1906 Camillo Golgi (ITA) and **Santiago Ramon y Cajal** (SPA). Work on structure of nervous system

1907 Charles Louis Alphonse Laveran (FRA). Work on role played by protozoa in causing diseases

1908 Ilja Il'jic Mechnikov (USSR) and **Paul Ehrlich** (GER). Work on immunity

1909 Emil Theodor Kocher (SWI). Work on physiology, pathology and surgery of thyroid gland

1910 Albrecht Kossel (GER). Cellular chemistry research

1911 Allvar Gullstrand (SWE). Work on the dioptics of the eye

1912 Alexis Carrel (FRA). Work on vascular suture and transplantation of blood-vessels and organs

1913 Charles Robert Richet (FRA). Work on anaphylaxis

1914 Robert Bárány (AUT). Work on vestibular apparatus of inner ear

1915–18 No awards

1919 Jules Bordet (BEL). Discoveries relating to immunity system

1920 August Steenberger Krogh (DEN). Discovery of capillary motor-regulating mechanism

1921 No award

1922 Archibald Vivian Hill (UK). Discovery relating to production of heat in the muscle

Otto Meyerhof (GER). Metabolism of lactic acid in muscles

On Christmas night in 1891, a young girl lay dying of diphtheria in a Berlin clinic. Dr Emil von Behring injected an experimental antitoxin derived from the diphtheria bacillus into the child. The girl's swift recovery seemed a miracle. Within three years 20 000 children in Berlin had been inoculated with a vaccination against diphtheria. For this remarkable achievement Behring (seen above left) was awarded the first Nobel Prize for Medicine in 1901.

1923 Sir Frederick Grant Banting and John James Richard Macleod (Can). Discovery of insulin

1924 Willem Einthoven (Neth). Discovery of electrocardiogram mechanism

1925 No award

1926 Johannes Andreas Grib Fibiger (Den). Cancer research

1927 Julius Wagner von Jauregg (Aut). Malaria inoculation in treatment of dementia paralytica

1928 Charles Jules Henri Nicolle (Fra). Work on typhus

1929 Christiaan Eijkman (Neth). Discovery of anti-neuritic vitamin

   Sir Frederick Gowland Hopkins (UK). Discovery of growth-stimulating vitamins

1930 Karl Landsteiner (US). Discovery of human blood groups

1931 Otto Heinrich Warburg (Ger). Discovery of nature and mode of action of respiratory enzyme

1932 Sir Charles Scott Sherrington and Lord Edgar Douglas Adrian (UK). Discoveries regarding functions of neurons

1933 Thomas Hunt Morgan (USA). Discoveries concerning role played by chromosomes in heredity

1934 George H. Whipple, George Richards Minot and William P. Murphy (USA). Discoveries concerning liver therapy in cases of anaemia

1935 Hans Spemann (Ger). Discovery of organiser effect in embryonic development

1936 Sir Henry Hallett Dale (UK) and Otto Loewi (Aut). Discoveries relating to chemical transmission of nerve impulses

1937 Albert Szent-Györgyi (Hun). Discoveries in connection with biological combustion

1938 Corneille Jean Heymans (Bel). Discovery of role played by sinus and aortic mechanisms in regulation of respiration

1939 Gerhard Domagk (Ger). Discovery of antibacterial effect of prontosil (Award declined – Hitler forbade Germans to accept Nobel prizes)

1940–42 No awards

The longest delay for the award of a Nobel Prize is 55 years. Francis Peyton Rous from America, who discovered a strain of cancer virus in 1910, was not awarded the Prize until 1966 at the ripe old age of 87.

1943 Henrik Carl Peter Dam (Den). Discovery of vitamin K

   Edward Adelbert Doisy (USA). Discovery of chemical nature of vitamin K

1944 Joseph Erlanger and Herbert Spencer Gasser (USA). Discoveries relating to highly differentiated functions of single nerve fibres

1945 Sir Alexander Fleming, Ernst Boris Chain and Lord Howard W. Florey (UK). Discovery of penicillin and its curative value in infectious diseases

1946 Hermann Joseph Muller (USA). Discovery of production of mutations by X-ray irradiation

1947 Carl Ferdinand Cori and Gerty Theresa Cori (née Radnitz) (USA). Discovery of catalytic conversion of glycogen

   Bernardo Alberto Houssay (Arg). Discovery of pituitary hormone function in sugar metabolism

1948 Paul Hermann Müller (Swi). Discovery of properties of DDT

1949 Walter Rudolf Hess (Swi). Discovery of functional organisation of midbrain as a co-ordinator of activities of internal organs

   Antonio Egas Moniz (Por). Discovery of therapeutic value of leucotomy in certain psychoses

1950 Edward Calvin Kendall, Philip S. Hench (USA) and Tadeus Reichstein (Swi). Discoveries relating to hormones of adrenal cortex, their structure and biological effects

1951 Max Theiler (SA). Discoveries concerning yellow fever and how to combat it

1952 Selman Abraham Waksman (USA). Discovery of streptomycin, the first antibiotic effective against tuberculosis

1953 Sir Hans Adolf Krebs (UK). Discovery of citric acid cycle

   Fritz Albert Lipmann (USA). Discovery of co-enzyme A and its importance for intermediary metabolism

1954 John Franklin Enders, Thomas Huckle Weller and Frederick Chapman Robbins (USA). Discovery of ability of poliomyelitis viruses to grow in various types of tissue cultures

1955 Axel Hugo Theodor Theorell (Swe). Discoveries concerning nature and mode of action of oxidation enzymes

1956 André Frédéric Cournand, Dickinson W. Richards (USA) and Werner Forssmann (Ger). Discoveries concerning heart catheterisation and pathological changes in circulatory system

1957 Daniel Bovet (Ita). Discoveries relating to synthetic compounds that inhibit action of certain body substances, and especially their action on vascular

system and skeletal muscles

1958 George Wells Beadle and Edward Lawrie Tatum (USA). Discovery that genes act by regulating definite chemical events

   Joshua Lederberg (USA). Discoveries concerning genetic recombination

1959 Severo Ochoa and Arthur Kornberg (USA). Discovery of production of artificial nucleic acids

1960 Sir Frank MacFarlane Burnet (Aus) and Sir Peter Brian Medawar (UK). Research into acquired immunity in tissue transplants

1961 Georg von Békésy (USA). Discoveries of physical mechanism of stimulation within inner ear

1962 Francis Harry Compton Crick, Maurice Hugh Frederick Wilkins (UK) and James Dewey Watson (USA). Discoveries concerning molecular structure of DNA

1963 Sir John Carew Eccles (Aus), Sir Alan Lloyd Hodgkin and Sir Andrew Fielding Huxley (UK). Research into transmission of nerve impulses along a nerve fibre

1964 Konrad Bloch (USA) and Feodor Lynen (Ger). Discoveries concerning mechanism and regulation of cholesterol and fatty acid metabolism

1965 François Jacob, André Lwoff and Jacques Monod (Fra). Research into regulatory activities of body cells

1966 Francis Peyton Rous (USA). Discovery of tumour-inducing viruses

   Charles Brenton Huggins (USA). Discoveries concerning hormonal treatment of prostatic cancer

1967 Ragnar A. Granit (Swe), Haldan Keffer Hartline and George Wald (USA). Discoveries concerning primary physiological and chemical visual processes in the eye

1968 Robert W. Holley, H. Gobind Khorana and Marshall W. Nirenberg (USA). Interpretation of genetic code and its function in protein synthesis

1969 Max Delbrück, Alfred D. Hershey and Salvador E. Luria (USA). Research into viruses and viral diseases

1970 Sir Bernard Katz (UK), Ulf von Euler (Swe) and Julius Axelrod (USA). Discoveries concerning humoral transmitters in nerve terminals and mechanism for their storage, release and inactivation

1971 Earl W. Sutherland (USA). Discoveries concerning action of hormones

1972 Gerald M. Edelman (USA) and Rodney R. Porter (UK). Discoveries concerning chemical structure of antibodies

1973 Karl von Frisch (Ger), Konrad

Lorenz (Aut) and **Nikolaas Tinbergen** (UK). Research into animal behaviour patterns

1974 **Albert Claude, George E. Palade** (USA) and **Christian de Duve** (Bel). Discoveries concerning structural and functional organisation of cells

1975 **David Baltimore, Renato Dulbecco** and **Howard Martin Temin** (USA). Discoveries concerning interaction between tumour viruses and genetic material of the cell

1976 **Baruch S. Blumberg** and **D. Carleton Gajdusek** (USA). Discoveries concerning origin and spread of infectious diseases

1977 **Roger Guillemin** and **Andrew V. Schally** (USA). Discoveries concerning brain peptide hormone production

Rosalyn S. Yalow (USA). Development of radio-immunoassay of peptide hormones

1978 **Werner Arber** (Swi), **Daniel Nathans** and **Hamilton O. Smith** (USA). Discovery of restriction enzymes and their application to problems of molecular genetics

1979 **Allan M. Cormack** (USA) and **Sir Godfrey N. Hounsfield** (UK). Development of computer-assisted tomography scanning

1980 **Baruj Benacerraf** (USA), **Jean Dausset** (Fra) and **George D. Snell** (USA). Discoveries concerning genetic control of the immune response to foreign substances

1981 **Roger W. Sperry** (USA). Discoveries concerning functional specialisation of cerebral hemispheres

David H. Hubel (USA) and **Torsten N. Wiesel** (Swe). Discoveries concerning visual information processing by the brain

1982 **Sune K. Bergström, Bengt I. Samuelsson** (Swe) and **Sir John R. Vane** (UK). Discoveries concerning prostaglandins and related biologically active substances

1983 **Barbara McClintock** (USA). Discovery of mobile plant genes which affect heredity

1984 **Niels K. Jerne** (UK/Den), **Georges J. F. Kohler** (Ger) and **Cesar Milstein** (Arg). Technique for producing monoclonal antibodies

1985 **Michael S. Brown** and **Joseph L. Goldstein** (USA). Discoveries concerning cell receptors involved in cholesterol metabolism

1986 **Stanley Cohen** (USA) and **Rita Levi-Montalcini** (Ita/USA). Discovery of chemical agents that help regulate cell growth

1987 **Susumu Tonegawa** (Jap). Research into genetic aspects of antibodies

1988 **Sir James W. Black** (UK), **Gertrude B. Ellison** and **George H. Hitchings** (USA). Development of new classes of drugs

1989 **Michael J. Bishop** and **Harold E. Varmus** (USA). Cancer research

1990 **Joseph E. Murray** and **E. Donnall Thomas** (USA). Discoveries concerning organ and cell transplantation in treatment of human disease

1991 **Erwin Neher** and **Bert Sakmann** (Ger). Cell biology, particularly understanding of disease mechanisms

1992 **Edmond Fischer** and **Edwin Krebs** (USA). Discovery (in the 1950s) of a cellular regulatory mechanism used to control a variety of metabolic processes

1993 **Richard Roberts** (UK) and **Phillip Sharp** (USA). Discovering how genes are arranged within DNA genetic material

Medicine/Psychology Nobel Prize Winners by Country

Country	Total	Year first awarded Prize
USA	72	1930
UK	22	1902
Germany*	14	1901
France	8	1907
Austria	6	1914
Sweden	6	1911
Denmark	5	1903
Switzerland	5	1909
Belgium	4	1919
Argentina	2	1947
Canada	2	1923
Italy	2	1906
Netherlands	2	1924
USSR	2	1904
Hungary	1	1937
Japan	1	1987
Portugal	1	1949
South Africa	1	1951
Spain	1	1906
Total	**157**	

*Includes both West and East Germany
Notes
1 Nobel Prizes are actually awarded to individuals rather than the countries from which they come.
2 Figures include 1993 prizewinners.

1993 Family Doctor of the Year

Jointly sponsored by *Practical Parenting* and *General Practitioner*, readers were asked to nominate doctors who had shown outstanding care and understanding, particularly towards children. From the many entries, a shortlist of 12 was drawn up, and from this an overall winner, Dr Kenneth Harper, aged 36, from Stoke-on-Trent, Staffs, was selected.

He had been nominated by Alison Blundred who praised his devotion to her daughter Natalie who is a Down's Syndrome child. Her nomination letter stated:

'I am writing with the hope of rewarding and thanking my wonderful GP. I have come into contact with many doctors over the years but none so caring and thoughtful as Dr Harper.

'Unlike so many doctors, he always talks to Natalie and explains what he is going to do. So many others have proceeded to examine her without a word and upset her.

'Dr Harper has never made me feel a nuisance and he always has a smile and sense of humour which I and many others appreciate.

'His genuine care, understanding and patience with Natalie and myself have made the past four years a lot easier.'

WORK ON THE COMMON COLD VIRUS LEADS TO 1993 NOBEL PRIZE

English-born Dr Richard Roberts and American Dr Phillip Sharp, working independently in America, came to a similar conclusion in 1977. Until that year it was thought that plant and animal genes were composed of continuous segments of DNA. The two doctors proved that far from being continuous they are broken up by pieces of DNA with no obvious purpose. Both men made this discovery while working on a common cold virus. Initially, scientists were not convinced of their claims, but soon 'split genes' were found in plants and animal cells everywhere.

This discovery contributed to work on understanding evolution. It was originally thought that random mutations in genes lead to gradual changes. However, because of this discovery, it became clear that mutations might also occur by gene segments shuffling about, thereby leading to much more rapid changes.

Dr Roberts, on receiving the $825 000 prize said: 'Everybody thought that genes were laid out in exactly the same way, and so it came as a tremendous surprise at the time. No one had anticipated it, it was one of the discoveries that come once in a lifetime, where dogma is completely overthrown.'

MEMORY FEATS

World Memory Championships

Dominic O'Brien retained his title of World Memory Champion in the second championships in 1993 with a total of 92.5 points out of a possible 100, finishing first in seven out of the ten events. He competed against 15 other contestants in events ranging from the memorisation of a randomly created 2000-digit number to the memorisation of 100 names and faces.

Dominic O'Brien's outstanding feats included the memorisation of eight shuffled packs of playing cards in one hour, the memorisation of 1002 binary digits in half an hour and, perhaps most impressively of all, the creation of a new world record by remembering 100 numbers which were read out at two-second intervals. He did this not once, but twice, making no mistakes. At the end of the 19th century, the best score achieved in this last feat was only 17. The previous world record, achieved by someone who had practised hard for many years, was 83. After the event, the BBC carried out some filming and this event was reconstructed. Dominic correctly recalled 104 digits, thus exceeding his previous record!

In the last event – memorising a pack of shuffled cards – Dominic's time was 119 seconds, way outside his own personal record of 55 seconds, but it was the end of a long hard weekend of events! Dominic started committing things to memory as a hobby but has now turned professional and spends his time developing new mnemonic schemes for committing numbers, objects or cards to memory.

The world record for memorising a single pack of shuffled cards is held by Mamoon Tariq from Pakistan who undertook the feat in 44.62 seconds at the School of Business, Florida Institute of Technology, USA, on 14 June 1993.

Dominic O'Brien, world memory champion, can memorise a randomly shuffled deck of cards in 55.4 seconds.

RESULTS

Memorisation event	Time allowed	Winner	Total achieved
1 2000-digit number: contestants recall this number by writing it down.	1 h	Dominic O'Brien	900 digits
2 100 names and faces: faces are presented in a certain order with names underneath. They are then presented in a new order without names. Contestants mark names on the new sheets.	15 min	Jonathan Hancock	100 names
3 List of 500 words: words are presented in columns of 50 and numbered. Contestants recall words in sequence by writing them down.	15 min	Dominic O'Brien	125 words
4 100-digit number spoken aloud at two-second intervals: recall by writing down and scored as number of digits correctly recalled before a mistake is made.	–	Dominic O'Brien	100 digits
5 12 packs of randomly-shuffled cards: contestants memorise as many cards as they can.	1 h	Dominic O'Brien	416 cards
6 Speed – 200-digit number: recall by writing numbers down.	5 min	Dominic O'Brien	132 digits
7 Paintings and images: contestants are given 24 images to memorise. They are then given a further 100 images of which the original 24 are a part. As each image is presented, contestants are asked to note whether or not it has appeared previously.	20 min	Creighton Carvello	18 images
8 Unknown text: contestants are given 40 lines of text to memorise and write down, including punctuation (see opposite).	15 min	Jonathan Hancock	12 lines
9 2000 randomly-generated binary numbers: contestants recall this number by writing it down.	1 h	Dominic O'Brien	1002 digit
10 A pack of shuffled cards: contestants are handed a shuffled pack of cards and timed to see who is the first to memorise and correctly recall the cards.	–	Dominic O'Brien	119 secon

The following championship results show how astounding Dominic is in comparison with some of the other competitors in scores and timings achieved (inaccuracies incurred time penalties):

Final placing	1 2000 digits	2 100 names	3 500 words	4 100 digits	5 12 packs	6 200 digits	7 24 images	8 40 lines	9 2000 binary	10 speed cards
1 D O'Brien	900	74	125	100	416	132	16	6	1002	119 s
2 J Hancock	160	100	114	35	312	17	15.5	12	200	189 s
3 P Bond	460	43.5	49	16	104	75	16	7	600	24 min
4 C Carvello	360	83.5	86.5	11	104	19	18	3	–	229 s
5 A Levy	120	86	42	7	53	36	17	9	162	13 min
6 K Wilshire	110	45.5	48.5	23	0	57	14.5	7	185	12 min
7 T Morton	320	62.5	87	8	0	57	9	3	–	17 min
8 N Diot	90	45	74	11	78	30	15	10	64	11 min

Grand totals

Each event scored 10 points for the winner, 9 for second placing, 8 for third, and so on

Dominic O'Brien	92.5
Jonathan Hancock	80.5
Philip Bond	67.5
Creighton Carvello	66.0
Alastair Levy	60.0
Ken Wilshire	54.5
Tom Morton	53.5
Natasha Diot	50.5

Alastair Levy is the 14-year-old world junior champion.

Paul Charles Morphy, world chess champion 1858–62.

An American chess master, Paul Charles Morphy (1837–84), was generally acknowledged at the age of 21 to be the greatest chess player in the world. He had an astounding memory which allowed him to achieve amazing success playing chess blindfold. Morphy was able, in a set of eight games of chess played simultaneously against eight different opponents, to memorise the positions of 256 chessmen which included having to revise his mental picture of each board after every move. He also had to plan his own attack and defences. The result of this amazing feat was to win six games, tie in one and lose one.

MEMORISATION OF UNKNOWN TEXT

Oxford University student Jonathan Hancock won the event with a text written especially for the championships by Ted Hughes, Poet Laureate. Jonathan memorised the first 12 lines, together with punctuation, in 15 minutes.

Anamnemonicker

A Knight in armour falls pushed off his star
By the crow of a cock. A wedding ring
Bounced off a coffin but a finger caught it.
A rapier dances away shining. A black
Cloak is flung aside while the owner
Flogs himself with nettles in a garden.
An *ignis fatui* face, pale, gray bearded,
Ponders a tuft of primroses. Too late
For the hoop of steel. Too late for the
    nightbird
Hurrying into the snare. A corpse in steel
Toppled by drunkards, calls from the foot of a
    cliff.
A sulphur coffin, the crypt's candelabra,
Warms the worm which serves as daily bread

For the mole. A different worm is dinner
To the carp which serves as brighter shadow
To the half-dressed and half-witted. A pair
Of Siamese Twins hunt with a pedigree
    Dachshund.
What was a passport is a twist of paper
Hiding a fiery poem and the egg of a blowfly.
Prison bars bend under a trumpet blast
Blown by the mask of a black knight who
    butchers
The ring-finger with a hammer of nettles.
A pigeon vomits a lily and a virgin
Hides her face in a bible of lies. A dagger
Slashes the air around its resting place.
Suddenly carves a nun out of nothing.
A rose devours itself and drops fragments.
A dark horse broods crow's eggs in a mare's
    nest.
It all comes out in a mirror. Even the dog
Dashes from its kennel, sniffs at a king
Sleeping on flowers bewailed by a laughing
    woman.
A mouse chokes on its fable. A royal stag

Stumbles under its arrow. The watchful flute
Refuses to make music for dancing weasels.
A cup of blood quenches heaven. Shackles
Are shaken at fear. Burbling, the new baby
Is invulnerable but the rat must perish.
A crown in a back pocket hurts as bad
As a boil that must be lanced. Maybe the
    ship
Will take it all away. A dripping sponge
Mops at the blood. But an angel adjusts
Its binoculars and all is recorded.
The army marches after a mad owl.
A sword burst into wild flowers, then flames,
Then melts, pouring into a mould. A letter
Dipped in ocean opens the two-faced door
To the serpent's fang that sleeps hidden
In a vial of tears wept by weeds.
A skull referees for two madmen
Fighting over a phantom . . . two idiots
Going off their heads in the front row.
A water skeeter becalms the storm brewing
Its pearl in the dregs of a teacup. A secretary
Reads out the minutes to a row of tombs.

Ted Hughes
Poet Laureate

MUSEUMS

Top 10 UK Museums and Galleries

		No. of visitors
1	**British Museum**, London	5 823 427
2	**National Gallery**, London	3 882 371
3	**Tate Gallery**, London	1 760 091
4	**Natural History Museum**, London	1 700 000
5	**Science Museum**, London	1 277 417
6	**Victoria and Albert Museum**, London	1 072 092
7	**Royal Academy**, London	922 135
8	**National Museum of Photography**, Bradford	853 784
9	**Glasgow Art Gallery and Museum**	796 380
10	**Jorvik Viking Centre**, York, N. Yorks	752 586

Source: English Tourist Board, 1993

British Museum's Topselling Postcards

The list of bestselling cards contains predominantly Egyptian subjects. The first four appear each year at the head of the list, with the Rosetta Stone card permanently at number one.

1 The Rosetta Stone
2 The front of the British Museum
3 The Gayer-Anderson cat
4 'Ginger', sand-dried body in reconstructed burial
5 Rembrandt drawing of Girl Sleeping, Rembrandt exhibition
6 View of the Egyptian Gallery
7 Wall painting 'Fowling in the Marshes'
8 Painted skeleton, The Skeleton at the Feast exhibition
9 Weighing of the heart, from Book of the Dead
10 Discus thrower, Roman marble copy of Greek bronze
11 Hieroglyphs, from temple of Ramesses II
12 Atomic apocalypse, Skeleton at the Feast exhibition
13 Mummy of an Egyptian cat
14 Funerary mask of a lady of high rank
15 Head of inner wooden coffin lid of the Libyan Pasenhor

Museum of the Year Award

This award was initiated in 1973 by National Heritage, a national charity launched in 1971 to support, encourage and protect museums and galleries in Britain. The award is made annually to the most enterprising and lively museum in the country. For many years it was sponsored by *The Illustrated London News,* and most recently by IBM. The winning museum receives a cheque and trophy, commissioned from Dame Elisabeth Frink, called the Easter Head which is housed by the winning museum for a year.

WINNERS

1973 Abbot Hall Museum, Kendal, Cumbria
1974 The National Motor Museum, Beaulieu, Hants
1975 The Weald & Downland Open Air Museum, Singleton, W. Sussex
1976 The Gladstone Pottery Museum, Stoke-on-Trent, Staffs
1977 The Ironbridge Gorge Museum, Telford, Salop
1978 The Museum of London, Erddig Hall, Wrexham, Clwyd
1979 Guernsey Museum and Art Gallery, St Peter Port
1980 British Museum (Natural History), London
1981 The Hunday Farm Museum, Stocksfield, Northd
1982 The City Museum & Art Gallery, Stoke-on-Trent, Staffs
1983 The Ulster Folk & Transport Museum, Holywood, Northern Ireland
1984 Quarry Bank Mill, Styal, Ches
1985 The Burrell Collection, Glasgow
1986 North of England Open-Air Museum, Beamish, Durham
1987 Manchester Museum
1988 National Museum of Photography, Film & Television, Bradford, W. Yorks
1989 National Portrait Gallery at Bodelwyddan Castle, Clwyd
1990 The Imperial War Museum, London
The Museum of Science & Industry, Manchester
1991 The National Railway Museum, York, N. Yorks
1992 Manx National Heritage, Douglas, Isle of Mann
1993 Jersey Museum, St Helier

As well as the main award, there are further subsidiary awards which vary from year to year. In 1993 five such awards were made as listed below (some details from the Judges' Report are included):

RIGHT The Easter Head, the National Heritage Museum of the Year trophy, by Dame Elisabeth Frink.

Best Museum of Industrial or Social History

Jewellery Quarter Discovery Centre, Birmingham

'Birmingham's new community museum opened in 1992 to celebrate a living industry and to contribute to the economic regeneration of the historic Jewellery Quarter. It combines careful restoration of a family jewellery firm with modern displays of Birmingham's jewellery trade – past present and future.'

Stockwood Craft Museum and Gardens, Luton, Beds

'At Stockwood Park there are agricultural items and a collection of Bedfordshire rural trades, shown in the converted stables. A group of crafts workshops provide working space for a potter, a book binder and a sculptor. The extensive grounds include a sculpture garden planned by Ian Hamilton Finlay.'

Best Museum of Fine or Applied Art

Ferens Art Gallery, Hull, Humberside

'This award is for three new exhibition galleries, an innovative 'Live Art Space' and a café. The octagonal galleries are flexible and it is heartening to see what excellent use is made of them. The important collection of Old Masters is stunning but the judges were also taken with the discerning purchases of modern art which allows this Gallery to offer a remarkably comprehensive view of British art.'

Best Museum Educational Initiative

South Shields Museum and Art Gallery, Tyne and Wear

'The Museum and Art Gallery is housed in a Victorian building on a central town site. It has archaeological, natural history, and art collections and historical displays which include a sequence of displays centred on Catherine Cookson's work. There is a large education room which is used to excellent effect on projects connected with the museum's collections. These projects include art, craft, and drama work, with particular encouragement given to the handicapped.'

Best Museum of Archaeological or Historical Interest

Tower Hill Pageant, London

'There are two elements of this new London attraction. First, the archaeological displays, and second a time-travellers' train which takes visitors through dioramas of London's history. The complex is a deft way of combining a use for secondary archaeological finds from riverside excavations with a popular entertainment.'

The Shoe String Award

For the museum achieving the best results with limited resources (sponsored by Museum Casts Ltd)

Amersham Museum, Bucks

'This small local history museum is housed in the restored part of a mid-fifteenth-century hall house with original hearth and timber frame structure. The excellent displays cover the history of Amersham and have been done in a most interesting and non-cluttered way. It must have been difficult to arrange them in such a diminutive space, but at no time do they obscure the architectural features. The museum is run entirely by volunteers and is a welcoming and heart-warming place with lots of visitors.'

The Blue Peter Children's Museum of the Year

Sponsored by IBM, this was a special award involving *Blue Peter*, the BBC children's programme. Viewers were asked to send in their votes for their favourite museum and 18 000 children competed to win one of three places on the panel of judges who visited a shortlist of three museums. The winner was the National Fishing Heritage Centre, Great Grimsby, Humberside. Opened in May 1991 it aims to celebrate Britain's fishing heritage. The museum gives visitors a chance to experience and appreciate the hardship and toil involved in the fishing industry by the dramatic use of temperature changes, movement, running water, sounds and smells which are used in the displays. The two runners-up were the Museum of Childhood, Edinburgh, and the Maritime Museum of the National Museums on Merseyside.

JERSEY MUSEUM – 1993 MUSEUM OF THE YEAR

The Jersey Museum at St Helier, in the Channel Islands, received the 1993 National Heritage award at a ceremony at the Science Museum. Michael Day, director, collected the trophy and a cheque for £2000.

The Jersey Museum opened as a national museum for the island in March 1992 in a new, three-storey granite building linked to the old museum, a 19th-century merchant's house. It displays a range of exhibits which draws out the story of the people who have lived on the island from the early settlers to the present day. The art gallery on the third floor exhibits the work of both local and visiting artists who have been inspired by the island and its natural beauty. The apt variety of layout, the distinction of presentation, the excellent standard of facilities all received praise in the judges' report and it was unanimously voted 'Museum of the Year'.

The front façade of the Jersey Museum, voted 1993 National Heritage Museum of the Year.

MUSIC

Masters of the Queen's (King's) Music

'Master of the King's Music' was the title given to the person who presided over the court musicians during the reign of Charles I. The first Master was appointed in 1626. Nowadays, the Master is expected to organise the music for state occasions and to write new music for them, although there are no fixed specific duties. The post is held for life and the Master receives an annual honorarium of £100.

1626 Nicholas Lanier (1588–1666)
1666 Louis Grabu (?–1674)
1674 Nicholas Staggins (1650–1700)
1700 John Eccles (1668–1735)
1735 Maurice Greene (1695–1755)
1755 William Boyce (1710–79)
1779 John Stanley (1713–86)
1786 Sir William Parsons (1746–1817)
1817 William Shield (1748–1829)
1829 Christian Kramer (?–1834)
1834 François (Franz) Cramer (1772–1848)
1848 George Anderson (?–1870)
1870 Sir William Cusins (1833–93)
1893 Sir Walter Parratt (1841–1924)
1924 Sir Edward Elgar (1857–1934)
1934 Sir Henry Walford Davies (1869–1941)
1941 Sir Arnold Bax (1883–1953)
1953 Sir Arthur Bliss (1891–1975)
1975 Malcolm Williamson (1931–)

The Gramophone Awards

Gramophone magazine celebrated its 70th year in 1993. It presented its first awards in 1977 in ten categories. Since then the categories have been increased and in their present form total 20. Nominations are derived from *Gramophone*'s reviews of over 2000 discs

> '*I thought Sarah Chang was the most wonderful, perfect, ideal violinist I had ever heard.*'
>
> Lord Menuhin OM KBE

David Mellor MP presents Anne Sofie von Otter with her Solo Vocal Award. She also won the Record of the Year award for the same disc, 'Grieg Songs'.

throughout the year. The magazine's critics then vote on these in two eliminating rounds, which establishes the winners in each category. The awards are given for excellence in classical music recordings.

1993 Awards

Artist of the Year Simon Rattle
Simon Rattle, born in Liverpool, began conducting at the age of 16. He is now Music Director of the City of Birmingham Symphony Orchestra. His recording career comprises a wide variety of works, ranging from the popular selection on 'The Jazz Album' to Mahler's 'Resurrection' Symphony No. 2 which won two *Gramophone* awards and was named 'Record of the Year' by *Gramophone* in 1988. Rattle's first complete opera recording, the Glyndebourne production of 'Porgy and Bess', was released in 1989 and brought him seven international awards. (Introduced in 1991, previous winners of Artist of the Year have been Luciano Pavarotti [1991] and Dame Kiri Te Kanawa [1992].)

Record of the Year and Solo Vocal Award: Anne Sofie von Otter
Anne Sofie von Otter is recognised as one of the finest mezzo-sopranos in the opera world. Born in Stockholm, she studied at the Guildhall School of Music and Drama in London and made her mark with the Basel Opera. She has sung with great success at the Metropolitan Opera in New York, La Scala Milan, the Deutsche Oper Berlin and the Bavarian State Opera and she has made acclaimed appearances in a variety of roles around the world. The 'Record of the Year' award was presented for her recording of Grieg Songs on the Deutsche Grammophon's record label (DG 437 521-2GH).

Young Artist of the Year Sarah Chang
Twelve-year-old New York violinist Sarah Chang is the youngest-ever recipient of a *Gramophone* award. She started to play the violin at the age of four and within a year had already performed with several orchestras in Philadelphia. At the age of eight, she auditioned for Zubin Mehta who was so impressed that he invited her to be a guest soloist with the New York Philharmonic just two days later. In May 1991, Chang received the 'Nan Pa' award, Korea's highest honour given to a musical artist. (Introduced in 1992, the previous winner was Bryan Terfel, bass baritone [1992].)

Lifetime Achievement Dietrich Fischer Dieskau
Dieskau is considered to be one of the greatest post-war interpreters of Austro-Germanic vocal repertoire. He was born in Berlin and studied there with Georg Walter, a noted singer. After the war he studied further with Herman Weissenborn before making his concert debut in Brahm's German Requiem at Freiburg in 1947. His stage debut was the following year as Posa in Don Carlos at the Berlin City Opera where he became a leading baritone. Since then he

GRAMOPHONE RECORD OF THE YEAR

1977 *Janáček* **Kata Kabanová**. Vienna State Opera Chorus, Vienna Philharmonic Orchestra / Sir Charles Mackerras (Decca 421 852-2DH2)

1978 *Puccini* **'La Fanciulla Del West'**. Chorus and orchestra of the Royal Opera House, Covent Garden / Zubin Mehta (DG 419 640-2GH2)

1979 *Haydn* **Piano Trios**. Beaux Arts Trio (Philips 432 061-2PM9)

1980 *Janáček* **'From the House of the Dead'**. Vienna State Opera Chorus, Vienna Philharmonic Orchestra / Sir Charles Mackerras (Decca 430 375-2DH2)

1981 *Wagner* **'Parsifal'**. Chorus of the Deutsche Oper, Berlin, Berlin Philharmonic Orchestra / Herbert von Karajan (DG 410 726-2GH2)

1982 *Tippett* **Triple Concerto**.

–1983 *Gyorgy Pauk* (violin), **Nobuko Imai** (viola), **Ralph Kirshbaum** (cello), London Symphony Orchestra / Sir Colin Davies (Philips 420 781-2PH)

1984 *Mahler* **Symphony No. 9**. Berlin Philharmonic Orchestra / Herbert von Karajan (DG 410 726-2GH2)

1985 *Elgar* **Violin Concerto**. Nigel Kennedy (violin), London Philharmonic Orchestra / Vernon Handley (EMI CDC7 42710-2)

1986 *Rossini* **'Il Viaggio A Reims'**. Prague Philharmonic Choir and Orchestra / Bernard Haitink (DG 415 498-2GH3)

1987 *Josquin Desprez* **'Masses; Pange Lingua; La sol fa re mi'**. The Tallis Scholars / Peter Phillips (Gimell CDGIM009)

1988 *Mahler* **Symphony No. 2 'Resurrection'**. City of Birmingham Symphony Orchestra and Chorus / Simon Rattle (EMI CDS7 47962-8)

1989 *Bartok* **String Quartets Nos. 1–6**. Emerson String Quartet (DG 423 657-2GH2)

1990 *Prokofiev* **'The Love for Three Oranges'**. Chorus and Orchestra of Lyon Opera / Kent Nagano (Virgin Classics VCD7 19084-2)

1991 *Beethoven* **Mass in D major, 'Missa Solemnis'**. Monteverdi Choir, English Baroque Soloists / John Eliot Gardiner (Archiv Production 429 779-2AH)

1992 *Beethoven* **Complete Symphonies**. Chamber Orchestra of Europe / Harnoncourt (Teldec 9031 75708-2)

1993 *Grieg* **Songs**. Anne Sofie von Otter, Bengt Forsberg (DG 437 521 2GH)

has built up an international reputation. (Introduced in 1991, previous winners of the Lifetime Achievement have been Joan Sutherland [1991] and Sir Georg Solti [1992].)

OTHER 1993 AWARDS

Baroque (non-vocal) Heinichen, Dresden Concertos. Musica Antiqua Köln / Reinhard Goebel (Archiv Produktion 437 549-2AH2)

Baroque Vocal Stradella, 'San Giovanni Battista'. Les Musiciens du Louvre / Marc Minkowski (Erato 2292-45739-2)

Bestselling Record Henryk Górecki, Symphony No. 3, 'Symphony of Sorrowful Songs'. Dawn Upshaw, London Sinfonietta / D. Zinman (Elektra Nonesuch 7559-79282-2) (Sold more than 200 000 copies in the UK and 650 000 worldwide in 1993)

Chamber Haydn, String Quartets, Op. 20. Mosaiques Quartet (Astrée Auvidis E8784)

Concerto Brahms, Piano Concerto No. 1, Two Songs, Op. 91. Stephen Kovacevich, London Philharmonic Orchestra / Wolfgang Sawallisch, Ann Murray, Nobuko Imai (EMI CDC7 54578-2)

Contemporary Macmillan, 'Confessions of Isobel Gowdie, Tryst'. BBC Scottish Symphony Orchestra / Jerzy Maksymiuk (Koch-Schwann 31050-2)

Early Music Venetian Vespers. Gabrieli Consort and Players / Paul McCreesh (Archiv Produktion 437 552-2AH2)

Engineering Debussy, 'Le Martyre de Saint Sébastian'. Leslie Caron, Sylvia McNair, Ann Murray, London Symphony Orchestra and Chorus / Michael Tilson Thomas (Sony Classical SK 48240)

Historic (non-vocal) Rachmaninov, The Complete Recordings. (RCA 09026 61265-2)

Historic Vocal Singers of Imperial Russia, Vols 1–4. Various (Pearl GEMMCD9997/9, 9001/3, 9004/6, 9007/9

Instrumental 80th birthday recital from Carnegie Hall. Shura Cherkassky (Decca 433 654-2DH)

Music Theatre Gershwin, George and Ira, 'Lady be Good'. Eric Stern (Elektra Nonesuch 7559-79308-2)

Opera Poulenc, 'Dialogues des Carmélites'. Lyon Opera / Kent Nagano (Virgin Classics VCD7 59227-2)

Orchestral Hindemith, 'Kammermusik'. Royal Concertgebouw Orchestra / Riccardo Chailly (Decca 433 816-2DH2)

Special Achievement Edward Greenfield, influential and widely read music critic writing in *The Guardian*, *Gramophone*, *The Penguin Guide*.

Video Wagner, 'Ring Cycle'. Bavarian State Opera / Wolfgang Sawallisch (LDX9 91275-1; VHS MVX9 91275-3)

The Classical Music Awards

These awards, inaugurated in 1994, aim to celebrate excellence and honour in international classical music, help to promote its success, and make it more familiar to a wider range of music lovers. The awards were devised by Bob Geldof and Irish television producer Ultan Guilfoyle, and they are sponsored by the Kenwood Corporation with *BBC Music Magazine* and *The Independent* as co-patrons.

An international jury selects from a list of nominated individuals, winners in 14 music categories covering every area of performance, recording and television, as well as composition and opera production. A 'Personality of the Year' was also polled among music lovers from readers of the *BBC Music Magazine* in the UK and USA, and *Ongaku no Tomo* ('Friend of Music') and *Record Geijutsu* ('Recording Art') from Ongaku no Tomo, the leading

10 Topselling UK Classical Albums, 1993

1 Górecki: Symphony No. 3	London Sinfonietta
2 The Essential Flute of James Galway	James Galway
3 Ti Amo – Puccini's Greatest Love Songs	Luciano Pavarotti
4 Diva! A Soprano at the Movies	Lesley Garrett
5 Jesus Blood Never Failed Me Yet	Gavin Bryars
6 With A Song in My Heart	José Carreras
7 The Piano	Michael Nyman
8 Glass: Low Symphony	Dennis Russell Davies / BFRO
9 The Seville Concert	John Williams, José Buenago / USS
10 Vivaldi: Four Seasons	Nigel Kennedy

Source: Compiled by MRIB, 1993

Górecki Symphony No. 3, 'Symphony of Sorrowful Songs' – No. 1 Bestseller

This 52-minute, classical recording, released by Warner Classics UK on the Elektra Nonesuch label in July 1992, was a phenomenal success, entering the Classic FM chart on 19 September 1992, toppling Nigel Kennedy from the No.1 spot where it remained for 35 weeks. The record reached No. 6 in the UK pop album charts and No. 1 in America's Billboard classical chart where it stayed for 37 weeks, remaining in the top 25 for 93 weeks. In 1993 the record sold 200 000 copies in the UK and 650 000 worldwide.

On 10 February 1993 Henryk Górecki, the 59-year-old Polish composer, was presented by Warner Classics with silver and gold discs for UK sales of 60 000 and 100 000 respectively. This was the first time in the history of the UK record industry that a contemporary classical composer had achieved this distinction.

Górecki wrote the symphony 17 years ago when Poland was cut off from the West. It was premièred at an avant-garde music festival in France in 1977 and surprised the audience who had expected to hear more of Górecki's 1960s atonal work. Instead they heard a work which was described as possessing 'profound emotional and spiritual quality'. As Communism in Poland crumbled during 1989, so Górecki's music spread. By 1990 Symphony No. 3 was being premièred by large orchestras from America to Australia and several recordings of it were made. However, it did not achieve fame until a recording made by the London Sinfonietta Orchestra, conducted by David Zinman and featuring the voice of Dawn Upshaw, was released.

The text of the first movement is a 15th-century Polish monastic lament, known as a Holy Cross lament, in which the Virgin Mary asks her dying son to share his wounds with her. The song in the second movement is taken from an inscription on a wall written by a young girl imprisoned by the Nazis during World War II. In English it reads: 'No Mother, do not weep. Most chaste Queen of Heaven. Support me always. Hail Mary.' The third movement is based on a 19th-century Polish folk melody, with a mother mourning the loss of her young soldier son during an uprising in the Silesian region of Poland, where Górecki was born.

The recording has won much acclaim including: 1993 *Gramophone* Award for Bestselling Record, 1994 Classical Music Award for Best Recording, and 1994 *Music Week* Award for Top Classical Album.

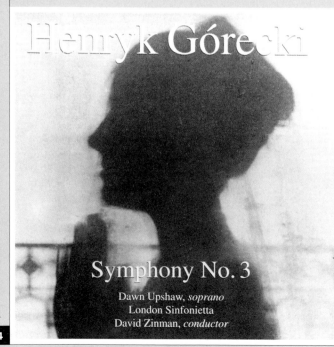

Henryk Górecki

Symphony No. 3

Dawn Upshaw, *soprano*
London Sinfonietta
David Zinman, *conductor*

Jacket cover of Górecki's bestselling record.

classical music publisher in Japan. The winners each received a copy of Dhruva Mistry's limited-edition award, an 11-inch bronze sculpture. The award ceremony was televised and shown on BBC2 and was scheduled to appear in 25 countries worldwide.

1994 AWARDS

Male Singer Thomas Hampson, USA
Female Singer Cecilia Bartoli, Italy
Instrumentalist Yuri Bashmet, Russia
Composition Witold Lutoslawski, Symphony No. 4, Poland
Orchestra New York Philharmonic, USA
Newcomer Sarah Chang, USA (aged 12)
Recording Henryk Górecki, Symphony No. 3, Elektra Nonesuch / Warner
Festival or Concert Series Tender is the North, The Barbican Centre, London
Chorus Arnold Schoenberg Choir, Vienna
Chamber Group Kronos Quartet, USA
Early Music Group Orchestra of the 18th Century, Netherlands
Conductor Valery Gergiev, Russia
Television Broadcast 'The Vampyr', BBC Television
Opera Production 'Oedipus Rex', Saito Kinen Festival, Japan
Personality José Carreras, Spain

The Harveys Leeds International Pianoforte Competition

Founded in 1963 by Fanny Waterman and Marion Thorpe, this

José Carreras, with his Classical Music Award trophy, 1994 Personality of the Year.

triennial competition offered £47 600 prize money in 1993, donated by various organisations and foundations. The winner received £10 000, the Princess Mary Gold Medal, and a programme of engagements and recital venues worldwide.

A further £10 000 was offered in 1993 to the winner of the Rachmaninoff Prize, which marked the 50th anniversary of the death of

POSSIBLY THE LEAST SUCCESSFUL PIANO RECITAL . . .

A promising American pianist gave a concert in the chamber music room of the Erewan Hotel in Bangkok in the early 1970s. He was only a few minutes into the recital when the high humidity caused the D above middle C to stick. It was ironic that his repertoire included Bach's D minor Toccata and Fugue, and Prelude and Fugue in D major.

A reviewer in the *Bangkok Post* commented in his review that there was also a problem with the piano stool which had been overgreased to the extent that in one of the more vigorous sections of the piece, the pianist suddenly found himself facing the audience!

Abandoning the Toccata the pianist moved on to Liszt's Fantasia in G minor, at which

point the G below middle C also became a casualty and began to stick. To try and free the notes the increasingly exasperated impresario started to kick the lower section of the piano with his foot which resulted in the piano's right leg giving way and the whole piano tilting through 35 degrees.

At this point he rose, bowed and left the stage to enthusiastic applause. He returned a few moments later with a fire axe in his hand and began to demolish the piano. On hearing the horrendous noise of splintering wood, the hotel manager, two security men and a passing policeman appeared and succeeded in disarming and dragging the man offstage.

the composer and pianist Sergei Rachmaninoff. His grandson, Alexandre Rachmaninoff, donated the prize; £5000 for the finest interpretations of the works of Rachmaninoff during the Competition and a further £5000 for the promotion of the career of the winner of the Prize following the Competition.

The 1993 competition attracted a record number of entrants: out of 232 applications, 88 were selected and 65 competitors between the ages of 15 and 30 played, with six being chosen to play in the finals which were broadcast on BBC2 with simultaneous broadcast on Radio 3. Simon Rattle, *Gramophone* 'Artist of the Year' (see above), conducted the City of Birmingham Symphony Orchestra to accompany the finalists.

Winners
1963 **Michael Roll** (UK)
1966 **Rafael Orozco** (Spa)
1969 **Radu Lupu** (Rom)
1972 **Murray Perahia** (USA)
1975 **Dmitri Alexeev** (Rus)
1978 **Michel Dalberto** (Fra)
1981 **Ian Hobson** (UK)
1984 **Jon Kimura Parker** (Can)
1987 **Vladimir Ovchinikov** (Rus)
1990 **Artur Pizarro** (Por)
1993 **Ricardo Castro** (Bra)

Ricardo Castro (seen above in the finals with Simon Rattle conducting) won the 1993 Leeds International Pianoforte Competition. Born in 1964 in Brazil, he started to play the piano at the age of three. He studied with Esther Cardoso, an exponent of the French piano school, with Maria Tipo at the Geneva Conservatoire, and then with Dominique Merlet in Paris. In 1983 he moved to Europe where he studied piano and conducting. He gave his first concert at the age of ten and has since played recitals in many countries, including Brazil, Europe, Japan and South America.

Pulitzer Prize

For a distinguished musical composition by an American, including chamber, orchestral, choral, opera, song, dance, or other form of musical theatre. (See separate section, Pulitzer Prizes.)
1943 **Secular Cantata No. 2**, William Schuman
1944 **Symphony No. 4, opus 34**, Howard Hanson
1945 **Appalachian Spring**, Aaron Copland
1946 **The Canticle of the Sun**, Leo Sowerby
1947 **Symphony No. 3**, Charles Ives
1948 **Symphony No. 3**, Walter Piston
1949 **Louisiana Story**, Virgil Thomson
1950 **The Consul**, Gian-Carlo Menotti
1951 **Giants in the Earth**, Douglas S. Moore
1952 **Symphony Concertante**, Gail Kubik
1953 No award
1954 **Concerto for Two Pianos and Orchestra**, Quincy Porter
1955 **The Saint of Bleecker Street**, Gian-Carlo Menotti

1956 **Symphony No. 3**, Ernst Toch
1957 **Meditations on Ecclesiastes**, Norman Dello Joio
1958 **The Score of Vanessa**, Samuel Barber
1959 **Concerto for Piano and Orchestra**, John la Montaine
1960 **Second String Quartet**, Elliott C. Carter, Jr
1961 **Symphony No. 7**, Walter Piston
1962 **The Crucible**, Robert Ward
1963 **Piano Concerto No. 1**, Samuel Barber
1964 No award
1965 No award
1966 **Variations for Orchestra**, Leslie Bassett
1967 **Quartet No. 3**, Leon Kirchner
1968 **Echoes of Time and the River**, George Crumb
1969 **String Quartet No. 3**, Karel Husa
1970 **Time's Economium**, Charles W. Wuorinen
1971 **Synchronisms No. 6**, Mario Davidovsky
1972 **Windows**, Jacob Druckman
1973 **String Quartet No. 3**, Elliott Carter

1974 **Notturno**, Donald Martino
1975 **From the Diary of Virginia Woolf**, Dominick Argento
1976 **Air Music, 10 études for orchestra**, Ned Rorem
1977 **Visions of Terror and Wonder**, Richard Wernick
1978 **Déjà vu for Percussion Quartet and Orchestra**, Michael Colgrass
1979 **Aftertones of Infinity**, Joseph Schwantner
1980 **In Memory of a Summer Day**, David del Tredici
1981 No award
1982 **Concerto for Orchestra**, Roger Sessions
1983 **Symphony No. 1 (Three Movements for Orchestra)**, Ellen T. Zwilich
1984 **Canti del Sole**, Bernard Rands
1985 **Symphony, RiverRun**, Stephen Albert
1986 **Wind Quintet IV**, George Perle
1987 **The Flight into Egypt**, John Harbison
1988 **12 New Etudes for Piano**, William Bolcom

1989 Whispers Out of Time, Roger Reynolds
1990 Duplicates: A Concerto for Two Pianos and Orchestra, Mel Powell
1991 Symphony, Shulamit Ran
1992 The Face of the Night, The Heart of the Dark, Wayne Peterson
1993 Trombone Concerto, Christopher Rouse
1994 Of Reminiscences and Reflections, Günther Schuller

The Grammy Awards

The Grammy Awards are organised by The National Academy of Recording Arts & Sciences in America. The Academy was founded in 1957 by recording artists, composers and craftsmen to advance the arts and sciences of recording. Grammy winners have been selected annually since 1958 by the voting members of the Academy whose members number over 7000 creative contributors to the field of recording. Awards are made to individuals who are acknowledged for their outstanding artistic and/or technical achievement in the recording field. At the first awards ceremony in 1958 there were 28 categories; in 1993 there were 81. A listing including Best Record, Album, Song, Pop Female and Male Vocal Performance follows:

Grammy Awards

	Record of the Year	Album of the Year	Song of the Year (Songwriter)	Best Pop Female Vocal Performance	Best Pop Male Vocal Performance
1958	Nel Blu Dipinto Di Blu (Volare) Domenico Modugno	The Music from Peter Gunn Henry Mancini	Nel Blu Dipinto Di Blu (Volare) Domenico Modugno	Ella Fitzgerald Sings the Irving Berlin Song Ella Fitzgerald	Catch a Falling Star Perry Como
1959	Mack The Knife Bobby Darin	Come Dance With Me Frank Sinatra	The Battle of New Orleans Jimmy Driftwood	But Not For Me Ella Fitzgerald	Come Dance With Me Frank Sinatra
1960	Theme From a Summer Place Percy Faith	Button Down Mind Bob Newhart	Theme from Exodus Ernest Gold	Mack the Knife Ella Fitzgerald	Georgia on my Mind Ray Charles
1961	Moon River Henry Mancini	Judy at Carnegie Hall Judy Garland	Moon River Henry Mancini, Johnny Mercer	Judy at Carnegie Hall (album) Judy Garland	Lollipops and Roses (single) Jack Jones
1962	I Left My Heart in San Francisco Tony Bennett	The First Family Vaughn Meader	What Kind of Fool Am I Leslie Bricusse, Anthony Newley	Ella Swings Brightly with Nelson Riddle (album) Ella Fitzgerald	I Left My Heart in San Francisco (album) Tony Bennett
1963	The Days of Wine and Roses Henry Mancini	The Barbra Streisand Album Barbra Streisand	The Days of Wine and Roses Henry Mancini, Johnny Mercer	The Barbra Streisand Album Barbra Streisand	Wives and Lovers (single) Jack Jones
1964	The Girl From Ipanema Stan Getz, Astrud Gilberto	Getz/Gilberto Stan Getz, Joao Gilberto	Hello, Dolly! Jerry Harman	People (single) Barbra Streisand	Hello, Dolly! (single) Louis Armstrong
1965	A Taste of Honey Herb Alpert and the Tijuana Brass	September of My Years Frank Sinatra	The Shadow of Your Smile (Love Theme from The Sandpiper) Paul Francis Webster, Johnny Mandel	My Name is Barbra (album) Barbra Streisand	It Was a Very Good Year (single) Frank Sinatra
1966	Strangers in the Night Frank Sinatra	Sinatra, A Man and His Music Frank Sinatra	Michelle John Lennon, Paul McCartney	If He Walked into My Life (single) Eydie Gorme	Strangers in the Night Frank Sinatra
1967	Up, Up and Away 5th Dimension	Sgt. Pepper's Lonely Hearts Club Band The Beatles	Up, Up and Away Jim Webb	Ode to Billie Joe (single) Bobbie Gentry	By the Time I Get to Phoenix (single) Glen Campbell
1968	Mrs Robinson Simon and Garfunkel	By the Time I Get To Phoenix Glen Campbell	Little Green Apples Bobby Russell	Do You Know the Way to San Jose (single) Dionne Warwick	Light My Fire (single) Jose Feliciano
1969	Aquarius/Let the Sunshine In 5th Dimension	Blood, Sweat & Tears Blood, Sweat & Tears	Games People Play Joe South	Is That All There Is (single) Peggy Lee	Everybody's Talkin' Harry Nilsson
1970	Bridge Over Troubled Water Simon and Garfunkel	Bridge Over Troubled Water Simon and Garfunkel	Bridge Over Troubled Water Paul Simon	I'll Never Fall in Love Again (album) Dionne Warwick	Everything is Beautiful (single) Ray Stevens

	Record of the Year	Album of the Year	Song of the Year (Songwriter)	Best Pop Female Vocal Performance	Best Pop Male Vocal Performance
1971	It's Too Late Carole King	Tapestry Carole King	You've Got a Friend Carole King	Tapestry (album) Carole King	You've Got a Friend (single) James Taylor
1972	The First Time Ever I Saw Your Face Roberta Flack	The Concert for Bangladesh George Harrison, Ravi Shanker, Bob Dylan . . .	The First Time Ever I Saw Your Face Ewan MacColl	I Am Woman (single) Helen Reddy	Without You (single) Nilsson
1973	Killing Me Softly With His Song Roberta Flack	Innervisions Stevie Wonder	Killing Me Softly With His Song Norman Gimbel, Charles Fox	Killing Me Softly With His Song (single) Roberta Flack	You Are The Sunshine of My Life (single) Stevie Wonder
1974	I Honestly Love You Olivia Newton-John	Fulfillingness' First Finale Stevie Wonder	The Way We Were Marilyn and Alan Bergman, Marvin Hamlisch	I Honestly Love You (single) Olivia Newton-John	Fulfillingness' First Finale (album) Stevie Wonder
1975	Love Will Keep Us Together Captain & Tennille	Still Crazy After All These Years Paul Simon	Send in the Clowns Stephen Sondheim	At Seventeen (single) Janis Ian	Still Crazy After All These Years (album) Paul Simon
1976	This Masquerade George Benson	Songs in the Key of Life Stevie Wonder	I Write the Songs Bruce Johnston	Hasten Down the Wind (album) Linda Ronstadt	Songs in the Key of Life (album) Stevie Wonder
1977	Hotel California Eagles	Rumours Fleetwood Mac	Love Theme From A Star is Born (Evergreen) Barbra Streisand, Paul Williams You Light Up My Life Joe Brooks	Love Theme From A Star is Born (Evergreen) (single) Barbra Streisand	Handy Man (single) James Taylor
1978	Just the Way You Are Billy Joel	Saturday Night Fever Bee Gees and others	Just the Way You Are Billy Joel	You Needed Me (single) Anne Murray	Copacabana (At the Copa) (single) Barry Manilow
1979	What A Fool Believes The Doobie Brothers	52nd Street Billy Joel	What A Fool Believes Kenny Loggins, Michael McDonald	I'll Never Love This Way Again (single) Dionne Warwick	52nd Street (album) Billy Joel
1980	Sailing Christopher Cross	Christopher Cross Christopher Cross	Sailing Christopher Cross	The Rose (single) Bette Midler	This Is It (track) Kenny Loggins
1981	Bette Davis Eyes Kim Carnes	Double Fantasy John Lennon and Yoko Ono	Bette Davis Eyes Donna Weiss, Jackie DeShannon	Lena Horne: The Lady and Her Music Live on Broadway (album) Lena Horne	Breakin Away (album) Al Jarreau
1982	Rosanna Toto	Toto IV Toto	Always on My Mind Johnny Christopher, Mark James, Wayne Carson	You Should Hear How She Talks About You (single) Melissa Manchester	Truly (single) Lionel Richie
1983	Beat It Michael Jackson	Thriller Michael Jackson	Every Breath You Take Sting	Flashdance What A Feeling (single) Irene Cara	Thriller (album) Michael Jackson
1984	What's Love Got To Do With It Tina Turner	Can't Slow Down Lionel Richie	What's Love Got To Do With It Graham Lyle, Terry Britten	What's Love Got To Do With It (single) Tina Turner	Against All Odds (Take A Look At Me Now) (single) Phil Collins
1985	We Are The World USA For Africa	No Jacket Required Phil Collins	We Are The World Michael Jackson, Lionel Ritchie	Saving All My Love For You (single) Whitney Houston	No Jacket Required (album) Phil Collins

	Record of the Year	Album of the Year	Song of the Year (Songwriter)	Best Pop Female Vocal Performance	Best Pop Male Vocal Performance
1986	Higher Love Steve Winwood	Graceland Paul Simon	That's What Friends Are For Dionne and friends	The Broadway Album (album) Barbra Streisand	Higher Love (single) Steve Winwood
1987	Graceland Paul Simon	Joshua Tree U2	Somewhere Out There Linda Ronstadt, James Ingram	I Wanna Dance with Somebody (Who Loves Me) (single) Whitney Houston	Bring on the Night (album) Sting
1988	Don't Worry Be Happy Bobby McFerrin	Faith George Michael	Don't Worry Be Happy Bobby McFerrin	Fast Car (single) Tracy Chapman	Don't Worry Be Happy (single) Bobby McFerrin
1989	Wind Beneath My Wings Bette Midler	Nick of Time Bonnie Raitt	Wind Beneath My Wings Larry Henley, Jeff Silbar	Nick of Time (track) Bonnie Raitt	How Am I Supposed to Live Without You (single) Michael Bolton
1990	Another Day in Paradise Phil Collins	Back on the Block Quincy Jones	From A Distance Bette Midler	Vision of Love (single) Mariah Carey	Oh Pretty Woman (single) Roy Orbison
1991	Unforgettable Natalie Cole	Unforgettable Natalie Cole	Unforgettable Irving Gordon	Something to Talk About (single) Bonnie Raitt	When A Man Loves A Woman (single) Michael Bolton
1992	Tears in Heaven Eric Clapton	Unplugged Eric Clapton	Tears in Heaven Eric Clapton, Will Jennings	Constant Craving (single) k.d. lang	Tears in Heaven (single) Eric Clapton
1993	I Will Always Love You Whitney Houston	The Bodyguard Whitney Houston	A Whole New World (*Aladdin*'s theme) Alan Menken, Tim Rice	I Will Always Love You (single) Whitney Houston	If I Ever Lose My Faith In You (single) Sting

GRAMMYS – MULTIPLE AWARD WINNERS

Winners of seven or more awards

30 Sir Georg Solti	Bobby McFerrin	Linda Ronstadt
26 Quincy Jones	Artur Rubinstein	Frank Sinatra
25 Vladimir Horowitz	Robert Woods	Barbra Streisand
20 Henry Mancini	**9** Count Basie	**7** Anita Baker
17 Stevie Wonder	James Blackwood (inc. Blackwood	Shirley Caesar
16 Leonard Bernstein	Bros)	Johnny Cash
Paul Simon (inc. Simon and Garfunkel)	Bill Cosby	Natalie Cole
15 Aretha Franklin	Alan Menken	Phil Collins
John T. Williams	Janis Siegel (inc. Manhattan Transfer)	Sir Colin Davis
14 Pierre Boulez	**8** George Benson	Bill Evans
Itzhak Perlman	Blackwood Brothers	Barry Gibb (inc. Bee Gees)
13 Ella Fitzgerald	Eric Clapton	George Harrison (inc. Beatles and
Leontyne Price	Chick Corea	Traveling Wilburys)
Robert Shaw (inc. Robert Shaw	Miles Davis	BB King
Chorale)	Art Garfunkel (inc. Simon and	John Lennon (inc. Beatles)
12 Chet Atkins	Garfunkel)	Marilyn McCoo (inc. 5th Dimension)
Ray Charles	Al Green	Car Peterson
Michael Jackson	Dave Grusin	André Previn
Sting (inc. Police)	Margaret Hillis	Bonnie Raitt
11 Duke Ellington	Erich Leinsdorf	Phil Ramone
James Mallinson	James Levine	Isaac Stern
Roger Miller	Yo-Yo Ma	Tina Turner (inc. Ike and Tina)
Thomas Z. Shepard	Manhattan Transfer	Maurice White (inc. Earth, Wind and
10 David Foster	Wynton Marsalis	Fire)
Paul McCartney (inc. Beatles and Wings)	Pat Metheny	

Sir Georg Solti, conductor, has won 30 Grammys (1958–93):

1962 Opera Recording *Verdi* Aida – Rome Opera House Orchestra and Chorus

1966 Opera Recording *Wagner – Die Walküre* – Vienna Philharmonic Orchestra

1972 Classical Album of the Year / Classical Choral Performance *Mahler* Symphony No. 8 – Chicago Symphony Orchestra, Vienna Boys Choir, Vienna State Opera Chorus, Vienna Singverein Chorus and soloists

Classical Orchestral Performance *Mahler* Symphony No. 7 – Chicago Symphony Orchestra (London)

1973 Classical Album of the Year / Classical Orchestral Performance *Berlioz* Symphonie Fantastique – Chicago Symphony Orchestra

Opera Recording *Puccini* La Bohème

1975 Classical Album of the Year *Beethoven* Symphonies (9) Complete – Chicago Symphony Orchestra

1976 Classical Orchestral Performance *Strauss* Also Sprach Zarathustra – Chicago Symphony Orchestra

1977 Classical Choral Performance (other than opera) *Verdi* Requiem – Chicago Symphony Orchestra

1978 Classical Choral Performance (other than opera) *Beethoven* Missa Solemnis – Chicago Symphony Orchestra and Chorus

1979 Classical Album / Classical Orchestral Recording *Brahms* Symphonies Complete – Chicago Symphony Orchestra

Classical Choral Performance (other than opera) *Brahms* A German Requiem – Chicago Symphony Chorus and Orchestra

1980 Classical Orchestral Recording *Bruckner* Symphony No. 6 in A major – Chicago Symphony Orchestra

1981 Classical Album / Classical Orchestral Recording *Mahler* Symphony No. 2 in C minor – Chicago Symphony Orchestra and Chorus

1982 Classical Choral Performance (other than opera) *Berlioz* La Damnation de Faust – Chicago Symphony Orchestra and Chorus

1983 Classical Album / Classical Orchestral Recording *Mahler* Symphony No. 9 in D major – Chicago Symphony Orchestra

Opera Recording *Mozart* Le Nözze di Figaro – London Philharmonic Orchestra

Classical Choral Performance (other than opera) *Haydn* The Creation – Chicago Symphony Orchestra and Chorus

1985 Opera Recording *Schoenberg* Moses und Aron Chicago Symphony Orchestra and Chorus

1986 Classical Orchestral Recording *Liszt* A Faust Symphony – Chicago Symphony Orchestra

1987 Orchestral Recording *Beethoven* Symphony No. 9 in D minor (choral) – Chicago Symphony Orchestra

1988 Opera Recording *Wagner* Lohengrin – Vienna State Opera Choir and Vienna Philharmonic Orchestra

Chamber Music Performance (instrumental or vocal) *Bartók* Son. for two pianos and percussion. *Brahms* Var. on a theme by Joseph Haydn for two pianos – Murray Perahia and Sir Georg Solti, pianos, with David Corkhill and Evelyn Glennie, percussion

1991 Performance of a Choral Work *Bach* Mass in B minor – Chicago Symphony Orchestra and Chorus

1992 Opera Recording *R. Strauss* Die Frau Ohne Schatten – Vienna Philharmonic Orchestra

---

Aladdin (US 92), Disney's most recent animated feature, was released in the US on 25 November 1992 and in the UK on 3 December 1993. The film won a number of music awards:

1992 Academy Awards
▌ Best Original Song for the theme song, 'A Whole New World', composed by Alan Menken and Tim Rice.
▌ Best Original Score to the composer, Alan Menken.

1994 Grammy Awards
▌ Song of the Year – songwriter(s) award, 'A Whole New World', Alan Menken and Tim Rice.
▌ Best Pop Performance by a Duo or Group with Vocal – 'A Whole New World', Peabo Bryson and Regina Belle.
▌ Best Musical Album for Children – 'Aladdin', the original motion picture soundtrack, Alan Menken and Tim Rice (producers).
▌ Best Instrumental Composition written for a Motion Picture or for Television – composer(s) award, 'Aladdin', the album, Alan Menken.
▌ Best Song Written Specifically for a Motion Picture or for Television – songwriter(s) award, 'A Whole New World', Alan Menken and Tim Rice.

1993 Golden Globe Awards
▌ Best Original Score.
▌ Best Original Song, 'A Whole New World'.
▌ Special Achievement Award – Robin Williams for the voice of the Genie.

Aladdin, his pet monkey, Abu, and Princess Jasmine, together with the Genie, take a ride on the Flying Carpet accompanied by the theme song 'A Whole New World'.

The bestselling record of all time is 'White Christmas', written by Irving Berlin and recorded by Bing Crosby on 29 May 1942. In 1987 it was announced that North American sales alone had reached 170 884 207 copies by 30 June 1987.

Topselling 1993 UK album.

₀ Topselling UK Singles, 1993

ι	I'd Do Anything for Love (But I Won't . . .)	Meat Loaf
₂	All That She Wants	Ace of Base
₃	(I Can't Help) Falling in Love With You	UB40
₄	Mr Blobby	Mr Blobby
₅	No Limit	2 Unlimited
₃	Babe	Take That
₇	Mr Vain	Culture Beat
₃	Pray	Take That
₃	Five Live E.P.	George Michael / Queen / Lisa Stansfield
₃	I Will Always Love You	Whitney Houston
ι	Dreams	Gabrielle
₂	Young at Heart	Bluebells
₃	Oh Carolina	Shaggy
₃	Boom! Shake the Room	Jazzy Jeff & Fresh Prince
₅	Tease Me	Chaka Demus & Pliers
₃	What is Love?	Haddaway
₇	Please Forgive Me	Bryan Adams
₃	Relight My Fire	Take That featuring Lulu
₃	True Love	Elton John & Kiki Dee
₃	Living On My Own	Freddie Mercury

urce: Compiled by MRIB, 1993

20 Topselling UK Albums, 1993

1	Bat Out of Hell II – Back Into Hell	Meat Loaf
2	The Bodyguard – Original Soundtrack	Various
3	Automatic for The People	R.E.M.
4	So Close	Dina Carroll
5	One Woman – The Ultimate Collection	Diana Ross
6	So Far So Good	Bryan Adams
7	Both Sides	Phil Collins
8	Promises and Lies	UB40
9	Unplugged	Eric Clapton
10	Everything Changes	Take That
11	Connected	Stereo MC's
12	Ten Summoner's Tales	Sting
13	Are You Gonna Go My Way	Lenny Kravitz
14	Diva	Annie Lennox
15	Zooropa	U2
16	Duets	Elton John / Various
17	Music Box	Mariah Carey
18	What's Love Got To Do With It	Tina Turner
19	Janet	Janet Jackson
20	The One Thing	Michael Bolton

Source: Compiled by MRIB, 1993

The International Committee of the Red Cross (ICRC)

The ICRC was awarded the Nobel Peace Prize in 1917, 1944 and 1963 (shared with the League of Red Cross Societies) – more times than any other individual or organisation. In 1901, the organisation's founder, Henry Dunant (1828–1910), also won the Prize for his work in setting up the movement. The Peace Prize is awarded to the person/organisation 'who shall have done the most or the best work for fraternity among nations, for the abolition or reduction of standing armies and for the holding and promotion of peace congresses'.

The Committee, a private independent institution, governed by Swiss nationals, works in

Henri Dunant, founder of the ICRC.

'The purpose of the Red Cross is not solely to succour the victims of war; by so doing, it serves another purpose no less important, that of saving from the torment and darkness of war the idea of human solidarity and of respect for the dignity of every human person, particularly in an age when the alleged necessities of war cause moral values to be relegated to the background.

'No organization intended to guarantee peace among nations can survive unless it is inspired by the idea of active solidarity among human beings, an idea which the Red Cross wishes to safeguard even in humanity's darkest hours.'

Max Huber, President, ICRC, Nobel Prize ceremony, Oslo, 10 December 1945

FACTS

■ The ICRC has a staff of 650 at its headquarters in Geneva, almost 1000 expatriate delegates, and 5000 locally-recruited staff working in 64 countries, more than 30 of those of which are experiencing conflict.

■ The ICRC is financed by voluntary contributions from governments, the EC, national societies and private individuals.

■ The ICRC is entitled, by its statutes, to take humanitarian initiatives to protect persons in situations not covered by the Conventions, such as internal tension or disturbances. The ICRC first made visits to so-called 'political' detainees in Russia in 1918 and Hungary in 1919. Since World War II, it has visited over half a million political detainees in almost 100 countries.

■ ICRC delegates, including a doctor, visit prisoners of war and people detained for political reasons, registering their names and making sure their conditions of detention are acceptable. In 1992, ICRC delegates visited 96 132 detainees in 2355 places of detention in 54 countries.

■ The ICRC's Central Tracing Agency has received over 45 600 requests and established the whereabouts of 32 000 persons. It has forwarded over 1 100 000 messages between persons separated by conflict, disturbances and tensions.

■ In 1992 the ICRC distributed more than 230 000 tons of relief supplies in 60 countries (food, clothing, blankets, tents, etc.) worth Sfr 214 million.

two ways, consistent with the guidelines laid down by its principal founder, Dunant. It is the 'promoter and guardian of the Geneva Conventions and of international humanitarian law; in addition, in all wars, it acts as a neutral intermediary between belligerents, helping and protecting victims of hostilities and alleviating their physical and moral suffering'.

On 24 June 1859, the armies of Imperial Austria and the Franco-Sardinian alliance fought a day-long battle near the northern Italian village of Solferino. The casualties were heavy – some 40 000 dead, wounded or missing. Military medical services at the time were virtually non-existent; as a result there was great suffering and many of the wounded died for lack of care.

The injured were brought to the surrounding villages for whatever treatment they could get. In the church at Castiglione, a young Swiss called Henri Dunant, horrified by the agony of the soldiers, began to organise help with the aid of the local people.

Returning home to Geneva, still haunted by what he had seen, he wrote a book about his experience. *Un Souvenir de Solferino* ('A Memory of Solferino'), published in 1862, was acclaimed throughout Europe. In it, Dunant put forward an idea for supplementing army medical services in times of war. This would be done through national relief societies which, in peacetime, would train their voluntary members for this work.

Thus the 'International Committee for Relief to the Wounded', later the International Committee of the Red Cross, was set up.

In response to an invitation from the International Committee, specialists from 16 countries met in Geneva in October 1863. They adopted ten resolutions that made up the founding charter of the Red Cross, defining the functions and working methods of the Committees for the Relief of the Wounded which Dunant had proposed.

In August 1864, delegates of 12 governments took part in a conference and adopted a draft treaty prepared by the International Committee. It was called the 'Geneva Convention for the Amelioration of the Condition of the Wounded in Armies in the Field'. This treaty, with its ten articles, was a milestone in the history of humanity. From this date, ambulances, military hospitals and medical staff were to be 'recognised as neutral and, as such, protected and respected by the belligerents . . . Wounded or sick combatants, to whatever nation they belong, shall be collected and cared for'.

The battle of Solferino.

Nobel Prize (continued)

1953 George C. Marshall (USA) – Politician. Marshall (European recovery) Plan

1954 Office of the United Nations High Commissioner for Refugees

1955-56 No awards

1957 Lester B. Pearson (CAN) – Politician. Efforts to solve the Suez Crisis (1956)

1958 Dominique Georges Pire (BEL) – Cleric and educationalist. Aid to displaced Europeans after World War II

1959 Philip Noel-Baker (UK) – Politician. Advocate of world disarmament

1960 Albert Lutuli (SA) – Former president, African National Congress. Non-violent struggle against apartheid

1961 Dag Hammarskjöld (SWE) – Secretary General of the United Nations. (posthumously awarded)

1962 Linus Pauling (USA) – Chemist. Campaigns for control of nuclear weapons and nuclear testing

1963 International Committee of the Red Cross. League of Red Cross Societies for relief work after natural disasters

1964 Martin Luther King Jr (USA) – Black civil rights leader.

1965 United Nations Children's Fund

1966–67 No awards

1968 René Cassin (FRA) – Jurist. Principal author of UN Declaration of Human Rights

1969 International Labour Organization

1970 Norman E. Borlaug (USA) – Agricultural scientist. Agricultural technology

1971 Willy Brandt (GER) – Politician. Reconciliation between West and East Germany

1972 No award

1973 Henry Kissinger (USA) – Politician.
Le Duc Tho (NV) – Politician. Peace settlement of the Vietnam War (Le Duc Tho declined the award)

1974 Eisaku Sato (JAP) – Prime Minister. Anti-nuclear policies
Sean MacBride (IRE) – Statesman. Campaign for human rights

1975 Andrei D. Sakharov (RUS) – Nuclear physicist. Advocacy of human rights and disarmament

1976 Mairead Corrigan (NI) and Betty Williams (NI). Campaign to end sectarian strife in Northern Ireland

1977 Amnesty International. Work to secure release of political prisoners

1978 Menachem Begin (ISR) – Prime Minister
Anwar el-Sadat (EGY) – President. Israel–Egypt peace treaty (1979)

1979 Mother Teresa of Calcutta (MACEDONIA) – Indian charity worker. Help with the destitute in India

1980 Adolfo Pérez Esquivel (ARG) – Sculptor and architect. Work for human rights in Latin America

1981 United Nations High Commissioner for Refugees.

1982 Alva Myrdal (SWE) – Diplomat
Alfonso Garcia Robles (MEX) – Diplomat. Advocacy of nuclear disarmament

1983 Lech Walesa (POL) – Politician and trade unionist. Solidarity movement

1984 Desmond Tutu (SA) – Anglican Archbishop. Peaceful anti-apartheid work

1985 International Physicians for the Prevention of Nuclear War.

1986 Elie Wiesel (FRA) – Writer and human rights activist

1987 Oscar Arias Sánchez (CR) – President. Promoting peace in Central America

1988 United Nations Peacekeeping Forces.

1989 The Dalai Lama (CHI) – Spiritual and exiled temporal leader of Tibet

1990 Mikhail Gorbachev (USSR) – President. Promoting greater openness in the Soviet Union, and helping to end the Cold War

1991 Aung San Suu Kyi (BUR) – Politician. Non-violent campaign for democracy

1992 Rigoberta Menchu (GUATEMALA) – Indian spokeswoman. Campaign for indigenous people

1993 Nelson Mandela and F. W. de Klerk (SA). Encouraging a peaceful end to apartheid

Peace Nobel Prize Winners by Country

Country	Total	Year first awarded Prize
USA	16	1906
France	9	1901
UK	7	1903
Germany*	5	1926
Sweden	5	1908
South Africa	4	1960
Belgium	3	1909
Switzerland	3	1901
Argentina	2	1936
Austria	2	1905
Northern Ireland	2	1976
Norway	2	1921
USSR	2	1975
Burma	1	1991
Canada	1	1957
China	1	1989
Costa Rica	1	1987
Denmark	1	1908
Egypt	1	1978
Guatemala	1	1992
Ireland	1	1974
Israel	1	1978
Italy	1	1907
Japan	1	1974
Macedonia	1	1979
Mexico	1	1982
Netherlands	1	1911
North Vietnam	1	1973
Poland	1	1983

In addition to the above, a number of international organisations have won the Peace Prize:

Organisation	Total	Year first awarded Prize
International Committee of the Red Cross	3	1917
Office of the United Nations High Commissioner for Refugees	2	1954
American Friends Service Committee	1	1947
Amnesty International	1	1977
Institute of International Law	1	1904
International Labour Organization	1	1969
International Peace Bureau	1	1910
International Physicians for the Prevention of Nuclear War	1	1985
Nansen International Office for Refugees	1	1938
United Nations Children's Fund	1	1965
United Nations Peacekeeping Forces	1	1988
Total	92	

*Includes both West and East Germany
Notes
1 Nobel Prizes are actually awarded to individuals rather than the countries from which they come.
2 Figures include 1993 prizewinners.

PERSONALITIES

Madame Tussaud's Popularity Poll

At the end of each year, Madame Tussaud's wax museum in London holds a popularity poll – asking visitors to name their heroes and heroines regardless of whether or not they are portrayed at Madame Tussaud's. Only one category asks visitors specifically to name their favourite waxwork figure. Recent results appear below:

Gérard Depardieu's wax portrait, amongst the top five favourite entertainment and arts category personalities.

Politics

1993	1992	1991	1990
1 ⎡Mikhail Gorbachev ⎣Margaret Thatcher	1 Margaret Thatcher	1 John Major	1 Margaret Thatcher
3 John Major	2 Mikhail Gorbachev	2 Margaret Thatcher	2 Mikhail Gorbachev
4 Bill Clinton	3 John Major	3 ⎡George Bush ⎣Mikhail Gorbachev	3 John Major
5 Nelson Mandela	4 Bill Clinton	5 Paddy Ashdown	4 ⎡Neil Kinnock ⎣Michael Heseltine
	5 George Bush		

Sport

1993	1992	1991	1990
1 Boris Becker	1 Paul Gascoigne	1 Boris Becker	1 Boris Becker
2 Nigel Mansell	2 Boris Becker	2 Gary Lineker	2 Peter Shilton
3 Will Carling	3 Gary Lineker	3 Paul Gascoigne	3 Paul Gascoigne
4 Paul Gascoigne	4 ⎡Daley Thompson ⎣Nigel Mansell	4 Daley Thompson	4 Gary Lineker
5 Johann Cruyff		5 John McEnroe	5 Stefen Edberg

Entertainment

1993	1992	1991	1990
1 Rowan Atkinson	1 Michael Jackson	1 Benny Hill	1 Eddie Murphy
2 Tom Cruise	2 Eddie Murphy	2 ⎡Cher ⎣Sylvester Stallone	2 Benny Hill
3 Madonna	3 Madonna	4 Eddie Murphy	3 Michael Jackson
4 Eddie Murphy	4 Gérard Depardieu	5 Lenny Henry	4 Lenny Henry
5 Lenny Henry	5 Dame Edna Everage		5 Dame Edna Everage

The Arts

1993	1992	1991	1990
1 Vincent van Gogh	1 Vincent van Gogh	1 Pablo Picasso	1 Pablo Picasso
2 Pablo Picasso	2 Pablo Picasso	2 Luciano Pavarotti	2 Mozart
3 Salvador Dali	3 Luciano Pavarotti	3 Salvador Dali	3 ⎡Vincent van Gogh ⎣Luciano Pavarotti
4 Luciano Pavarotti	4 Gérard Depardieu	4 ⎡Vincent van Gogh ⎣William Shakespeare	5 William Shakespeare
5 Ludwig van Beethoven	5 Mozart		

Beauty and Glamour

1993	1992	1991	1990
1 Cindy Crawford	1 Cindy Crawford	1 Jerry Hall	1 Jerry Hall
2 Elizabeth Taylor	2 Cher	2 Cher	2 Cher
3 Princess of Wales	3 Joan Collins	3 Marilyn Monroe	3 Marilyn Monroe
4 Joan Collins	4 Princess of Wales	4 Princess Diana	4 Madonna
5 Claudia Schiffer	5 Jerry Hall	5 Joan Collins	5 Joan Collins

Most Hated and Feared

1993	1992	1991	1990
1 Saddam Hussein	1 Saddam Hussein	1 Adolf Hitler	1 Saddam Hussein
2 Adolf Hitler	2 Adolf Hitler	2 Saddam Hussein	2 Adolf Hitler
3 Jack the Ripper	3 Margaret Thatcher	3 Margaret Thatcher	3 Margaret Thatcher
4 Hannibal Lecter	4 Colonel Gadaffi	4 Colonel Gadaffi	4 Jack the Ripper
5 Charles Manson	5 Jack the Ripper	5 Freddie Kruger	5 Freddie Kruger

Alexander Müller (Swi). Discovery of superconductivity in ceramic materials

1988 Leon M. Lederman, Melvin Schwartz and Jack Steinberger (USA). Researched subatomic particles

1989 Norman F. Ramsey (USA). Invention of separated oscillatory field method and its use in the hydrogen maser and other atomic clocks

Hans G. Dehmelt (USA) and Wolfgang Paul (Ger). Development of the ion trap technique

1990 Jerome I. Friedman, Henry W. Kendall (USA) and Richard E. Taylor (Can). Investigations concerning deep inelastic scattering of electrons on protons and bound neutrons, which have been of essential importance for development of the quark model in particle physics

1991 Pierre-Gilles de Gennes (Fra). Studies in changes in liquid crystals

1992 George Charpak (Fra). Devised an electronic detector that reads trajectories of sub-atomic particles

1993 Russell Hulse and Joseph Taylor (USA). Discovered first indirect proof of existence of gravity waves

Physics Nobel Prize Winners by Country

Country	Total	Year first awarded Prize
USA	58	1907
UK	21	1904
Germany*	16	1901
France	10	1903
Netherlands	6	1902
USSR	6	1958
Sweden	4	1912
Austria	3	1933
Denmark	3	1922
Italy	3	1909
Japan	3	1949
Switzerland	3	1920
China	2	1957
Canada	1	1990
India	1	1930
Ireland	1	1951
Pakistan	1	1979
Total	**142**	

*Includes both West and East Germany
Notes
1 Nobel Prizes are actually awarded to individuals rather than the countries from which they come.
2 Figures include 1993 prizewinners.

The wonder of holography – invented by Englishman Dennis Gabor who was awarded the Nobel Prize for Physics for his discovery in 1971. A boy admires circular holograms at the Museum of La Villette in Paris.

POETRY

Poets Laureate

There is no official record of the origin of the office of Poet Laureate of England. The poet of the royal household is so called because of the laurel wreath which was awarded to eminent poets in the Graeco-Roman world. The laureate is elected and serves to write commemorative verses to celebrate major public occasions.

According to Thomas Warton, historian and poet laureate, in the reign of Henry III (1216–72) there was a Versificator Regis or King's Poet who was paid 100 shillings a year. The history of early poets with unofficial status include Geoffrey Chaucer (1340–1400), who in 1389 got a royal grant of a yearly allowance of wine; John Kay (during Edward IV's reign [1461–83]); Andrew Bernard (Henry VII [1485–1509]); John Skelton (Henry VIII [1509–47]); Edmund Spenser; Samuel Daniel (appointed 1599); and Ben Jonson (1619). Godson of William Shakespeare, William D'Avenant, was appointed in 1637.

Alfred Tennyson, longest-serving poet laureate.

■ Thomas Shadwell was involved in a violent feud with the poet John Dryden, whom he attacked in *The Medal of John Bayes* (1682). He succeeded Dryden as poet laureate in 1688.

■ The longest-serving poet laureate was Alfred Tennyson who was appointed on 19 November 1850 and died in office on 6 October 1892 – a total of 41 years 322 days.

■ The oldest poet laurate was William Wordsworth who was 73 years old when he succeeded Robert Southey on 6 April 1843.

■ The youngest poet laureate was Laurence Eusdan who succeeded on 24 December 1718 at the age of 30 years 3 months.

In 1668 the post was officially established. There is an annual stipend payable of £70 plus £27 in lieu of the traditional butt of sack (cask of wine). Poets laureate since 1668 have been:

1668 John Dryden (1631–1700)
1688 Thomas Shadwell (1642–92)
1692 Nahum Tate (1652–1715)
1715 Nicholas Rowe (1674–1718)
1718 Laurence Eusden (1688–1730)
1730 Colley Cibber (1671–1757)
1757 William Whitehead (1715–85). Appointed after Thomas Gray declined
1785 Thomas Warton (1728–90)
1790 Henry James Pye (1745–1813)
1813 Robert Southey (1774–1843)
1843 William Wordsworth (1770–1850)
1850 Alfred, Lord Tennyson (1809–92). Appointed after Samuel Russell declined
1896 Alfred Austin (1835–1913)
1913 Robert Bridges (1844–1930)
1930 John Masefield (1878–1967)
1968 Cecil Day Lewis (1904–72)
1972 Sir John Betjeman (1906–84)
1984 Ted Hughes (1930–)

Pulitzer Prize

Awarded for a distinguished volume of verse by an American author (see separate section, Pulitzer Prizes).
1918 *Love Songs*, Sara Teasdale
1919 *Corn Huskers*, Carl Sandburg; *Old Road to Paradise*, Margaret Widdemer
1920 No award
1921 No award
1922 *Collected Poems*, Edwin Arlington Robinson
1923 *The Ballad of the Harp-Weaver; A Few Figs from Thistles*; eight sonnets in *American Poetry 1922, A Miscellany*, Edna St. Vincent Millay
1924 *New Hampshire: A Poem with Notes and Grace Notes*, Robert Frost
1925 *The Man Who Died Twice*, Edwin Arlington Robinson
1926 *What's O'Clock*, Amy Lowell
1927 *Fiddler's Farewell,* Leonora Speyer
1928 *Tristram,* Edwin Arlington Robinson
1929 *John Brown's Body*, Stephen Vincent Benet
1930 *Selected Poems*, Conrad Aiken
1931 *Collected Poems*, Robert Frost
1932 *The Flowering Stone,* George Dillon

185

Term		Party	Length of office
1970–74	Edward Heath	Conservative	3 years 9 months
1974–76	Harold Wilson	Labour	2 years 1 month
1976–79	James Callaghan	Labour	3 years 1 month
1979–90	Margaret Thatcher	Conservative	11 years 6 months
1990–	John Major	Conservative	(Took office 28 November 1990)

American Presidential Elections (since 1900)

	Presidential candidates	Party	Electoral vote	Popular vote
1900	William McKinley	Republican	292	7 219 530
	William J. Bryan	Dem People's	155	6 358 071
	Eugene V. Debs	Social Democratic	0	94 768
1904	Theodore Roosevelt	Republican	336	7 628 834
	Alton B. Parker	Democratic	140	5 084 491
	Eugene V. Debs	Socialist	0	402 400
1908	William H. Taft	Republican	321	7 679 006
	William J. Bryan	Democratic	162	6 409 106
	Eugene V. Debs	Socialist	0	420 820
1912	Woodrow Wilson	Democratic	435	6 286 214
	Theodore Roosevelt	Progressive	88	4 126 020
	William H. Taft	Republican	8	3 483 922
	Eugene V. Debs	Socialist	0	897 011
1916	Woodrow Wilson	Democratic	277	9 129 606
	Charles E. Hughes	Republican	254	8 538 221
	A. L. Benson	Socialist	0	585 113
1920	Warren G. Harding	Republican	404	16 152 200
	James M. Cox	Democratic	127	9 147 353
	Eugene V. Debs	Socialist	0	917 799
1924	Calvin Coolidge	Republican	382	15 725 016
	John W. Davis	Democratic	136	8 385 586
	Robert M. LaFollette	Progressive, Socialist	13	4 822 856
1928	Herbert Hoover	Republican	444	21 392 190
	Alfred E. Smith	Democratic	87	15 016 443
	Norman Thomas	Socialist	0	267 420
1932	Franklin D. Roosevelt	Democratic	472	22 821 857
	Herbert Hoover	Republican	59	15 761 841
	Norman Thomas	Socialist	0	884 781
1936	Franklin D. Roosevelt	Democratic	523	27 751 597
	Alfred M. Landon	Republican	8	16 679 583
	Norman Thomas	Socialist	0	187 720
1940	Franklin D. Roosevelt	Democratic	449	27 244 160
	Wendell L. Willkie	Republican	82	22 305 198
	Norman Thomas	Socialist	0	99 557
1944	Franklin D. Roosevelt	Democratic	432	25 602 504
	Thomas E. Dewey	Republican	99	22 006 285
	Norman Thomas	Socialist	0	80 518
1948	Harry S Truman	Democratic	303	24 179 345
	Thomas S. Dewey	Republican	189	21 991 291
	J. Strom Thurmond	States' Rights Dem	39	1 176 125
	Henry A. Wallace	Progressive	0	1 157 326
	Norman Thomas	Socialist	0	139 572
1952	Dwight D. Eisenhower	Republican	442	33 936 234
	Adlai E. Stevenson	Democratic	89	27 314 992
1956	Dwight D. Eisenhower	Republican	457	35 590 472
	Adlai E. Stevenson	Democratic	73	26 022 752
1960	John F. Kennedy	Democratic	303	34 226 731
	Richard M. Nixon	Republican	219	34 108 157

'A politician should have three hats. One for throwing in the ring, one for talking through, and one for pulling rabbits out of if elected.'

Carl Sandburg

'Every government carries a health warning.'

Anon

'Elections are won by men and women chiefly because most people vote against somebody, rather than for somebody.'

Franklin P. Adams

'Well I have one consolation. No candidate was ever elected ex-president by such a large majority!'

William Howard Taft, US statesman, referring to his disastrous defeat in the 1912 presidential election

Presidential candidates	Party	Electoral vote	Popular vote
1964 Lyndon B. Johnson	Democratic	486	43 129 484
Barry M. Goldwater	Republican	52	27 178 188
1968 Richard M. Nixon	Republican	301	31 785 480
Hubert H. Humphrey	Democratic	191	31 275 166
George C. Wallace	American Ind	46	9 906 473
1972 Richard M. Nixon	Republican	520	47 169 911
George McGovern	Democratic	17	29 170 383
John G. Schmitz	American	0	1 099 482
1976 Jimmy Carter	Democratic	297	40 828 657
Gerald R. Ford	Republican	240	39 145 520
Eugene J. McCarthy	Independent	0	756 605
1980 Ronald Reagan	Republican	489	43 209 016
Jimmy Carter	Democratic	49	34 921 696
John Anderson	Independent	0	5 581 710
1984 Ronald Reagan	Republican	525	54 281 858
Walter F. Mondale	Democratic	13	37 457 215
1988 George Bush	Republican	426	48 881 221
Michael S. Dukakis	Democratic	111	41 805 422
1992 Bill Clinton	Democratic	370	44 908 254
George Bush	Republic	168	39 102 343
H. Ross Perot	Independent	0	19 741 065

Note: The popular vote is the vote of the people which determines the senators and representatives to which each state is entitled. The electoral vote is the presidential vote by ballot of the senators and representatives, which determines the next president.

The longest American presidential inaugural address lasted nearly two hours and was composed of 8445 words. It was delivered by a hatless, coatless William Henry Harrison during a snowfall in 1841. He died of pneumonia exactly a month later.

Parliamentarians of the Year

These awards have been given since 1984 and are sponsored and organised by *The Spectator* and Highland Park. The main award, Parliamentarian of the Year, has gone to the following:

1984 David Owen
1985 John Biffen
1986 John Smith
1987 Nigel Lawson
1988 Edward Heath
1989 John Smith
1990 Douglas Hurd
1991 Robin Cook
1992 Betty Boothroyd
1993 George Robertson
Geoffrey Hoon

The principal task of an opposition is to defeat the Government. In July 1993 a combination of the opposition parties and Conservative rebels did just that, on the question of the opt-out from the Social Chapter of the Maastricht Treaty. The 1993 award was made jointly to George Robertson, Labour's European spokesman, and Geoffrey Hoon, a backbench Labour lawyer, for constructing the trap that forced the Government to allow a vote on this question. When the Government lost, only a vote of confidence tied to the question saved the Prime Minister. The judges had great regard for the way in which the opposition outwitted the Government.

Other 1993 awards were made as follows:

Member to Watch Nicholas Soames
'. . . He is one of the most effective and popular ministers in the Government. He is an outstanding communicator. At the dispatch box his persuasive skills and wit disarm even the most hostile opponent. As a minister with politics in his blood, he embodies many of the old virtues of public service. The judges viewed him not only as a man who merits promotion, but also as one likely to achieve high office in his party.'

Backbencher of the Year Sir Peter Tapsell
'. . . First elected in 1959 he has, apart from a brief spell in the 1970s, never held any sort of office. Yet, in the 1955 General Election, he was right-hand man to Sir Anthony Eden. He is exactly the sort of backbencher the whips cannot tolerate. He makes a point, in his frequent interventions, of confirming that he is not asking planted questions. He is a completely independent man and demonstrates this by frequently asking the question the Prime Minister least wants to hear. He is still famed for a remark he made more than a decade ago to Dr David Owen, who said of a particular policy that "history will judge". "Has the Rt. Hon. gentleman not considered," said Tapsell, "that history may have something better to do?"'

Debater of the Year Kenneth Clarke
'. . . He has been described by no less an expert than Lady Thatcher as "a bruiser". The House of Commons is littered with men who bear the marks of his verbal batterings. When executing probably the finest U-turn in modern political history, in tearing up large parts of the last Criminal Justice Act, he did so with a brutalist shamelessness that left his normally eloquent opponent, Tony Blair, almost gasping. Later in the same debate, he memorably advised Robert MacLennan of the Liberal Democrats to go and lie down in a darkened room and keep taking the pills.'

(The judges state that 'their awards do not claim any superior authority. They are offered only in affection and respect for the Houses of Parliament.')

Hull	Camb'ge U	11		
Leyton O	Burnley	12		
Reading				
Rotherham				
Chest'field				
Crewe	Bury	16		

Littlewoods Pools was launched with a capital of £150 in 1923 as a part-time venture by three young Manchester Post Office telegraphists – Colin Askham, Bill Hughes and John Moores. They rented a single top-floor room in Church Street, Liverpool. Feeling that their employers would disapprove of their venture, they decided to use the surname Askham had before he was adopted – Littlewood.

They found a printer and secretary and commissioned schoolboys to distribute coupons on the terraces. Four thousand copies of the first coupon were printed and distributed outside Manchester United football ground. Only 35 of these coupons were returned and the total amount of money invested was only £4 7s 6d, with a first payout of just £2 12s 0d. A little later, 10 000 coupons were distributed at a major football fixture in Hull and only one was returned.

At the end of its first season in operation, Littlewoods Pools had incurred losses amounting to £600, and two of the partners decided to withdraw. John Moores, the surviving partner, decided to carry on and buy out the partners for £200 each, persuading his brother, Cecil, and their two sisters to join the company – a decision that was to make him a millionaire before he was 35.

In 1928 the total pool for one week reached the £10 000 mark, by 1934 the figure had risen to £200 000, and in 1939 it had topped £400 000. Today, Littlewoods handles approximately seven million coupons, which represents 70 per cent of the pools' market (Vernons and Zetters share the other 30 per cent) and pays out dividends amounting to over £3 000 000 every week.

					£6.60	8 from 12	12

Barry Mallett from Harwich, Essex, and his father who share the record £2 255 387.40 won in February 1994 with a stake of only 60p.

In 1983, when there were widespread redundancies in Liverpool, John Moores swopped his Rolls-Royce for a Ford Cortina. His fellow executives asked him why he bothered – the whole of Liverpool knew he was a billionaire. 'Yes,' he replied, 'but do they know I *care* about them?'

FACTS

■ Over seven million coupons are received weekly.

■ Littlewoods is the biggest pools company, paying out £6 every second . . . £360 every minute . . . £21 600 every hour . . .

■ All pools wins are tax free.

■ The fastest jackpot on record came in 1979 when Irene Powell, an unemployed hairdresser from Port Talbot, W. Glam, filled in her first ever coupon and won £882 528.

■ Littlewoods pays out £3.5 million every week – it is the number of draws and where they are placed on the coupon which decides how big the dividends are and whether or not there is a jackpot.

■ The collectors' service for the coupons took off with the postal strike in the early 1970s, when people looked for an alternative way of handing in their coupons. Today, some 70 000 collectors nationwide handle 90 per cent of the coupons.

Record Wins on the Pools

Date	Amount	Details
1923–36		No records kept
1937	£30 780	Record 4 aways dividend paid to R. Levy, London
1947	£64 450	Record Penny Points Pool dividend
1948	£75 000	First ever win of this amount on Treble Chance, F. Chivers, Aldershot, Hants
1950	£100 000	Winner on the Treble Chance Pool, Mrs E. Knowlson, Manchester
1957	£200 000	N. McGrail, Stockport
1959	£300 000	Belfast man
1971	£400 000	Leeds man
1972	£512 683	K. Grimes, Liss, Hants
March 1979	£882 528	Miss Irene Powell, Port Talbot, W. Glam
February 1980	£953 874.10	New record – Dave Preston of Burton-on-Trent, Staffs hits the jackpot on both Littlewoods and Vernons in the same week
October 1984	three x £750 000	Three £750 000 jackpots won in consecutive weeks. The first was Jack Calvert, Sale, Cheshire; the second, an anonymous Scotsman; the third, Neil Hembling, Dunstable, Beds
December 1984	£776 735	First ever double jackpot. Syd Barnard, Brighton (£776 735) and Cec Carr and his group of City of London Bank workers (£784 411)
April 1985	£784 411	First ever double jackpot. Syd Barnard, Brighton (£776 735) and Cec Carr and his group of City of London Bank workers (£784 411)
	£937 807.36	First £900 000 plus win, Dennis Turner, Stoke-on-Trent, Staffs receives a world record cheque for a 36p stake on ten random numbers
April 1986	£1 017 890	First £1 million Pools win and the biggest ever prize in any British competition. Nursing Sister Margaret Francis and ten colleagues win with an 8 from 11 perm costing £1.32.
April 1987	£1 032 088.40	Anonymous Bexley housewife wins a record jackpot with a 40p stake
July 1987	£1 339 358.30	Jimmy Anderson, 51-year-old lorry driver
January 1990	£1 501 405	Four Marks and Spencer warehousemen from Llandudno, Gwynedd scoop this record sum with a *Sun* Plan 40
January 1990	£1 505 443	Heating engineer Alan Hepden sets a new record only three weeks later by winning with an 8 from 10 perm costing just 45p.
March 1990	£1 515 589.05	Former policeman from Cumbria
June 1990	£1 111 346	For the first time ever, two people win £1 million each in the same week. Retired waitress Mona Skidmore (£1 111 346) and a Norfolk man (£1 131 012)
August 1990	£1 131 012	For the first time ever, two people win £1 million each in the same week. Retired waitress Mona Skidmore (£1 111 346) and a Norfolk man (£1 131 012)
1991	£1 556 070.75	Eight West Midlands engineering workers
October 1991	£1 646 108.20	Great-grandmother, Peggy Regan, scoops a world record jackpot cheque with an 8 from 10 perm costing just 45p
1992	£2 072 220	Romanian born Rodi Woodcock became the first person to win more than £2 million with an 8 from 10 perm, costing 54p
1992	£2 137 917	A South London office worker wins with an 8 from 12 perm costing £5.94
January 1994	£2 246 113	Bournemouth man
	£2 255 387.40	Barry Mallett, from Harwich, Essex, with a stake of only 60p, wins with a full perm 8 from 10. He shares the win with his father.

Premium Entries

PLANS
THE

29

| 58 | Stenh'muir |

PUBS

CAMRA *Pub of the Year*

The Campaign for Real Ale (CAMRA) award was first given in 1989, and seeks to recognise the ambience and character of the British pub with both regional winners and a national champion. The national winners have been:

1989 Boar's Head, Kinmuck, Aberdeen
1990 Cap and Feathers, Tillingham, Essex
1991 Bell, Aldworth, Berks
1992 Great Western, Wolverhampton, W. Midlands
1993 Fisherman's Tavern, Broughty Ferry, Tayside
Three Kings, Hanley Castle, Hereford and Worcs

The 1994 Good Pub Guide *Awards*

The 1994 Good Pub Guide, edited by Alisdair Aird, provides a guide to recommended pubs. All entries in the book go through a two-stage process before inclusion. First, some 2000 correspondents regularly report on pubs, and nearly double that number report occasionally. Each pub, before inclusion, is anonymously visited by the book's editor or deputy editor, or both. To warrant inclusion in the book, the pub has to have some special quality that would make strangers enjoy visiting it. What often marks a pub out for special attention is good value food (anything from a well-made sandwich to imaginative cooking outclassing most restaurants in the area); or drinks that are out of the ordinary (pubs with several hundred whiskies, with remarkable wine lists, home-made country wines or good beer or cider made on the premises). There may be a special appeal about it as a place to stay, with good bedrooms, or maybe the building itself or its surroundings are exceptional.

From these entries the following have been designated winners within the following categories. Details have been taken from the *Guide*.

Pub of the Year

Royal Oak, Appleby, Cumbria 'This pub keeps eight to ten real ales on handpump at any one time, several malt whiskies, and a carefully chosen wine list. Part of the long, low building dates back to the 14th century. Fresh and home-made, the enterprising menu typically includes superb soup with home-made bread, lunchtime sandwiches, Cumberland sausage (made by hand by the local butcher's wife), green pancakes, good salads, real brown Lancashire shrimps and vegetarian dishes. There are adventurous daily specials, children's meals, and puddings; the breakfasts, if staying overnight, are gigantic. In summer the outside is very colourful, with seats on the front terrace among masses of flowers in tubs, troughs and hanging baskets.'

Landlord of the Year

Stephen Waring, Wenlock Edge Inn,

The Royal Oak at Appleby, Cumbria – 1994 Pub of the Year.

Salop 'A tremendously favoured pub where you will be greeted by a wonderful welcome. The marvellously special atmosphere is down to the very friendly Warings, for whom nothing is too much trouble. The cosy feel is perhaps at its best on Mondays – story-telling night, when the right-hand bar is packed with locals telling tales, some true, others somewhat dubious. There's a big woodburning stove in an inglenook in here, as well as a shelf of high plates. The consistently excellent fresh home-made bar food includes, for example, soup, prawn salad, steak and mushroom pie, and good old-fashioned puddings such as lemon pudding, fruit crumble or treacle tart. If you stay the night and shower it will be in mineral water as the pub's water comes from its own 119-foot well.'

Dining Pub of the Year

Blue Lion, East Witton, Yorks 'Besides sandwiches and soup, a wide choice of enterprising home-made bar food might include tagliatelle carbonara, excellent poached fillet of salmon with a chive and cucumber beurre blanc, sautéed duck-leg confit with butterbeans cooked in tomato and smoked-bacon sauce, pheasant rolled in bacon with sage sauce, and puddings such as treacle sponge, white-chocolate mousse and apple crumble with brown-bread ice cream. The big squarish bar has high-backed antique settles, old Windsor chairs and round tables on the turkey rugs and flagstones.'

Scottish Dining Pub of the Year

Riverside, Canonbie, Dumfries and Galloway 'Comfortable and restful communicating rooms in the bar have a peaceful atmosphere. The bar menu, chalked up by the bar staff each lunchtime, might include soups like fish and shellfish, herring in oatmeal, a dozen langoustines, cod fillets in beer batter, venison, and lots of puddings such as spiced brown bread and butter pudding with toffee sauce or baked rhubarb cheesecake with rhubarb and orange sauce. There are careful touches like virgin olive oil for the salad dressings, bread baked on the premises, and a concentration on "organic" foods.'

Welsh Dining Pub of the Year

Walnut Tree, Llandewi, Skirrid, Gwent The small white-walled bar has polished settles and country chairs around tables, and a flagstone floor. It opens into an airy and relaxed dining lounge where a typical menu might include starters such as gazpacho soup,

tagliolini with courgette flowers and truffle paste, bruschetta with seafood, half a dozen oysters. To follow, items such as fillet of Dover sole brodettato, lamb sweetbreads, mushrooms marsala and parma ham, breast of guinea fowl, or roast monkfish with samphire coulis and deep-fried seaweed. Puddings include chocolate brandy loaf and coffee-bean sauce, or coconut parfait with mango sauce.'

London Dining Pub of the Year

The Eagle, Farringdon Road, EC1 'Unusually for a London pub, food is the reason to come here. There's an emphasis on Mediterranean dishes (particularly Spanish and Italian). The open kitchen forms part of the bar, and furnishings are simple – school chairs and circular tables on bare boards. The menu changes twice daily and all produce used is of the highest quality: ribollita (Tuscan beans, bacon and Swiss chard soup with bread and olive oil), Greek salad, spaghetti with courgettes, garlic, chilli, basil and pine kernels, roast red onions and mashed potato, marinated rumpsteak and ciabatta sandwich. Puddings such as apricot and cherry frangipani tart or strawberries macerated with red wine are offered.'

Cellarman of the Year

Graham Titcombe, Blackwood Arms, Littleworth Common, Bucks 'This unspoilt country pub has a friendly atmosphere and a marvellous choice of constantly changing real ales. The landlord only deals with small independent brewers and on the five handpumps may have up to 60 different beers a week, for example Black Sheep Special, Clarks Festival, Hambleton Goldfields, Hop Back Summer Lightning, Orkney Skull Splitter and Woodfordes Nelsons Revenge. They also serve Belgian draught and bottled beers, a constantly changing farm cider, and a good choice of malt whiskies.'

Own-brew Pub of the Year

Rising Sun, Shraleybrook, Staffs 'It's the range of beers that attract people to this pub. Their own ales are produced in the brewery behind the pub, which currently supplies five bitters – Rising, Setting, Sunlight, Sunstroke, Solar Flare, and a stronger brew fittingly called Total Eclipse. Guest beers might include Adnams, Badger, Courage Directors, Hadrian Gladiator and Centurion, Robinwood Old Fart and Titanic. There are also around 125 malts, 12 cognacs, 100 liqueurs, and foreign beers from

Belgium, Germany, Singapore, Spain and Australia. The bar has a warm open fire, beams and timbers, dim lighting, curtains made from beer drip towels sewn together, and there may be a minibus service to get you home!'

Wine Pub of the Year

Fox, Lower Oddington, Glos 'There's an exceptionally good choice of wines here – the owners are in partnerships with a very highly regarded wine guru as shippers. The building is elegant, carefully restored, with simple, spotlessly furnished rooms, flagstones and an open fire.'

Whisky Pub of the Year

Wight Mouse Bar, Clarendon Hotel, Chale, Isle of Wight 'Named after a ship wrecked just off the shore here in the Great Storm of 1836, this bar stocks a good range of drinks including well-kept Boddingtons, Marstons Pedigree, Whitbreads Castle Eden and Strong Country on handpump, an outstanding choice of around 365 whiskies, nearly 50 wines, and some uncommon brandies, madeiras and country wines.'

Fish Pub of the Year

Half Moon, Kirdford, Sussex 'Three generations of one family took over this 17th-century pub in 1992. As the family have ties with Billingsgate going back 130 years, fresh fish is very much the speciality (they have become the leading UK importer of fresh exotic species from around the world). Their menu might include tile fish, porgy, parrot fish, soft-shell crabs, Morton Bay bugs, scabbard fish, razor shells, mahi mahi, and baramundi.'

Best Vegetarian Pub Cooking

Royal Oak, Barrington, Cambs 'A good choice of vegetarian dishes in this interesting thatched and heavily-timbered pub might include chestnut and cashew pâté, nut and date curry or walnut spiral, lager mushrooms and pineapple fritter with sweet and sour sauce on a pillow of rice, pecan mango and mushroom stroganoff or basil strudel with a lime glaze.'

Best Traditional English Cooking

Green Man, Gosfield, Essex 'This friendly pub has a fine atmosphere in its two little bars and extremely good English food. This might include good leek and potato or superb game with sherry soups, liver and bacon, salads with home-cooked tongue, beef or turkey carved by the landlord, braised oxtail, duck with gooseberry sauce; and well-made home-made puddings like treacle pudding or spotted dick. The vegetables are fresh and the chips home-made.'

Top Yorkshire Pudding Pub

Half Moon, Skidby, Humberside 'Plenty of pubs in this area and further afield have yorkshire pudding on the menu, but we single out this establishment as doing the best. Their unique speciality loaf-size but feather-light Yorkshire puddings with various fillings are deservedly popular – so much so that their creation involes some 70 000 eggs and 7000 lb of flour a year. The choice goes from onion gravy, through chilli and curry to roast beef.'

Best Home-made Pudding

Duke of York, Berrow, Hereford & Worcs 'If you love puddings, then this is the pub for you. It offers 20 home-made varieties, ranging from bread and butter pudding to treacle tart, fruit pies and crumbles to gâteaux. It is an old, friendly, well-run pub – in the 15th century it was used by pilgrims who were making their way from Tewkesbury to Hereford, and was later a meeting point for local Yorkists in the Wars of the Roses.'

Cheese Pub of the Year

Royal Oak, Didsbury, Manchester 'Over the last 30 years, the enthusiastic landlord has been tracking down cheeses from all over the place, and you'd be hard pushed to find one he doesn't keep.'

Good Value Cheap Food Award

Admiral, St Helier, Channel Islands Recently opened, this big pub has interesting decorations, such as old telephones, a clocking-in machine, copper milk churn, enamel advertising signs and nice touches such as the daily papers to read and an old penny What the Butler Saw machine. Very good-value food includes filled rolls, home-made soup (£1.30), half a spit-roasted chicken (£1.95), cottage pie (£2.50), pizzas (from £2.50) and mushroom pie (£2.95). Sunday lunch costs £5.95.'

Warmest Welcome of the Year

Lathkill, Over Haddon, Derbys 'The setting here is marvellous – you can walk straight out into the wooded pastures of Lathkill Dale, and if you follow the footpath to the east of the pub you can see the River Lathkill far below flowing over a series of weirs; there's even a place in the lobby on your return for muddy boots. The airy room on the right has old-fashioned settles with upholstered cushions or plain wooden chairs and big windows. On the left is a spacious and sunny family dining area which doubles as a restaurant in the evenings.'

Unspoilt Pub of the Year

Bell, Aldworth, Berks 'Marvellously old-fashioned and simple, this welcoming 14th-century country pub has been in the same family for over 200 years. The cosy bar has beams in the shiny ochre ceiling, benches around its panelled walls, a woodburning stove, an ancient one-handed clock, and a glass-panelled hatch rather than a bar counter for service. The quiet, old-fashioned garden is lovely in summer.'

County Dining Pubs of the Year

Alisdair Aird, Editor of *The 1994 Good Pub Guide*, has included for the first time a list of 'Dining Pubs of the Year' for almost every county. These pubs offer an outstanding combination of excellent cooking with attractive surroundings and atmosphere.

Berkshire	Harrow, West Ilsley
Buckinghamshire	Old Crown, Skirmett
Cambridgeshire	Three Tuns, Fen Drayton
Cheshire	Cholmondeley Arms, nr Bickley Moss
Cumbria	Bay Horse, Ulverston
Derbyshire	Druid, Birchover
Devon	Drew Arms, Broadhembury
Dorset	Manor Hotel, West Bexington
Essex	Queens Head, Littlebury
Gloucester	Kings Head, Bledington
Hampshire	Wykeham Arms, Winchester
Hereford and Worcs	Lough Pool, Sellack
Hertfordshire	George & Dragon, Watton at Stone
Humberside	Pipe & Glass, South Dalton
Isle of Wight	Seaview Hotel, Seaview
Kent	George, Newnham
Lancashire	Bushells Arms, Goosnargh
Leicestershire	Peacock, Redmile
Lincolnshire	George, Stamford
Nottinghamshire	Martins Arms, Colston Bassett
Norfolk	Saracens Head, Erpingham
Northamptonshire	Falcon, Fotheringhay
Northumbria	Fox & Hounds, Cotherstone
Oxfordshire	Lamb, Shipton-under-Wychwood
Shropshire	Stables, Hope
Somerset	Notley Arms, Monksilver
Staffordshire	Olde Dog & Partridge, Tutbury
Suffolk	Crown, Southwold
Surrey	Woolpack, Elstead
Sussex	Griffin, Fletching
Warwickshire	Bell, Alderminster
Wiltshire	Silver Plough, Pitton

The largest UK pub is the 'Downham Tavern' in Bromley, Kent. It was built in 1930 and has two large bars, each 45 ft (13.7 m) in length accommodating 1000 customers in total. The smallest pub is the ground floor of 'The Nutshell' in Bury St Edmunds, Suffolk, measuring 15 ft 10 in x 7 ft 6 in (4.82 x 2.28 m).

The Bell Aldworth Berks.

The Bell, Aldworth, Berks – Unspoilt Pub of the Year.

PULITZER PRIZES

Joseph Pulitzer (1847–1911) was an American editor and publisher who contributed greatly towards creating a model for the modern newspaper with such features as sports sections, women's pages, comics and illustrations. He also introduced promotional campaigns featuring stunts and contests. He was born in Makó, Hungary on 10 April 1847 and educated in Budapest. In 1864 he went to Boston, Massachusetts, USA, where he enlisted in the Union Army and served until 1865. In 1867 he took up American citizenship and a year later went to work as a reporter for a German-language newspaper owned by Carl Schurz in St Louis, Missouri.

Pulitzer was elected as a Republican to Missouri in 1869 and was prominent in Horace Greeley's presidential campaign in 1872. He then joined the Democratic party where he remained for the rest of his life. He also read law but never went into practice.

In 1878 Pulitzer bought the bankrupt St Louis *Dispatch* and merged it with the St Louis *Evening Post*, becoming sole owner and renaming it the St Louis *Post-Dispatch*. Five years later, he bought the New York *World* which became a platform for the Democratic party in America. In 1885 he was elected to the US House of Representatives but resigned after a few months. In 1887 he founded another New York daily paper, the *Evening World*.

In his will, Pulitzer provided for the endowment of the Columbia School of Journalism, which opened in 1912, and a gift of $500 000 for the creation of the Pulitzer Prizes which have been awarded to American citizens since 1917. They have been awarded each spring since 1947 by the trustees of Columbia University and administered by the University's Graduate School of Journalism. The recipients of the awards are decided by a 14-member Advisory Board which was created under the terms of Pulitzer's will. Each award carries a $3000 prize (apart from the recipient of the Public Service Journalism Award

which carries a gold medal). The Board acts on findings by juries who are appointed by the university. In 1994 the following awards were made:

Journalism (see p. 136)

1 Public Service – for a distinguished example of meritorious public service by a newspaper through the use of its journalistic resources, which may include editorials, cartoons and photographs, as well as reporting.

2 Spot News Reporting – for a distinguished example of local reporting of spot news.

3 Investigative Reporting – for a distinguished example of investigative reporting within a newspaper's area of circulation by an individual or team, presented as a single article or series.

4 Explanatory Journalism – for a distinguished example of explanatory journalism that illuminates significant and complex issues.

5 Beat Reporting – for a distinguished example of beat reporting.

6 National Reporting – for a distinguished example of reporting on national affairs.

7 International Reporting – for a distinguished example of reporting on international affairs, including a United Nations correspondence.

8 Feature Writing – for a distinguished example of feature writing, giving prime consideration to high literary quality and originality.

9 Commentary – for distinguished commentary.

10 Criticism – for distinguished criticism.

11 Editorial Writing – for distinguished editorial writing, the test of excellence being clearness of style, moral purpose, sound reasoning, and power to influence public opinion in what the writer conceives to be the right direction, due account being taken of the whole volume of the editorial writer's work during the year.

12 Editorial Cartooning – for a distinguished example of a cartoonist's work, the determining qualities being that the cartoon shall embody an idea made clearly apparent, shall show good drawing and striking pictorial effect, and shall be intended to be helpful to some commendable cause of public

importance, due account being taken of the whole volume of the artist's work during the year.

13 Spot News Photography – for a distinguished example of spot news photography in black and white or colour, which may consist of a photograph or photographs, a sequence or an album.

14 Feature Photography – for a distinguished example of feature photography in black and white or colour, which may consist of a photograph or photographs, a sequence or an album.

Literature

1 Fiction – for distinguished fiction by an American author, preferably dealing with American life. (See p. 51.)

2 Drama – for a distinguished play by an American author, preferably original in its source and dealing with American life. (See p. 236.)

3 History – for a distinguished book on the history of the United States.

4 Biography – for a distinguished biography or autobiography by an American author.

5 Poetry – for a distinguished volume of verse by an American author. (See p. 185.)

6 General Non-Fiction – for a distinguished book of non-fiction by an American author that is not eligible for consideration in any other category (awarded since 1962). (See p. 52.)

Music

For distinguished musical composition by an American in any of the larger forms, including chamber, orchestral, choral, opera, song, dance, or other forms of musical theatre, which has had its first performance in the United States during the year (awarded since 1943). (See p. 156.)

'One of the chief difficulties with journalism is to keep the news instinct from running rampant over the restraints of accuracy and conscience.'

Joseph Pulitzer

QUIZ

Mastermind

The first transmission of Mastermind, held at Liverpool University, was broadcast by BBC Television on Monday 11 September 1972 at 10.45 p.m. It was aimed at a minority audience of academics but soon became compulsive viewing for millions of people.

Magnus Magnusson chairs the programme and is now well known for his 'I've started so I'll finish' questionmaster's repost. The very first contestant's question was on visual arts: 'Picasso's "Guernica" was a protest about the bombing by Spanish planes of a village. In what year did the event take place that inspired the painting?' (Answer: 1937).

Each series consists of a number of programmes, four contestants appearing on each, who compete in two two-minute rounds, answering questions on their own specialist subject and then on general knowledge.

FACTS

■ In 1982, to celebrate the first decade of Mastermind, a Champion of Champions contest was organised for all former winners. It was won by Sir David Hunt, the 1977 champion.

■ The highest-ever specialist round score was 22, achieved in 1979 by Joe West, a helicopter pilot, answering questions on 'Nelson'. The second highest was 21 by Hendy Farquhar-Smith in 1986, answering questions on 'David Wilkie'.

■ The highest-ever general knowledge round score was 22, achieved by Jennifer Keaveney, in the 1986 final.

■ The record for the highest total score ever achieved – 40 points – is held jointly by two women: Jennifer Keaveney (answering questions on 'The life and work of E. Nesbit'), in the fourth semi-final and the final in 1986; Mary Elizabeth Raw (answering questions on 'The life and works of Elizabeth Gaskell'), in one of the 1989 heats. The second highest was 38, scored by Margaret Harris in the 1984 final.

■ There have been 7 women and 15 men winners. The ratio of men to women competitors is usually three to one; in 1994 it was more than four to one. However, the first three winners (1972–1974) were all women.

■ By the end of 1993, an estimated 52 500 questions had been answered or 'passed' on, and 1092 contestants had participated.

■ Unusual specialist subjects have included: Pigs; Life-cycle of the honey bee; Burial grounds of London; Notable British poisoners; Doctor Who; The Moomintrolls.

■ Rejected specialist subjects have included: Cremation practice and law in Britain; Routes to anywhere in mainland Britain from Letchworth by road; Orthopaedic bone cement in total hip replacement; Iron graveslabs of England; The banana industry; Farm wagons and carts of England and Wales.

■ The programme's theme music is entitled 'Approaching Menace', composed by Neil Richardson.

Winners	Occupation	Specialist subjects
1972 Nancy Wilkinson	Part-time lecturer	Music, 1550–1900
1973 Patricia Owen	Lecturer in English	Byzantine art and opera
1974 Elizabeth Horrocks	Housewife	Shakespeare, Tolkien, Jane Austen, Dorothy L. Sayers
1975 John Hart	Schoolmaster	Ancient Athens, Rome in the age of Cicero
1976 Roger Prichard	Civil servant	Duke of Wellington
1977 Sir David Hunt	Retired ambassador	Roman Revolution, History of Cyprus, North African Campaign, Alexander the Great, Italian Campaign
1978 Rosemary James	Teacher	Greek and Roman mythology, author Frederick William Rolfe
1979 Philip Jenkins	Research assistant	Early Christianity, medieval Wales, Vikings in Ireland and Scotland
1980 Fred Housego	Licensed taxi driver	Henry II, Westminster Abbey, The Tower of London
1981 Leslie Grout	Schoolmaster	St George's Chapel, Windsor Castle, London burial grounds
1982 Not held (see Fact box)		
1983 Christopher Hughes	Underground train driver	British steam locomotives, Flashman novels
1984 Margaret Harris	Deputy headmistress	Cecil Rhodes, Postal history and philately of South Africa 1853–1960
1985 Ian Meadows	Hospital driver	Astronomy up to 1700
1986 Jennifer Keaveney	Careers information officer	Mrs Gaskell, E. Nesbit
1987 Jeremy Bradbrooke	General practitioner	Franco-Prussian war
1988 David Beamish	House of Lords clerk	Lady Astor and the Hanoverian royal family
1989 Mary Elizabeth Raw	Veterinary surgeon	Charles I, Prince Albert
1990 David Edwards	Schoolmaster	Lives of physicists
1991 Stephen Allen	Actor	Henry VII, Sir Francis Drake
1992 Steve Williams	Computer programmer	Surrealist art between the wars, Peter the Great, Pre-Socratic philosophy
1993 Gavin Fuller	Part-time archivist, HMS *Warrior*, Fareham	The Crusades 1095–1154
1994 Dr George Davidson	University Senior Lecturer, Chemistry	The Life and Works of John Dalton

More than 2000 people apply every year and the producer selects 300 candidates to interview, spending three months travelling round the UK, holding auditions.

Each audition lasts about 20 minutes and includes a brief interview with would-be contestants about themselves and the information form they have filled in.

They are also given an informal oral general knowledge quiz. From this, the final contestants are selected and winners receive the Mastermind engraved bowl of Caithness glass.

QUIZ

THE 1993 MASTERMIND FINAL

Gavin Fuller won the 1993 Mastermind Championship. In the final he scored 17 points (1 pass) in the specialist round; 15 points (1 pass) in the general knowledge round; making a total of 32 points (2 passes). The questions and whether he answered them correctly are listed below (the answers appear in Solutions, p. 252).

Specialist Subject The Crusades 1095–1154

1 In March 1095, at which Church Council held by Urban II did Byzantine envoys seek the help of western knights? (Correct)

2 Who wrote the *Alexiad,* the main Greek source on the First Crusade? (Correct)

3 In June 1097, to which ruler did Nicaea surrender, thus depriving the crusading forces? (Correct)

4 Who was the knight, known as 'the Penniless', who led part of the 'People's Crusade' in 1096? (Correct)

5 On what day was Baldwin crowned King of Jerusalem in 1100? (Correct)

6 In May 1104, which Italian fleet helped Baldwin capture Acre? (Correct)

7 In the First Crusade, which French noble led the army comprising mainly Provençals and Burgundian soldiers? (Correct)

8 Who was freed by the payment of a huge ransom to the Danishmend emir in 1103? (Correct)

9 In 1099, whose vision revealed that Jerusalem would fall if the crusading army fasted and processed round the city walls? (Pass)

10 Who was the Muslim governor of Jerusalem who managed to escape when the city was captured? (Wrong)

11 In 1118, to which group of knights did Baldwin I grant rooms in the royal palace? (Correct)

12 Who accompanied his overlord Stephen of Blois to Constantinople and later became Chaplain to Baldwin I and chronicler of the First Crusade? (Correct)

13 What did the Crusaders call the battle of June 1119, in which Roger of Antioch and his finest knights were killed by Muslim forces? (Correct)

14 Which sect was behind the murders of the Muslim leader Mawdud and the Crusader Count Raymond II of Tripoli? (Correct)

15 Around 1143, which castle outside Tripoli was given to the Hospitallers? (Wrong)

16 Which brief patriarch of Jerusalem is said to have discovered the greater part of the True Cross after the fall of Jerusalem? (Correct)

17 In June 1908, which renegade captain treacherously admitted Bohemond and his knights into Antioch? (Correct)

18 Which Byzantine Emperor made a truce with the Seldjuk Sultan of Konya in 1147? (Correct)

19 In April 1154, which city opened its gates to Nur-ad Din as its citizens objected to their ruler's alliance with the Christians? (Correct)

20 Which 'honey-tongued teacher' did Pope Eugenius and Louis VII of France entrust to promote the cause of the Second Crusade? (Correct)

General Knowledge

1 Which building material is formed from a mixture of cement, sand, gravel and water? (Wrong)

2 Which dynasty was the ruling house of Imperial Germany from 1871 to 1918? (Correct)

3 According to a saying attributed by Mark Twain to Disraeli, there are three kinds of lies: Lies, damned lies – and what else? (Correct)

4 In March 1993, which Scottish rugby player was appointed captain of the British Lions for the New Zealand tour? (Correct)

5 James Edward Stuart, known as the Old Pretender, was the son of which king? (Correct)

6 What is the name of the hidden Tibetan lamasery in James Hilton's novel *Lost Horizon*, which is used to describe an earthly paradise? (Correct)

7 In which modern country is the site of the ancient city of Babylon? (Correct)

8 The viral disease hard pad, which affects dogs, is known by what other name? (Pass)

9 According to the Old Testament, which birds brought bread and meat to Elija by the brook of Cherith? (Wrong)

10 Which co-founder of the National Trust, who campaigned for improved housing conditions, wrote *Homes of the London Poor* (published in 1875)? (Correct)

11 Which of Mozart's operas features the characters Tamino and Pamina? (Wrong)

12 Which Norse god, noted for his cunning and trickery, was responsible for the death of Baldr? (Correct)

13 On which river does the city of Winchester stand? (Correct)

14 What was the nationality of the artist Gustav Klimt? (Wrong)

15 The name of which eighteenth-century war commemorates an incident in which Spanish officials allegedly mutilated a British merchant captain? (Correct)

16 Of which administrative region in central Italy is Florence the capital? (Correct)

17 In mathematics, a tetrahedron is a solid figure with how many plane faces? (Correct)

18 Which Irish author, noted for his tales of mystery and terror, wrote the collection entitled *In a Glass Darkly*? (Wrong)

19 What name is given to the tower on the upper deck of a submarine from which the vessel is directed when it is on or near the surface? (Correct)

20 In the early 1930s, which Indian leader gave to the Untouchables the name *Harijan*, meaning 'Children of God'? (Correct)

21 With which fruit is the liqueur Cointreau flavoured? (Correct)

RAILWAYS

The Railway Heritage Awards

The Best Restored Station Competition started in 1979 for restored railway buildings in private ownership. In 1985 the competition became the Ian Allan Railway Heritage Awards and it was extended to include public sector owned property. Any restored railway structures may be entered, either large or small, and also new structures built in traditional style and workmanship. In 1989 the first prize money was offered for both winners and runners-up. In 1993 this amounted to £5000. The awards are sponsored by Ian Allan Ltd, British Rail, The Railway Heritage Trust and Westinghouse Signals Ltd.

Owners submit an application form to the awards committee, and judges, usually architects interested in the subject, are sent out to anonymously report on the buildings. If the report and marks are high enough, a second visit, and possibly even a third, is made, before the winners are finally decided.

Detail of the restored roof on the main station building at Stoke-on-Trent, which won the 1993 Railway Heritage Trust Award. The task of restoration involved totally reroofing with 100 000 clay roof and ridge tiles, made to the same size as the original. They were handmade in the Potteries in Staffordshire Blue and Red to achieve the correct colour banding of the original 1840s station roof.

Other 1993 awards

Railway Heritage Trust Award Stoke-on-Trent, Staffs, main station building roof (British Rail Property Board)

Westinghouse Signalling Award Muston signalbox, at Murton Park, York (Great Yorkshire Railway Preservation Society)

***Railway World* Commendation Isfield station**, East Sussex (Lavender Line Preservation Society)

British Rail Premier Award / Private Sector

		Entered by
1979	Oakworth Station	Keighley & Worth Valley Railway
1980	Staverton Station	Dart Valley Railway
1981	Ropley Station	Mid-Hants Railway
1982	Highley Station	Severn Valley Railway
1983	Arley Station	Severn Valley Railway
1984	Damems Station	Keighley & Worth Valley Railway
1985	Bo'Ness Station	Scottish Railway Preservation Society
1986	Haven Street Station	Isle of Wight Steam Railway
1987	Kidderminster Town	Severn Valley Railway
1988	Rowden Mill Station House	The Wilkinson Family
1989	Ingrow Station	Keighley & Worth Valley Railway
1990/1991	Errol Station	Errol Station Trust
1992	Bowes-Lyon Bridge, Crich	Tramway Museum Society
1993	Scotscalder Station House	Daniel Brittain-Catlin

Ian Allan Award/Public and Commercial Sector

		Entered by
1985	N. Woolwich Station	Passmore Edwards Museum
1986	Wellingboro' Station	BR London Midland Region
1987	St Denys Station	BR Southern Region
1988	Glasgow Central	ScotRail Architects
1989	Lewes Station	BR Department of Architecture & Design
1990/1991	Wicker Arch, Sheffield	BR Regional Civil Engineers, York
1992	Cathedral Arches, Salford	BR Property Board & Craft-Kind Ltd
1993	Ribblehead Viaduct	Regional Railways North East (*et al.*)

Scotscalder Station House, located south of Thurso on the ScotRail line from Inverness, owned by Daniel Brittain-Catlin, won the 1993 Private Sector Premier award for best-restored station. The station is privately owned and unstaffed but the line running past is the Inverness to Wick line and is owned by British Rail. The train will stop at the station only if passengers make a request to the driver or guard.

The station was used by BR until 1974, having also been used as a post office and storage area. After lying empty for 15 years it was extensively restored by Mr Brittain-Catlin as a private dwelling. An interesting feature of the renovated building is the restoration of various rooms to represent the style and decor of different periods since the building was constructed in 1874. For instance, one bedroom has been decorated in the style of the 1870s, another the 1910s; the kitchen and the lounge reflect the 1930s.

Mr Brittain-Catlin received a gilded green Westmorland slate plaque presented by British Rail's Community Unit and a cheque for £1500. He intends to spend the prize money on fixing hanging baskets of flowers along the line.

First Class Awards Chesham station, Bucks (London Underground Ltd), **Gloucester Road station**, London (London Underground Ltd), **Ramsbottom station**, Lancs (East Lancashire Railway) **Certificates of Commendation** Oakworth station, N. London (Keighley and Worth Valley Railway), **Boston station portico**, Lincs (Regional Railways Central)

British Rail Best Station Award

For many years, competitions have been held between Britain's railway stations competing for titles such as Best Kept Station and Best Station Garden. These often started out as local events, spreading to a regional level and, on occasions, nationwide. In 1986 British Rail relaunched the Best Station Award. All aspects of station facilities and customer services are included, rather than concentrating on gardens and floral displays, and for the first time independent judges were brought in. Stations are judged in three categories–small, medium and large–with one station receiving an overall Best Station Award. Regional judging takes place in stages throughout the year, with the final winners being decided by a panel of national judges.

In 1991 a fourth category was introduced for unstaffed stations, covering those without permanent railway staff which are often looked after by the local community. This was won by Dolau Station, Powys, in 1991 and 1992, and Lingwood, Norfolk, in 1993.

The Best Kept London British Rail Terminus

The London Regional Passengers' Commitee/Cartner Award has been given annually since 1987 for the best kept London British Rail station. Members of the Committee and staff visit all London terminus stations and complete a checklist and report, awarding points in various categories such as litter control, clarity of information, helpfulness, presentation of staff, and cleanliness. The reliability and frequency of trains is not taken into consideration. All the information is analysed by the Committee to establish the winner, who receives a large wall plaque which can be displayed for one year, and a miniature solari indicator.

WINNERS

1987 Waterloo
1988 London Bridge
1989 King's Cross
1990 Euston
1991 Fenchurch Street
1992 King's Cross
1993 Liverpool Street

The 1993 win for Liverpool Street comes two years after a multi-million pound facelift to improve the 19th-century station. A new section of roof was built, platforms were extended and a parade of shops and restaurants opened on a new high-level balcony overlooking the main concourse. A special team of eight staff was set up to improve the overall standard of service to the station's 200 000 daily users.

BELOW Liverpool Street, Best Kept London British Rail Terminus in 1993.

	Overall	Small station	Medium station	Large station
1986	Dumfries, D&G	Windermere, Cumbria	Dumfries, D&G	Waterloo, London
1987	Dumfries, D&G	Templecombe, Somerset	Dumfries, D&G	Waterloo, London
1988	Templecombe, Somerset	Templecombe, Somerset	Stratford-on-Avon, Warks	York, N. Yorks
1989	Stoke-on-Trent, Staffs	Aberdour, Fife	Stoke-on-Trent, Staffs	Glasgow Central, Strathclyde
1990	Aberdour, Fife	Templecombe, Somerset	Salisbury, Wilts	York, N. Yorks
1991	Templecombe, Somerset	Pevensey & Westham, E. Sussex	Fenchurch Street, London	York, N. Yorks
1992	Stoke Mandeville, Bucks	Elsenham, Essex	Cambridge, Cambs Birmingham Int., W. Mid	York, N. Yorks
1993	Euston, London	Mexborough, S. Yorks	Ipswich, Suffolk	Doncaster, S. Yorks

Table caption: BRITISH RAIL BEST STATION AWARD WINNERS

BEST LONDON UNDERGROUND STATION GARDEN

Chesham Station on the Metropolitan Line won the 1993 Best Garden prize in London Underground's Station Gardens competition. The garden was judged top on visual impact, design, care and choice of plants. The station supervisors, Barbara Brown of Croxley Green and Mark Stephenson of Chesham, received a cash prize of £150 and hold the Station Gardens Challenge Trophy for a year, and the station received a permanent winner's plaque. In previous years, Barbara and Mark have been awarded Certificates of Merit for their hanging basket displays. They spend about 15 hours each week on the garden.

RESTAURANTS

Egon Ronay/Cellnet Restaurant of the Year

This award is given for the best restaurant whose consistent excellence or enterprise is found to be outstanding.

WINNERS

1969 Thornbury Castle, Thornbury, Avon
1970 Le Poulbot, London
1971 Box Tree Cottage, Ilkley, W. Yorks
1972 Le Gavroche, London
1973 Kildwick Hall, Kildwick, Yorks
1974 Shezan, London
1975 Wilton's, London
1976 Horn of Plenty, Gulworthy, Devon
1977 Carrier's, London
1978 McCoy's, Staddle Bridge, N. Yorks
1979 Les Quat'Saisons, Oxford
1980 Sharrow Bay Country House Hotel Restaurant, Ullswater, Cumb
1981 The Waterside Inn, Bray-on-Thames, Berks
1982 La Tante Claire, London
1983 The Dorchester Grill Room, London
1984 Chez Nico, London
1985 Le Manoir aux Quat'Saisons, Great Milton, Oxon
1986 No award
1987 Walnut Tree Inn, Abergavenny, Gwent
1988 Morels, Haslemere, Surrey
1989 L'Arlequin, London
1990 The Waterside Inn, Bray-on-Thames, Berks
1991 L'Ortolan, Shinfield, Berks
1992 Bibendum, London
1993 The Carved Angel, Dartmouth, Devon
1994 Le Soufflé Restaurant, Inter-Continental Hotel, London

The Top 20 London Restaurants

Fay Maschler, author of the Evening Standard *London Restaurant Guide 1994,* has put together her own list of favourite restaurants. The Eros award was given to 20 London restaurants and the list reflects 'not just the best cooking in London but something more; a recognition of the restaurants that joyfully succeed in what they set out to do, be that classic French food served with grace and style, a neighbourhood place all neighbourhoods would like to have, consistent high standards in a notoriously fluctuating area, postive enlightenment concerning authenticity, or regionality of a cuisine'. Eros awards for 1994 with Fay Maschler's overall comment (figure in brackets is a guide to the cost of a three-course meal for one person with half a bottle of wine [or appropriate drink], tax and service):

Beth's, NW3 –'Where my sister cooks' (£25)
Bibendum Restaurant and Oyster Bar, SW3 – 'My choice of a desert island restaurant' (£60 [restaurant] £25 [oyster bar])
Bistrot Bruno, W1 –'Some of the most inventive cooking in London' (£25)
The Brackenbury, W6 – 'A paragon among modern restaurants with modest prices and vivid food' (£20)
Le Caprice, SW1 – 'See and be seen with good food and slick service' (£35–£40)
Chez Moi, W11 –'Long-established genteel restaurant with some tearaway food' (£35)
Chutney Mary, SW10 –'One of the more delicious results of the British presence in India' (£35)
The French House Dining Room, W1 – 'One of the best things to happen to Soho' (£23)
Fung Shing, WC2 – 'The most reliably good Cantonese place in Chinatown' (£25)
Le Gavroche, W1 – 'For serious lovers of food and luxury' (£40 [lunch] (£70 [dinner])
The Ivy, WC2 –'Beautifully managed theatrical restaurant' (£34)
Le Petit Max, Hampton Wick – 'Twins from Essex cook fine French food' (£21)
Quaglino's, SW1 – 'The closest in London so far to La Coupole' (£30)
Riva, SW13 – 'A great Italian in Barnes' (£25)
The River Café, W6 – 'Where the Italian restaurant revolution started' (£35)
Les Saveurs, W1 –'Joel Antunès is a chef's name that should be tripping off tongues' (£31 [lunch] £40 [dinner])
Le Suquet, SW3 –'An incorrigibly French fish restaurant' (£30)
La Tante Claire, SW3 – 'Now endorsed by The Michelin Men as "exceptional cuisine, worth a special journey"' (£35–£70)
The White Tower, W1 –'A charmer in an almost unbroken line from 1938 – and the birthplace of taramasalata in London' (£30)
Zen Central Restaurant, W1 –'Capable of the best, chic Chinese food in town' (£40)

EGON RONAY/CELLNET 1994 RESTAURANT OF THE YEAR

The editorial for this culinary delight at the Le Soufflé Restaurant at the Inter-Continental Hotel, London, reads as follows in the Guide:

'Subtle improvements to the decor have been made, the restaurant retaining its elegantly modern and ultra-stylish decor of cool cream and pale turquoise. Lighting is very kind, being softly diffused. A white baby grand now occupies the centre of the room, a pianist playing soothing renditions of light classics and popular music. This fine setting is the perfect backdrop to Peter Kromberg's extraordinary talents. Now in his 18th year here he continues as a leader, nurturing and encouraging new talents as in his current team of excellent sous chefs headed by Richard Thompson. Together they produce menus of superbly constructed complexity, the individual dishes creating genuine frissons of delight. Each day sees a new stunning eight-course gourmet menu, the different dishes all perfectly balanced and complementing one another . . . There is an underlying classicism to the cooking though combinations are such that the dishes are far removed from traditional concepts. The results are ethereal as in a salad of grilled green asparagus spears flavoured with a citrus fruit vinaigrette with a light crème fraîche, a smooth fluffy smoked salmon bavarois and slices of the softest, most delicate smoked salmon creating a dish of pure enchantment . . . Main courses are exemplified by a pan-fried supreme of Lunesdale duck, the skin replaced by crisply cooked potato scales and served with a Cabernet Sauvignon vinegar sauce, apples cooked in cider and cream, artichokes, fresh broad beans and a dice of beetroot – a wealth of mouthwatering flavours and textures.'

The table d'hôte luncheon menu includes a choice of three starters, three main courses, a selection of cheeses and either the soufflé of the day or a dessert, coffee and petit fours and is priced at £25.50. The evening seven-course 'choix du chef' menu is priced at £43 (1994 Guide prices).

ROYALTY

Longest-Reigning British Monarchs

	Reign	No. of years	Age at succession	Age at death
Victoria	20 Jun 1837–22 Jan 1901	63 years 7 months	18	81
George III	25 Oct 1760–29 Jan 1820	59 years 3 months	22	81
Henry III	28 Oct 1216–16 Nov 1272	56 years 1 month	9	64
Edward III	25 Jan 1327–21 Jun 1377	50 years 5 months	14	64
Elizabeth I	17 Nov 1558–24 Mar 1603	44 years 4 months	25	69
Elizabeth II	6 Feb 1952–to date (1994)	42 years-	25	
Henry VI	1 Sep 1422–4 Mar 1461	38 years 6 months	8 months	49
Henry VIII	22 Apr 1509–28 Jan 1547	37 years 9 months	17	55
Charles II	30 Jan 1649–6 Feb 1685	36 years 1 month	19	54
Ethelred II	Mar 978–1014	36 years	?	?
Henry I	5 Aug 1100–1 Dec 1135	35 years 4 months	31	66

Shortest-Reigning British Monarchs

	Reign	Length of reign
Jane	6–19 Jul 1553	14 days
Edward V	9 Apr–25 Jun 1483	75 days
Edward VIII	20 Jan–11 Dec 1936	325 days
Richard III	26 Jun 1483–22 Aug 1485	2 years 2 months
Harthacnut	1040–8 Jun 1042	2 years 6 months
Edward the Martyr	Jul 975–18 Mar 978	2 years 8 months
Ethelbald	858–60	3 years
James II	6 Feb 1685–11 Dec 1688	3 years 10 months
Edwy	Nov 955–1 Oct 959	3 years 11 months

Order of Succcession to the British Throne

1. **HRH Prince Charles of Wales,** elder son of HM Queen Elizabeth II
2. **HRH Prince William of Wales,** elder son of Prince Charles
3. **HRH Prince Henry of Wales,** younger son of Prince Charles
4. **HRH Prince Andrew,** second son of HM Queen Elizabeth II
5. **HRH Princess Beatrice of York,** elder daughter of Prince Andrew
6. **HRH Princess Eugenie of York,** younger daughter of Prince Andrew
7. **HRH Prince Edward,** youngest son of HM Queen Elizabeth II
8. **HRH Princess Anne,** only daughter of HM Queen Elizabeth II
9. **Peter Phillips,** son of Princess Anne
10. **Zara Phillips,** daughter of Princess Anne

Queen Victoria at the age of 78, three years before her death. Her reign of 63 years 7 months made her Britain's longest-reigning monarch.

SLOGANS

Winning Advertising Slogans

Over the years, companies have devised advertising slogans to sell their products. Some have not only proved remarkably successful at the time, but have moved into the arena of permanent 'catch phrases'. Below are a selection chosen by the author of the more enduring successes:

▌ **'Drinka Pinta Milka Day'**. The aim was to get everybody to drink a pint of milk a day. The term 'a pinta' originating in the sixties even entered the *Chambers Twentieth Century Dictionary*.

▌ **'Go to work on an egg'**. This 1957 slogan was said to have been created by Fay Weldon, novelist, who was a copywriter on the British Egg Marketing Board account at the time.

▌ **'Guinness is good for you'**. Arthur Guinness, Son & Co., after 170 years without advertising, enlisted the S. H. Benson agency in 1929 who undertook consumer research (unusual in those days) into why people drunk Guinness; the result was that they thought it did them good. Today, people still connect with the slogan even though it was discontinued in the early forties.

▌ **'Full of eastern promise'**. A slogan for Fry's Turkish Delight used in the 1950s. It was one of the longest-running British television advertisements. The first showed a male slave unrolling a carpet containing a woman captive.

▌ **'A Double Diamond works wonders'**. Used in 1952, it was sung to the tune of 'There's a Hole in my Bucket' which has made it one of the best-known slogans ever.

▌ **'Don't be vague – ask for Haig'**. Used to advertise Haig whisky since the mid-thirties. Other slogans used were 'Don't be vague, order Haig' and 'Why be vague? Ask for Haig'.

▌ **'Don't forget the fruit gums, mum!'**. An advert for Rowntree's Fruit Gums in the late fifties. It was devised from market research which discovered that women mostly bought the product which was then eaten by children. Later the 'Mum' was changed to 'chum'.

▌ **'Don't say Brown – say Hovis'**. Used originally in the 1930s, the company produced its own paper bags which showed a radio announcer saying:

Don't forget the FRUIT GUMS Mum!

ROWNTREE'S FRUIT GU

Gums that last a

'Here's a rather important correction . . . I should have said Hovis and not just "brown"'. It was introduced in the fifties in its present form.

▌ **'Heineken refreshes the parts other beers cannot reach'**. This slogan was introduced in the mid-seventies and is considered to be one of the most popular slogans ever used. The 'refreshing' qualities of the beer were demonstrated

with items such as the raised nose of Concorde and a policeman's toes. Margaret Thatcher at the Conservative Party Conference in 1980 said: 'When I think of our much-travelled Foreign Secretary I am reminded of . . . the peer that reaches those foreign parts other peers cannot reach!'

▌ **'Put a tiger in your tank'**. This Esso slogan, advertising petrol, originated in the USA and was taken from the lyrics of a popular rhythm and blues song. It arrived in Britain in 1964 in a cartoon version. The idea took off and became a national craze with people attaching tiger tails to their petrol caps.

▌ **'Heinz 57 varieties'.** A brand name which became a slogan, it has been used by Heinz tinned products since 1896. Henry Heinz first thought of the idea while travelling through New York City on the overhead railway. He saw an advert offering 21 styles of shoe, and worked out that Heinz had approximately 58 products, but settled for 57 since he considered it sounded better.

Top 10 Prizewinning Slogans

Competitors Companion, a publication covering aspects of competition entry, has produced three volumes on 'Great British Prizewinning Slogans'. From this the editors have produced the following list of winning slogans in the 1990s:

1 WINNER – Wonderful Invigorating, Nearly Neat, Exciting Reading
2 Experts perfect it, connoisseurs select it
3 Specialists perfect them, perfectionists select them
4 It gives a gastronomic thrill, not an astronomic bill
5 Their range is extensive, but never expensive
6 Their superb selection is taste perfection
7 The cost is nominal and the taste phenomenal
8 [Product] reigns supreme, setting standards seldom seen
9 It's wholesome, nutritious and tastes quite delicious
10 [Product] delights me, [prize] excites me, hope [store] invites me

HOVIS – WHAT'S IN A NAME?

'Smith's Patent Germ Flour' did little to sell the product, and in 1890 Richard Smith, creator of wheatgerm bread, and Thomas Fitton, managing director of S. Fitton and Son, a milling company, organised a national competition to find a better brand name. After agonising for some time over the likely sales appeal of 'Yum Yum', they finally awarded the £25 prize to a London student, Herbert Grime, for a neat derivation of the Latin '*hominis vis*', meaning 'the strength of man – thus Hovis was born. Herbert Grime went on to become an Inspector of Schools. On his death the Hovis company paid his widow a pension as a tribute to the creator of the name which has become a household trade name.

SONGS

The Eurovision Song Contest

A Song for Europe

Annually, the BBC runs a series of programmes in which Britain's songs for Europe are featured. Viewers vote for their favourite choice to represent Britain in that year's Eurovision Song Contest. Songs that have been chosen are:

FACTS

■ The UK has entered 37 contests and has won four times – 1967, 1969 (joint), 1976, 1981; second 14 times; and third twice.

■ Four British songs made it to number one in the British singles chart: 'Puppet on a String' (27 April 1967); 'Congratulations' (10 April 1968); 'Save Your Kisses For Me' (27 March 1976); 'Making Your Mind Up' (18 April 1981).

■ 'Puppet on a String' was the most successful Eurovision song in the British singles chart. It reached number one and remained in the charts for 18 weeks.

■ 'Save Your Kisses For Me' sold over six million singles, reached number one and spent a total of 16 weeks in the British singles chart.

■ Frances Ruffelle, the UK's 1994 singer, is best known for her Tony award-winning performance as Eponine in the original Broadway production of *Les Misérables*. She is the second star from this show to represent the UK – Michael Ball also appeared in this production and came second in the 1993 contest.

■ In 1994, 'Lonely Symphony' sung by Frances Ruffelle received 99 946 votes in the Song for Europe selection out of a total of 248 082 votes rung in by British viewers.

	Title	Artist	Eurovision placing	Highest British singles chart placing	Total weeks in chart
1956	No entry				
1957	All	Patricia Bredin	7th	–	–
1958	No entry				
1959	Sing Little Birdie	Teddy Johnson and Pearl Carr	2nd	12	8
1960	Looking High, High, High	Bryan Johnson	2nd	20	11
1961	Are you Sure?	The Allison Brothers	2nd	2	16
1962	Ring-a-Ding Girl	Ronnie Carroll	4th	46	3
1963	Say Wonderful Things	Ronnie Carroll	4th	6	14
1964	I Love the Little Things	Matt Monro	2nd	–	–
1965	I Belong	Kathy Kirby	2nd	36	3
1966	A Man Without Love	Kenneth McKellar	9th	30	4
1967	Puppet on a String	Sandie Shaw	1st	1	18
1968	Congratulations	Cliff Richard	2nd	1	13
1969	Boom Bang-a-Bang	Lulu	Joint 1st	2	13
1970	Knock, Knock, Who's There?	Mary Hopkin	2nd	2	14
1971	Jack in the Box	Clodagh Rodgers	4th	4	10
1972	Beg, Steal or Borrow	The New Seekers	2nd	2	13
1973	Power to All Our Friends	Cliff Richard	3rd	4	12
1974	Long Live Love	Olivia Newton-John	Joint 4th	11	8
1975	Let Me Be The One	The Shadows	2nd	12	9
1976	Save Your Kisses For Me	Brotherhood of Man	1st	1	16
1977	Rock Bottom	Lynsey de Paul and Mike Moran	2nd	19	7
1978	The Bad Old Days	Co-Co	11th	13	7
1979	Mary Ann	Black Lace	7th	42	4
1980	Love Enough for Two	Prima Donna	3rd	48	4
1981	Making Your Mind Up	Bucks Fizz	1st	1	12
1982	One Step Further	Bardo	7th	2	8
1983	I'm Never Giving Up	Sweet Dreams	6th	21	7
1984	Love Games	Belle and the Devotions	7th	11	8
1985	Love is . . . (A Feeling)	Vikki	4th	49	3
1986	Runner in the Night	Ryder	Joint 7th	–	–
1987	Only the Light	Rikki	13th	–	–
1988	Go	Scott Fitzgerald	2nd	52	2
1989	Why Do I Always Get it Wrong	Live Report	2nd	73	1
1990	Give a Little Love Back to the World	Emma	6th	33	6
1991	A Message to Your Heart	Samantha Janus	10th	30	3
1992	One Step Out of Time	Michael Ball	2nd	20	7
1993	Better the Devil You Know	Sonia	2nd	15	7
1994	Lonely Symphony	Frances Ruffelle	10th	25	6

The worst song entry in the history of the Eurovision Song Contest must be deemed to be 'Mile After Mile', the 1978 Norwegian entry sung by Jan Teigan. The voting from all panels was unanimous – nil! However, it proved to be to Teigan's advantage – the next day the papers were full of his achievement, the winner hardly got a mention. 'This was my greatest success', he said, 'I have done what no one ever did before me. I'm the first Norwegian to get zero points. Since the concert I've had lots of offers for TV appearances, tours and interviews. I've never known as much interest taken in me.'

Jacqueline Boyer performing her song 'Tom Pillibi' for France which won the 1960 Eurovision Song Contest. Katie Boyle (centre) presented the programme.

The Eurovision Song Contest

Held annually since 1956, artists from different European countries compete by singing their country's chosen song which is then judged and voted on by all participating countries. The Contest, especially the voting, was watched avidly by an estimated 8.3 million UK viewers in 1994. There are several fan clubs in Britain devoted to the Contest and all the superlatives, facts and figures that surround the event.

A comedy produced by Andrew Lloyd Webber entitled *Eurovision* opened in 1993 in London. The star, Anita Dobson, played Katia Europa, a song contest hostess who, possessed by the Spirit of Europe, gives a televised lecture to the world on the glories of European harmony. The opening night was attended by former song contestants Bucks Fizz, Rose Marie and The Brotherhood of Man, together with the contest's real-life hostess for many years, Katie Boyle. Unfortunately, the play scored 'nil points' from the critics and proceeded to post closure notices up within four days of opening, with a predicted loss of £275 000.

WINNERS

Year	Song	Artist	Country
1956	Refrain	Lys Assia	Switzerland
1957	Net Als Toen	Corry Brokken	Netherlands
1958	Dors Mon Amour	André Claveau	France
1959	Een Beetje	Teddy Scholten	Netherlands
1960	Tom Pillibi	Jacqueline Boyer	France
1961	Nous, Les Amoureux	Jean-Claude Pascal	Luxembourg
1962	Un Premier Amour	Isabelle Aubret	France
1963	Dansevise	Grethe and Jorgen Ingmann	Denmark
1964	Now ho L'Età per Amarti	Gigliola Cinquetti	Italy
1965	Poupée de Cire, Poupée	France Gall de Son	Luxembourg
1966	Merci Chérie	Udo Jürgens	Austria
1967	Puppet on a String	Sandie Shaw	UK
1968	La, La, La	Massiel	Spain
1969	Un Jour, Un Enfant	Frida Boccara	France
	De Troubadour	Lennie Kuhr	Netherlands
	Vivo Cantando	Salome	Spain
	Boom Bang-a-Bang	Lulu	UK
1970	All Kinds of Everything	Dana	Ireland
1971	Un Banc, Un Arbre, Une Rue	Severine	Monaco
1972	Après Toi	Vicky Leandros	Luxembourg
1973	Tu Te Reconnaîtras	Anne-Marie David	Luxembourg
1974	Waterloo	Abba	Sweden
1975	Ding-Dinge-Dong	Teach-In	Netherlands
1976	Save Your Kisses For Me	Brotherhood of Man	UK
1977	L'Oiseau et l'Enfant	Marie Myriam	France
1978	A-Ba-Ni-Bi	Izhar Cohen and Alphabeta	Israel

■ In 1969 four songs remarkably scored the same number of points and tied in first place.

■ Since 1956, 35 different countries have participated in the contest. Most wins – six: Ireland (1970, 1980, 1987, 1992, 1993, 1994). Five wins: Luxembourg (1961, 1965, 1972, 1973, 1983); and France (1958, 1960, 1962, 1969 (joint), 1977). Four wins: UK (1967, 1969 (joint), 1976, 1981); and the Netherlands (1957, 1959, 1969 (joint), 1975).

■ Johnny Logan was the first to win the Contest twice (1980 and 1987). He also wrote the winning song, 'Why Me', in 1992.

The most successful year for Eurovision entries in the UK singles chart was 1974:

■ Waterloo / Abba (UK)
No. 1: 9 weeks in chart

■ Go / Gigliola Cinquetti (Italy)
No. 8: 10 weeks in chart

■ I See A Star / Mouth and MacNeal (Netherlands)
No. 8: 10 weeks in chart

■ Long Live Love / Olivia Newton-John (UK)
No. 11: 8 weeks in chart

Songs of Praise *Top Ten*

Songs of Praise, the flagship of BBC's religious programmes, is watched every week by between five and seven million viewers, mostly aged over 45. The following listing gives the most popular hymns.

1 Dear Lord and Father of Mankind
2 Day Thou Gavest Lord is Ended
3 The Old Rugged Cross
4 How Great Thou Art
5 Abide With Me
6 Shine Jesus Shine
7 Make Me a Channel of Your Peace
8 The Lord's My Shepherd
9 Love Divine All Loves Excelling
10 Great is Thy Faithfulness

1979	Hallelujah	Gali Atari and Milk and Honey	Israel
1980	What's Another Year	Johnny Logan	Ireland
1981	Making Your Mind Up	Bucks Fizz	UK
1982	Ein bisschen Frieden	Nicole	Germany
1983	Si La Vie est Cadeau	Corinne Hermes	Luxembourg
1984	Diggi-Loo, Diggi-Ley	Herrey's	Sweden
1985	La det Swinge	Bobbysocks	Norway
1986	J'Aime La Vie	Sandra Kim	Belgium
1987	Hold Me Now	Johnny Logan	Ireland
1988	Ne Partez pas Sans Moi	Céline Dion	Switzerland
1989	Rock Me	Riva	Yugoslavia
1990	Insieme: 1992	Toto Cutugno	Italy
1991	Fangad av en Stormvind	Carola	Sweden
1992	Why Me	Linda Martin	Ireland
1993	In Your Eyes	Niamh Kavanagh	Ireland
1994	Rock 'n' Roll Kids	Paul Harrington and Charlie McGettigan	Ireland

Most Successful Eurovision Songs

The following is a list of the winning songs which have made an appearance in the British singles chart. The list is arranged in descending order from the most successful.

Date entered	Winning song / Artist	Highest placing	Total weeks in chart
March 1967	Puppet on A String / Sandie Shaw	1	18
March 1976	Save Your Kisses For Me / Brotherhood of Man	1	16
April 1970	All Kinds of Everything / Dana	1	15
(July 1970	Re-entry	47	1)
March 1981	Making Your Mind Up / Bucks Fizz	1	12
April 1974	Waterloo / Abba	1	9
May 1982	Ein bisschen Frieden (entitled 'A Little Peace' in chart) / Nicole	1	9
May 1980	What's Another Year / Johnny Logan	1	8
April 1972	Après Toi (entitled 'Come What May' in chart) / Vicky Leandros	2	16
May 1987	Hold Me Now / Johnny Logan	2	11
March 1969	Boom Bang-a-Bang / Lulu	2	13
April 1979	Hallelujah / Gali Atari and Milk and Honey	5	8
April 1971	Un Banc, Un Arbre, Une Rue / Severine	9	11
April 1973	Tu Te Reconnaîtras (entitled 'Wonderful Dream' in chart) / Anne-Marie David	13	9
April 1975	Ding-Dinge-Dong (entitled Ding-A-Dong in chart) / Teach-In	13	7
April 1964	Non ho L'Età per Amarti / Gigliola Cinquetti	17	17
May 1978	A-Ba-Ni-Bi / Izhar Cohen and Alphabeta	20	7
May 1993	In Your Eyes / Niamh Kavanagh	24	5
April 1960	Tom Pillibi / Jacqueline Boyer	33	2
April 1968	La, La, La / Massiel	35	4
May 1977	L'Oiseau et L'Enfant / Marie Myriam	42	4
May 1985	La det Swinge (entitled 'Let It Swing' in chart) / Bobbysocks	44	4
May 1984	Diggi Loo, Diggi Ley / Herrey's	46	3
May 1992	Why Me / Linda Martin	59	2

SPORT

Daily Express *Sports Awards*

The *Daily Express* Sports Awards were first given in 1946, and are the longest established sports awards in Britain. 'Sportsman of the Year' was introduced first, followed six years later by 'Sportswoman of the Year'. The winners are selected by *Daily Express* readers who nominate and vote for their favourite sports personalities of the year.

The awards have been sponsored by Yardley Gold, a division of the cosmetic company, since 1990 and their Yardley Gold Cup for special achievement has gone to Gary Lineker (1990), Kriss Akabusi (1991), Steve Redgrave (1992), and Jack Charlton (1993).

MEN	WOMEN
1946 Bruce Woodcock (boxing)	
1947 Denis Compton (cricket)	
1948 Denis Compton (cricket)	
1949 Reg Harris (cycling)	
1950 Reg Harris (cycling)	
1951 Geoffrey Duke (motorcycling)	
1952 Len Hutton (cricket)	Jeanette Altwegg (ice skating)
1953 Gordon Pirie (athletics)	Pat Smythe (show jumping)
1954 Roger Bannister (athletics)	Pat Smythe (show jumping)
1955 Gordon Pirie (athletics)	Pat Smythe (show jumping)
1956 Chris Brasher (athletics)	Judy Grinham (swimming)
1957 Derek Ibbotson (athletics)	Diane Wilkinson (swimming)
1958 Ian Black (swimming)	Judy Grinham (swimming)
1959 John Surtees (motorcycling)	Mary Bignal (athletics)
1960 Don Thompson (walking)	Anita Lonsbrough (swimming)
1961 Johnny Haynes (football)	Angela Mortimer (lawn tennis)
1962 Brian Phelps (diving)	Anita Lonsbrough (swimming)
1963 Jim Clark (motor racing)	Dorothy Hyman (athletics)
1964 Robbie Brightwell (athletics)	Mary Rand (née Bignal) (athletics)
1965 Tommy Simpson (cycling)	Marion Coakes (show jumping)
1966 Bobby Moore (football)	Ann Jones (lawn tennis)
1967 Harvey Smith (show jumping)	Beryl Burton (cycling)
1968 Lester Piggott (horse racing)	Marion Coakes (show jumping)
1969 Tony Jacklin (golf)	Ann Jones (lawn tennis)
1970 Henry Cooper (boxing)	Lillian Board (athletics)
1971 Jackie Stewart (motor racing)	HRH the Princess Anne (equestrian three-day event)
1972 Gordon Banks (football)	Mary Peters (athletics)
1973 Jackie Stewart (motor racing)	Ann Moore (show jumping)
1974 Willie John McBride (rugby union)	Virginia Wade (lawn tennis)
1975 David Steele (cricket)	Virginia Wade (lawn tennis)
1976 James Hunt (motor racing)	Debbie Johnsey (equestrian three-day event)
1977 Geoff Boycott (cricket)	Virginia Wade (lawn tennis)
1978 Steve Ovett (athletics)	Sharron Davies (swimming)
1979 Sebastian Coe (athletics)	Caroline Bradley (show jumping)
1980 Sebastian Coe (athletics)	Lindsay Macdonald (athletics)
1981–1989 No awards	No awards
1990 Paul Gascoigne (football)	Tracy Edwards (yachting)
1991 Graham Gooch (cricket)	Liz McColgan (athletics)
1992 Nigel Mansell (motor racing)	Sally Gunnell (athletics)
1993 Damon Hill (motor racing)	Sally Gunnell (athletics)

Most wins MEN 2 – Denis Compton (1947, 1948), Reg Harris (1949, 1950), Gordon Pirie (1953, 1955), Jackie Stewart (1971 1973), Sebastian Coe (1979, 1980).

WOMEN 3 – Pat Smythe (1953-55), Virginia Wade (1974, 1975, 1977); **2** – Judy Grinham (1956, 1958), Mary Rand (née Bignal) (1959, 1964), Anita Lonsbrough (1960, 1962), Marion Coakes (1965, 1968), Ann Jones (1966, 1969), Sally Gunnell (1992, 1993).

Sports Writers' Association Annual Awards

The Sports Writers' Association was formed in 1948 as an affiliation to the international body AIPS (Association Internationale de la Press Sportive). Its aim is to promote and maintain a high professional standard, to obtain the best possible working conditions for its members at various events, to welcome sports journalists from abroad, and to promote social activity among members.

The Association held its first dinner in December 1949 to honour some of Britain's reigning men world champions. In 1950 invitations were offered to a select number of leading international competitors. The annual ballot among members to elect the Sportsman of the Year began in 1951.

Irregular, separate functions for leading sportswomen had been held since 1951, but it was not until 1959 that the Sportswoman of the Year poll was instituted, and in 1963 the major annual Association function, previously a men-only night, became a dinner-dance for both sports men and women.

> '*My dad once said you meet a much nicer class of person there, but I'm not so sure.*'
>
> Damon Hill finding himself at the back of the grid for the Portuguese Grand Prix

Sports Writers' Association Awards

The athletes Linford Christie and Sally Gunnell – Sports Writers' Association Sportsman and Sportswoman of the year in both 1992 and 1993. **ABOVE** Linford Christie wins the 100 metres at the 1992 Olympic Games in Barcelona. **BELOW** Sally Gunnell wins the 400-metre hurdles in the 1992 Olympic Games in Barcelona.

MEN

1949 James Dear (rackets)
    Reg Harris (cycling)
    Johnny Leach (table tennis)
    Freddie Mills (boxing)
    Tommy Price (speedway)
1950 Geoffrey Duke (motor cycling)
    Reg Harris (cycling)
    Jack Holden (athletics)
    Harry Llewellyn (show jumping)
    John Parlett (athletics)
    Reg Parnell (motor racing)
1951 Randolph Turpin (boxing)
1952 Len Hutton (cricket)
1953 Gordon Pirie (athletics)
1954 Roger Bannister (athletics)
1955 John Disley (athletics)
1956 Chris Brasher (athletics)
1957 Derek Ibbotson (athletics)
1958 Ian Black (swimming)
1959 John Surtees (motor cycling)
1960 Don Thompson (walking)
1961 Terry Downes (boxing)
1962 Brian Kilby (athletics)
1963 Jim Clark (motor racing)
1964 Lynn Davies (athletics)
1965 Tommy Simpson (cycling)
1966 England World Cup XI (football)
1967 Mike Hailwood (motor cycling)
1968 David Hemery (athletics)
1969 Tony Jacklin (golf)
1970 Tony Jacklin (golf)
1971 Ken Buchanan (boxing)
1972 Richard Meade (three-day event)
1973 Jackie Stewart (motor racing)
1974 John Conteh (boxing)
1975 David Wilkie (swimming)
1976 James Hunt (motor racing)
1977 Barry Sheene (motor cycling)

WOMEN

Mary Bignal (athletics)
Anita Lonsbrough (swimming)
Angela Mortimer (tennis)
Anita Lonsbrough (swimming)
Dorothy Hyman (athletics)
Mary Rand (née Bignal) (athletics)
Marion Coakes (show jumping)
Linda Ludgrove (swimming)
Beryl Burton (cycling)
Lillian Board (athletics)
Ann Jones (tennis)
Mary Gordon Watson (three-day event)
HRH the Princess Anne (three-day event)
Mary Peters (athletics)
Ann Moore (show jumping)
Gillian Gilks (badminton)
Lucinda Prior-Palmer (three-day event)
Gillian Gilks (badminton)
Virginia Wade (tennis)

1978	Daley Thompson (athletics)	Sharron Davies (swimming)
1979	Sebastian Coe (athletics)	Caroline Bradley (show jumping)
1980	Sebastian Coe (athletics)	Sharron Davies (swimming)
1981	Sebastian Coe (athletics)	Jayne Torvill (ice dancing)
1982	Daley Thompson (athletics)	Wendy Norman (modern pentathlon)
1983	Steve Cram (athletics)	Jo Durie (tennis)
1984	Sebastian Coe (athletics)	Tessa Sanderson (athletics)
1985	Steve Cram (athletics)	Virginia Holgate (equestrianism)
1986	Lloyd Honeyghan (boxing)	Fatima Whitbread (athletics)
1987	Nick Faldo (golf)	Fatima Whitbread (athletics)
1988	Sandy Lyle (golf)	Liz McColgan (athletics)
1989	Nick Faldo (golf)	Yvonne Murray (athletics)
1990	Nick Faldo (golf)	Tracy Edwards (yachting)
1991	Kriss Akabusi (athletics)	Liz McColgan (athletics)
1992	Linford Christie (athletics)	Sally Gunnell (athletics)
1993	Linford Christie (athletics)	Sally Gunnell (athletics)

Most wins MEN 4 – Sebastian Coe (1979, 1980, 1981, 1984); **3** – Nick Faldo (1987, 1989, 1990). **WOMEN 2** – Mary Rand (née Bignal) (1959, 1964), Anita Lonsbrough (1960, 1962), Gillian Gilks (1974, 1976), Sharron Davies (1978, 1980), Fatima Whitbread (1986, 1987), Liz McColgan (1988, 1991), Sally Gunnell (1992, 1993).

BBC Sports Personality of the Year

First awarded in 1954, this prestigious British award for sportsmen and women is given at the end of each year. Winners are established by television viewers sending in their votes. Prior to the awards ceremony, the awards details are included in televised sports programmes. A suggested list of nominees is drawn up by the BBC sports department, although viewers can nominate anybody.

1954	Chris Chataway (athletics)
1955	Gordon Pirie (athletics)
1956	Jim Laker (cricket)
1957	Dai Rees (golf)
1958	Ian Black (swimming)
1959	John Surtees (motorcycling)
1960	David Broome (show jumping)
1961	Stirling Moss (motor racing)
1962	Anita Lonsbrough (swimming)
1963	Dorothy Hyman (athletics)
1964	Mary Rand (athletics)
1965	Tommy Simpson (cycling)
1966	Bobby Moore (football)
1967	Henry Cooper (boxing)
1968	David Hemery (athletics)
1969	Ann Jones (tennis)
1970	Henry Cooper (boxing)
1971	HRH the Princess Anne (equestrianism)
1972	Mary Peters (athletics)
1973	Jackie Stewart (motor racing)
1974	Brendan Foster (athletics)
1975	David Steele (cricket)
1976	John Curry (ice-skating)
1977	Virginia Wade (lawn tennis)
1978	Steve Ovett (athletics)
1979	Sebastian Coe (athletics)
1980	Robin Cousins (ice skating)
1981	Ian Botham (cricket)
1982	Daley Thompson (athletics)
1983	Steve Cram (athletics)
1984	Jayne Torvill and Christopher Dean (ice dancing)
1985	Barry McGuigan (boxing)
1986	Nigel Mansell (motor racing)
1987	Fatima Whitbread (athletics)
1988	Steve Davis (snooker)
1989	Nick Faldo (golf)
1990	Paul Gascoigne (football)
1991	Liz McColgan (athletics)
1992	Nigel Mansell (motor racing)
1993	Linford Christie (athletics)

Most wins 2 – Henry Cooper (1967, 1970), Nigel Mansell (1986, 1992).

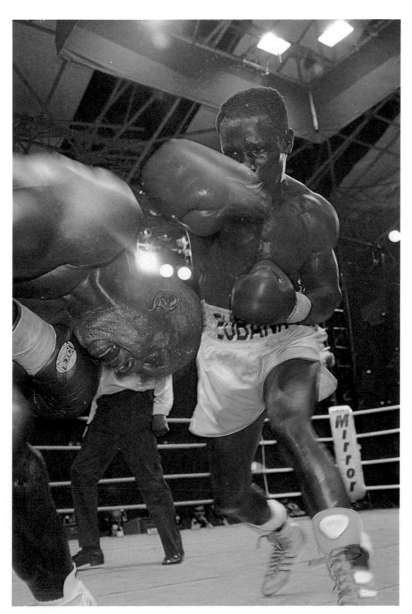

LEFT The Eubank v Benn fight, which attracted a record 1993 television audience, on 9 October in Manchester – the fight was declared a draw after 12 rounds.

Sport's Top Television Audiences, 1993

Event	Date	Average (million)
1 Eubank v Benn (ITV) – middleweight boxing	9 Oct	16.35
2 The Grand National (BBC)	3 Apr	15.17
3 Holland v England (ITV) – World Cup qualifier	13 Oct	14.07
4 Bruno v Williams (BBC) – prize fight	24 Apr	13.99
5 FA Cup final replay (BBC)	20 May	13.44
6 San Marino v England (BBC) – World Cup qualifier	17 Nov	11.8
7 World athletics (BBC) (inc. men's 100 m final)	15 Aug	11.49
8 *Grandstand* final score (BBC) (on Grand National day)	3 Apr	11.27
9 FA Cup final (BBC)	15 May	10.92
10 Linford Christie v Carl Lewis (ITV) – 100 metres	20 Feb	10.06

Source: Viewing figures supplied by BARB

Football Writers' Association Footballer of the Year

The Football Writers' Association was founded in 1947 and since 1947/48 its members have voted for their Footballer of the Year.

1948 Stanley Matthews (Blackpool)
1949 Johnny Carey (Manchester United)
1950 Joe Mercer (Arsenal)
1951 Harry Johnston (Blackpool)
1952 Billy Wright (Wolverhampton Wanderers)
1953 Nat Lofthouse (Bolton Wanderers)
1954 Tom Finney (Preston North End)
1955 Don Revie (Manchester City)
1956 Bert Trautmann (Manchester City)
1957 Tom Finney (Preston North End)
1958 Danny Blanchflower (Tottenham Hotspur)
1959 Syd Owen (Luton Town)
1960 Bill Slater (Wolverhampton Wanderers)
1961 Danny Blanchflower (Tottenham Hotspur)
1962 Jimmy Adamson (Burnley)
1963 Stanley Matthews (Stoke City)
1964 Bobby Moore (West Ham United)
1965 Bobby Collins (Leeds United)
1966 Bobby Charlton (Manchester United)
1967 Jackie Charlton (Leeds United)
1968 George Best (Manchester United)
1969 Tony Book (Manchester City)
Dave Mackay (Derby County)
1970 Billy Bremner (Leeds United)
1971 Frank McLintock (Arsenal)
1972 Gordon Banks (Stoke City)
1973 Pat Jennings (Tottenham Hotspur)
1974 Ian Callaghan (Liverpool)
1975 Alan Mullery (Fulham)
1976 Kevin Keegan (Liverpool)
1977 Emlyn Hughes (Liverpool)
1978 Kenny Burns (Nottingham Forest)
1979 Kenny Dalglish (Liverpool)
1980 Terry McDermott (Liverpool)
1981 Frans Thijssen (Ipswich Town)
1982 Steve Perryman (Tottenham Hotspur)
1983 Kenny Dalglish (Liverpool)
1984 Ian Rush (Liverpool)
1985 Neville Southall (Everton)
1986 Gary Lineker (Everton)
1987 Clive Allen (Tottenham Hotspur)
1988 John Barnes (Liverpool)
1989 Steve Nicol (Liverpool)
1990 John Barnes (Liverpool)
1991 Gordon Strachan (Leeds United)
1992 Gary Lineker (Tottenham Hotspur)
1993 Chris Waddle (Sheffield W)
1994 Alan Shearer (Blackburn Rovers)

Most wins 2 – Stanley Matthews (1948, 1963), Tom Finney (1954, 1957), Danny Blanchflower (1958, 1961), Kenny Dalglish (1979, 1983), John Barnes (1988, 1990).

Professional Footballers' Association Player of the Year

Since 1974, at the end of each season, the professional players vote for their Player of the Year, a trophy highly regarded by its winners. A Young Player of the Year trophy is also awarded annually.

Player of the Year

1974 Norman Hunter (Leeds United)
1975 Colin Todd (Derby County)
1976 Pat Jennings (Tottenham Hotspur)
1977 Andy Gray (Aston Villa)
1978 Peter Shilton (Nottingham Forest)
1979 Liam Brady (Arsenal)
1980 Terry McDermott (Liverpool)
1981 John Wark (Ipswich Town)
1982 Kevin Keegan (Southampton)
1983 Kenny Dalglish (Liverpool)
1984 Ian Rush (Liverpool)
1985 Peter Reid (Everton)
1986 Gary Lineker (Everton)
1987 Clive Allen (Tottenham Hotspur)
1988 John Barnes (Liverpool)
1989 Mark Hughes (Manchester United)
1990 David Platt (Aston Villa)
1991 Mark Hughes (Manchester United)
1992 Gary Pallister (Manchester United)
1993 Paul McGrath (Aston Villa)
1994 Eric Cantona (Manchester United)
Most wins 2 - Mark Hughes (1989, 1991).

Young Player of the Year

1974 Kevin Beattie (Ipswich Town)
1975 Mervyn Day (West Ham United)
1976 Peter Barnes (Manchester City)
1977 Andy Gray (Aston Villa)
1978 Tony Woodcock (Nottingham Forest)
1979 Cyrille Regis (West Bromwich Albion)
1980 Glenn Hoddle (Tottenham Hotspur)
1981 Gary Shaw (Aston Villa)
1982 Steve Moran (Southampton)
1983 Ian Rush (Liverpool)
1984 Paul Walsh (Luton Town)
1985 Mark Hughes (Manchester United)
1986 Tony Cottee (West Ham United)
1987 Tony Adams (Arsenal)
1988 Paul Gascoigne (Newcastle United)
1989 Paul Merson (Arsenal)
1990 Matthew Le Tissier (Southampton)
1991 Lee Sharpe (Manchester United)
1992 Ryan Giggs (Manchester United)
1993 Ryan Giggs (Manchester United)
1994 Andy Cole (Newcastle United)

Most wins 2 – Ryan Giggs (1992, 1993)

Mark Hughes, playing for Manchester United, has won the Professional Footballers' Association Player of the Year trophy twice (1989, 1991).

International Athletes of the Year

Organised since 1988, the International Amateur Athletic Federation (IAAF) undertakes a poll to find the International Athletes of the Year. The poll includes votes from IAAF members, media representatives, organisers and sponsors.

	MEN	WOMEN
1988	Carl Lewis (USA)	Florence Griffith-Joyner (USA)
1989	Roger Kingdom (USA)	Anna Quirot (CUB)
1990	Steve Backley (UK)	Merlene Ottey (JAM)
1991	Carl Lewis (USA)	Katrin Krabbe (GER)
1992	Kevin Young (USA)	Heike Henkel (GER)
1993	Colin Jackson (UK)	Sally Gunnell (UK)

Most wins 2 - Carl Lewis (1988, 1991).

Wisden *Cricketers of the Year*

The award dates back to 1889 and has been in its present form – five cricketers named each year – since 1927. No one is given the award twice. Recipients are announced in the *Wisden Cricketers' Almanack* each year on publication. Winners since 1947:

1947 A. V. Bedser, L. B. Fishlock, V. (M. H.) Mankad, T. P. B. Smith, C. Washbrook
1948 M. P. Donnelly, A. Melville, A. D. Nourse, J. D. Robertson, N. W. D. Yardley
1949 A. L. Hassett, W. A. Johnston, R. R. Lindwall, A. R. Morris, D. Tallon
1950 T. E. Bailey, R. O. Jenkins, J. G. Langridge, R. T. Simpson, B. Sutcliffe
1951 T. G. Evans, S. Ramadhin, A. L. Valentine, E. D. Weekes, F. M. M. Worrell
1952 R. Appleyard, H. E. Dollery, J. C. Laker, P. B. H. May, E. A. B. Rowan
1953 H. Gimblett, T. W. Graveney, D. S. Sheppard, W. S. Surridge, F. S. Trueman
1954 R. N. Harvey, G. A. R. Lock, K. R. Miller, J. H. Wardle, W. Watson

1955 B. Dooland, Fazal Mahmood, W. E. Hollies J. B. Statham, G. E. Tribe
1956 M. C. Cowdrey, D. J. Insole, D. J. McGlew, H. J. Tayfield, F. H. Tyson
1957 D. Brookes, J. W. Burke, M. J. Hilton, G. R. A. Langley, P. E. Richardson
1958 P. J. Loader, A. J. W. McIntyre, O. G. Smith, M. J. Stewart, C. L. Walcott
1959 H. L. Jackson, R. E. Marshall, C. A. Milton, J. R. Reid, D. Shackleton
1960 K. F. Barrington, D. B. Carr, R. Illingworth, G. Pullar, M. J. K. Smith
1961 N. A. T. Adcock, E. R. Dexter, R. A. McLean, R. Subba Row, J. V. Wilson
1962 W. E. Alley, R. Benaud, A. K. Davidson, W. M. Lawry, N. C. O'Neill
1963 D. Kenyon, Mushtaq Mohammad, P. H. Parfitt, P. J. Sharpe, F. J. Titmus
1964 D. B. Close, C. C. Griffith, C. C. Hunte, R. B. Kanhai, G. S. Sobers
1965 G. Boycott, P. J. Burge, J. A. Flavell, G. D. McKenzie, R. B. Simpson
1966 K. C. Bland, J. H. Edrich, R. C. Motz, P. M. Pollock, R. G. Pollock
1967 R. W. Barber, B. L. D'Oliveira, C. Milburn, J. T. Murray, S. M. Nurse
1968 Asif Iqbal, Hanif Mohammad, K. Higgs, J. M. Parks, Nawab of Pataudi jun
1969 J. G. Binks, D. M. Green, B. A Richards, D. L. Underwood, O. S Wheatley
1970 B. F. Butcher, A. P. E. Knott, Majid Khan, M. J. Procter, D. J. Shepherd
1971 J. D. Bond, C. H. Lloyd, B. W. Luckhurst, G. M. Turner, R. T. Virgin
1972 G. G. Arnold, B. S. Chandrasekhar, L. R. Gibbs, B. Taylor, Zaheer Abbas
1973 G. S. Chappell, D. K. Lillee, R. A. L. Massie, J. A. Snow, K. R. Stackpole
1974 K. D. Boyce, B. E. Congdon, K. W. R. Fletcher, R. C. Fredericks, P. J. Sainsbury
1975 D. L. Amiss, M. H. Denness, N. Gifford. A. W. Greig, A. M. E. Roberts
1976 I. M. Chappell, P. G. Lee, R. B. McCosker, D. S. Steele, R. A. Woolmer
1977 J. M. Brearley, C. G. Greenidge, M. A. Holding, I. V. A. Richards, R. W. Taylor
1978 I. T. Botham, M. Hendrick, A. Jones, K. S. McEwan, R. G. D. Willis
1979 D. I. Gower, J. K. Lever, C. M. Old, C. T. Radley, J. N. Shepherd
1980 J. Garner, S. M. Gavaskar, G. A. Gooch, D. W. Randall, B. C. Rose
1981 K. J. Hughes, R. D. Jackman, A. J. Lamb, C. E. B. Rice, V. A. P. van der Bijl
1982 T. M. Alderman, A. R. Border, R. J. Hadlee, Javed Miandad, R. W. Marsh
1983 Imran Khan, T. E. Jesty, A. I. Kallicharran, Kapil Dev, M. D. Marshall
1984 M. Amaruath, J. V. Coney, J. E. Emburey, M. W. Gatting, C. L. Smith

1985 M. D. Crowe, H. A. Gomes, G. W. Humpage, J. Simmons, S. Weittimuny
1986 P. Bainbridge, R. M. Ellison, C. J. McDermott, N. V. Radford, R. T. Robinson
1987 J. H. Childs, G. A. Hick, D. B. Vengsarkar, C. A. Walsh, J. J. Whitaker
1988 J. P. Agnew, N. A. Foster, D. P. Hughes, P. M. Roebuck, Salim Malik
1989 K. J. Barnett, P. J. L. Dujon, P. A. Neale, F. D. Stephenson, S. R. Waugh
1990 S. J. Cook, D. M. Jones, R. C. Russell, R. A. Smith, M. A. Taylor
1991 M. A. Atherton, M. Azharuddin, A. R. Butcher, D. L. Haynes, M. E. Waugh
1992 C. E. L. Ambrose, P. A. J. DeFreitas, A. A. Donald, R. B. Richardson, Waqar Younis
1993 N. E. Briers, M. D. Moxon, I. D. K. Salisbury, A. J. Stewart, Wasim Akram
1994 D. C. Boon, I. A. Healy, M. G. Hughes, S. K. Warne, S. L. Watkin

Harry Vardon Trophy

Harry Vardon won the British Open a record six times (1896, 1898, 1899, 1903, 1911, 1914). This trophy, named after him, has been awarded annually since 1937 by the Professional Golfers Association (PGA) to the leading player in the Order of Merit. (Players are British, except where indicated otherwise.)

1937 Charles Whitcombe
1938 Henry Cotton
1939 Reg Whitcombe
1940–1945 No awards
1946 Bobby Locke (SA)
1947 Norman von Nida (AUS)
1948 Charles Ward
1949 Charles Ward
1950 Bobby Locke (SA)
1951 John Panton
1952 Harry Weetman
1953 Flory van Donck (BEL)
1954 Bobby Locke (SA)
1955 Dai Rees
1956 Harry Weetman
1957 Eric Brown

1958 Bernard Hunt
1959 Dai Rees
1960 Bernard Hunt
1961 Christy O'Connor (IRE)
1962 Christy O'Connor (IRE)
1963 Neil Coles
1964 Peter Alliss
1965 Bernard Hunt
1966 Peter Alliss
1967 Malcolm Gregson
1968 Brian Huggett
1969 Bernard Gallacher
1970 Neil Coles
1971 Peter Oosterhuis
1972 Peter Oosterhuis
1973 Peter Oosterhuis
1974 Peter Oosterhuis
1975 Dale Hayes (SA)
1976 Severiano Ballesteros (SPA)
1977 Severiano Ballesteros (SPA)
1978 Severiano Ballesteros (SPA)
1979 Sandy Lyle
1980 Sandy Lyle
1981 Bernhard Langer (GER)
1982 Greg Norman (AUS)
1983 Nick Faldo
1984 Bernhard Langer (GER)
1985 Sandy Lyle
1986 Severiano Ballesteros (SPA)
1987 Ian Woosnam
1988 Severiano Ballesteros (SPA)
1989 Ronan Rafferty (NIR)
1990 Ian Woosnam
1991 Severiano Ballesteros (SPA)
1992 Nick Faldo
1993 Colin Montgomerie

Most wins 6 – Severiano Ballesteros (1976–78, 1986, 1988, 1991); **4** – Peter Oosterhuis (1971–74); **3** – Bobby Locke (1946, 1950, 1954), Bernard Hunt (1958, 1960, 1965), Sandy Lyle (1979, 1980, 1985).

Horse Racing – Timeform Ratings

Timeform Ratings for racehorses measure, by a series of scientific calculations, the performance of each horse in a particular season, and are therefore a useful means of comparing champions of different eras, on the Flat and over the jumps. In the following list, horses are ranked according to their best ever annual Timeform Rating with the year this was achieved and their age in that year.

Flat

Colts
145 Sea-Bird 1965 (3 yr, FRA)
144 Tudor Minstrel 1947 (3 yr, GB)
Brigadier Gerard 1972 (4 yr, GB)

Severiano Ballesteros, six times leading player in the Harry Vardon Trophy Order of Merit, here seen playing in the 1994 Tyrespaña Masters in Jerez, Spain.

142 Abernant 1950 (4 yr, GB)
Windy City 1951 (2 yr, IRE)
Ribot 1956 (4 yr, ITA)
141 Mill Reef 1971 (3 yr, GB); 1972 (4 yr, GB)
140 Vaguely Noble 1968 (3 yr, FRA)
Shergar 1981 (3 yr, GB)
Dancing Brave 1986 (3 yr, GB)
139 Pappa Fourway 1955 (3 yr, GB)
Reference Point 1987 (3 yr, GB)
Generous 1991 (3 yr, GB)
138 Alycidon 1949 (4 yr, GB)
Exbury 1963 (4 yr, FRA)
Nijinsky 1970 (3 yr, IRE)
Alleged 1978 (4 yr, IRE)
137 Pinza 1953 (3 yr, GB)
Never Say Die 1954 (3 yr, GB)
Princely Gift 1955 (4 yr, GB)
Right Boy 1959 (5 yr, GB)
Molvedo 1961 (3 yr, ITA)

Ragusa 1963 (3 yr, IRE)
Reliance 1965 (3 yr, FRA)
Rheingold 1973 (4 yr, GB)
Apalachee 1973 (2 yr, IRE)
Grundy 1975 (3 yr, GB)
Troy 1979 (3 yr, GB)
Moorestyle 1980 (3 yr, GB)
Zilzal 1989 (3 yr, GB)
Dayjur 1990 (3 yr, GB)
136 My Babu 1947 (2 yr, GB); 1949 (4 yr, GB)
Black Tarquin 1949 (4 yr, GB)
Tantième 1950 (3 yr, FRA)
Haffiz 1956 (4 yr, FRA)
Crepello 1957 (3 yr, GB)
Ballymoss 1958 (4 yr, IRE)
Alcide 1959 (4 yr, GB)
Herbager 1959 (3 yr, FRA)
Floribunda 1961 (3 yr, IRE)
Relko 1963 (3 yr, FRA); 1964 (4 yr, FRA)

Thatch 1973 (3 yr, IRE)
Bustino 1975 (4 yr, GB)
Northjet 1981 (4 yr, FRA)
El Gran Senor 1984 (3 yr, IRE)
Slip Anchor 1985 (3 yr, GB)
Bering 1986 (3 yr, FRA)
Warning 1988 (3 yr, GB)
Old Vic 1989 (3 yr, GB)
Suave Dancer 1991 (3 yr, FRA)

Fillies

138 Star of India 1955 (2 yr, GB)
136 Texana 1957 (2 yr, FRA)
Allez France 1974 (4 yr, FRA)
Habibti 1983 (3 yr, GB)

Jumping

Hurdlers

182 Night Nurse 1976/77 (6 yr, GB)
180 Monksfield 1978/79 (7 yr horse, IRE)
179 Persian War 1968/69 (6 yr, GB)
178 Comedy of Errors 1974/75 (8 yr, GB)
177 Lanzarote 1974/75 (7 yr, GB)
176 Bula 1971/72 (7 yr, GB)
Birds Nest 1975/76 (6 yr, GB); 1976/77 (7 yr, GB)
Golden Cygnet 1977/78 (6 yr, IRE)
175 Salmon Spray 1965/66 (8 yr, GB)
Sea Pigeon 1976/77 (7 yr, GB); 1977/78 (8 yr, GB); 1978/79 (9 yr, GB); 1979/80 (10 yr, GB); 1980/81 (11 yr, GB)
Gaye Brief 1982/83 (6 yr, GB)
174 Magic Court 1964/65 (7 yr, GB)
Lanzarote 1976/77 (9 yr, GB)
Dramatist 1976/77 (6 yr, GB)
For Auction 1981/82 (6 yr, IRE)
Morley Street 1990/91 (7 yr, GB)
173 Dawn Run 1983/84 (6 yr mare, IRE)
See You Then 1985/86 (6 yr, GB); 1986/87 (7 yr, GB)
172 Bannow Rambler 1975/76 (7 yr, IRE)
Boreen Prince 1982/83 (6 yr, IRE)
Browne's Gazette 1984/85 (7 yr, GB)
Prideaux Boy 1985/86 (8 yr, GB)
Flatterer 1986/87 (8 yr, USA)
Beech Road 1988/89 (7 yr, GB)
171+ Daring Run 1980/81 (6 yr, IRE)
171 Pollardstown 1980/81 (6 yr, GB)
Barnbrook Again 1986/87 (6 yr, GB)
170 Comedy of Errors 1975/76 (9 yr, GB)
Celtic Shot 1987/88 (6 yr, GB)
Mighty Mogul 1992/93 (6 yr, GB)
169 Kybo 1978/79 (6 yr, GB)
Ekbalco 1981/82 (6 yr, GB)
Rustle 1988/89 (7 yr, GB)
Kribensis 1989/90 (6 yr, GB)
168 Flash Imp 1975/76 (7 yr, GB)
Beacon Light 1976/77 (6 yr, GB)
Broadsword 1981/82 (5 yr horse, GB)

Beech Road 1989/90 (8 yr, GB)
Nomadic Way 1990/91 (6 yr, GB)
167 Tree Tangle 1975/76 (7 yr, GB)
Master Monday 1976/77 (7 yr, IRE)
Starfen 1980/81 (5 yr, GB)
Celtic Ryde 1981/82 (7 yr, GB)
Very Promising 1983/84 (6 yr, GB)
Ruling 1990/91 (5 yr, GB)
Granville Again 1992/93 (7 yr, GB)
166 Supernova 1975/76 (6 yr mare, GB)
Cima 1983/84 (6 yr, GB)
Celtic Chief 1987/88 (5 yr, GB)
Classical Charm 1987/88 (5 yr, IRE)
Royal Derbi 1992/93 (8 yr, GB)
166? River Ceiriog 1986/87 (6 yr, GB)
165 Royal Vulcan 1982/83 (5 yr horse, GB)
Nohalmdun 1985/86 (5 yr, GB); 1986/87 (6 yr, GB)
Galmoy 1986/87 (8 yr, IRE)
Deep Idol 1986/87 (7 yr, IRE)
Stepaside Lord 1986/87 (5 yr, IRE/GB)
Past Glories 1989/90 (7 yr, GB)
Muse 1992/93 (6 yr, GB)
165* Connaught Ranger 1979/80 (6 yr, GB); 1980/81 (7 yr, GB)
Flown 1992/93 (6 yr, GB)
164 Derring Rose 1980/81 (6 yr, GB)
Heighlin 1981/82 (6 yr, GB)
Floyd 1986/87 (7 yr, GB)
Cloughtaney 1987/88 (7 yr, IRE)
Kingsmill 1988/89 (6 yr, IRE)
King's Curate 1990/91 (7 yr, GB)
164** Royal Gait 1991/92 (9 yr, GB)

Steeplechasers

212 Arkle 1965/66 (9 yr, IRE)
210 Flyingbolt 1965/66 (7 yr, IRE)
191 Mill House 1964/65 (8 yr, GB)
187 Desert Orchid 1989/90 (11 yr, GB)
186 Dunkirk 1965/66 (9 yr, GB)
184 Burrough Hill Lad 1984/85 (9 yr, GB)
182 Captain Christy 1975/76 (9 yr, IRE)
Desert Orchid 1988/89 (10 yr, GB)
Carvill's Hill 1991/92 (10 yr, GB)
179 Badsworth Boy 1982/83 (8 yr, GB)
178 Pendil 1972/73 (8 yr, GB)
177 The Dikler 1972/73 (10 yr, GB)
Bregawn 1982/83 (9 yr, GB)
176 Saffron Tartan 1960/61 (10 yr, GB)
Buona Notte 1964/65 (8 yr, GB)
Titus Oates 1970/71 (9 yr, GB)
Little Owl 1980/81 (7 yr, GB)
175 Pas Seul 1960/61 (8 yr, GB)
Frenchmans Cove 1961/62 (7 yr, GB)
Kinloch Brae 1969/70 (7 yr, GB)
L'Escargot 1970/71 (8 yr, IRE)
Brown Lad 1975/76 (10 yr, IRE)
Night Nurse 1980/81 (10 yr, GB)
Silver Buck 1981/82 (10 yr, GB)
Wayward Lad 1983/84 (9 yr, GB)
174 Bula 1975/76 (11 yr, GB)
Pearlyman 1987/88 (9 yr, GB)
Barnbrook Again 1989/90 (9 yr, GB)

174** Jodami 1992/93 (8 yr GB)
173 Captain John 1982/83 (9 yr, GB)
Blazing Walker 1990/91 (7 yr, GB)
Remittance Man 1991/92 (8 yr, GB)
172 Brown Chamberlin 1983/84 (9 yr, GB)
Katabatic 1991/92 (9 yr, GB)
Rushing Wild 1992/93 (8 yr, GB)
171 Anaglogs Daughter 1980/81 (8 yr mare, IRE)
Charter Party 1987/88 (10 yr, GB)
Nupsala 1987/88 (9 yr, FRA)
Garrison Savannah 1990/91 (8 yr, GB)
The Fellow 1990/91 (6 yr, FRA)
Cool Ground 1991/92 (10 yr, GB)
170 Ten Up 1975/76 (9 yr, IRE)
Rathgorman 1981/82 (10 yr, GB); 1982/83 (11 yr, GB)
The Mighty Mac 1983/84 (9 yr, GB)
Combs Ditch 1985/86 (10 yr GB)
Playschool 1987/88 (10 yr, GB)
Kildimo 1987/88 (8 yr, GB)
Celtic Shock 1990/91 (9 yr, GB)
Docklands Express 1991/92 (10 yr, GB)
169** Carvill's Hill 1988/89 (7 yr, IRE)
169 Spartan Missile 1980/81 (9 yr, GB)
Sunset Cristo 1981/82 (8 yr, GB)
Fifty Dollars More 1982/83 (8 yr, GB); 1983/84 (9 yr, GB)
Forgive'N Forget 1985/86 (9 yr, GB); 1986/87 (10 yr, GB); 1987/88 (11 yr, GB)
Yahoo 1988/89 (8 yr, GB)
168 Diamond Edge 1979/80 (9 yr, GB); 1980/81 (10 yr, GB); 1981/82 (11 yr, GB)
Run and Skip 1985/86 (8yr, GB)
Very Promising 1986/87 (9 yr, GB)
Barnbrook Again 1988/89 (8 yr, GB)
Nortons Coin 1989/90 (9 yr, GB)
Waterloo Boy 1991/92 (9 yr, GB)
168? Beau Ranger 1988/89 (11 yr, GB)
167 Lough Inagh 1975/76 (9 yr, IRE)
Jack of Trumps 1979/80 (7 yr, IRE); 1980/81 (8 yr, IRE)
Drumgora 1981/82 (10 yr, IRE)
Dawn Run 1985/86 (8 yr mare, IRE)
Cavvies Clown 1987/88 (8 yr, GB)
Toby Tobias 1989/90 (8 yr, GB)
166** The Thinker 1986/87 (9 yr, GB)
166 Tingle Creek 1975/76 (10 yr, GB)
Nick the Brief 1989/90 (8 yr, GB)
Royal Athlete 1992/93 (10 yr, GB)

KEY

+ the horse's form may be rather better than rated.

* a horse who is unreliable, either for temperamental or for other reasons who may run up to its rating on occasions but cannot be trusted.

** the horse is likely to make more than normal progress and to improve on his rating.

? the horse's rating is suspect.

STAMPS

Royal Mail Sherlock Holmes Stamps

On 12 October 1993, the Royal Mail celebrated the centenary of Sherlock Holmes's fictitious death with the launch of a set of five 24p special stamps depicting scenes from Sir Arthur Conan Doyle's stories.

The stamps were unusual, not only in depicting fictional characters, but also in containing an element of mystery. Certain clues were included in the stamps to add intrigue and character, not specifically designed for use in a competition. Subsequently, however, *The Independent* over five days, in association with the Royal Mail, ran two competitions featuring the stamps.

The readers' first task was to find a letter hidden in each stamp. These five letters had to be rearranged into an order to make a word with strong Holmesian connections (see Solutions, p. 252, for the answer). The second task was to solve five clues, one of which was given each day in the paper. These clues, written by *The Independent*, concentrated more on the general detective / Sherlock Holmes theme than the stamp clues.

The competition was won by Andrew Charters of Manchester. The clues were as follows (solutions appear on p. 252):

Stamp 1 Sherlock Holmes & Dr Watson: 'The Reigate Squire'. This stamp shows Holmes and Dr Watson in a scene from the story *The Reigate Puzzle*, originally featured in the 1894 *Memoirs of Sherlock Holmes*. Holmes uses his powers of deduction to unmask the murderers of the Cunningham family's coachman.

Clue 'Talking of Reigate,' said Dr Watson, 'reminds me of the Giant Rat of Sumatra. Whatever happened to that rodent?' He gestured towards the instrument on the table. 'I suppose your violin playing frightened it off?' 'My violin?' queried Holmes in surprise. 'I fancy that some sort of rat Aids virus is the answer.'

Question What had Holmes been playing?

Stamp 2 Sherlock Holmes & Sir Henry: 'The Hound of the Baskervilles'. This stamp celebrates perhaps the best known of the Sherlock Holmes stories in which the desperate Sir Henry Baskerville called Holmes and Watson to Dartmoor to pit their wits against the dreadful Hound of the Baskervilles.

Clue 'That hound Baskerville has disappeared,' said Dr Watson angrily. 'We must track him down by examining the clues one by one.' 'Initially two at a time, I fancy,' replied Sherlock Holmes. 'Will the stamp help?' asked Watson. Sherlock Holmes thought for a moment before saying, enigmatically: 'Undoubtedly it edifies. Stamps attract esoterics.'

Question Where had Baskerville fled to?

Stamp 3 Sherlock Holmes & Lestrade: 'The Six Napoleons'. This stamp shows Sherlock Holmes and Inspector Lestrade in a scene from *The Six Napoleons*. Lestrade appears in many of the Holmes stories and with his unimaginative and dogged methods provides a foil to Sherlock's ingenuity.

Clue 'We've cracked the case,' said Lestrade. 'First class!' 'Like the stamps,' said Holmes, 'Indeed I do,' replied Lestrade, 'but how much did you pay for the bust of Napoleon?' 'There were five coins involved in the transaction,' explained Holmes, 'including both payment and any change that may have been given; and the sum was the smallest that could not have been so attained with exactly four coins.'

Question Using current British coinage, what sum fulfils Holmes's description?

Stamp 4 Sherlock Holmes & Mycroft: 'The Greek Interpreter'. This stamp shows Holmes in a scene with his brother Mycroft, who helps him to discover the whereabouts of Mr Melas, the Greek interpreter, and save him from a room filled with charcoal fumes.

Clue 'Having trouble with the knot, Sherlock?' asked Mycroft. 'Perhaps I might be of assistance.' 'O, that hemp is sensible,' exclaimed the great detective, pulling at the rope. 'What I cannot grasp,' said Mycroft, 'is how you knew where to find the Greek interpreter.' 'When you have eliminated the impossible,' said Holmes, 'whatever remains, however improbable, must be the truth.'

Question Where did Holmes find the interpreter?

Stamp 5 Sherlock Holmes & Moriarty: 'The Final Problem'. *The Final Problem* chronicles the death of Sherlock Holmes, plunging into the Reichenbach Falls locked in mortal combat with his arch-enemy Professor Moriarty. It was this story that prompted thousands of fans to threaten Conan Doyle for killing off this incredibly popular character. The public outcry that followed Holmes's 'death' was so great that Conan Doyle was compelled to 'revive' him in 1903. Two more decades of adventures followed before the author's death finally killed off his greatest creation once and for all.

Clue 'CJM RVLQPMQR QY TNSEM,' said Watson. 'And you say that's the coded message that saved you?' 'It told me what to beware,' answered Holmes. 'But how did you break the code?' asked the doctor. 'I surmised it was based on a simple letter substitution table,' explained the detective, 'and was intended for myself alone.' He picked up a pen and wrote eight letters on a sheet of paper. He paused, then added five more letters from the beginning of the alphabet, never repeating any letter already used. He continued the process in a second row of 13 letters immediately beneath the first. 'And that cracked the code,' concluded Holmes.

Question What was the decoded message?

STRENGTH

World's Strongest Man

Since 1977 Transworld has annually organised the search for the world's strongest man. There are only about 20 athletes in the world of this calibre and Transworld seeks advice from the Federation of International Strength Athletes which gives advice on who these top athletes are. They are then approached to see if they would like to participate.

Preliminary rounds are held until eight contestants are selected to appear in the final. The winner receives £10 000 and a silver Tonka toy truck. Top three placings are given below:

	Location	First	Second	Third
1977	USA	Bruce Wilhelm (USA)	Don Reinhoudt (USA)	Lou Ferrigno (USA)
1978	USA	Bruce Wilhelm (USA)	Don Reinhoudt (USA)	Lars Hedlund (SWE)
1979	USA	Don Reinhoudt (USA)	Lars Hedlund (SWE)	Bill Kazmaier (USA)
1980	USA	Bill Kazmaier (USA)	Lars Hedlund (SWE)	Geoff Capes (GB)
1981	USA	Bill Kazmaier (USA)	Geoff Capes (GB)	Dave Waddington (USA)
1982	USA	Bill Kazmaier (USA)	Tom Magee (CAN)	John Gamble (USA)
1983	New Zealand	Geoff Capes (GB)	Jon Pall Sigmarsson (ICE)	Siem Wulfse (NET)
1984	Sweden	Jon Pall Sigmarsson (ICE)	Ab Wolders (NET)	Geoff Capes (GB)
1985	Portugal	Geoff Capes (GB)	Jon Pall Sigmarsson (ICE)	Cees de Vreugd (NET)
1986	France	Jon Pall Sigmarsson (ICE)	Geoff Capes (GB)	Ab Wolders (NET)
1987	No contest			
1988	Hungary	Jon Pall Sigmarsson (ICE)	Bill Kazmaier (USA)	Jamie Reeves (GB)
1989	Spain	Jamie Reeves (GB)	Ab Wolders (NET)	Jon Pall Sigmarsson (ICE)
1990	Finland	Jon Pall Sigmarsson (ICE)	O. D. Wilson (USA)	Ikka Nummisto (FIN)
1991	Canary Islands	Magnus ver Magnusson (ICE)	Henning Thorsen (DEN)	Gary Taylor (GB)
1992	Iceland	Ted van der Parre (NET)	Jamie Reeves (GB) / Magnus ver Magnusson (ICE)	
1993	France	Gary Taylor (GB)	Magnus ver Magnusson (ICE)	Riku Riri (FIN)

▌ Jon Pall Sigmarsson from Iceland has won the title most – 4 times (1984, 1986, 1988, 1990). He was 24 years old when he first won the title. He was then 6 ft 3 in (1.9 m) tall, weighed 294 lb (133 kg), and his vital statistics were: chest 57 in (145 cm), waist 40 in (102 cm), upper arm 20.5 in (52 cm) and thigh 30 in (76 cm).

▌ The first win for Great Britain was in 1983 when Geoff Capes won the title. He also won second place in 1981 and 1986 and third in 1980, and 1984.

▌ The record vital statistics for contestants are: Height – 6 ft 6 in (1.98 m), Geoff Capes (GB); Weight – 438 lb (199 kg), James Perry (USA); Chest measurement – 65 in (165 cm), Grizzly Brown (USA); Waist – 55 in (140 cm), James Perry (USA); Upper arm – 25 in (63 cm), Manfred Hoeberl (Aut) and James Perry (USA); Thigh – 39 in (99 cm), Berend Veneberg (Hol).

1993 EVENTS

1 The Juggernaut. A truck weighing approximately 7 tonnes had to be pulled over a hard-surfaced course, 25 metres long, by a harness. Maximum time allowed: 90 seconds.

2 The Leviathan Lift. Repeated lifting of a log weighing approx 100 kg. The log had to be lifted from the chest to an overhead position. Maximum time allowed: 90 seconds.

3 Samson's Barrow. A heavy loaded barrow with a single front wheel had to be pushed as fast as possible over a course. Maximum time allowed: 90 seconds.

4 Clash of the Titans. Contestants, in pairs, faced each other, and with two rope hand-holds on a heavy pole, tried to manoeuvre the opposition out of the marked arena.

5 Car Walk. A car weighing 440 kg, with roof and floor removed so that the contestant could stand inside the car in order to lift and carry it with the aid of straps placed over the shoulders, was lifted and carried along a measured distance. The car's wheels had to remain clear of the floor.

6 Hercules Hold (The Crucifix). The competitors had to stand with arms extended sideways, horizontally in line with the shoulders, and the hands had to grip handles which supported two barrels over a pulley, weighing 130 kg each. The barrels were hydraulically lifted and the competitor had to keep the barrels in a position off the floor for as long as possible.

7 The Trojan Wall. Contestants had to throw a 'stone' block weighting 20 kg over a wall, the height of which was increased after each round. If a competitor failed in three consecutive throws, he was eliminated. The maximum height of the wall was determined to be 20 ft (6.1 m).

8 The Atlas Stones. Five stones weighing 95 kg, 105 kg, 115 kg, 125 kg, and 135 kg had to be lifted and carried in ascending order of weight, to be placed on 52-inch (132-cm) high barrels in the shortest time possible.

Gary Taylor – The World's Strongest Man

Gary Taylor was 32 years old when he won the strongest man title. A Welshman, he lives in London and works as a PE instructor at Wandsworth Jail. He boasts a 54-in (137-cm) chest, 38-in (96-cm) waist, 22-in (56-cm) arm circumference, 31-in (79-cm) upper thighs, and weighs 21 stone (133 kg). He became interested in body building having seen a magazine on the subject in 1980 and started working out with weights five or six times a week. At the 1984 Los Angeles Olympics, he won a silver medal for weightlifting, followed by fourth place in the Mr Universe competition.

Gary keeps his strength up by eating six or seven large meals a day in a combination of 65% carbohydrates, 20% proteins and 15% fats – a total of six to nine thousand calories in all.

For breakfast he usually has four rashers of bacon, four or five eggs, toast and butter, baked beans, finishing with an 8-ounce (225-g) bowl of oat porridge with milk and sucrose and a pint of skimmed milk to drink. Mid-morning he has four or five chicken and salad cream sandwiches and a pint of semi-skimmed milk, and for lunch, rice, vegetables and chicken, cooked with onions and spices. Mid-afternoon he has a protein drink consisting of three-quarters of a pint of milk, with three eggs, two egg whites and a banana which he makes in a blender, and at teatime a pasta dish or jacket potato. To round the day off he has another plate of rice and chicken for dinner, and, finally, before going to bed, he has three shredded wheat with a tin of pineapple poured over, plus milk over the top. His food bill comes to approximately £150 a week.

He trains with weights for two hours, twice a day, six days a week, and rests for a week before a competition. His training schedule before the event was: Monday – 1½ hours upper body strength training; Tuesday – 1½ hours explosive power and lower back strength training; Thursday – 1½ hours explosive power and shoulder strength training; Friday – 1½ hours leg and back strength training; and Sunday – 1 hour fitness training.

Gary Taylor, 1993 Strongest Man, lifting one of the Atlas stones in the last round of the competition.

TELEVISION & RADIO

Top 50 TV Programmes, 1993

	Programme	Channel	Day	Date	Viewing figures (millions)
1	EastEnders	BBC1	Thu/Sun	7/10 Jan	23.21
2	Coronation Street	ITV	Mon/Wed	22/24 Nov	22.04
3	One Foot in the Algarve	BBC1	Sun	26 Dec	20.00
4	Only Fools and Horses	BBC1	Sat	25 Dec	19.59
5	Birds of a Feather	BBC1	Sat	25 Dec	19.39
6	Inspector Morse	ITV	Wed	13 Jan	18.77
7	Ghost (US 90)	BBC1	Sat	25 Dec	18.53
8	You've Been Framed	ITV	Sun	4 Dec	18.48
9	One Foot in the Grave	BBC1	Sun	28 Feb	18.39
10	Neighbours	BBC1	Wed	13 Jan	18.29
11	Heartbeat	ITV	Sun	5 Dec	17.77
12	The Bill	ITV	Fri	26 Mar	17.73
13	Wish You Were Here	ITV	Mon/Wed	11/13 Jan	17.09
14	Keeping Up Appearances	BBC1	Sun	26 Dec	17.07
15	Casualty	BBC1	Sun	26 Dec	17.03
16	News and Weather	BBC1	Sun	26 Dec	16.66
17	This Is Your Life	ITV	Wed	3 Feb	16.36
18	Big Fight Live	ITV	Sat	9 Oct	16.35
19	London's Burning	ITV	Sun	5 Dec	16.22
20	Strike It Lucky Special	ITV	Mon	27 Dec	15.67
21	Darling Buds of May	ITV	Sun	21 Mar	15.46
22	Noel's House Party	BBC1	Sat	2 Jan	15.45
23	Barrymore	ITV	Sat	13 Feb	15.23

F A C T S

▌ Channel 4 and BBC2 do not get a mention in the 'Top 50' listing. Their top three programmes in 1993 were as follows: BBC2 – *Michael Jackson* (Mon 15 Feb) 11.52 million; *Only Fools and Horses* (Sun 3 Jan) 7.72; 'Wimbledon Men's Final' (Sun 4 Jul) 7.56. Channel 4 – *Nuns on The Run* (GB 90) (Sun 18 Apr) 9.20; *Brookside* (Wed / Sat 3 / 6 Nov) 8.27; *Bill and Ted's Excellent Adventure* (US 88) (Sun 11 Apr) 7.29.

BELOW The cast of *EastEnders*, the programme with the highest viewing figures in 1993.

Programme	Channel	Day	Date	Viewing figures (millions)
24 *Grand National 1993*	BBC1	Sat	3 Apr	15.17
25 *Pretty Woman* (US 90)	ITV	Sun	5 Sep	15.16
26 *It'll Be Alright On The Night*	ITV	Sat	9 Jan	15.09
27 *Home and Away*	ITV	Mon	11 Jan	15.01
28 *Royal Variety Performance*	ITV	Sat	20 Nov	14.95
29 *Ghostbusters II* (US 89)	ITV	Wed	10 Mar	14.79
30 *Auntie's Bloomers*	BBC1	Sat	27 Feb	14.67
31 *Year in Provence*	BBC1	Sun	28 Feb	14.52
32 *Mr Bean in Room 426*	ITV	Wed	17 Feb	14.31
33 *Prime Suspect 3*	ITV	Sun	19 Dec	14.27
34 *Crimewatch UK*	BBC1	Thu	18 Feb	14.20
35 *Big Break*	BBC1	Sat	11 Dec	14.18
36 *World Cup Football*	ITV	Wed	13 Oct	14.07
37 *Live Boxing*	BBC1	Sat	24 Apr	13.99
38 *Gladiators*	ITV	Sat	4 Dec	13.97
39 *Family Fortunes*	ITV	Fri	19 Nov	13.91
40 *Back To The Future III* (US 90)	BBC1	Sat	25 Dec	13.74
41 *British Comedy Awards*	ITV	Sun	12 Dec	13.60
42 *Emmerdale Farm*	ITV	Tue/Thu	26/28 Oct	13.50
43 *Second Worst Night*	ITV	Sat	3 Apr	13.48
44 *Taggart*	ITV	Tue	16 Feb	13.47
45 *Soldier Soldier*	ITV	Tue	16 Nov	13.46
46 *Watching*	ITV	Sun	4 Apr	13.46
47 *Match of the Day*	BBC	Thu	20 May	13.44
48 *Blind Date*	ITV	Sat	2 Oct	13.20
49 *The Upper Hand*	ITV	Mon	22 Feb	13.01
50 *A Question of Sport*	BBC1	Tue	28 Dec	12.80

Source Viewing figures supplied by BARB
Note Programmes are only listed once, the top viewing figure being used in each case.

Golden Rose of Montreux

This annual international contest for television light entertainment was first held in 1961. The event is organised by the Swiss Broadcasting Corporation in cooperation with the town of Montreux, under the patronage of the European Broadcasting Union.

Awards are made in three categories – Humour, Music and Miscellaneous – and there is a first and second prize (Silver and Bronze). The programmes accepted for the competition are shown to three international juries – one for each category. The juries are composed of television professionals and journalists appointed by the organisers of the contest. The Golden Rose of Montreux is awarded by the Grand Jury to one of the first prize winners. The Grand Jury is composed of the three juries under the chairmanship of an international entertainer.

BRITISH TELEVISION WINNERS

Golden Rose

1961 *Black and White Minstrel Show* (BBC)
1967 *Frost Over England* (BBC)
1972 *Marty: The Best of the Comedy Machine* (ITV)
1977 *The Muppet Show* (ITV)
1982 *Dizzy Feet* (ITV)
1985 *The Paul Daniels Magic Easter Show* (BBC)
1988 *The Comic Strip Presents . . . The Strike* (Channel 4)
1989 *Hale and Pace* (ITV)
1990 *Mr Bean* (ITV)
1991 *A Night on Mount Edna* (ITV)

Silver Rose

1969 *Marty* (BBC)
1971 *Monty Python's Flying Circus* (BBC)
1972 *The Goodies* (BBC)

1974 *Barbra Streisand and other Musical Instruments* (ITV)
1975 *The Goodies* (BBC)
1978 *Dave Allen at Large* (BBC)
1980 *It'll Be Alright on the Night* (ITV)
1983 *Three of a Kind* (BBC)
1990 *Norbert Smith – A Life* (Channel 4)
1992 *KYTV – Good Morning Calais* (BBC)

Bronze Rose

1976 *The Picnic* (BBC)
1980 *Not the Nine O'Clock News* (BBC)
1985 *Spitting Image* (ITV)
1987 *Torvill and Dean's Fire and Ice* (ITV)
1994 The All New Alexei Sayle Show (BBC), **Noel's House Party** (BBC)

Press Prize

1963 *It's A Square World* (BBC)
1967 *Frost Over England* (BBC)
1980 *The Plank* (ITV)
1983 *Three of a Kind* (BBC)
1987 *Now – Something Else* (BBC)
1988 *The Comic Strip Presents . . . The Strike* (Channel 4)
1989 *Hale and Pace* (ITV)

Special Prize

1968 *The World of Charlie Drake* (BBC)
1972 *Marty: The Best of the Comedy Machine* (ITV)
1983 *It's Your Move* (ITV)
1984 *The Benny Hill Show* (ITV)
1990 *Mr Bean* (ITV)

British Academy of Film and Television Arts Awards

Formerly the Society of Film and Television Arts, this organisation was formed in 1959 by the amalgamation of the British Film Academy (founded in September 1948) and the Guild of Television Producers and Directors (formed in 1954). Membership is open to senior creative workers in both industries. A further reorganisation in 1975 resulted in a change in title to the British Academy of Film and Television Arts (BAFTA). Branches of the Academy exist throughout the world with the aim of raising standards in all aspects of film-making and television.

Each year BAFTA presents a series of awards in various categories. Formerly, these were given as The British Film Academy Awards (1947–68), The Society of Film and Television Arts Awards (1969–74) and, from 1975, the

> '*I hate television. I hate it as much as peanuts. But I can't stop eating peanuts.*'
>
> Orson Welles

BAFTA awards. Winners from selected categories follow.

Alan Clarke Award

Awarded for outstanding creative contribution to television. Prior to 1991 known as the Desmond Davis Award.

1960 Richard Dimbleby, CBE
1961 Michael Barry, OBE
1962 Cecil McGivern, CBE
1963 Joan Kemp-Welch
1964 No award
1965 Humphrey Burton
1966 Alan Chilvers
1967 Sydney Newman
1968 Ken Russell
1969 Richard Cawston
1970 David Attenborough
1971 Jeremy Isaacs
1972 Nigel Ryan
1973 James MacTaggart
1974 Denis Mitchell
1975 Jack Gold
1976 Bill Ward
1977 Norman Swallow
1978 Christopher Ralling
1979 Herbert Wise
1980 Roger Mills
1981 David Croft

1982 Philip Saville
1983 James Goddard
1984 Christopher Morahan
1985 Leslie Woodhead
1986 David Rose
1987 Julia Smith
1988 Stuart Burge
1989 John Lloyd
1990 Ray Fitzwalter
1991 Robert Young
1992 Kenith Trodd
1993 Stephen Frears

Richard Dimbleby Award

For the year's most important personal contribution to factual television.

1963 Bernard Braden
1964 Alan Whicker
1965 Malcolm Muggeridge
1966 Alastair Burnet
1967 David Frost
1968 Julian Pettifer
1969 Kenneth Clark
1970 Alastair Burnet
1971 Desmond Wilcox
1972 Alistair Cooke
1973 Jonathan Dimbleby
1974 Robin Day
1975 Robert Kee

1976 Frank Bough
1977 Alan Whicker
1978 David Bellamy
1979 Alastair Burnet
1980 Barry Norman
1981 Tim Sebastian
1982 Brian Hanrahan
     Michael Nicholson
1983 John Tusa
1984 Mark Tully
1985 Brian Walden
1986 Melvyn Bragg
1987 Esther Rantzen
1988 Ludovic Kennedy
1989 Kate Adie
1990 John Pilger
1991 John Simpson
1992 John Cole
1993 Joan Bakewell

> '*A box that has changed children from an irresistible force into an immovable object.*'
>
> Anon

The longest-running British drama serial is Granada's *Coronation Street* which was first broadcast live on 9 December 1960, running twice-weekly until 29 October 1989, when it was broadcast three times a week. It appeared in black and white until 1970 when it appeared in colour for the first time. The storyline was an original idea conceived by Tony Warren, aged 23. He was working on an adaptation of W. E. Johns's *Biggles* stories for Granada at the time. He wrote the first episode and approached Granada who employed him at £30 a week to develop the idea. His original title was *Florizel Street* but this was changed before it reached the screen on the grounds that Florizel sounded like a detergent. He set the series in Weatherfield, a fictitious district of Manchester. The cast was made up and included actors such as Doris Speed (playing Annie Walker), Violet Carson (Ena Sharples), Pat Phoenix (Elsie Tanner) and William Roache (Ken Barlow) who has played the character without a break for over 30 years.

On Sunday 2 December 1990 the very first episode, written by its creator, Tony Warren, was repeated. The scene opens with Elsie Lappin (played by Maudie Edwards) handing over the corner shop to Florrie Lindley (Betty Alberge) and Ena Sharples makes her first appearance – 'Are you a widder woman? Ah'll have a packet of bakin'powder.'

The Barlow family – Deidre (Anne Kirkbridge), Ken (William Roache) and Tracey (Dawn Acton) in a scene from Granada's *Coronation Street* – Britain's longest-running drama serial.

The highest accolade for the Street was on 5 May 1982 when HM The Queen visited the cast on the set outside television's most famous pub, The Rover's Return.

Coronation Street has also sold the greatest number of episodes of any television programme ever. *The Guinness Book of Records* states that on 31 May 1971, 1144 episodes were sold by Granada Television to CBKST Saskatoon, Saskatchewan, Canada. This constituted 20 days 15 h 44 min of continuous viewing. A further 728 episodes (covering the period January 1974 to January 1981) were sold to CBC in the USA in August 1982.

BAFTA Awards (since 1968)

	Single Play / Drama	Drama Series / Serial	Factual Series	Light Entertainment Programme	Comedy Series	Best Actor	Best Actress
1968	*Parachute* Anthony Page	No award	*This Week* (ITV) Philip Whitehead and production team	*Marty* (BBC), *'Till Death Us Do Part* (BBC) Dennis Main Wilson	No award	Roy Dotrice *Brief Lives*	Wendy Craig *Not in Front of the Children*
1969	*The Letter* (Somerset Maugham series), *Nora, You've Made Your Bed Now Lie on It* Christopher Morahan	Somerset Maugham series Verity Lambert	*News at Ten* ITN production team	*Just Pet* Yvonne Littlewood	*Please Sir* (ITV) Mark Stuart	Edward Woodward *Callan* (ITV), *A Dream Divided* (*Omnibus*) (BBC), *A Bit of a Holiday*	Margaret Tyzack *The First Churchills*
1970	*The Lie* (BBC) Alan Bridges	No award	No award	*Dad's Army* (BBC) David Croft and production team	No award	Keith Michell *The Six Wives of Henry VIII* (BBC), *An Ideal Husband*	Annette Crosbie *Catherine of Aragon* (*The Six Wives of Henry VIII*) (BBC)
1971	*Edna, The Inebriate Woman* (BBC) Ted Kotcheff	*Upstairs, Downstairs* (ITV) John Hawkesworth	*World in Action* (ITV) Jeremy Wallington and production team	*The Benny Hill Show* (BBC) John Robins, David Bell	No award	John Le Mesurier *Traitor*	Patricia Hayes *Edna, The Inebriate Woman* (BBC)
1972	*Stockers Copper* Jack Gold	*Country Matters* (ITV) Derek Granger	*Horizon* Peter Goodchild and production team	*Monty Python's Flying Circus* (BBC) Ian McNaughton and production team	*My Wife Next Door* (BBC) Graeme Muir	Anthony Hopkins *War and Peace* (ITV)	Billie Whitelaw *The Sextet*
1973	*Kisses at Fifty* Michael Apted	*Upstairs, Downstairs* (ITV) John Hawkesworth	*World in Action* (ITV) Gus MacDonald	*The Stanley Baxter Big Picture Show* (ITV) David Bell	*Whatever Happened to the Likely Lads?* (BBC) James Gilbert	Frank Finlay *The Adventures of Don Quixote, Candide, The Death of Adolf Hitler* (ITV)	Celia Johnson *Mrs Palfry at the Claremont*
1974	*Antony & Cleopatra* Jon Scofield	*South Riding* (ITV) James Ormerod	*Horizon* Peter Goodchild, Bruce Norman	*The Stanley Baxter Moving Picture Show* David Bell (ITV)	*Porridge* (BBC) Sydney Lotterby	Peter Barkworth *Crown Matrimonial*	Lee Remick *Jennie*
1975	*The Evacuees* Alan Parker	*Edward the Seventh* (ITV) Cecil Clarke, John Gorrie	*Disappearing World* (ITV) Brian Moser	*The Two Ronnies* (BBC) Terry Hughes	*Fawlty Towers* (BBC) John Howard Davies	John Hurt *The Naked Civil Servant, Nijinsky– God of the Dance*	Annette Crosbie *Edward the Seventh* (ITV)
1976	*Bar-Mitzvah Boy* Michael Tuchner	*Rock Follies* (ITV) Andrew Brown	*Sailor* (BBC) John Purdie, Roger Mills	*The Muppett Show* (ITV) Production team	*Porridge* (Special) (BBC) Sydney Lotterby	Derek Jacobi *I Claudius* (BBC)	Sian Phillips *I Claudius* (BBC), *How Green Was My Valley*
1977	*Spend, Spend, Spend* John Goldschmidt	*Madame Curie* Peter Goodchild, John Glenister	*The South African Experience* Antony Thomas	*The Morecambe and Wise Christmas Show* (ITV) Ernest Maxin	*Rising Damp* (ITV) Ronnie Baxter	Peter Barkworth *Professional Foul, The Country Party*	Penelope Keith *The Norman Conquests*
1978	*Licking Hitler* David Hare	*Edward and Mrs Simpson* (ITV) Andrew Brown, Waris Hussein	*The Voyage of Charles Darwin* (BBC) Christopher Ralling	*The Kenny Everett Video Show* (ITV) David Mallet	*Going Straight* (BBC) Sydney Lotterby	Edward Fox *Edward and Mrs Simpson* (ITV)	Francesca Annis *Lillie* (ITV), *The Comedy of Errors*
1979	*Blue Remembered Hills* (BBC) Brian Gibson	*Testament of Youth* (BBC) Jonathan Powell, Moira Armstrong	*Circuit Eleven Miami* (BBC) Mark Anderson	*Ripping Yarns* (BBC) Alan Bell, Jim Franklin	*Fawlty Towers* (BBC) Douglas Argent, Bob Spiers	Alec Guinness *Tinker, Tailor, Soldier, Spy* (BBC)	Cheryl Campbell *Testament of Youth* (BBC), *The Duke of Wellington, Malice Aforethought*
1980	*Caught on a Train* (BBC) Peter Duffell	*Oppenheimer* Peter Goodchild, Barry Davis	*Strangeways* (BBC) Rex Bloomstein	*Not the Nine O'Clock News* (BBC) John Lloyd, Sean Hardie, Bill Wilson	*Yes Minister* (BBC) Sydney Lotterby	Denholm Elliott *Gentle Folk, In Hiding, Blade on the Feather, The Stinker*	Peggy Ashcroft *Caught on a Train* (BBC), *Cream in My Coffee* (ITV)
1981	*Going Gently* (BBC) Stephen Frears	*Brideshead Revisited* (ITV) Derek Granger, Charles Sturridge, Michael Lindsay-Hogg	*Ireland–A Television History* (episodes 5–13) Jeremy Isaacs	*The Stanley Baxter Series* David Bell, John Kaye Cooper	*Yes Minister* (BBC) Peter Whitmore	Anthony Andrews *Brideshead Revisited* (ITV)	Judi Dench *Going Gently, A fine Romance* (ITV), *The Cherry Orchard*
1982	*The Ballroom of Romance* Pat O'Connor	*Boys From the Blackstuff* Michael Waring, Philip Saville	*Police* (BBC) Roger Graef, Charles Stewart	*Three of a Kind* (BBC) Paul Jackson	*Yes Minister* (BBC) Peter Whitmore	Alec Guinness *Smiley's People* (BBC)	Beryl Reid *Smiley's People* (BBC)
1983	*An Englishman Abroad* John Schlesinger	*Kennedy* (ITV) Andrew Brown, Jim Goddard	*40 Minutes* (BBC) Roger Mills	*Carrott's Lib* (BBC) Geoff Posner	*Hi-De-Hi* (BBC) John Kilby	Alan Bates *An Englishman Abroad*	Coral Browne *An Englishman Abroad*
1984	*Threads* Mick Jackson	*The Jewel in the Crown* Christopher Morahan, Jim O'Brien	*River Journeys* Roger Laughton, David Wallace	*Another Audience with Dame Edna Everage* Richard Drewett	*The Young Ones* (BBC) Paul Jackson	Tim Pigott-Smith *The Jewel in the Crown*	Peggy Ashcroft *The Jewel in the Crown*

BELOW Helen Mirren won the BAFTA Best Actress award in both 1991 and 1992 for her part in Granada's *Prime Suspect 1* and *2*.

RIGHT Julie T. Wallace in one of her many guises in *The Life and Loves of a She Devil* (BBC), 1986 BAFTA Best Drama Series. The series was adapted from Fay Weldon's novel of the same name. The programme also appears at No. 8 in the BBC's list of bestselling drama programmes.

	Single Play / Drama	Drama Series / Serial	Factual Series	Light Entertainment Programme	Comedy Series	Best Actor	Best Actress
85	*Shadowlands* Norman Stone, David Thompson	*Edge of Darkness* (BBC) Michael Waring, Martin Campbell	*40 Minutes* Edward Mirzoeff, Roger Mills	*Victoria Wood as Seen on TV* (BBC) Geoff Posner	*Only Fools and Horses* (BBC) Ray Butt	Bob Peck *Edge of Darkness* (BBC)	Claire Bloom *Shadowlands*
86	*Hôtel Du Lac* Giles Foster, Sue Birtwistle	*The Life and Loves of a She Devil* (BBC) Sally Head, Philip Saville	*World in Action* (ITV) Ray Fitzwalter	*Victoria Wood as Seen on TV* (BBC) Geoff Posner	*Just Good Friends* (BBC) Ray Butt, Sue Bush	Michael Gambon *The Singing Detective*	Anna Massey *Hôtel du Lac*
87	*Lifestory* Mick Jackson	*Tutti Frutti* Andy Park, Tomy Smith	*The Duty Men* Paul Hamann	*Victoria Wood on TV Special* (BBC) Geoff Posner	*Blackadder the Third* (BBC) John Lloyd, Mandie Fletcher	David Jason *Porterhouse Blue*	Emma Thompson *Fortunes of War*, *Tutti Frutti*
88	*Tumbledown* (BBC) Charles Wood, Richard Broke, Richard Eyre	*A Very British Coup* Alan Plater, Anne Skinner, Sally Hibbin, Mick Jacks	*Arena* Nigel Finch, Anthony Wall	*An Audience with Victoria Wood* (BBC) David G. Hillier	*Only Fools and Horses* (BBC) John Sullivan, Gareth Gwenlan, Tony Dow	Ray McAnally *A Very British Coup*	Thora Hird *A Cream Cracker Under the Settee*
89	*The Accountant* Geoffrey Case, Paul Knight, Les Blair	*Traffik* Simon Moore, Brian Eastman, Alastair Reid	*40 Minutes* (series 1) Edward Mirzoeff	*Clive James on the 80s* (BBC) Elaine Bedell, Richard Drewett	*Blackadder Goes Forth* (BBC) John Lloyd, Richard Boden, Ben Elton, Richard Curtis	John Thaw *Inspector Morse* (ITV)	Diana Rigg *Mother Love*
90	*News Hounds* Les Blair, Sarah Curtis	*Oranges are not the Only Fruit* (BBC) Jeanette Winterson, Phillipa Giles, Beeban Kidron	*The Trials of Life* (BBC) Peter Jones	*Whose Line is it Anyway?* (ITV) Dan Patterson, Chris Bould	*The New Statesman* Laurence Marks, Maurice Gran, David Reynolds, Geoffrey Sax	Ian Richardson *House of Cards* (BBC)	Geraldine McEwan *Oranges Are Not The Only Fruit* (BBC)
91	*A Question of Attribution* Alan Bennett, Innes Lloyd, John Schlesinger	Serial: *Prime Suspect* (ITV) Lynda La Plante, Don Leaver, Christopher Menaul Series: *Inspector Morse* (ITV) David Lascelles	*Naked Hollywood* Nicolas Kent	*Have I Got News For You?* (BBC) Harry Thompson	*One Foot in The Grave* (BBC) David Renwick, Susan Belbin	Robert Lindsay *G.B.H.*	Helen Mirren *Prime Suspect* (ITV)
92	*An Ungentlemanly Act* Bradley Adams, Stuart Urban	Serial: *Anglo-Saxon Attitudes* Andrew Brown, Diarmuid Lawrence, Andrew Davies Series: *Inspector Morse* Deidre Keir	*Pandora's Box* (BBC) Adam Curtis	*Noel's House Party* (BBC) Michael Leggo	*Absolutely Fabulous* (BBC) Jon Plowman, Bob Spiers, Jennifer Saunders	John Thaw *Inspector Morse* (ITV)	Helen Mirren *Prime Suspect 2* (ITV)
93	*Safe* David M. Thompson, Antonia Bird, Al Ashton	Serial: *Prime Suspect 3* (ITV) Paul Marcus, David Drury, Lynda La Plante	*The Ark* Molly Dineen	*Rory Bremner . . . Who Else?* (Channel 4) Geoff Atkinson, Elaine Morris, SteveConnelly, Tom Poole	*Drop the Dead Donkey* (Channel 4) Andy Hamilton, Guy Jenkin, Liddy Oldroyd	Robbie Coltrane *Cracker* (ITV)	Helen Mirren *Prime Suspect 3* (ITV)

Longest-Running Programmes on BBC Television

		First broadcast
1	*Come Dancing**	29 Sep 1950
2	*Panorama*	11 Nov 1953
3	*The Sky at Night*	24 Apr 1957
4	*Grandstand*	11 Oct 1958
5	*Blue Peter*	16 Oct 1958
6	*Songs of Praise*	1 Oct 1961
7	*Dr Who*	23 Nov 1963
8	*Top of the Pops*	1 Jan 1964
9	*Horizon*	2 May 1964
10	*Match of the Day*	22 Aug 1964

*See section on Dance

Broadcasting Press Guild Television and Radio Awards

The Broadcasting Press Guild is an association of journalists who specialise in writing about television, radio and the media generally. The association was formed in 1973 by members of the television section of the Critics Circle who wanted the freedom to organise, among other activities, their own annual awards.

The first awards were presented in 1974 and they have been awarded annually since then. All television awards, apart from the Harvey Lee Award for Outstanding Contribution to Broadcasting

One of the most memorable incidents at an award ceremony was in 1979 when Dennis Potter, who normally shunned public appearances, came to receive his BPG Best Drama Series award for *Pennies From Heaven*. His producer, Kenith Trodd, had bet Potter that the series would not get into the top ten ratings – it did and Trodd paid up at the awards ceremony – in pennies!

(which is chosen by committee) are voted for by the membership as a whole. The awards are valued in the industry because they are considered to be impartial. The recipients receive framed printed certificates.

Recipients of the awards have included the late Dame Peggy Ashcroft, Sir David Attenborough (twice), Peter Barkworth, Alan

Bestselling BBC Programmes, by Country

		No. countries programme has been sold to	First broadcast
1	**The Living Planet** David Attenborough's 12-part portrait of the Earth	77	19 Jan 1984
2	**Dr Who** Science-fiction series, travelling through time with the Doctor	74	23 Nov 1963
3	**Flight of the Condor** Natural history programme on plight of the condor	74	14 Feb 1982
4	**Animal Olympians** Natural history documentary showing the animal kingdom and its parallel in the Olympic sports	66	24 Jun 1980
5	**The Six Wives of Henry VIII** Drama series starring Keith Michell	66	1 Jan 1970
6	**The Onedin Line** Drama series concerning a 19th-century shipping family in Liverpool	66	15 Oct 1971
7	**Supersense** Documentary, narrated by Andrew Sachs, exploring the senses of animals and fish	63	5 Dec 1988
8	**The Impossible Bird** *Wildlife on One* series – the Ostrich	63	17 Jan 1980
9	**Tender is the Night** F. Scott Fitzgerald drama	62	23 Sep 1985
10	**Ascent of Man** Documentary, presented by Dr Jacob Bronowski, tracing the history of man's ideas from prehistoric times to the present	62	5 May 1973

Source: BBC Enterprises International

Bestselling BBC Drama Programmes, by Country

		No. countries programme has been sold to	First broadcast
1	*The Ginger Tree* Romantic saga set in Japan	32	26 Nov 1989
2	*House of Cards* Political thriller, starring Ian Richardson	30	18 Nov 1990
3	*Christabel* Dennis Potter's version of Christabel Bielenberg's autobiography	28	16 Nov 1988
4	*Never Come Back* Action espionage thriller starring James Fox	26	21 Mar 1990
5	*First Born* Charles Dance rearing hybrid species born to a gorilla	25	30 Oct 1988
6	*Mother Love* Psycho-drama starring Diana Rigg and David McCallum	24	29 Oct 1989
7	*Lovejoy* Rather shady antiques dealer played by Ian McShane	20	10 Jan 1986
8	*The Life and Loves of a She-Devil* Dramatisation of Fay Weldon's dark novel of retribution	18	8 Oct 1986
9	*The Dark Angel* Chilling adaptation of Gothic romance, *Uncle Silas*, starring Peter O'Toole and Jane Lapotaire	17	4 Jan 1989
10	*Ashenden* Somerset Maugham First World War espionage thriller, starring Alan Bennett	15	17 Nov 1991

Source: BBC Enterprises International

Bennett, Melvyn Bragg, Kenneth Branagh, Alistair Cooke, Sir Robin Day, Sir Alec Guinness, Barry Humphries, Jeremy Isaacs, Derek Jacobi, Helen Mirren (twice), Michael Palin (twice) and the late Brian Redhead (three).

1993 WINNERS

Single Drama *The Snapper* (BBC)

Drama Series / Serial *Cracker* (Granada for ITV)

Documentary Series *Thatcher: The Downing Street Years* (Fine Art Productions for BBC)

Single Documentary *Arena: Graham Greene Trilogy* (BBC)

Entertainment *Rory Bremner: Who Else?* (Kudos for Channel 4)

News and Current Affairs *Cutting Edge* (Channel 4)

Actor Robbie Coltrane, *Cracker* (ITV)

Actress Helen Mirren, *Prime Suspect 3* (ITV)

TV Performance in a Non-Acting Role Michael Barrymore (LWT for ITV)

Writer's Award Jimmy McGovern, *Cracker* (ITV)

Radio Programme of the Year *Knowing Me, Knowing You* (BBC Radio 4)

Radio Broadcaster of the Year Brian Redhead (*Today* and other Radio 4 programmes)

Harvey Lee Award for Outstanding Contribution to Broadcasting Sir David Attenborough (for many BBC programmes)

Top 20 Bestselling BBC Television Videos

1. *Watch With Mother*
2. *Whole Body Programme 1 – Rosemary Conley*
3. *Postman Pat: Big Video*
4. *Mr Blobby*
5. *Fawlty Towers: The Germans*
6. *Fawlty Towers: The Kipper and the Corpse*
7. *Fawlty Towers: Basil The Rat*
8. *Postman Pat 1*
9. *Black Adder 2: Bells, Head, Potato*
10. *Fawlty Towers: The Psychiatrist*
11. *Black Adder 2: Money, Beer, Chains*
12. *Pingu*
13. *Postman Pat 2*
14. *Noddy and the Naughty Tail*
15. *Postman Pat 3*
16. *Red Dwarf 1 – The End*
17. *History of Liverpool FC*
18. *Black Adder: Foretelling*
19. *Black Adder: Private Plane*
20. *Postman Pat's New Video*

Source: BBC Enterprises Ltd, 1994

> *'TV is an invention that permits you to be entertained in your living room by people you wouldn't have in your home.'*
>
> David Frost (1971)

Doctor Who, the world's longest-running television science fiction series, and also the second bestselling BBC programme – 74 different countries have bought the series. It was created by Sydney Newman and developed at the BBC as a semi-educational programme for the family by bringing history to life and considering the future. It was first broadcast on 23 November 1963 in black and white, and in colour from 1970, and ran until 1989 – a total of 695 episodes. The Doctor travelled through time in a police box known as the TARDIS (originally said to stand for 'Time and Relative Dimension In Space'). In 1983 BBC Enterprises bought the exclusive rights to the police box from the Metropolitan Police Force.

The Doctor was played originally by William Hartnell, followed by Patrick Troughton, Jon Pertwee, Tom Baker, Peter Davison, Colin Baker and Sylvester McCoy. The series was finally axed in 1989 when its ratings sank to 4.5 million and the BBC resisted the lobbying of thousands of fans worldwide to make a new series. Through various series having been sold, it has an estimated audience of 110 million in 74 countries and has created an estimated revenue of £10 million for the BBC through sales of videos, chess sets, T-shirts and other merchandise.

HERE'S ONE I MADE EARLIER...

Blue Peter, first broadcast on 16 October 1958, celebrated its 35th birthday on 29 September 1993, having produced 2626 shows. The programme was created after John Hunter Blair had been asked to devise an item for children who had grown out of *Watch With Mother* (which was first broadcast on 11 July 1950). Hunter called it *Blue Peter* after the flag which is raised as a signal that a ship is leaving port and, somewhat dubiously, 'blue was a child's favourite colour, Peter the name of a child's friend'. The first presenters were Christopher Trace (once stand-in for Charlton Heston in *Ben Hur* (US 59)) and Leila Williams (Miss Great Britain 1957). The first 15-minute show broadcast was introduced by the signature tune still played today – 'Barnacle Bill'. *Blue Peter* has had 20 presenters during its lifetime and now attracts over five million viewers each week.

The original presenters of *Blue Peter* (BBC), Leila Williams (right) and Christopher Trace (above) with 'do-it-yourself' Dalek, designed by Raymond Cusick, original designer of the Daleks for the *Dr Who* serial.

British Comedy Awards

These annual awards were established in 1990 to pay tribute to the hitherto neglected areas of television, stage, film and radio comedy. In conjunction with the Writers' Guild of Great Britain (WGGB) and selected groups of industry professionals, categories are drawn up and then voted upon. Recent years have seen the introduction of a viewers' telephone poll to determine the winners of two categories – Best Entertainment Series and Best Comedy Series – which prompted over 300 000 calls, demonstrating the audience's enthusiasm to participate in the voting procedure.

The awards ceremony takes place live in front of a studio audience of celebrities drawn from the world of comedy and show business and it attracts in excess of 12 million viewers (13.60 million in 1993, appearing in 41st position in the top 50 programmes), making it the most popular awards ceremony shown on British television.

1993 WINNERS

Television Comedy Personality Joanna Lumley
WGGB Award for Top Comedy Writer Richard Curtis

Comedy Film *Groundhog Day* (US 93)
Television Comedy Drama *The Snapper* (BBC)
BBC Sitcom *One Foot in the Grave*
ITV Sitcom *Watching*
Channel 4 Sitcom *Drop the Dead Donkey*
Lifetime Achievement Award Ken Dodd
Variety Award Ken Dodd
Live Stand-up Comedian Eddie Izzard
Entertainment Series *Barrymore*
New Television Comedy *Absolutely Fabulous* (BBC)
Television Comedy Newcomer Steve Coogan
Television Comedy Actor Rik Mayall
Television Comedy Actress Joanna Lumley
ITV Entertainment Presenter Michael Barrymore
BBC Entertainment Presenter Noel Edmonds
Channel 4 Entertainment Presenter Chris Evans
Female Comedy Performer French & Saunders
Male Comedy Performer Dave Allen
Radio Comedy *Knowing Me, Knowing You . . .* with Alan Partridge
Comedy Series *The Smell of Reeves and Mortimer*

Television and Radio Industries Club Awards

In the early days of broadcasting, a radio manufacturers' association gave monthly lunches at the Savoy Hotel, to which were invited leading wholesalers and distributors, and speakers of varying quality. The most formidable and frequent speaker was the BBC's Sir John Reith, who used to harangue his captive audience about the need to educate his listeners, rather than simply to make money out of them. Eight of these wholesalers formed

The main children's series produced by the BBC in the early days of television was *For the Children*, introduced by Annette Mills since 1946. It featured puppets such as Louise the lamb, Sally the Sea-lion, and the much-loved Muffin the Mule. In 1950 *Watch With Mother* was introduced at 3.45 p.m. on Tuesdays, Wednesdays and Thursdays. From 1955 these transmissions went out daily, featuring *Picture Book* (Monday), *Andy Pandy* (Tuesday), *The Flowerpot Men* (Wednesday), *Rag, Tag and Bobtail* (Thursday) and *The Woodentops* (Friday). This remained unchanged until the 1960s when they alternated on a Monday and other children's programmes were introduced for the rest of the week. In 1980, after 30 years, the title was changed to *See-Saw*. The nostalgic element contributed to the success of the video released in 1988 containing extracts from the 1950s programmes and in 1994 it was the BBC's topselling video (see p. 227).

French & Saunders in their own version of *Gone With The Wind*. They received a British Comedy Award in 1993 for Best Female Comedy Performers.

the Radio Industries Club for that purpose in 1931 and gave a lunch every month at the Connaught Rooms, providing a speaker. In 1980 the association changed its name to The Television and Radio Industries Club.

The objective of the association has been to provide a neutral, relaxed and friendly forum, helping to promote mutual understanding and goodwill amongst those engaged in the audio, visual and allied industries. The Club's 1994/95 president was Bob Monkhouse OBE and HRH Prince Michael of Kent, the patron. In 1969 the Club instigated its annual celebrity awards for radio and television – the TRIC Awards. Forms are sent to members each year and the votes are counted to establish the winners.

1994 WINNERS
BBC Personality Noel Edmonds
ITV / Channel 4 Personality Michael Barrymore
Radio Personality Melvyn Bragg
TV Theme Music Mike Moran, *Taggart* (ITV)
Newscaster / Reporter Carol Barnes, ITN
Sports Presenter Steve Rider
Factual or Science-Based Programme *Thatcher: The Downing Street Years* (BBC)
Television Sitcom *Absolutely Fabulous* (BBC)
New Television Talent Paul McKenna
Satellite Television Programme / Channel CNN International
Radio Programme *The Masterson Inheritance* (BBC Radio 4)
BBC Television Programme *To Play the King*
ITV / Channel 4 Television Programme *Prime Suspect 3*

Sony Radio Awards

Sponsored since 1983 by Sony, these awards are given annually to radio broadcasters, programme makers and those responsible for outstanding achievements and performances in all aspects of

> 'I find television very educating. Every time someone turns on the set I go into the other room and read a book.'
>
> Groucho Marx

Jane Horrocks, Julia Sawalha, Joanna Lumley and Jennifer Saunders in *Absolutely Fabulous* – the BBC award-winning comedy series.

national and regional British radio. The awards 'celebrate the quality, creativity and excellence of those whose work in radio brings enjoyment to millions of listeners'. The judges work in the profession and included in 1993 Matthew Bannister, Simon Brett, Sarah Dickinson, Bryan Gould MP, David Mellor MP and Mike Smith. Winners of the Gold Award for outstanding contribution to radio over the years and Personality / Broadcaster of the Year follow:

	Gold Award	Personality/Broadcaster of the Year
1983	Frank Muir	Brian Johnston
	Denis Norden	Sue MacGregor
1984	David Jacobs	Brian Matthew
		Margaret Howard
1985	British Forces Broadcasting Service	Jimmy Young
1986	John Timpson	Douglas Cameron
1987	*The Archers*	Derek Jameson
1988	Gerard Mansell	Alan Freeman
1989	Tony Blackburn	Sue Lawley
1990	Roy Hudd	Chris Tarrant
1991	Charlie Gillett	James Naughtie
1992	Sir James Savile	Danny Baker
1993	Humphrey Lyttelton	John Peel

Royal Television Society Awards

The Television Society was formed on 7 September 1927, nine years before the first public service broadcast from Alexandra Palace. It began as a small group of enthusiasts intent on furthering the new scientific discovery and is today The Royal Television Society representing one of the most important communications mediums in the world. The Society was granted its royal title in 1966 and now represents over 3000 members from the entire spectrum of the broadcasting industry.

Today, about 80 awards are made annually in five areas: Journalism, Main Programmes, Design and Commercials, Technology, and Education. The Main Programme awards since 1990:

RIGHT Penelope Wilton, Ian Holm and Rebecca Callard in *The Borrowers* which received the children's award for drama and entertainment in 1992.

	1990	1991	1992	1993
Children's Awards Drama and entertainment	*Press Gang* (ITV)	*Dodgem* (BBC)	*The Borrowers* (BBC) *What's That Noise!* (BBC)	*Just Us* (ITV) *Old Bear Stories* (ITV)
Factual	*The Lowdown: Today I am A Man* (BBC)	*Mozart is Alive and Well in Milton Keynes* (BBC)	*Newsround Special – SOS: The Suffering of Somalia* (BBC)	*It'll Never Work* (BBC)
Single Drama	*Shoot to Kill*	*Prime Suspect* (ITV)	*Hedd Wyn* (S4C) (ITV)	*The Snapper* (BBC)
Drama Series	*Inspector Morse* (ITV)	*Casualty* (BBC)	*Between the Lines – Out of the Game* (BBC)	*Cracker* (ITV)
Drama Serial	*Oranges Are Not the Only Fruit* (BBC)	*Children of the North* (BBC)	*Goodbye Cruel World* (BBC)	*Tales of the City* (Channel 4)
Single Documentary	*Red Hot* (ITV)	*The Leader, His Driver and the Driver's Wife* (Channel 4)	*Katie and Eilish – Siamese Twins* (ITV)	*We Are All Neighbours – Disappearing World* (ITV)
Documentary Series	*Hello, Do You Hear Us?* (Channel 4)	*Secret History* (Channel 4)	*Pandora's Box – The League of Gentlemen* (BBC)	*The Plague* (Channel 4)
Situation Comedy	*Rab C. Nesbitt* (ITV)	*One Foot in the Grave – The Man in the Long Black Cloak* (BBC)	*One Foot in the Grave – The Worst Horror of All* (BBC)	*One Foot in the Grave* (BBC)
Entertainment	*French & Saunders* (BBC)	*Vic Reeves Big Night Out* (Channel 4)	*Victoria Wood's All Day Breakfast Show* (BBC)	*Barrymore* (ITV)
Arts	*Bookmark: From Moscow to Pietushki* (BBC)	*Bookmark: Dostoevsky's Travels* (BBC)	*Bookmark: Miss Pym's Day Out* (BBC)	*Without Walls: The Wonderful Horrible Life of Leni Riefenstahl* (Channel 4)
Outside Broadcasts	*90 Glorious Years* (BBC)	*As it Happens; Moscow New Year* (Channel 4)	*Last Night of the Proms* (BBC)	*Stiffelio* (BBC)
Technique	Mike Blakeley *Disappearing World* (ITV)	Thames TV *The Bill – They Also Serve* (ITV)	Lee Eynon, BBC VT editing of Barcelona Olympics – British Medals sequence	–
Regional Programme	*First Sight: Baby Alex* (BBC South & East)	*Scotch & Wry* (BBC Scotland)	*The Snow Show* (BBC Scotland)	*Selected Exits* (BBC Wales)
Regional Documentary	–	*Summer on the Estate – Episode 1* (ITV)	*Tuesday Special – Caution – Our Hands are Tied* (ITV)	*This Mine is Ours* (ITV)
Team Award	–	–	*The Big Breakfast* (Channel 4)	*This Morning* (ITV)
Performance Award	Charlotte Coleman Ian Richardson	Helen Mirren Robert Lindsay	Julia Sawalha David Jason	Kathy Burke Robbie Coltrane
Writer's Award	Ben Elton	Lynda La Plante	Andy Jenkin, Guy Hamilton *Drop the Dead Donkey* (Channel 4)	Roddy Doyle *The Snapper* (BBC)

THEATRE & DRAMA

Longest Running London Current Productions

	Production	Category	First performance
1	*The Mousetrap*	Whodunnit	November 1952
2	*Cats*	Musical	May 1981
3	*Starlight Express*	Musical	March 1984
4	*Les Misérables*	Musical	October 1985
5	*The Phantom of the Opera*	Musical	October 1986
6	*Blood Brothers*	Musical	July 1988
7	*The Woman in Black*	Thriller	February 1989
8	*Miss Saigon*	Musical	September 1989
9	*Buddy*	Musical	October 1989
10	*Five Guys Named Moe*	Musical	December 1990
11	*Don't Dress For Dinner*	Comedy	March 1991
12	*Joseph and the Amazing Technicolor Dreamcoat*	Musical	June 1991
13	*Travels with My Aunt*	Play	November 1992
14	*An Inspector Calls*	Play	January 1993
15	*Crazy For You*	Musical	February 1993

As at end March 1993

THE MOUSETRAP

Agatha Christie's *The Mousetrap* is the world's longest running play. It opened on 25 November 1952 at the Ambassadors Theatre and after 8862 performances transferred to the St Martin's Theatre where it reopened on 25 March 1974. On Thursday 25 November 1993 it celebrated its 41st birthday and could claim the following:

▌ 17 067 performances

▌ More than ten million people had seen the play

▌ 263 actors and actresses had appeared in the play

▌ 122 understudies had been employed

▌ 76 miles of shirts had been ironed

▌ Over 300 tons of ice cream and approximately 63 000 gallons of minerals had been consumed

▌ The play had been presented in 44 different countries and had been translated into 24 different languages

▌ Box-office takings in the West End alone totalled over £25 million.

The play opened in 1952 with Richard Attenborough and Sheila Sims in the leading roles. During its life, the set, furnishings and curtains have all had to be replaced, but two things remain which were in use on the first night – a leather armchair which is occupied by Mrs Boyle, one of the characters, and a clock on the mantelshelf.

The original poster for 'The Mousetrap' starring Richard Attenborough and Sheila Sim (above) and a scene from the current production starring Beth Tuckey, Nigel Fairs and Paul Bacon. The picture also shows the clock and leather armchair that are the only items on the set that have remained unchanged since the first performance.

In March 1956 Sir Peter Saunders, the producer, sold the film rights of the play to Romulus Films, with the proviso that the film could not be released until six months after the end of the London stage run. The film has yet to be made.

In June 1965 Sir Peter Saunders formed *The Mousetrap* Club and since then 'male mice' who have been connected with the production have been presented with a special tie. It has a dark-blue background with a little red mouse motif and a white 'T'. For the play's 33rd birthday a new tie in pink was made with the same insignia on it and at this time females were 'admitted' to the Club with a silver pendant in the form of a mousetrap. To date there are 459 members of the Club.

Top 20 Longest Running London Productions

		Theatre	Opened	Performanc
1 *The Mousetrap*	thriller by Agatha Christie	Ambassadors	25 November 1952	
		St Martins	25 March 1974	17 213
2 *No Sex Please, We're British*	farce by Anthony Marriott and Alistair Foot	Strand	3 June 1971	
		Garrick	18 January 1982	
		Duchess	2 September 1986	6 691
3 *Run for Your Wife*	farce by Ray Cooney	Shaftesbury	29 March 1983	
		Criterion	12 December 1983	
		Whitehall	6 March 1989	
		Aldwych	17 May 1990	
		Duchess	17 September 1990	5 800
4 *Cats*	musical by Andrew Lloyd Webber from poems by T. S. Eliot	New London	11 May 1981	5 391
5 *The Black and White Minstrel Show*		Victoria Palace	25 May 1962	4 344
6 *Starlight Express*	musical by Andrew Lloyd Webber and Richard Stilgoe	Apollo Victoria	27 March 1984	4 144
7 *Oh! Calcutta*	revue devised by Kenneth Tynan	Royalty	28 January 1970	
		Duchess	18 January 1974	3 918
8 *Les Misérables*	musical by Alain Boublil and Claude Schönberg, English lyrics by Herbert Kretzmer	Palace	4 December 1985	3 452
9 *Jesus Christ Superstar*	musical by Andrew Lloyd Webber and Tim Rice	Palace	9 August 1972	3 357
10 *Me and My Girl*	revival of musical by Noel Gay and L. A. Rose, adapted by Stephen Fry	Adelphi	12 February 1985	3 305
11 *The Phantom of the Opera*	musical by Andrew Lloyd Webber and Charles Hart	Her Majesty's	9 October 1986	3 189
12 *The Business of Murder*	thriller by Richard Harris	Duchess	2 April 1981	
		May Fair	10 May 1982	2 965
13 *The Rocky Horror Show*	musical by Richard O'Brien	Theatre Upstairs	19 June 1973	
		Classic, Chelsea	14 August 1973	
		Kings Road	31 October 1973	
		Comedy	6 April 1979	2 960
14 *Evita*	musical by Andrew Lloyd Webber and Tim Rice	Prince Edward	21 June 1978	2 900
15 *Oliver!*	musical by Lionel Bart	New	30 June 1960	2 618
16 *There's a Girl in My Soup*	comedy by Terence Frisby	Globe	15 June 1966	
		Comedy	18 August 1969	2 547
17 *Pyjama Tops*	farce by Mawby Green and Ed Feilbert, from *Moumou* by Jean de Letraz	Whitehall	22 September 1969	2 498
18 *The Sound of Music*	musical by Richard Rodgers and Oscar Hammerstein II	Palace	18 May 1961	2 386
19 *Sleuth*	thriller by Anthony Shaffer	St Martin's	12 February 1970	
		Garrick	6 March 1972	
		Fortune	9 October 1973	2 359
20 *Salad Days*	musical by Julian Slade and Dorothy Reynolds	Vaudeville	5 August 1954	2 283

* indicates production still running
Note: As at 1 April 1994

The Laurence Olivier Awards

These awards are presented by The Society of London Theatre in recognition of distinguished artistic achievement in West End theatre. The Society of London Theatre, founded in 1908 by Sir Charles Wyndham, is the trade association which acts for the producers, managers and owners of London's West End theatres.

The awards were established in 1976 as The Society of West End Theatre Awards. Lord Olivier agreed to have his name associated with them in 1984 and they were subsequently renamed. The awards are organised on behalf of the Society members by an Awards Committee which was chaired by Bill Kenwright in 1994. The awards are judged by three separate panels; for theatre, opera and dance. The Theatre Panel comprises seven people chosen for their specialist knowledge and six members of the theatre-going public. The Opera and Dance Panels each include three professional members and two members of the public. Members of the public apply each year to be included on the panels and undergo a rigorous selection procedure. Any productions that open in the year previous to the awards ceremony are eligible for consideration. All productions are seen by members of the relevant panel, and then voted on. A selection of awards (winners since inception – the awards have not always been given in each year

The bronze Laurence Olivier Award which is presented to all winners. It was specially commissioned by The Society of London Theatre from the sculptor Harry Franchetti and represents the young Laurence Olivier as Henry V at the Old Vic in 1937.

and sometimes they are awarded under a different title):

The BBC Award for Best Play
1976 *Dear Daddy*, Denis Cannan
1977 *The Fire That Consumes*, Henry de Montherlant; English version by Vivian Cox with Bernard Miles
1978 *Whose Life is it Anyway?*, Brian Clark
1979 *Betrayal*, Harold Pinter
1980 *The Life and Adventures of Nicholas Nickleby*, Charles Dickens; adapted by David Edgar
1981 *Children of a Lesser God*, Mark Medoff
1982 *Another Country*, Julian Mitchell
1983 *Glengarry Glen Ross*, David Mamet
1984 *Benefactors*, Michael Frayn
1985 *Red Noses*, Peter Barnes
1986 *Les Liaisons Dangereuses*, Christopher Hampton

Sweeney Todd – 1994 Best Musical Revival, Laurence Olivier Awards.

1987 *Serious Money*, Caryl Churchill
1988 *Our Country's Good*, Timberlake Wertenbaker
1989/1990 *Racing Demon*, David Hare
1991 *Dancing at Lughnasa*, Brian Friel
1992 *Death and the Maiden*, Ariel Dorfman
1993 *Six Degrees of Separation*, John Guare
1994 *Arcadia*, Tom Stoppard

Best Revival
1991 *Pericles*, William Shakespeare
1992 *Hedda Gabler*, Henrik Ibsen
1993 *An Inspector Calls*, J. B. Priestley
1994 *Machinal*, Sophie Treadwell

Best Entertainment
1991 *Five Guys Named Moe*, Clarke Peters
1992 *Talking Heads*, Alan Bennett
1993 *Travels with My Aunt*, Graham Greene; adapted by Giles Havergal
1994 *A Christmas Carol*, Charles Dickens; adapted by Patrick Stewart

Musical of the Year
1976 *A Chorus Line*, Marvin Hamlisch (music), Edward Kleban (lyrics)
1977 *The Comedy of Errors*, Guy Woolfenden (music) William Shakespeare (lyrics)
1978 *Evita*, Andrew Lloyd Webber (music), Tim Rice (lyrics)
1979 *Songbook*, Monty Norman (music), Julian More (lyrics)
1980 *Sweeney Todd*, Stephen Sondheim
1981 *Cats*, Andrew Lloyd Webber (music), T. S. Eliot (lyrics)
1982 *Poppy,* Monty Norman (music), Peter Nichols (lyrics)
1983 *Blood Brothers*, Willy Russell
1984 *42nd Street*, Harry Warren (music), Al Dubin (lyrics)
1985 *Me and My Girl*, Noel Gay (music), L. Arthur Rose (lyrics)
1986 *The Phantom of the Opera*, Andrew Lloyd Webber (music), Charles Hart, Richard Stilgoe (lyrics)
1987 *Follies*, Stephen Sondheim
1988 *Candide*, Leonard Bernstein (music), Richard Wilbur (lyrics)
1989/1990 *Return to the Forbidden Planet*, Bob Carlton
1991 *Sunday in the Park with George*, Stephen Sondheim

> *'The play was a great success, but the audience was a disaster.'*
>
> Oscar Wilde, referring to a play that had recently failed

1992 *Carmen Jones*, Oscar Hammerstein II
1993 *Crazy For You*, George and Ira Gershwin
1994 *City of Angels*, Cy Coleman (music), David Zippel (lyrics)

Best Musical Revival
1991 *Show Boat*, Jerome Kern (music), Oscar Hammerstein II (lyrics)
1992 *The Boys from Syracuse*, Richard Rodgers (music), Lorenz Hart (lyrics)
1993 *Carousel*, Richard Rodgers (music), Oscar Hammerstein II (lyrics)
1994 *Sweeney Todd*, Stephen Sondheim

Best Comedy
1976 *Donkey's Years*, Michael Frayn
1977 *Privates on Parade*, Peter Nichols
1978 *Filumena*, Eduardo de Filippo; adapted by Keith Waterhouse and Willis Hall
1979 *Middle Age Spread*, Roger Hall
1980 *Educating Rita*, Willy Russell
1981 *Steaming*, Nell Dunn
1982 *Noises Off*, Michael Frayn
1983 *Daisy Pulls if Off*, Denise Deegan
1984 *Up 'n' Under*, John God by Alan Ayckbourn
1986 *When We Are Married*, J. B. Priestley
1987 *Three Men on a Horse*, John Cecil Holm and George Abbott
1988 *Shirley Valentine*, Willy Russell
1989/1990 *Single Spies*, Alan Bennett
1991 *Out of Order*, Ray Cooney
1992 *La Bête*, David Hirson
1993 *The Rise and Fall of Little Voice*, Jim Cartwright
1994 *Hysteria*, Terry Johnson

Most Outstanding Achievement in Opera
1977 Glyndebourne Festival Opera, *Don Giovanni*
1978 English National Opera for their enterprising repertoire
1979 The Royal Opera, *The Rake's Progress*
1980 English National Opera, *Così Fan Tutte*
1981 The Royal Opera, *Les Contes D'Hoffman*
1982 English National Opera, *Rigoletto*
1986 English National Opera, *Doctor Faust*; Graham Clark and Thomas Allen specially commended
1987 English National Opera, *Lady Macbeth of Mtsensk*
1988 Leontina Vaduva for her performance in *Manon* (Royal Opera)
1989/1990 Die Komische Oper, *Orpheus and Eurydice*
1991 Mark Elder for conducting English National Opera's *Duke Bluebeard's Castle*; *Macbeth*; *Pelléas & Mélisande*;

Wozzeck
1992 The Royal Opera, *Mitridate*; *Rè Di Ponto*
1993 Sir Edward Downes for conducting *The Fiery Angel* and *Stiffelio* at the Royal Opera House and the preparation of the performing edition for *Stiffelio*
1994 English National Opera orchestra for *Lohengrin* and *Inquest of Love*

Most Outstanding Achievement in Dance
1977 London Festival Ballet, *Romeo and Juliet*
1978 Robert Cohan, Artistic Director, London Contemporary Dance Theatre
1979 Peter Schaufuss for *La Sylphide*
1980 The Royal Ballet, *Gloria*
1981 Stuttgart Ballet, *Forgotten Lane*
1982 Le Ballet de L'Opéra de Paris, *Le Songe d'Une Nuit d'Eté*
1986 The Ballet Rambert for their 60th Anniversary Season
1987 Trisha Brown for her season at Sadler's Wells
1988 The Dancers of the Kirov Ballet for their London season
1989/1990 London Contemporary Dance Theatre for their production of Kim Brandstrup's *Orfeo*
1991 Twyla Tharp and Jennifer Tipton for choreography and lighting of The American Ballet Theatre, *In the Upper Room*
1992 *In the Middle, Somewhat Elevated* for William Forsythe's choreography and performance by the Royal Ballet
1993 Siobhan Davies for choreography of Rambert Dance Company's *Winnsboro Cotton Mill Blues*
1994 London Contemporary Dance Theatre dancers for their season at Sadler's Wells

Best Actor
1985 Antony Sher, *Richard III*; *Torch Song Trilogy*
1986 Albert Finney, *Orphans*
1987 Michael Gambon, *A View from the Bridge*
1989/1990 Oliver Ford Davies, *Racing Demon*
1991 Ian McKellen, *Richard III*
1992 Nigel Hawthorne, *The Madness of George III*
1993 Robert Stephens, *Henry IV, Parts 1 and 2*
1994 Mark Rylance, *Much Ado About Nothing*

Best Actress
1985 Yvonne Bryceland, *The Road to Mecca*
1986 Lindsay Duncan, *Les Liaisons Dangereuses*

1987 Judi Dench, *Antony and Cleopatra*
1989/1990 Fiona Shaw, *Electra; As You Like It; The Good Person of Sichuan*
1991 Kathryn Hunter, *The Visit*
1992 Juliet Stevenson, *Death and The Maiden*
1993 Alison Steadman, *The Rise and Fall of Little Voice*
1994 Fiona Shaw, *Machinal*

Best Comedy Performance
1976 Penelope Keith, *Donkey's Years*
1977 Dennis Quilley, *Privates on Parade*
1978 Ian McKellen, *The Alchemist*
1979 Barry Humphries, *A Night with Dame Edna*
1980 Beryl Reid, *Born in the Gardens*
1981 Rowan Atkinson, *Rowan Atkinson in Revue*
1982 Geoffrey Hutchings, *Poppy*
1983 Griff Rhys Jones, *Charley's Aunt*
1984 Maureen Lipman, *See How They Run*
1988 Alex Jennings, *Too Clever by Half*
1989/1990 Michael Gambon, *Man of the Moment*
1991 Alan Cumming, *Accidental Death of an Anarchist*
1992 Desmond Barrit, *The Comedy of Errors*
1993 Simon Cadell, *Travels with My Aunt*
1994 Griff Rhys Jones, *An Absolute Turkey*

Best Actor in a Supporting Role
1977 Nigel Hawthorne, *Privates on Parade*
1978 Robert Eddison, *Twelfth Night*
1979 Patrick Stewart, *Antony and Cleopatra*
1980 David Threlfall, *Nicholas Nickleby*
1981 Joe Melia, *Good*
1982 David Healy, *Guys and Dolls*
1983 Alan Devlin, *A Moon for the Misbegotten*
1984 Edward Petherbridge, *Strange Interlude*
1991 David Bradley, *King Lear*
1992 Oleg Menshikov, *When She Danced*
1993 Julian Glover, *Henry IV, Parts 1 and 2*
1994 Joseph Mydell, *Perestroika*

Best Actress in a Supporting Role
1977 Mona Washbourne, *Stevie*
1978 Elizabeth Spriggs, *Love Letters on Blue Paper*
1979 Doreen Mantle, *Death of a Salesman*
1980 Suzanne Bertish, *Nicholas Nickleby*
1981 Gwen Watford, *Present Laughter*
1982 Anna Massey, *The Importance of Being Earnest*

1983 Abigail McKern, *As You Like It*
1984 Marcia Warren, *Stepping Out*
1991 Sara Crowe, *Private Lives*
1992 Frances de la Tour, *When She Danced*
1993 Barbara Leigh-Hunt, *An Inspector Calls*
1994 Helen Burns, *The Last Yankee*

Best Actor in a Musical or Entertainment
1979 Anton Rodgers, *Songbook*
1980 Denis Quilley, *Sweeney Todd*
1981 Michael Crawford, *Barnum*
1982 Roy Hudd, *Underneath the Arches*
1983 Denis Lawson, *Mr Cinders*
1984 Paul Clarkson, *The Hired Man*
1985 Robert Lindsay, *Me and My Girl*
1986 Michael Crawford, *The Phantom of the Opera*
1987 John Bardon and Emil Wolk, *Kiss Me Kate*
1988 Con O'Neill, *Blood Brothers*
1989/1990 Jonathan Pryce, *Miss Saigon*
1991 Philip Quast, *Sunday in the Park with George*
1992 Alan Bennet, *Talking Heads*
1993 Henry Goodman, *Assassins*
1994 Alun Armstrong, *Sweeney Todd*

Best Actress in a Musical or Entertainment
1979 Virginia McKenna, *The King and I*
1980 Gemma Craven, *They're Playing Our Song*
1981 Carlin Glynn, *The Best Little Whorehouse in Texas*
1982 Julia McKenzie, *Guys and Dolls*
1983 Barbara Dickson, *Blood Brothers*
1984 Natalia Makarova, *On Your Toes*
1985 Patti Lupone, *Les Misérables; The Cradle Will Rock*
1986 Lesley Mackie, *Judy*
1987 Nichola McAuliffe, *Kiss Me Kate*
1988 Patricia Routledge, *Candide*
1989/1990 Lea Salonga, *Miss Saigon*
1991 Imelda Staunton, *Into the Woods*
1992 Wilhelmenia Fernandez, *Carmen Jones*
1993 Joanna Riding, *Carousel*
1994 Julia McKenzie, *Sweeney Todd*

Best Supporting Performance in a Musical
1991 Karla Burns, *Show Boat*
1992 Jenny Galloway, *The Boys from Syracuse*
1993 Janie Dee, *Carousel*
1994 Sara Kestelman, *Cabaret*

Best Set Designer
1991 Mark Thompson, *The Wind in the Willows*
1992 Mark Thompson, *The Comedy of Errors*

1993 Ian MacNeil, *An Inspector Calls*
1994 Mark Thompson, *Hysteria*

Best Lighting Designer
1991 Jean Kalman, *Richard III; White Chameleon*
1992 Mark Henderson, *Murmuring Judges; Long Day's Journey into Night*
1993 Howell Binkley, *Kiss of the Spider Woman*
1994 Rick Fisher, *Hysteria; Machinal; Moonlight*

Best Costume Designer
1991 Jasper Conran, *The Rehearsal*
1992 Mark Thompson, *The Comedy of Errors*
1993 William Dudley, *Heartbreak House; Pygmalion; The Rise and Fall of Little Voice*
1994 Gerald Scarfe, *An Absolute Turkey*

Best Director of a Play
1976 Jonathan Miller, *The Three Sisters*
1977 Clifford Williams, *Wild Oats*
1978 Terry Hands, *Henry VI*
1979 Michael Bogdanov, *The Taming of the Shrew*
1980 Trevor Nunn and John Caird, *Nicholas Nickleby*
1981 Peter Wood, *On The Razzle*
1982 Richard Fyre, *Guys and Dolls*
1983 Terry Hands, *Cyrano de Bergerac*
1984 Christopher Morahan, *Wild Honey*
1985 Bill Bryden, *The Mysteries*
1986 Bill Alexander, *The Merry Wives of Windsor*
1987 Declan Donnellan, *The Cid, Twelfth Night, Macbeth*
1988 Deborah Warner, *Titus Andronicus*
1989/1990 Michael Bogdanov, *The Wars of the Roses*
1991 David Thacker, *Pericles*
1992 Deborah Warner, *Hedda Gabler*
1993 Stephen Daldry, *An Inspector Calls*
1994 Stephen Daldry, *Machinal*

Best Director of a Musical
1991 Richard Jones, *Into the Woods*
1992 Simon Callow, *Carmen Jones*
1993 Nicholas Hytner, *Carousel*
1994 Declan Donnellan, *Sweeney Todd*

> 'A play is like a cigar. If it is a failure no amount of puffing will make it draw. If it is a success everybody wants a box.'
>
> Henry J. Bryan

Best Choreographer
1991 Charles Augins, *Five Guys Named Moe*
1992 Rafael Aguilar, *Matador*
1993 Susan Stroman, *Crazy For You*
1994 Luke Cresswell and Steve McNicholas, *Stomp*

Special Award for Lifetime Achievement
1993 The late Sir Kenneth Macmillan
1994 The late Sam Wanamaker

Pulitzer Prize

For a distinguished play by an American author, preferably original in its source and dealing with American life. (See separate section, Pulitzer Prizes.)
1918 Jesse Lynch Williams, *Why Marry?*
1919 No award
1920 Eugene O'Neill, *Beyond the Horizon*
1921 Zona Gale, *Miss Lulu Bett*
1922 Eugene O'Neill, *Anna Christie*
1923 Owen Davis, *Icebound*
1924 Hatcher Hughes, *Hell-Bent for Heaven*
1925 Sidney Howard, *They Knew What They Wanted*
1926 George Kelly, *Craig's Wife*
1927 Paul Green, *In Abraham's Bosom*
1928 Eugene O'Neill, *Strange Interlude*
1929 Elmer Rice, *Street Scene*
1930 Marc Connelly, *The Green Pastures*
1931 Susan Glaspell, *Alison's House*
1932 George S. Kaurman, Morris Ryskind and Ira Gershwin, *Of Thee I Sing*
1933 Maxwell Anderson, *Both Your Houses*
1934 Sidney Kingsley, *Men in White*
1935 Zoe Akins, *The Old Maid*
1936 Robert E. Sherwood, *Idiot's Delight*
1937 George S. Kaurman and Moss Hart, *You Can't Take It With You*
1938 Thornton Wilder, *Our Town*
1939 Robert E. Sherwood, *Abe Lincoln in Illinois*
1940 William Saroyan, *The Time of Your Life*
1941 Robert E. Sherwood, *There Shall Be No Night*
1942 No award
1943 Thornton Wilder, *The Skin of Our Teeth*
1944 No award
1945 Mary Chase, *Harvey*
1946 Russel Crouse and Howard Lindsay, *State of the Union*
1947 No award
1948 Tennessee Williams, *A Streetcar Named Desire*

1949 Arthur Miller, *Death of a Salesman*
1950 Richard Rodgers, Oscar Hammerstein (II) and Joshua Logan, *South Pacific*
1951 No award
1952 Joseph Kramm, *The Shrike*
1953 William Inge, *Picnic*
1954 John Patrick, *Teahouse of the August Moon*
1955 Tennessee Williams, *Cat on a Hot Tin Roof*
1956 Frances Goodrich and Albert Hackett, *The Diary of Anne Frank*
1957 Eugene O'Neill, *Long Day's Journey Into Night*
1958 Ketti Frings, *Look Homeward, Angel*
1959 Archibald MacLeish, *J.B.*
1960 George Abbott, Jerome Weidman, Sheldon Harnick and Jerry Bock, *Fiorello*
1961 Tad Mosel, *All the Way Home*
1962 Frank Loesser and Abe Burrows, *How To Succeed in Business Without Really Trying*
1963 No award
1964 No award
1965 Frank D. Gilroy, *The Subject was Roses*
1966 No award
1967 Edward Albee, *A Delicate Balance*
1968 No award
1969 Howard Sackler, *The Great White Hope*
1970 Charles Gordon, *No Place to be Somebody*
1971 Paul Zindel, *The Effect of Gamma Rays on Man-in-the-Moon Marigolds*
1972 No award
1973 Jason Miller, *That Championship Season*
1974 No award
1975 Edward Albee, *Seascape*
1976 Michael Bennett, James Kirkwood, Nicholas Dante, Marvin Hamlisch, Edward Kleban, *A Chorus Line*
1977 Michael Cristofer, *The Shadow Box*
1978 Donald L. Coburn, *The Gin Game*
1979 Sam Shepard, *Buried Child*
1980 Lanford Wilson, *Talley's Folly*
1981 Beth Henley, *Crimes of the Heart*
1982 Charles Fuller, *A Soldier's Play*
1983 Marsha Norman, *Night, Mother*
1984 David Mamet, *Glengarry Glen Ross*
1985 Stephen Sondheim (music and lyrics) and James Lapine (book), *Sunday in the Park With George*
1986 No award
1987 August Wilson, *Fences*
1988 Alfred Uhry, *Driving Miss Daisy*
1989 Wendy Wasserstein, *The Heidi Chronicles*

1990 August Wilson, *The Piano Lesson*
1991 Neil Simon, *Lost in Yonkers*
1992 Robert Schenkkan, *The Kentucky Cycle*
1993 Tony Kushner, *Angels in America: Millennium Approaches*
1994 Edward Albee, *Three Tall Women*

Tony Awards

The Tony, named in honour of Antoinette Perry, is one of the theatre's most coveted awards and is given annually for 'distinguished achievement' in the theatre in the United States by the League of New York Theatres.

Antoinette Perry made her first entry into the theatre in 1906, when she was only eighteen. She played opposite David Warfield in *Music Master* and, the following year, in David Belasco's *A Grand Army Man*. Her dedication and tireless efforts to broaden the scope of theatre through the American Theatre Wing, of which she was Chairman of the Board, affected hundreds of people. After she died, it was decided to institute a memorial to her in the form of the Antoinette Perry Awards.

The first awards were made at a dinner in the Grand Ballroom of the Waldorf Astoria on Easter Sunday, 6 April 1947. Antoinette Perry's successor as Chairwoman, Vera Allen, presided, and the evening included dining, dancing and a programme of entertainment including Mickey Rooney, Herb Shriner and Ethel Waters.

During the first two years there was no official Tony award. The winners were presented with a cigarette lighter (for men) or a compact (for women) as well as a scroll. The United Scenic Artists sponsored a contest for a suitable design for the award and Herman Rosse's entry, depicting the masks of comedy and tragedy on one side and the profile of Antoinette Perry on the other, was selected. In 1949 the medallion was presented at the third annual dinner.

From 1967 the League of American Theatres and Producers Inc. was authorised by the American Theatre Wing to present the Tony Awards, when the ceremonies were moved from the traditional hotel ballroom setting to a Broadway theatre.

In 1947 the first committee devised a voting system whose eligible voters were members of the Board of the American Theatre Wing, representing management, and the performer and craft unions of the entertainment field. In 1954 voting eligibility was expanded to include theatre professionals who were not members of the American Theatre Wing. Today, the system has been further enlarged to include members of the governing boards of the Actors' Equity Association, the Dramatists Guild, The Society of Stage Directors and Choreographers, the United Scenic Artist, those persons whose names appear on the first and second night press lists, and the membership of the League of American Theatres and Producers; a total of approximately 650. Winners for the last ten years:

Best Play

Awarded to author(s) and producer(s)

1983 *Torch Song Trilogy*, Harvey Fierstein. **Producers** Kenneth Waissman, Martin Markinson, Lawrence Lane, John Glines, BetMar and Donald Tick

1984 *The Real Thing*, Tom Stoppard. **Producers** Emanuel Azenberg, The Shubert Organization, Icarus Productions, Byron Goldman, Ivan Bloch, Roger Berlind and Michael Codron

1985 *Biloxi Blues*, Neil Simon. **Producers** Emanuel Azenberg, Center Theater Group/Ahmanson Theatre, Los Angeles

1986 *I'm Not Rappaport*, Herb Gardner. **Producers** James Walsh, Lewis Allen and Martin Heinfling

1987 *Fences*, August Wilson. **Producers** Carole Shorenstein Hays, The Yale Repertory Theatre

1988 *M. Butterfly*, David Henry Hwang. **Producers** Stuart Ostrow, David Geffen

1989 *The Heidi Chronicles*, Wendy Wasserstein. **Producers** The Shubert Organization, Suntory International Corp., James Walsh, Playwrights Horizons

1990 *The Grapes of Wrath*, Frank Galati. **Producers** The Shubert Organization, Steppenwolf Theatre Company, Suntory International Corp., Jujamcyn Theaters

1991 *Lost in Yonkers*, Neil Simon. **Producer** Emanuel Azenberg

1992 *Dancing at Lughnasa*, Brian Friel. **Producers** Noel Pearson, Bill Kenwright, Joseph Harris

1993 *Angels in America: Millennium Approaches*, Tony Kushner. **Producers** Jujamcyn Theaters, Mark Taper Forum/ Gordon Davidson, Margo Lion, Susan Quint Gallin, Jon B. Platt, The Baruch-Frankel Viertel Group, Frederick Zollo, Herb Alpert

Best Musical

Awarded to producer(s)

1983 *Cats*, Cameron Mackintosh, The Really Useful Company, Inc., David Geffen and The Shubert Organization

1984 *La Cage aux Folles*, Allan Carr, Kenneth D. Greenblatt, Marvin A. Krauss, Steward F. Lane, James M. Nederlander, Martin Richards, Barry Brown, Fritz Holt

1985 *Big River*, Rocco Landesman, Heidi Landesman, Rick Steiner, M. Anthony Fisher, Dodger Productions

1986 *The Mystery of Edwin Drood*, Joseph Papp

1987 *Les Misérables*, Cameron Mackintosh

1988 *The Phantom of the Opera*, Cameron Mackintosh, The Really Useful Theatre Company Inc.

1989 *Jerome Robbins' Broadway*, The Shubert Organization, Roger Berlind, Suntory International Corp., Byron Goldman, Emanuel Azenberg

1990 *City of Angels*, Nick Vanoff, Roger Berlind, Jujamcyn Theaters, Suntory International Corp., The Shubert Organization

1991 *The Will Rogers Follies*, Pierre Cossette, Martin Richards, Sam Crothers, James M. Nederlander, Stewart F. Lane, Max Weitzenhoffer, Japan Satellite Broadcasting Inc.

1992 *Crazy For You*, Roger Horchow, Elizabeth Williams

1993 *Kiss of the Spider Woman – The Musical*, Livent (US) Inc.

RIGHT The cast in a scene from the award-winning musical, *Les Misérables*.

THEATRICAL DISASTER

Several productions share the distinction of being opened and closed in one evening, but perhaps the record should go to Lord Lytton's play, *The Lady of Lyons* which opened on Boxing Day 1888 at the Shaftesbury Theatre, London. In fact it never really opened – the play never started. After waiting for an hour the management asked the audience, who had become increasingly impatient, to go home. The reason: no one could raise the safety curtain.

Tony Awards

PLAYS

	Leading Actor	Leading Actress	Featured Actor	Featured Actress	Direction
1983	Harvey Fierstein *Torch Song Trilogy*	Jessica Tandy *Foxfire*	Matthew Broderick *Brighton Beach Memoirs*	Judith Ivey *Steaming*	Gene Saks *Brighton Beach Memoirs*
1984	Jeremy Irons *The Real Thing*	Glenn Close *The Real Thing*	Joe Mantegna *Glengarry Glen Ross*	Christine Baranski *The Real Thing*	Mike Nichols *The Real Thing*
1985	Derek Jacobi *Much Ado About Nothing*	Stockard Channing *Joe Egg*	Barry Miller *Biloxi Blues*	Judith Ivey *Hurlyburly*	Gene Saks *Biloxi Blues*
1986	Judd Hirsch *I'm Not Rappaport*	Lily Tomlin *The Search for Signs of Intelligent Life in the Universe*	John Mahoney *The House of Blue Leaves*	Swoosie Kurtz *The House of Blue Leaves*	Jerry Zaks *The House of Blue Leaves*
1987	James Earl Jones *Fences*	Linda Lavin *Broadway Bound*	John Randolph *Broadway Bound*	Mary Alice *Fences*	Lloyd Richards *Fences*
1988	Ron Silver *Speed-The-Plow*	Joan Allen *Burn This*	B. D. Wong *M. Butterfly*	L. Scott Caldwell *Joe Turner's Come and Gone*	John Dexter *M. Butterfly*
1989	Philip Bosco *Lend Me A Tenor*	Pauline Collins *Shirley Valentine*	Boyd Gaines *The Heidi Chronicles*	Christine Baranski *Rumors*	Jerry Zaks *Lend Me A Tenor*
1990	Robert Morse *Tru*	Maggie Smith *Lettice and Lovage*	Charles Durning *Cat on a Hot Tin Roof*	Margaret Tyzack *Lettice and Lovage*	Frank Galati *The Grapes of Wrath*
1991	Nigel Hawthorne *Shadowlands*	Mercedes Ruehl *Lost in Yonkers*	Kevin Spacey *Lost in Yonkers*	Irene Worth *Lost in Yonkers*	Jerry Zaks *Six Degrees of Separation*
1992	Judd Hirsch *Conversations With My Father*	Glenn Close *Death and the Maiden*	Larry Fishburne *Two Trains Running*	Brid Brennan *Dancing at Lughnasa*	Patrick Mason *Dancing at Lughnasa*
1993	Ron Leibman *Angels in America: Millennium Approaches*	Madeline Kahn *The Sisters Rosenzweig*	Stephen Spinella *Angels in America: Millennium Approaches*	Debra Monk *Redwood Curtain*	George C. Wolfe *Angels in America: Millennium Approaches*

MUSICALS

	Book	Original Score	Leading Actor	Leading Actress	Featured Actor	Featured Actress	Direction
1983	*Cats* T. S. Eliot	*Cats* Music: Andrew Lloyd Webber Lyrics: T. S. Eliot	Tommy Tune *My One and Only*	Natalia Makarova *On Your Toes*	Charles 'Honi' Coles *My One and Only*	Betty Buckley *Cats*	Trevor Nunn *Cats*
1984	*La Cage aux Folles* Harvey Fierstein	*La Cage aux Folles* Jerry Herman	George Hearn *La Cage aux Folles*	Chita Rivera *The Rink*	Hinton Battle *The Tap Dance Kid*	Lila Kedrova *Zorba*	Arthur Laurents *La Cage aux Folles*
1985	*Big River* William Hauptman	*Big River* Roger Miller	No award	No award	Ron Richardson *Big River*	Leilani Jones *Grind*	Des McAnuff *Big River*
1986	*The Mystery of Edwin Drood* Rupert Holmes	*The Mystery of Edwin Drood* Rupert Holmes	George Rose *The Mystery of Edwin Drood*	Bernadette Peters *Song & Dance*	Michael Rupert *Sweet Charity*	Bebe Neuwirth *Sweet Charity*	Wilford Leach *The Mystery of Edwin Drood*
1987	*Les Misérables* Alain Boublil, Claude-Michel Schönberg	*Les Misérables* Music: Claude-Michel Schönberg Lyrics: Herbert Kretzmer, Alain Boublil	Robert Lindsay *Me and My Girl*	Maryann Plunkett *Me and My Girl*	Michael Maguire *Les Misérables*	Frances Ruffelle *Les Misérables*	Trevor Nunn, John Caird *Les Misérables*
1988	*Into the Woods* James Lapine	*Into the Woods* Stephen Sondheim	Michael Crawford *The Phantom of the Opera*	Joanna Gleason *Into the Woods*	Bill McCutcheon *Anything Goes*	Judy Kaye *The Phantom of the Opera*	Harold Prince *The Phantom of the Opera*

	Book	Original Score	Leading Actor	Leading Actress	Featured Actor	Featured Actress	Direction
1989	No award	No award	Jason Alexander *Jerome Robbins' Broadway*	Ruth Brown *Black and Blue*	Scott Wise *Jerome Robbins' Broadway*	Debbie Shapiro *Jerome Robbins' Broadway*	Jerome Robbins *Jerome Robbins' Broadway*
1990	*City of Angels* Larry Gelbart	*City of Angels* Music: Cy Coleman Lyrics: David Zippel	James Naughton *City of Angels*	Tyne Daly *Gypsy*	Michael Jeter *Grand Hotel, The Musical*	Randy Graff *City of Angels*	Tommy Tune *Grand Hotel, The Musical*
1991	*The Secret Garden* Marsha Norman	*The Will Rogers Follies* Music: Cy Coleman Lyrics: Betty Comden, Adolph Green	Jonathan Pryce *Miss Saigon*	Lea Salonga *Miss Saigon*	Hinton Battle *Miss Saigon*	Daisy Eagan *The Secret Garden*	Tommy Tune *The Will Rogers Follies*
1992	*Falsettos* William Finn and James Lapine	*Falsettos* William Finn	Gregory Hines *Jelly's Last Jam*	Faith Prince *Guys and Dolls*	Scott Waara *The Most Happy Fella*	Tonya Pinkins *Jelly's Last Jam*	Jerry Zaks *Guys and Dolls*
1993	*Kiss of the Spider Woman – The Musical* Livent Us Inc.	*Kiss of the Spider Woman – The Musical* Music: John Kander Lyrics: Fred Ebb *The Who's Tommy* Pete Townshend	Brent Carver *Kiss of the Spider Woman – The Musical*	Chitz Rivera *Kiss of the Spider Woman – The Musical*	Anthony Crivello *Kiss of the Spider Woman – The Musical*	Andrea Martin *My Favorite Year*	Des McAnuff *The Who's Tommy*

Other Tony awards given, but not listed here: Best Scenic Design, Best Costume Design, Best Lighting Design, Best Choreography, Best Revival – Play or Musical, Special Awards.

Martini / TMA Regional Theatre Awards

Organised by The Theatrical Management Association (TMA) and sponsored by Martini & Rossi since 1990, these awards are given annually. They were initiated by the TMA to recognise achievement, and draw attention to and compare regional theatre on a national level. The TMA was founded in 1894 by Sir Henry Irving, the first actor to be awarded a knighthood. It represents the interests of all sectors of British theatre outside the West End of London.

The awards are given as a result of votes submitted by TMA members and 87 TMA regional panellists – experienced theatregoers – who are enlisted to serve for up to two years. Each region is divided up so that a TMA theatre can expect to be visited by an average of three panellists. Voting forms are submitted for hundreds of productions from the panellists and all these are counted at the end of each year to ascertain the award winners in each category.

Most Welcoming Theatre
1991 The Watermill, Newbury
1992 The Swan Theatre, Worcester
1993 Royal Theatre, Northampton

Best Regional Theatre Critic
1991 Penny Simpson, *South Wales Echo*
1992 Charles Roberts, *Eastern Daily Press*, Norwich
1993 David Isaacs, *Evening Chronicle*, Newcastle upon Tyne

Best Show for Children and Young People
1991 *Monty Moonbeams Magnificent Mission,* Christopher Lillicrap and Jeanette Ranger, Swan Theatre, Worcester
1992 *The Magic Storybook,* Renata Allen, Oxford Stage Company and Oxford Playhouse
1993 *Mr A's Amazing Maze Plays,* Alan Ayckbourn, on tour

Best Touring Production
1991 *The Winter's Tale,* William Shakespeare, English Shakespeare Company
1992 *Shadowlands,* William Nicholson, Armada Productions and Carnival Theatre
1993 *Anna Karenina,* Leo Tolstoy, adapted by Helen Edmundson, Shared Experience Theatre

Best Musical
1991 *Sweeney Todd,* Stephen Sondheim, Oldham Coliseum
1992 *Into the Woods,* Stephen Sondheim, Wolsey Theatre, Ipswich
1993 *Me and My Girl,* Noel Gay

(music), L. Arthur Rose and Douglas Furber (lyrics), on tour

Best Designer
1991 Simon Vincenzi for *Thérèse Raquin,* Nottingham Playhouse
1992 Neil Warmington (set), Ben Ormerod (lighting), Mic Pool (sound), *Life is a Dream,* West Yorkshire Playhouse, Leeds
1993 Charles Cusick-Smith, *The Plough and the Stars,* Haymarket, Leicester

Best Actress in a Supporting Role
1991 Sian Thomas, *Uncle Vanya,* Renaissance Theatre Company
1992 Liza Sadovy, *Mrs Klein,* Royal Theatre, Northampton, and *The Secret Rapture,* Bristol Old Vic
1993 Alison Fiske, *Relative Values,* Chichester Festival Theatre

Best Actor in a Supporting Role
1991 Ben Thomas, *Antony and Cleopatra,* Talawa Theatre Company
1992 Jud Meyers as Arnold Epstein, *Biloxi Blues,* Library Theatre, Manchester
1993 Tim Sabel, *For Services Rendered,* Salisbury Playhouse

Best Director
1991 Patrick Sandford, *The Winter Wife* and *Much Ado About Nothing,* Nuffield Theatre, Southampton
1992 Gregory Hersov, *Romeo and Juliet* and *A View from the Bridge,* Royal

Exchange Theatre, Manchester
1993 David Glass, *Gormenghast*, on tour

Best Actor
1991 Stephen Hattersley, *Kingdom of Earth*, Redgrave Theatre, Farnham
1992 David Fielder, *The Choice*, Salisbury Playhouse
1993 Niall Buggy, *Juno and the Paycock*, on tour

Best Actress
1991 Cheryl Campbell, *A Streetcar Named Desire*, Leicester Haymarket
1992 Gillian Hanna, *Wallflowering*, West Yorkshire Playhouse, Leeds, and *A View from the Bridge*, Royal Exchange Theatre, Manchester
1993 Josette Bushell-Mingo, *From the Mississippi Delta*, Contact Theatre, Manchester

Best New Play
1991 *Donny Boy*, Robin Glendinning, Royal Exchange Theatre, Manchester
1992 *The Choice*, Claire Luckham, Salisbury Playhouse
1993 *Lost in Yonkers*, Neil Simon, on tour

Most Outstanding Contribution to Theatrical Life
1991 Toby Robertson, Artistic Director, Theatr Clwyd Mold
1992 The Alhambra Theatre, Bradford
1993 Giles Havergal, Robert David MacDonald and Philip Prowse, Citizens Theatre, Glasgow

Martini Special Award for Best Overall Production
1991 *Hobson's Choice*, Harold Brighouse, Derby Playhouse
1992 *Gaudeamus after Construction Battalion* by Sergei Kaladin, toured by the Maly Drama Theatre of St Petersburg
1993 *Juno and the Paycock*, Sean O'Casey, Carnival Theatre and Rainbow Productions by arrangement with The Gate Theatre, Dublin, on tour

The Scotsman *Fringe Firsts*

These awards have been presented since 1973 to outstanding new

'A drama critic is a person who surprises the playwright by informing him what he meant.'

Wilson Mizner, US writer

drama, performed during the three weeks of the Edinburgh Festival Fringe in August each year. Recently, new adaptations of classic works have also been eligible. Originally, the Fringe Board, headed by Jonathan Miller (theatre and opera director), perceived a need to highlight new work and the then administrator of the Fringe, John Milligan, collaborated with *The Scotsman*'s arts editor, Allen Wright, in drawing up a scheme which would reward new plays.

The shows which are eligible for an award (i.e. new scripts and shows which have not had more than six preview performances) are marked with a star in the Fringe programme and *The Scotsman* undertakes to have all eligible shows reviewed – several hundred are reviewed by up to 40 reviewers.

Usually between four and six awards are given in each of the three weeks of the Fringe. There is no set panel of judges, the procedure being that a reviewer will report back to the arts editor of *The Scotsman* that a show is of particular quality and may be worthy of an award. At least one other senior and experienced critic will then anonymously visit the show and write a report. Further opinions are then canvassed before a final list is drawn up.

The awards take the form of an inscribed copper plaque. No cash prize is given but winning groups invariably find an increase in box-office takings as the public use the awards as a reliable guide to quality amid the bewildering mass of the Fringe (582 companies with 1643 shows and 14 108 performances in 1993).

1993 WINNERS (*Scotsman* Fringe Firsts)

Week 1 *Tonight I'm Entertaining Richard Gere*, Cecilia Delatori
Accustomed to Her Face, presented by Clyde Unity Theatre
The Tender Mercies, Sladjana Vujovic
Port and Lemon, John Cargill Thompson
Storybook, Richard Davidson

Week 2 *The Truman Capote Talk Show*, Bob Kingdom
Dead Fish, Gordon Steele, presented by Stockton Youth Theatre
One Moment, Jeremy Weller, presented by The Grassmarket Project
Bloodstream, Andrew Buckland

Week 3 *The Woman on a Tree on The Hill*, presented by Theatreworks, Singapore
The Legend of St Julian, Gerry Mulgrew, presented by Communicado
Roll-a-Pea, presented by Wierszalin, Poland
The Admiral Jones, Frederick Mohr, performed by James Chisholm, presented by Dumfries and Galloway Arts
The Audition, A. L. Kennedy, performed by Mike Hayward, presented by Borderline
Klytemnestra's Bairns, a Scots version of *The Oresteia* by Bill Dunlop

---

John Whiting Award

This award was instituted in 1965 and first given in 1966 by the Arts Council to commemorate the late John Whiting and his contribution to post-war British theatre. He was a member of the Arts Council Drama Panel from 1955 until his death in 1963. The award is intended to help further the careers and enhance the reputations of British playwrights and to draw attention to the importance of writers in contemporary theatre.

The award is given by a panel of independent judges who are not members or associated with the Arts

Council. It is made to the writer whose play, in the judges' opinion, most nearly satisfies the following description: writing is of special quality, is of relevance and importance to contemporary life, and is of potential value to British theatre. The winner receives £6000.
1966 Wole Soyinka, *The Lion and the Jewel*; *Trials of Brother Jero*. **Tom Stoppard**, *Rosencrantz and Guildenstern are Dead*
1967 Peter Nicholls, *A Day in the Death of Joe Egg*. **Peter Terson**, *The Ballad of the Artificial Mash*; *Zigger Zagger*
1968 Peter Barnes, *The Ruling Class*. **Edward Bond**, *Narrow Road to the Deep North*

1969 Howard Brenton, *Revenge; Christie in Love*, etc. **The Freehold Company** (director Nancy Meckler), *Antigone*
1970 Heathcote Williams, *AC/DC*
1971 Mustapha Matura, *As Time Goes By*
1972 John Arden and Margaretta D'Arcy
1973 David Rudkin, *Ashes*
1974 John McGrath, but not accepted on a technicality
1975 David Edgar, *Destiny*
1976 David Lan, *The Winter Dancers*
1977 David Halliwell, *Prejudice*. Snoo Wilson, *The Glad Hand*
1978 Vince Foxall, *Gestures*
1979 Stephen Bill, *The Old Order*
1980 No award
1981 David Pownall, *Beef*
1982 Peter Flannery, *Our Friends in the North*
1983 Karim Alrawi, *Migrations*
1984 Ron Hutchinson, *Rat in the Skull*
1985 Guy Hibbert, *On the Edge*. Heidi Thomas, *Shamrocks and Crocodiles*
1986 Nick Dear, *The Art of Success*
1987 Iain Heggie, *American Bagpipes*
1988 Billy Roche, *A Handful of Stars*
1989 Lucy Gannon, *Keeping Tom Nice*
1990 Terry Johnson, *Imagine Drowning*
1991 Rod Wooden, *Your Home in the West*
1992 Martin Crimp, *The Treatment*

Barclays Music Theatre Awards

Launched in 1986 and sponsored by Barclays Bank in association with *The Times Educational Supplement* (TES), these awards intend to encourage the performance of multi-art form productions in schools and youth theatres and participation by as many young people as possible. The awards have three patrons: Trevor Nunn, Stephen Sondheim and Sir Michael Tippet. All performers under 19 years of age are eligible, performing any combination of music and drama. Auditions are held annually and 11 groups go forward to the finals where awards totalling £7000 are presented to the winners.

The judges for 1993 were Richard Stilgoe (songwriter), Denise Coffey (actress, director and author), Alan Fluck (director of Youth and Music), Jeremy-James Taylor (artistic director of National Youth Music Theatre) and Wendy Toye (choreographer).

1993 WINNERS (Barclay Music Theatre Awards)

Category	Theatre Company	Play
Best overall production		
Junior	Young East Warwickshire Theatre, Yewth, Rugby	*Polo and The Khan*
Senior	Northern Theatre Company, Hull	*Sanctus*
Outstanding Choreographic Performance		
Junior	Stage '84, Bradford	*Joseph and His Amazing Technicolor Dreamcoat*
Senior	JSS Ensemble, Worthing	*Witch*
Outstanding Dramatic Performance		
Junior	Stage '84, Bradford	*Joseph and His Amazing Technicolor Dreamcoat*
Senior	Northern Theatre Company, Hull	*Sanctus*
Outstanding Musical Performance		
Junior	Young East Warwickshire Theatre, Yewth, Rugby	*Polo and the Khan*
Senior	Woking College	*Half a Sixpence*
TES Best Original Work		
Junior	Ashfield Junior School, Workington, Cumbria	*Sea Saga II*
Senior	Harrow School Rattigan Society, Harrow, Middlesex	*Ain't Life Good*
Judges Special Award		
Junior	Ashbourne Pneu School, Derbys	*All Aboard*
Senior	Woking College	*Half a Sixpence*

SHORTEST RUN

The Intimate Review opened at the Duchess Theatre, London, on 11 March 1930, and managed one incomplete performance before closing. The curtain rose to reveal a stage so cluttered that there was hardly room for any actors. Because each sketch had so much scenery, each change took up to 20 minutes to effect and, as *The Times* critic said: 'Every time the curtains parted, squads of scene-shifters might be seen in action or in horrid precipitate flight.' Apparently, the first time this happened the audience found it amusing, but, when it repeatedly happened, hysteria set in. In Miss Florence McHugh's 'Hawaiin Idyll' sketch, while she strode along the beach, declaring the pains of love, clearly visible through the transparent blue backdrop two scene-shifters were hard at work in the sea behind her.

With the scene changes taking so long, the management had to scrap seven scenes to get the finale on before midnight. The following day, a brief statement appeared in the *Evening Standard* from the cast: 'Everyone concerned was so much in agreement with the criticism of last night's performance that its closure was decided upon promptly. In regard to the accommodation on stage there was certainly an appearance of overcrowding.'

SHORTEST PRODUCTION

One of the briefest productions ever staged was *Breath* written by the Nobel Prize winning Irish writer, Samuel Beckett. It was a skit – a dramatic presentation of breathing and light. It was offered to Ken Tynan by the author in 1969 and at its first showing took only 35 seconds to perform.

Evening Standard *Drama Awards*

These awards have been given annually since 1955 in various categories for outstanding contributions to the theatre. The winners are decided by a panel of judges composed of newspaper editors and critics. Winners from 1973 of Best Play, Musical, Comedy (given from 1970), Actor, Actress, Sydney Edwards Award for Best Director (given from 1979) are listed overleaf:

The Evening Standard Drama Awards

	Play	Musical	Comedy	Actor	Actress	Director (Sydney Edwards Award)
1973	*Saturday, Sunday, Monday* Eduardo de Filippo	*Rocky Horror Show*	*Absurd Person Singular* Alan Ayckbourn	Alec McCowen	Janet Suzman	
1974	*Norman Conquests* Alan Ayckbourn	*John, Paul, George, Ringo & Bert*	*Travesties* Tom Stoppard	John Wood	Claire Bloom	
1975	*Otherwise Engaged* Simon Gray	*A Little Night Music*	*Alphabetical Order* Michael Frayn	Sir John Gielgud	Dorothy Tutin	
1976	*Weapons of Happiness* Howard Brenton	*A Chorus Line*	*The Thoughts of Chairman Alf* Johnny Speight	Albert Finney	Janet Suzman	
1977	*Just Between Ourselves* Alan Ayckbourn	*Elvis*	*Privates on Parade* Peter Nichols	Donald Sinden	Alison Steadman	
1978	*Night and Day* Tom Stoppard	*Annie*	*Gloo-Joo* Michael Hastings	Alan Howard	Kate Nelligan	
1979	*Amadeus* Peter Shaffer	*Songbook*	*A Day in Hollywood, A Night in the Ukraine*	Warren Mitchell	Vanessa Redgrave	Trevor Nunn *Once in a Lifetime*
1980	*The Dresser* Ronald Harwood	*Sweeney Todd*	*Make and Break* Michael Frayn	Tom Courtenay	Judi Dench Frances de La Tour	Trevor Nunn, John Caird *Nicholas Nickleby*
1981	*Passion Play* Peter Nichols	*Cats*	*Goose-Pimples* Mike Leigh	Alan Howard	Maggie Smith	Sir Peter Hall *The Oresteia*
1982	*The Real Thing* Tom Stoppard	*Windy City*	*Noises Off* Michael Frayn	Alec McCowen	Judi Dench	Richard Eyre *Guys and Dolls*
1983	*Master Harold and the Boys* Athol Fugard	*Little Shop of Horrors*	*Tales from Hollywood* Christopher Hampton	Derek Jacobi	Geraldine McEwan	Yuri Lyubimov *Crime and Punishment*
1984	*Benefactors* Michael Frayn	*42nd Street*	*Stepping Out* Richard Harris	Ian McKellen	Maggie Smith	Christopher Morahan *Wild Honey*
1985	*Pravda* David Hare, Howard Brenton	*Are You Lonesome Tonight?*	*A Chorus of Disapproval* Alan Ayckbourn	Antony Sher	Vanessa Redgrave	Bill Bryden *The Mysteries*
1986	*Les Liaisons Dangereuses* Christopher Hampton	*The Phantom of the Opera*	*A Month of Sundays* Bob Larbey	Albert Finney	Julia McKenzie	Nuria Espert *The House of Bernarda Alba*
1987	*A Small Family Business* Alan Ayckbourn	*Follies*	*Serious Money* Caryl Churchill	Michael Gambon	Judi Dench	Peter Hall *Antony and Cleopatra*
1988	*Aristocrats* Brian Friel	No award	*Lettice and Lovage* Peter Shaffer	Eric Porter	Lindsay Duncan	Deborah Warner *Titus Andronicus*
1989	*Ghetto* Joshua Sobol	*Miss Saigon*	*Henceforward* Alan Ayckbourn	Ian McKellen	Felicity Kendal	Nicholas Hytner *Ghetto; Miss Saigon*
1990	*Shadowlands* William Nicholson	*Into The Woods*	*Man of the Moment* Alan Ayckbourn *Jeffrey Bernard is Unwell* Keith Waterhouse	Richard Harris	Josette Simon	Clare McIntyre *My Heart's A Suitcase*
1991	*Dancing at Lughnasa* Brian Friel	*Carmen Jones*	*Kvetch* Steven Berkoff	John Wood	Vanessa Redgrave	Trevor Nunn *Timon of Athens*
1992	*Angels in America* Tony Kushner	*Kiss of the Spiderwoman*	*The Rise and Fall of Little Voice* Jim Cartwright	Nigel Hawthorne	Diana Rigg	Stephen Daldry *An Inspector Calls*
1993	*Arcadia* Tom Stoppard	*City of Angels*	*Jamais Vu* Ken Campbell	Ian Holm	Fiona Shaw	Terry Hands *Tamburlaine the Great*

TOYS

Toy of the Year

The British Association of Toy Retailers has organised this award annually since 1965 when it was won by 007 Aston Martin – James Bond's car made by Mettoy. At the end of each year, retailers are asked to nominate their top ten toys and the judging panel sits in January to evaluate the results and decide on the top toy for the previous year. The criteria is not necessarily based on products which make most money but those which appear to have most popular appeal. The winner receives a trophy in the shape of a jigsaw piece, made out of marble.

1965 007 Aston Martin car
1966 Action Man
1967 Spirograph
1968 Sindy doll
1969 Hot Wheels
1970 Sindy doll
1971 Katie Kopycat
1972 Plasticraft
1973 Master Mind
1974 Lego – family-size kit
1975 Lego – basic kit
1976 Peter Powell Kites
1977 Playpeople
1978 Combine Harvester
1979 Legoland Space
1980 Rubik's Cube
1981 Rubik's Cube
1982 Star Wars figures and vehicles
1983 Star Wars figures and vehicles
1984 Masters of the Universe figures
1985 Transformers
1986 Transformers
1987 Sylvanian Families
1988 Sylvanian Families
1989 Sylvanian Families
1990 Turtles
1991 Nintendo Gameboy
1992 WWF Wrestlers
1993 Tracy Island (part of Thunderbirds range)

Hamley's Bestselling Toys

Hamleys of Regent Street, London, founded in 1760, is given as being the world's oldest, largest and best-stocked toyshop in *The Guinness*

THE SYLVANIAN FAMILIES

The Sylvanian Families range is the only product to have won the 'Toy of the Year' title three times (1987–89). The idea for the Sylvanian Families was conceived by Epoch of Japan in 1984 and the product was launched in the UK and the Republic of Ireland by Tomy at the 1987 Toy Fair. As a result of success in the UK, the range is now available worldwide, including Australia, the Middle East, USA, Scandinavia, Spain, Portugal, Italy, Greece.

A vast range of animal families has been sold over the years together with accessories, such as a nursery tree house, the Sylvanian Harvester Restaurant, a post office, windmill, country cottage, etc. The current range includes the Squirrel Family (Douglas, Kenneth, Emma and Greta Furbanks); the Hedgehog Family (Maxwell, Mortimer, Eleanor and Abigail Bramble); the Bear Family (Ottilee, Margot, Maurice and

Oscar Marmalade); the Otter Family (Brook, Becky, Eddy, Flo, Ebb, and Spring Vandyke); and the Koala Family (Rolf, Matilda, Kylie and Jason Billabong). A vast range of furniture is sold, including a bedroom furniture set, a 'real sound' flushing toilet, bath and shower set, patio table, chairs and barbeque and a fridge with accessories.

The approximate unit sales figures for 1993 were: figures and families 400 000; furniture and accessories 300 000; houses and shops 150 000; and token collectors products (collectors tokens are available on all Sylvanian Families packs) 900 000.

The bestselling families have been (with approximate sales figures): The Babblebrooks (grey rabbits) 760 000; The Timbertops (brown bears) 740 000; The Waters (beavers) 640 000; The Brambles (hedgehogs) 500 000.

This canal boat, from the Sylvanian Families range, is described in the Tomy catalogue as: 'For fun, adventure and happy Sylvanian holidays you could do no better than the Rose of Sylvania. A traditional canal boat with a galley kitchen, a bathroom with shower, bunk beds, clever places to stow things and all the other little accessories you need for a life on the water – such as an anchor, bucket, washing line, fishing rod, boathook and other maritime essentials.' On board are two members of the Vandyke Otter Family while Ottilee and Oscar Marmalade, members of the Bear Family, watch them depart.

Book of Records. Each Christmas it produces a list of bestselling gifts which for 1993 was:

1 Sega Computer Games – Sega Mega Drive, £129.99; Game Gear £99.99
2 Squiggle Wiggle Writer, £4.99
3 Self-tying shoelaces, £3.99
4 Nintendo computer games – Super

NES, £99.99; Game Boy/Tetris £49.99
5 Changeable colouring pens , £3.99
6 Rapidough boxed game, £25.99
7 Tomy Char-G radio-controlled car, £14.99
8 Barbie – Hollywood Hair, £11.99; TeenTalk, £16.99
9 Air Art Blitzter, £7.99
10 Lego Castle range

TRAVEL & TOURISM

Top 20 UK Attractions Charging Admission

		No. of visitors
1	**Alton Towers**, Staffs	2 618 365
2	**Madame Tussaud's**, London	2 449 627
3	**Tower of London**	2 332 468
4	**St Paul's Cathedral**, London	1 900 000
5	**Natural History Museum**, London	1 700 000
6	**Chessington World of Adventures**, London	1 495 000
7	**Thorpe Park**, Surrey	1 327 000
8	**Science Museum**, London	1 277 417
9	**Tower World**, Blackpool	1 250 000
10	**Drayton Manor Park**, Tamworth, Staffs	1 060 000
11	**Edinburgh Castle**	1 049 693
12	**Flamingo Land**, Kirby Misperton, N. Yorks	958 000
13	**Kew Gardens**, London	940 035
14	**Royal Academy**, London	922 135
15	**Roman Baths and Pump Room**, Bath	898 142
16	**London Zoo**	863 352
17	**Chester Zoo**	814 883
18	**Windsor Castle**, State Apartments, Berks	813 059
19	**American Adventure**, Ilkeston, Derbys	800 000
20	**Jorvik Viking Centre**, York	752 586

Source: English Tourist Board, 1993

Top 20 UK Attractions Charging Admission, Opened Since 1988

		No. of visitors
1	**Granada Studios Tour**, Manchester (1988)	700 000
2	**Pleasure Island**, Liverpool (1992)	680 000
3	**Sea Life Centre**, Blackpool (1990)	595 000
4	**Rock Circus**, London (1989)	554 483
5	**Metroland**, Gateshead, Tyne & Wear (1988)	450 000
6	**Cadbury World**, Bournville, W. Midlands (1990)	416 000
7	**Museum of the Moving Image**, London (1988)	374 692
8	**Eurotunnel Exhibition Centre**, Folkestone (1988)	295 000
9	**Sea Life Centre**, Scarborough, N. Yorks (1991)	293 000
10	**Eureka!**, The Museum of Children, Halifax, W. Yorks (1992)	256 000
11	**Sea Life Centre**, Brighton (1991)	250 000
12	**Kingdom of the Sea**, Great Yarmouth, Norfolk (1990)	225 700
13	**Palms Tropical Oasis**, Stapely, Ches (1988)	223 660
14	**Sea Life Centre**, Hastings, E. Sussex (1990)	216 000
15	**White Cliffs Experience**, Dover (1991)	206 628
16	**White Post Modern Farm Centre**, Farns Field, Notts (1988)	190 397
17	**Kingdom of the Sea**, Hunstanton, Norfolk (1989)	168 201
18	**Tullie House**, Carlisle, Cumbria (1991)	165 866
19	**Plymouth Dome** (1989)	164 756
20	**Canterbury Tales**, Canterbury (1988)	160 000

Source: English Tourist Board

'Revolution' at night on Blackpool Pleasure Beach, the UK's most visited leisure park. It receives in excess of 6½ million visitors a year.

The Runaway Mine Train ride at Alton Towers, the UK's most popular attraction, charging admission. It receives more than 2½ million visitors a year.

Top 10 UK Historic Properties

		No. of visitors
1	Tower of London	2 332 468
2	Edinburgh Castle	1 049 693
3	Roman Baths and Pump Room, Bath	898 142
4	Windsor Castle, State Apartments	813 059
5	Warwick Castle	751 026
6	Stonehenge, Wilts	668 607
7	Shakespeare's Birthplace, Stratford	606 697
8	Hampton Court Palace, London	576 664
9	Leeds Castle, Kent	533 000*
10	Beaulieu, Hants	481 223

*estimated
Source: English Tourist Board, 1993

Top 10 UK Leisure Parks and Piers

		No. of visitors
1	Blackpool Pleasure Beach	6 750 000*
2	Palace Pier, Brighton, E. Sussex	3 500 000*
3	Alton Towers, Staffs	2 618 365
4	Pleasure Beach, Great Yarmouth, Norfolk	2 400 000*
5	Pleasureland, Southport, Merseyside	2 000 000*
6	Chessington World of Adventures, London	1 495 000
7	Thorpe Park, Surrey	1 327 000
8	Frontierland, Morecambe, Lancs	1 300 000*
9	Tower World, Blackpool, Lancs	1 250 000
10	Hornsea Pottery, Hornsea, Humbers	200 000*

*estimated
Source: English Tourist Board, 1993

Leading UK Tourist Attractions by Category

	No. of visitors (millions)
Museums and galleries	79
Historic properties	78
Country parks	48
Leisure parks	37
Wildlife attractions	22
Gardens	15.2
Visitor centres	12.8
Workplaces	10.2
Farms	6
Steam railways	5
Miscellaneous	43.8
Total	357.0

Source: English Tourist Board

Top 10 London Attractions

		No. of visitors (millions)
1	British Museum	6.3
2	National Gallery	4.3
3	Madame Tussaud's	2.3
4	Tower of London	2.2
5	Natural History Museum	1.7
6	Tate Gallery	1.6
7	St Paul's Cathedral	1.4
8	Science Museum	1.2
9	Chessington World of Adventures	1.2
10	Victoria and Albert Museum	1.2

1993s Top Travel Companies

The *Weekend Telegraph* asked readers to vote for their favourite travel companies. A total of 17 253 readers did just that, casting 34 466 votes for travel companies in 10 categories. The paper asked which companies had impressed travellers the most over the past 12 months – whether they had enjoyed efficient service, value for money and whether they actually received the holiday they had expected. Thomson streaked ahead of all the travel companies, winning four out of the ten categories.

WINNERS

Skiing	Ski Thomson
Cruising	P & O Cruises
Exotic Holidays	Kuoni
Short Breaks, Europe	Thomson Citybreaks
Short Breaks, UK	Forte Hotels
Ferry Company	P & O Ferries
Family Holidays	Thomson Holidays
Self-Catering, Europe	Thomson Holidays
Self-Catering, UK	English Country Cottages
Activity Holidays	HF Holidays

The National Trust's Most Visited Properties

Fountains Abbey and Studley Royal, North Yorks	285 823
Stourhead Garden, Wilts	251 820
Wakehurst Place, W. Sussex	229 250
Polesden Lacey, Surrey	204 873
St Michael's Mount, Cornwall	191 673
Sissinghurst Garden, Kent	175 513
Bodiam Castle, E. Sussex	172 435
Chartwell, Kent	170 256
Bodnant Garden, Gwynedd	168 398
Corfe Castle, Dorset	154 501

1993 figures

FACTS

■ The National Trust has 2 120 576 members.

■ In 1993, 10 506 685 people visited Trust properties that charge an entrance fee.

■ 136 Trust properties, including gardens, mansions and parks, had more than 20 000 paying visitors in 1993.

■ 25 000 volunteers worked a total of 1¼ million hours for the National Trust in 1993.

Thomas Cook Travel Book Awards

Thomas Cook (1808–92), who was a printer before becoming an excursion agent, was a great believer in the written word. To advertise his tours, ticket systems, hotel coupons and circular notes (early travellers cheques) he initiated the publication of a magazine, *The Excursionist*, later called *The Traveller's Gazette*, which was published from 1851 to 1939. In 1880 Cook also launched a series of guide books which were published until 1939.

In 1980 Thomas Cook revived its interest in travel books by launching two Travel Book Awards. These were intended to encourage and reward travel books with literary merit and informative and imaginative guide books. Up to 1988 there were two categories of entry (travel and guide), and since then, three – travel (£7500 prize), guide (£2500) and illustrated guide (£1500).

The books were judged in 1993 by: Sir John Ure (Thomas Cook), Alex Hamilton (Travel Editor, *The Guardian*), Douglas Schatz (Stanfords Bookshop), Sarah Anderson (Travellers Book Shop), and Harriet Harvey (British Council).

Travel

1980 *Tracks*, Robyn Davidson
1981 *Old Glory*, Jonathan Raban
1982 *The Sinbad Voyage*, Tim Severin
1983 *From Heaven Lake*, Vikram Seth
1984 *To the Frontier*, Geoffrey Moorhouse
1985 *So Far From God*, Patrick Marnham
1986/1987 *Between the Woods and the Water*, Patrick Leigh Fermor
1988 *Behind the Wall*, Colin Thubron
1989 *Riding the Iron Rooster*, Paul Theroux
1990 *Our Grandmothers' Drums*, Mark Hudson
1991 *Hunting Mister Heartbreak*, Jonathan Raban
1992 *A Goddess in the Stones*, Norman Lewis
1993 *The Heart of the World*, Nik Cohn

Guide

1980 *The 1980 South American Handbook*, John Brooks (ed.)
1981 *China Companion*, Evelyn Garside
1982 *India*, G. Crowther, Pa Raj and T. Wheeler

Buckingham Palace's first season 'open to the public' raised a total £2.2 million in revenue towards the restoration of Windsor Castle. Over the 56-day period (7 August–1 October 1993), 377 000 visitors passed through the gates paying £8 a head (£4 for children) generating 1.4 million. They then proceeded to the gift shop and spent £800 000 on souvenirs. The number of visitors compares favourably with Windsor Castle which only received 813 059 visitors in 1993.

1983 *Companion Guide to New York*, Michael Leapman
1984 *Cruising French Waterways*, Hugh McKnight
1985 *Shell Guide to Nottinghamshire*, Henry Thorold
1986/1987 *Fontana/Hatchette Guide to France* 1986
1988 *The Tibet Guide*, Stephen Batchelor
1989 *Landscapes of Madeira*, John and Pat Underwood
1990 *Blue Guide Turkey*, Bernard McDonagh
1991 *Caribbean Islands Handbook*, Ben Box and Sarah Cameron
1992 *London's American Past*, Fran Hazelton
1993 *Thailand (Rough Guides)*, Paul Gray and Lucy Ridout

Illustrated Guide

1988 *Languedoc*, Charlie Waite and James Bentley
1989 *The Marco Polo Expedition*, Richard B. Fisher and Tom Ang
1990 *What the Traveller Saw*, Eric Newby
1991 No award
1992 *Eyes to the Hills*, Gordon Stainforth
1993 No award

England for Excellence Awards

Since 1988 the English Tourist Board (ETB) has made annual awards to the domestic tourist industry to 'reward and recognise the highest standards and excellence in major sectors of the English tourism industry'. Entry forms are submitted by entrants to either the ETB or the Regional Tourist Boards. The judging panels, which contain ETB staff and external experts relevant to each category, look for the highest standards in a number of different areas such as facilities,

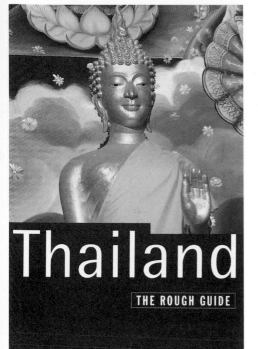

The Rough Guide to 'Thailand', winner of the 'Guide' category in the 1993 Thomas Cook Travel Book Awards.

service, training and marketing activities.

In total there have been 84 winners, only three organisations winning the award on more than one occasion: Bournemouth – Resort of the Year 1989 and 1992; Center Parcs – Tourism Destination 1988, Green Tourism Award 1990; and Butlins – English Travel Company of the Year 1990, 1992. Each year various categories are included; in 1993 there were 12:

1993 WINNERS
Outstanding Contribution to English Tourism Award
Bob Scott, Chairman, Manchester's Olympic Committee For his valiant bid to bring the 2000 Olympics to Manchester.

Caravan Holiday Park of the Year
New Forest Country Holidays, Godshill, Fordingbridge, Hants Purchased by Ernest Westlake in 1919 to save the trees, New Forest Country Holidays has been steadily developed and is now run by third and fourth generations of the Westlake family. Care has been taken to blend the latest facilities in with the natural environment. The park caters for privately-owned holiday homes, timber lodges and caravans for hire, and offers many facilities, including indoor and outdoor swimming pools, restaurant, adventure playground, riding stables, fishing, cycling, archery and laser shooting.

Bed and Breakfast of the Year
Halfway House, Crayke, York, N. Yorks Situated midway between the Georgian market town of Easingwold and the village of Crayke, this former working farm pays attention to detail and has high standards. The restored house offers accommodation for a maximum of six guests and includes a tennis court, orchard and secluded gardens. All bedrooms have individual colour schemes and towels, flowers, pictures, tissues, notepaper, bath accessories and china which are all colour matched.

Holiday Destination of the Year
Nottingham City and Nottinghamshire County Councils A wealth of attractions, events and historical connections are offered which are promoted at a variety of exhibitions to the travel trade and public. The marketing campaign attracted a large number of extra visitors and benefited the tourism industry which employs 15 000 people plus 2200 hotel staff.

Hotel of the Year
Swallow Hotel, Hagley Road, Birmingham Located in the heart of Birmingham, the hotel opened in March 1990 after five years of work and a £15 million investment. It is the flagship of Swallow Hotels, Britain's sixth largest hotel group. Employing 133 full-time and part-time staff, the hotel offers traditional values such as personal service, good customer care and warm hospitality. There are 98 bedrooms and the hotel has two award-winning Egon Ronay restaurants.

Self-Catering Holiday of the Year
Longlands, Cartmel, Cumbria Eight separate cottages are offered in this holiday retreat in the Lake District National Park situated in the grounds of a restored 200-year-old Georgian country house. Innovation is shown in the flexibility of service offered – a complete self-catering holiday with the option of full 'serviced facilities', including daily maid service and meals.

Travel and Tourism Award
Haven Warner, Hemel Hempstead, Herts Haven Warner, a major subsidiary of The Rank Organisation plc, is the UK's biggest domestic holiday company with over 60 holiday parks and villages around the country providing over one million holidays each year. The Haven parks and Warner villages offer a range of facilities, services and entertainment programmes to suit all age groups. The activities and entertainment elements are included in the price and as such are a major sales feature within the market.

Tourism and Environment Award
'Eco-hull', British Waterways, Watford and Alvechurch Boat Centres, Birmingham British Waterways, a nationalised industry, employs 1950 staff and operates over 2000 miles of canals and river navigations mostly in England for the benefit of the nation. The canals are more than 200 years old and are an outstanding feature of this country's heritage. Over 158 million visits are made annually, by boaters, anglers, walkers, cyclists, etc. Alvechurch Boat Centres has designed a boat, 'Eco-hull', with a new type of hull. Designed with the environment in mind, the boat produces less wash and so causes less erosion of the banks. New engine technology, combined with the smoother-flowing shape of the new hull, means that smaller more efficient engines can be used. Known as the 'Green Star Boats' potential customers of the canals are being targeted.

Tourism for All Award
Plymouth Dome, The Hoe, Plymouth, Devon Opened in March 1989 and sited on Plymouth Hoe, overlooking Plymouth

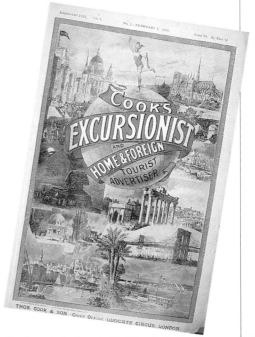

The Excursionist, launched by Thomas Cook in 1851.

Sound, the centre uses a variety of techniques to interpret the history of Plymouth and the famous voyages that have sailed from here, from actors to audio visuals, from Elizabethan smells to interactive computers. The Dome attracts around 170 000 visitors each year.

Tourism Training Award

White Rose Line, Lendal Bridge, York, N. Yorks White Rose Line operates daily sightseeing cruises and private charters, including food and beverage service, on the Yorkshire Ouse through historic York. In the last four years the business has grown rapidly from two vessels and one full-time employee to six double-deck passenger vessels employing 30 people.

Tourist Information Centre of the Year Award

Pickering Tourist Information Centre, Eastgate Car Park, North Yorks Located in a converted market auctioneer's office in Eastgate town, it is operated by one full-time and three part-time staff. It was highly commended in the 1992 Awards.

A view of the courtyard at Longlands, Cartmel, winner of the Self-Catering Holiday of the Year title in the England for Excellence Awards.

This illustration shows a giant mouth on display at Eureka! The Museum for Children, in Halifax, W. Yorks. The museum was voted 1993 'Visitor Attraction of the Year' by the English Tourist Board in its 'England for Excellence Awards'. Eureka! was specifically devised for children, parents and teachers; children from across Britain were involved in the research and development phase of the museum and still are involved in assessing the success of projects.

There are three main exhibitions: 'Me and My Body' (see picture right), 'Living and Working Together', and 'Inventing and Creating'. The 'Me and My Body' section explores children's knowledge of themselves; how the body and senses work. Children register their likes and dislikes, find out how the choices they make affect their well-being, and experience what it is like to have a disability.

'Living and Working Together' provides an environment where the child can discover the mysteries and commonplace complexities of daily life. They can explore a Town Square – a group of buildings which include a house, shop, bank, garage, factory and recycling centre.

'Inventing and Creating' provides opportunities for children to use their imagination, and share skills and knowledge to solve problems. They can find out about the world of communications from different locations, such as a desert island, a yacht in distress and a television studio. They can

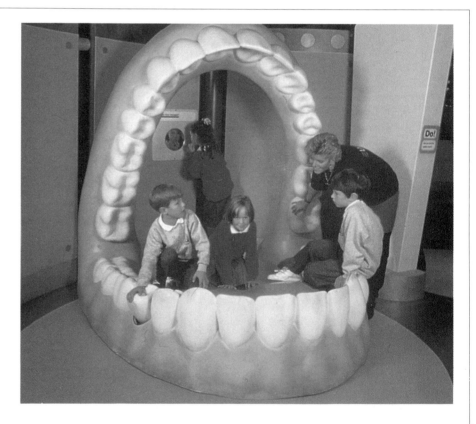

discover the latest technology by using two video phones, making a newspaper and using a fax machine.

The brochure designed for children says it all: 'Find out what makes your heart beat, what goes on under the streets in your town and what made Archimedes shout 'Eureka!'.

Wherever you go in Eureka! you can touch, listen and smell, as well as look. You can work on a factory production line, feed the giant Mouth Machine to find out what happens to the food you eat, and venture into the Hazard Dome, a unique audio-visual experience about safety in the home.'

Visitor Attraction of the Year Award

Eureka! The Museum for Children, Halifax, W. Yorks This is the first interactive museum in Britain wholly designed to teach children about the world in which we live. A private charity, Eureka!, was opened by HRH the Prince of Wales in July 1992 and employs 50 to 70 staff. The new stone, steel and glass building houses a gift shop, café and theatre as well as the main exhibitions.

Seaside Award and European Blue Flag

The European Blue Flag campaign was introduced in 1987, the European Year of the Environment. It acknowledges beaches with good management which have attained the water standards set in 1976 by the EC Bathing Water Directive EEC/76/160. In 1992 the water quality criterion for the Blue Flag changed from the mandatory to the higher guideline standard of this Directive.

The Seaside Award was introduced in 1992 to complement the European Blue Flag by providing the public with information about a wider range of UK beaches with more emphasis on the standard of land-based facilities, beach management, safety, and the provision of information such as the latest bathing water results. The land-based criteria are judged at the very beginning of the season, and the water quality is taken as the previous year's results (the water must be sampled and tested at least 20 times a year).

The Seaside Award recognises two categories of beach: resort and rural. Where the bathing water reaches the mandatory (good) standard of the Directive and fulfils several land-based criteria, the beach may fly the light blue and yellow Seaside Award flag for one year. Where the water quality has exceeded the Directive, the darker blue and yellow Premier Seaside Award flag may be flown. The beach is monitored during the summer to confirm that all criteria are being fulfilled, and, if they are not, the flag is removed until all criteria have again been satisfied. A resort beach must fulfil 28 land-based criteria, and a rural beach, 12.

European Blue Flag Winners, 1993

In 1993, 1204 beaches and 277 marinas out of the 1595 cases presented to the European Jury were given the right to raise the Blue Flag on 3 June as follows:

Country	Beaches	Marinas	Total
Spain	229	51	280
Italy	215	39	254
Greece	237	6	243
France	193	43	236
Denmark	125	81	206
Portugal	102	1	103
Ireland	61	0	61
Germany	0	27	27
Netherlands	19	3	22
United Kingdom	20	0	20
Finland	0	19	19
Turkey	0	7	7
Belgium	3	0	3
Total	**1204**	**277**	**1481**

UK Blue Flag Beaches

The following 20 beaches were eligible to fly the Blue Flag in 1993:

1 **Longsands South**, Tynemouth, Tyne & Wear
2 **Hunstanton**, Norfolk
3 **Southwold**, Suffolk
4 **Beach Street**, Sheerness, Kent
5 **West Hayling Island**, Hants
6 **Colwell Bay**, Isle of Wight
7 **Bournemouth**, Dorset
8 **Sandbanks**, Poole, Dorset
9 **Dawlish Warren**, Devon
10 **Oddicombe**, Torbay, Devon
11 **Meadfoot**, Torquay, Devon
12 **Crinnis**, Cornwall
13 **Sennen Cove**, Cornwall
14 **Porthmeor**, Cornwall
15 **Woolacombe**, Devon
16 **Cefn Sidan**, Pembrey Country Park, Wales
17 **Tenby North**, Dyfed, Wales
18 **Whitesands**, St Davids, Dyfed
19 **West Bay Strand**, Portrush, Northern Ireland
20 **Benone**, Northern Ireland

Top UK Beaches

The 18 beaches listed below were eligible to fly both the European Blue Flag and the Premier Seaside Award in 1993.

Beach Street, Sheerness, Kent
Benone, Northern Ireland
Bournemouth, Dorset
Cefn Sidan, Pembrey Country Park, Wales
Colwell Bay, Isle of Wight
Crinnis, Cornwall
Hunstanton, Norfolk
Longsands South, Tynemouth, Tyne & Wear
Meadfoot, Torquay, Devon
Oddicombe, Torbay, Devon
Porthmeor, Cornwall
Sandbanks, Poole, Dorset
Sennen Cove, Cornwall
Tenby North, Dyfed, Wales
West Bay Strand, Portrush, Northern Ireland
West Hayling Island, Hants
Whitesands, St Davids, Dyfed
Woolacombe, Devon

F A C T S ■ Only three beaches have been eligible to fly the European Blue Flag since its inception in 1987: Crinnis, Cornwall; Oddicombe, Torbay, Devon; and Sandbanks, Poole, Dorset. They all also received a Premier Seaside Award in 1992 and 1993.

All-Time Top 10 UK Beaches – Most Awards

	Beach	Total	Blue Flag	Premier Seaside Award	Seaside Award
1	Crinnis, Cornwall	9	7 (1987–93)	2 (1992–93)	–
	Oddicombe, Torbay, Devon	9	7 (1987–93)	2 (1992–93)	–
	Sandbanks, Poole, Dorset	9	7 (1987–93)	2 (1992–93)	–
4	Cefn Sidan, Pembrey Country Park, Wales	8	6 (1987–88, 1990–93)	2 (1992–93)	–
5	Porthmeor, Cornwall	8	6 (1987–91, 1993)	1 (1993)	1 (1992)
	Weymouth Central, Dorset	8	6 (1987–92)	1 (1992)	1 (1993)
7	Sennen Cove, Cornwall	7	5 (1989–93)	2 (1992–93)	–
8	Bournemouth, Dorset	7	5 (1988–91, 1993)	1 (1993)	1 (1992)
	Meadfoot, Torquay, Devon	7	5 (1988, 1990–93)	1 (1992)	1 (1993)
10	Redgate, Anstey's Cove, Devon	7	5 (1987–91)	–	2 (1992–93)

Note: All figures relate to the period from the inception of both schemes (Blue Flag [1987], Premier and Seaside Awards 1992) to end 1993.

RESORT BEACH

Defined as a beach which actively encourages visitors; has developed its facilities and provides varied recreational opportunities; is adjacent or within reach and reasonable access to the urban community. Typically, it would include all the following facilities: café or restaurant, shop, toilets, public transport, supervision, first aid, public telephone. Briefly, the requirements are:

Water Quality

1 Attained mandatory standard of Directive (if guideline standard, beach will receive 'Premier' Award).
2 No industrial or sewage discharges affecting beach area
3 No gross pollution
4 No algal or other vegetation materials accumulating or decaying
5 No oil pollution

Safety

6 Lifeguards on duty during the summer season and / or adequate safety provision, including lifesaving equipment
7 Times and area patrolled by lifeguards is clearly marked.
8 Clearly signposted first-aid facilities
9 Daily beach supervision through the holiday season
10 Record of all emergency incidents.

Management

11 Beach is actively managed and promoted by owners
12 Local emergency plans to cope with pollution incidents
13 Easy and safe access to beach for all, including disabled people where possible
14 No unauthorised driving, dumping and camping
15 The needs of the different users is managed well, e.g. zoning for swimmers, surfers, windsurfers, motorised craft, nature conservation
16 Dogs banned throughout the summer season
17 Dog refuse bins available along seafront where all dogs should be kept on a lead
18 Clearly marked and protected source of drinking water
19 Public telephones, checked daily, within easy access
20 Adequate toilet facilities, cleaned and maintained daily, including facilities for disabled
21 All buildings and equipment maintained to a high standard
22 Adequate access and parking facilities with marked spaces and suitable access for disabled people.

1 9 9 3 SEASIDE AWARD BEACHES

KEY P = PREMIER SEASIDE AWARD

LOCATION	TYPE
SCOTLAND	
1 NAIRN	RESORT
2 SANDEND	RURAL
3 INVERBOYNDIE	RURAL
4 FRASERBURGH	RESORT
5 PETERHEAD LIDO	RESORT
6 BALMEDIE	RURAL
7 STONEHAVEN	RESORT
8 ST. ANDREWS	RESORT
9 GULLANE BENTS	RURAL
NORTH EAST	
10 BAMBURGH	RURAL P
11 BEADNELL BAY	RURAL P
12 NEWTON HAVEN	RURAL P

LOCATION	TYPE
13 WARKWORTH	RURAL P
14 TYNEMOUTH – LONGSANDS STH.	RESORT P
15 SANDHAVEN	RESORT
YORKSHIRE AND HUMBERSIDE	
16 RUNSWICK BAY	RURAL
17 SANDSEND	RURAL
18 WHITBY WEST CLIFF	RESORT P
19 SCARBOROUGH NORTH BAY	RESORT
20 SCARBOROUGH SOUTH BAY	RESORT
21 FILEY	RESORT
22 BRIDLINGTON NORTH	RESORT
23 BRIDLINGTON SOUTH	RESORT
EAST ANGLIA	
24 SNETTISHAM	RURAL

LOCATION	TYPE
25 HUNSTANTON	RESORT P
26 WELLS-NEXT-THE-SEA	RESORT
27 LOWESOFT SOUTH	RESORT
28 KESSINGLAND	RURAL
29 SOUTHWOLD	RESORT P
30 DUNWICH	RURAL
31 ALDEBURGH	RURAL P
32 SHOEBURYNESS	RURAL P
33 SOUTHEND-ON-SEA	RESORT
SOUTH EAST	
34 SHEERNESS (BEACH ST.)	RESORT P
35 MARGATE	RESORT
36 VIKING BAY, BROADSTAIRS	RESORT
37 DYMCHURCH	RURAL
38 ROMNEY SANDS	RURAL
39 CAMBER	RURAL
40 WINCHELSEA	RURAL
41 BEXHILL	RESORT
42 PEVENSEY BAY	RURAL
43 EASTBOURNE	RESORT
44 BIRLING GAP	RURAL P
45 LITTLEHAMPTON	RESORT
46 BOGNOR REGIS	RESORT
47 HAYLING ISLAND WEST	RESORT P
48 SOUTHSEA	RESORT
49 LEPE	RURAL
50 EAST COWES	RURAL
51 RYDE EAST	RESORT
52 SPRINGVALE	RURAL
53 YAVERLAND	RURAL
54 SANDOWN	RESORT
55 COLWELL BAY	RESORT P
CHANNEL ISLANDS – GUERNSEY	
56 PORT SOIF	RURAL
57 PEMBROKE	RURAL
SOUTH WEST	
58 FRIARS CLIFF	RESORT
59 HIGHCLIFFE CASTLE	RURAL
60 BOSCOMBE	RESORT
61 BOURNEMOUTH	RESORT P
62 POOLE, SANDBANKS	RESORT P
63 SWANAGE BAY	RESORT
64 WEYMOUTH	RESORT
65 DAWLISH WARREN	RESORT P
66 MAIDENCOMBE	RURAL P
67 WATCOMBE	RURAL
68 ODDICOMBE	RESORT P
69 REDGATE	RESORT
70 MEADFOOT	RESORT
71 PAIGNTON	RESORT
72 GOODRINGTON STH. SANDS	RESORT P
73 BROADSANDS	RESORT
74 STRETE GATE	RURAL
75 BLACKPOOL SANDS	RURAL P
76 TORCROSS	RURAL P
77 BANTHAM	RURAL P
78 CRINNIS	RESORT P

LOCATION	TYPE
79 SENNEN COVE	RESORT P
80 PORTHMEOR	RESORT
81 TREYARNON	RURAL P
82 CONSTANTINE BAY	RURAL
83 HARLYN BAY	RURAL
84 POLZEATH	RURAL
85 TREBARWITH STRAND	RURAL
86 WIDEMOUTH SAND	RURAL P
87 CROOKLETS	RURAL
88 SANDYMOUTH	RURAL
89 WOOLACOMBE	RESORT P
WALES	
90 SOUTHERNDOWN	RURAL
91 REST BAY, PORTHCAWL	RURAL
92 PORT EYNON	RURAL P
93 CEFN SIDAN (PEMBREY)	RESORT P
94 AMROTH	RURAL P
95 LYDSTEP	RURAL P
96 SKRINKLE	RURAL P
97 MANORBIER	RURAL P
98 TENBY NORTH	RESORT P
99 TENBY SOUTH	RURAL
100 BARAFUNDLE	RURAL P
101 BROADHAVEN	RURAL P
102 WEST ANGLE BAY	RURAL P
103 DALE	RURAL P
104 BROADHAVEN (HAVERFORDWEST)	RURAL P
105 NEWGALE	RURAL P
106 CAERFAI, ST. DAVIDS	RURAL P
107 WHITESANDS, ST. DAVIDS	RESORT P
108 ABEREIDDY	RURAL P
109 NEWPORT	RURAL P
110 POPPIT	RURAL
111 MWNT	RURAL P
112 TRESAITH	RURAL
113 PENBRYN	RURAL
114 CWMTYDU	RURAL
115 LLANGRANNOG	RURAL
116 TRAETHGWYN, CEI NEWYDD	RURAL
117 YR HARBWR, CEI NEWYDD	RURAL
118 CEI BACH	RURAL
119 TRAETH Y DE, ABERAERON	RURAL
120 GILFACH YR HALEN	RURAL
121 TRAETH Y GOGLEDD	RESORT
122 BORTH	RURAL
123 LLANDANWG	RURAL
124 ABERDARON	RURAL P
125 MORFA DINLLE	RURAL P
126 RHOSNEIGR	RURAL P
127 TREARDDUR BAY	RURAL
128 BENLLECH	RURAL
NORTH WEST	
129 AINSDALE	RESORT
NORTHERN IRELAND	
130 CRANFIELD	RURAL
131 WEST BAY STRAND, PORTRUSH	RESORT P
132 BENONE	RESORT P

Cleansing

23 Adequate cleansing of beach
24 Appropriate litter bins, emptied at least daily

Information and Education

25 Prompt public warning if beach is to become grossly polluted or unsafe
26 Liaison with local conservation organisations on protected sites or rare protected species
27 Laws covering beach use easily available to public
28 Public display of bathing water quality, car parks, safety information, etc.
29 Ability to demonstrate that authority encourages promotional / educational activities through the year relating to coastal environment in area.

RURAL BEACH

Defined as a beach which has limited facilities and has neither been actively managed and developed as a resort, nor is part of any significant development. Briefly, the requirements are as follows:

Water Quality

1 See 1 above
2 See 2 above

Beach and Intertidal Area

3 See 3 above

Safety

4 Beach is considered locally as being relatively safe for swimmers and visitors
5 Appropriate lifesaving equipment provided
6 Beach users warned of potential hazards of swimming and advised of appropriate behaviour close to water

Management

7 Beach is actively managed under a scheme of 'guardianship' by a local group, school, parish or individual
8 Access is safe and well maintained
9 See 14 above
10 Any buildings and equipment are adequately maintained

Cleansing

11 Provision of properly secured litter bins in adequate numbers, where appropriate. Litter and animal waste should not be allowed to accumulate on beach or surrounding area

Information and Education

12 Information point giving advice about nearest telephone, hospital / surgery / first aid point / police, coastguard, etc.
13 Visitors actively encouraged to protect and conserve beach.

Britain in Bloom

Britain in Bloom is a nationwide annual competition organised since 1964 which encourages environmental improvement through the use of imaginative landscaping, trees, shrubs and flowers. It was first organised by Roy Hay, a horticultural journalist, who, while on holiday in France, noticed that everywhere he looked there were pots, tubs, window boxes, hanging baskets and gardens overflowing with plants and flowers. When he made enquiries, he discovered that it was part of the 'Fleurissement de France', a make-France-more-beautiful campaign, initiated by General de Gaulle. On his return to England, Roy, with the support of the British Tourist Authority, set up a campaign to run a version of this in England – Britain in Bloom.

Since 1983 the event has been organised by the Tidy Britain Group, an independent environmental charity concerned with the eradication of litter and the physical improvement of the environment.

The competition takes place in two stages: Regions in Bloom; and National Britain in Bloom. In the first stage, Britain in Bloom is divided into 12 English regions and Scotland, Northern Ireland, Wales, Isle of Man and Jersey. These are judged by an independent panel during June and July. In the second stage, selected winners from the regions compete and are rejudged on a national basis by the judges in late August/early September.

The first winner in 1964 was Bath. For the last three years, trophies have been presented in the following categories:

	Population	1991	1992	1993
Large city	over 150 000	Bournemouth	Oxford	Birmingham
City	70 001–150 000	Cheltenham	Eastbourne	Rotherham
Inner city	–		Birmingham	Sunderland
Large town	25 001–70 000	Guildford	Harrogate	Perth
Town trophy	10 001–25 000	St Helier	Hawick	St Ives & Carbis Bay
Small town	5001–10 000	St Ives	Keswick	Moira
Small country town	2001–5000	–	Usk	Kirkby Lonsdale
Large village	601–2000	Bampton	Saintfield	Broughshane
Village	600 max.	–	Thorpe Salvin	Beddgelert
Urban community	2001–10 000	Cambuskenneth	Port Sunlight	Darley Abbey

Britain in Bloom – Most Wins since 1964

	No. of wins	Category	Winning years
Aberdeen	9	City	1965, 1969, 1970, 1971, 1973, 1974, 1977, 1979, 1987
Bath	9	City	1964, 1968, 1972, 1975, 1976, 1978, 1981, 1984, 1990
Harrogate	7	Town	1976, 1977, 1979, 1981, 1983, 1986, 1992
Falmouth	4	Town	1970, 1971, 1973, 1979
Douglas	3	Large town	1978, 1980, 1987
Forres	3	Small town	1982, 1986, 1989
Sidmouth	3	Town	1975, 1978, 1984

View of a cottage in Kirkby Lonsdale, 1993 trophy winner in Britain in Bloom.

SOLUTIONS

CROSSWORDS

The Times Crossword Championship
(p. 77)

Across
- 1 Reappraise
- 6 Ides
- 9 Philistine
- 10 Flea
- 12 Kith
- 13 Uniformed
- 15 Tigerish
- 16 Indaba
- 18 Ramrod
- 20 Machismo
- 23 Bandicoot
- 24 Half
- 26 Urge
- 27 Streetwise
- 28 Dada
- 29 Dawn Chorus

Down
- 1 Rapt
- 2 Abiding
- 3 Philharmonic
- 4 Altruism
- 5 Sunlit
- 7 Dilemma
- 8 Snapdragon
- 11 Down the hatch
- 14 Stormbound
- 17 Pantheon
- 19 Managed
- 21 Soldier
- 22 Portia
- 25 Zeus

First Modern Crossword (p.78)

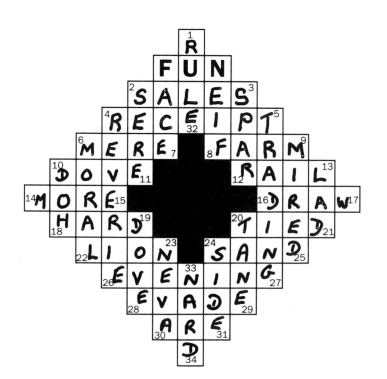

Quiz

Mastermind (p. 199)
Specialist Subject: The Crusades 1095–1154
1. The Council of Piacenza
2. Anna Comnena
3. Alexius I
4. Walter Sans-Avoir
5. 25 December
6. The Genoese (or Genoans)
7. Raymond of Toulouse (or Raymond of St Giles)
8. Bohemond (of Antioch)
9. Peter Desiderius
10. Iftikhar
11. The Knights Templar
12. Fulcher of Chartres
13. Ager Sanguinis – the Field of Blood
14. The Assassins or Hashishi(in)
15. Krak des Chevaliers
16. Arnulf of Rohes
17. Firuz
18. Manuel I
19. Damascus
20. Bernard of Clairvaux

General Knowledge
1. Concrete
2. Hohenzollern
3. Statistics
4. Gavin Hastings
5. James II
6. Shangri La
7. Iraq
8. (Canine) distemper
9. Ravens
10. Octavia Hill
11. Die Zauberflöte *or* The Magic Flute
12. Loki
13. Itchen
14. Austrian
15. The War of Jenkins' Ear
16. Tuscany *or* Toscana
17. Four
18. Sheridan Le Fanu
19. Conning tower *or* sail
20. (Mohandras Karamchand) Gandhi
21. Orange

Stamps

Royal Mail Sherlock Holmes Stamps (p. 218)

1 The word spelt out by the five stamps is: DOYLE
   Stamp 1 'The Reigate Squire'
   The letter 'E' appears on the book above Watson's right shoulder
   Stamp 2 'The Hound of the Baskervilles'
   The letter 'D' appears on the ground by Baskerville
   Stamp 3 'The Six Napoleons'
   The letter 'L' appears on the book on the table
   Stamp 4 'The Greek Interpreter'
   The letter 'Y' appears behind the rope tying Melas's feet
   Stamp 5 'The Final Problem'
   The letter 'O' appears on Holmes's cuff

2 The answers to the five clues are:
   Stamp 1 The Reigate Squire
   Answer Stradivarius
   Explanation An anagram of (indicated by 'some form of') 'rat Aids virus'.
   Stamp 2 The Hound of the Baskervilles
   Answer United States
   Explanation: Two letters from the start of each word (indicated by 'Initially two at a time') from Holmes's second sentence.

Stamp 3 The Six Napoleons
Answer £1.33
Explanation Holmes said: 'There were five coins involved in the transaction, including both payment and any change that may have been given; and the sum was the smallest that could not have been so attained with exactly four coins'.

The key point is the phrase, 'including both payment and any change'. The sum of 38p, the most common incorrect answer, can be attained in a four-coin transaction in several ways: 20p + 20p tendered, 1p + 1p change; or 20p + 10p + 10p tendered, 2p change. The sum of 38p is indeed the smallest amount that cannot be tendered in four coins, but that was not the question.

The correct answer of £1.33 may be most simply arrived at by considering the analogous question with one coin fewer. With three coins it can quickly be shown that the smallest sum that cannot be attained is 33p. Since 1p to 32p can be attained with three coins, it follows (by adding 1p) that 2p to 33p can be done with four. And 21p to 52p can be attained by adding 20p, while the ranges 51p to 82p and £1.01 to £1.32 are covered by adding 50p. The missing 83p to 99p segment is covered by tendering £1 and receiving a three-coin 1p to 17p in change, which leaves only 1p and £1 (both of which are easily done) to complete every value from 1p to £1.32 in exactly four coins.

Finally, rejecting any suggestion that the £2 commemorative coin should be considered current coinage, it can easily be shown that £1.33 cannot be produced as a four-coin transaction unless 33p can be done in three coins.

Stamp 4 The Greek Interpreter
Answer Athens
Explanation Remove (indicated by 'eliminate') letters in 'the impossible' from 'O that hemp is sensible' and 'Athens' remains.

Stamp 5 The Final Problem
Answer The Napoleon of Crime
Explanation The key to the code is:
SHERLOCKABDFG
IJMNPQTUVWXYZ
'A simple letter substitution table.'

INDEX

PICTURE CREDITS